Sr. Mary Salucci
Carmelite Monastery
1381 University Ave
Bronx n.y. 10452

METHOD IN THEOLOGY

BERNARD J. F. LONERGAN, S. J.

METHOD
IN
THEOLOGY

Herder and Herder

1972

Herder and Herder New York
232 Madison Avenue, New York 10016

ISBN: 665–00033–2
Library of Congress Catalog Card Number: 78–181008

© 1972 by Bernard J. F. Lonergan

Printed in Great Britain

CONTENTS

CONTENTS

CONTENTS

PREFACE

THIS book has long been in the making. The development of my investigation up to 1965 has been studied by David Tracy in his *Achievement of Bernard Lonergan*. In that year for reasons of health I retired from the Gregorian University and, since then, I have enjoyed the hospitality of Regis College which has met all my needs and left me free to think and write without asking any service in return. To Regis College, then, and to the good fellowship of its staff and students during the past six years my profound gratitude.[1]

I have also the duty of thanking the friends that helped with the proofs and the index: Timothy Fallon, Mattew Lamb, Philip McShane, Conn O'Donovan, William Reiser, Richard Roach, Willian Ryan, and Bernard Tyrrell.

Bernard Lonergan

Harvard Divinity School
November 15, 1971

---

[1] Inevitably my lectures and papers in recent years echo the contents of this book. But explicit mention should perhaps be made of the following. Chapter Five has appeared in *Gregorianum* 50 (1969), 485–505. Chapter Twelve contributed much to *Doctrinal Pluralism*, the Père Marquette Theology Lecture for 1971, published by the Marquette University Press. Chapter Seven is due to appear in the first issue of a new review, *Cultural Hermeneutics*, published at Boston College probably in the fall of 1971. Chapters Four and Twelve were drawn on for my part in a symposium held at Villanova University, June 14–19, 1971. The symposium will be edited by Joseph Papin with the title: *The Pilgrim People*.

INTRODUCTION

A THEOLOGY mediates between a cultural matrix and the significance and role of a religion in that matrix. The classicist notion of culture was normative: at least *de jure* there was but one culture that was both universal and permanent; to its norms and ideals might aspire the uncultured, whether they were the young or the people or the natives or the barbarians. Besides the classicist, there also is the empirical notion of culture. It is the set of meanings and values that informs a way of life. It may remain unchanged for ages. It may be in process of slow development or rapid dissolution.

When the classicist notion of culture prevails, theology is conceived as a permanent achievement, and then one discourses on its nature. When culture is conceived empirically, theology is known to be an ongoing process, and then one writes on its method.

Method is not a set of rules to be followed meticulously by a dolt. It is a framework for collaborative creativity. It would outline the various clusters of operations to be performed by theologians when they go about their various tasks. A contemporary method would conceive those tasks in the context of modern science, modern scholarship, modern philosophy, of historicity, collective practicality and coresponsibility.

In such a contemporary theology we envisage eight distinct tasks: research, interpretation, history, dialectic, foundations, doctrines, systematics, and communications. How each of these tasks is to be performed, is treated now in greater and now in less detail in the nine chapters that form the second part of this work. In the first part are treated more general topics that have to be presupposed in the second part. Such are method, the human good, meaning, religion, and functional specialties. Of these, the last, functional specialties, explains how we arrived at our list of eight distinct tasks.

In general, what we shall have to say, is to be taken as a model. By a model is not meant something to be copied or imitated. By a model is not meant a description of reality or a hypothesis about reality. It is simply an intelligible, interlocking set of terms and relations that it may be well to have about when it comes to describing reality or to forming hypotheses. As the proverb, so the model is something worth keeping in mind when one confronts a situation or tackles a job.

However, I do not think I am offering merely models. On the contrary, I hope readers will find more than mere models in what I shall say. But it is up to them to find it. For the first chapter on method sets forth what they can discover in themselves as the dynamic structure of their own cognitional and moral being. In so far as they find that, they also will find something that is not open to radical revision. For that dynamic structure is the condition of the possibility of any revision. Moreover, subsequent chapters are in the main prolongations of the first. They presuppose it. They complement it, indeed, but they do so by drawing attention to further aspects or fuller implications or added applications. However, just as each one has to find in himself the dynamic structure indicated in the first chapter, so too he has to satisfy himself about the validity of the further additions in the subsequent chapters. As already I have said, method offers not rules to be followed blindly but a framework for creativity.

If I hope many readers will find in themselves the dynamic structure of which I write, others perhaps will not. Let me beg them not to be scandalized because I quote scripture, the ecumenical councils, papal encyclicals, other theologians so rarely and sparingly. I am writing not theology but method in theology. I am concerned not with the objects that theologians expound but with the operations that theologians perform.

The method I indicate is, I think, relevant to more than Roman Catholic theologians. But I must leave it to members of other communions to decide upon the extent to which they may employ the present method.

PART ONE
BACKGROUND

I

METHOD

THOUGHT on method is apt to run in some one of three channels. In the first, method will be conceived more as an art than as a science. It is to be learnt not from books or lectures but in the laboratory or in the seminar. What counts is the example of the master, the effort to do likewise, his comments on one's performance. Such, I think, must be the origin of all thought on method for such thought has to be reflection on previous achievement. Such, also, will always remain the one way in which the refinements and subtleties proper to specialized areas will be communicated.

There are, however, bolder spirits. They select the conspicuously successful science of their time. They study its procedures. They formulate precepts. Finally, they propose an analogy of science. Science properly so called is the successful science they have analyzed. Other subjects are scientific in the measure they conform to its procedures and, in the measure they do not, they are something less than scientific. So Sir David Ross remarked of Aristotle: "Throughout the whole of his works we find him taking the view that all other sciences than the mathematical have the name of science only by courtesy, since they are occupied with matters in which contingency plays a part."[1] So too today the English word, science, means natural science. One descends a rung or more in the ladder when one speaks of behavioral or human sciences. Theologians finally often have to be content if their subject is included in a list not of sciences but of academic disciplines.

[1] W. D. Ross, *Aristotle's Prior and Posterior Analytics*, Oxford, 1949, p. 14. Cf. pp. 51 ff.

3

Clearly enough, these approaches to the problem of method do little to advance the less successful subjects. For in the less successful subject, precisely because it is less successful, there is a lack of masters to be followed and of models to be imitated. Nor will recourse to the analogy of science be of any use, for that analogy, so far from extending a helping hand to the less successful, is content to assign them a lower rank in the pecking order. Some third way, then, must be found and, even though it is difficult and laborious, that price must be paid if the less successful subject is not to remain a mediocrity or slip into decadence and desuetude.

To work out the basis for such a third way is the purpose of the present chapter. First, we shall appeal to the successful sciences to form a preliminary notion of method. Secondly, we shall go behind the procedures of the natural sciences to something both more general and more fundamental, namely, the procedures of the human mind. Thirdly, in the procedures of the human mind we shall discern a transcendental method, that is, a basic pattern of operations employed in every cognitional enterprise. Fourthly, we shall indicate the relevance of transcendental method in the formulation of other, more special methods appropriate to particular fields.

1. A PRELIMINARY NOTION

A method is a normative pattern of recurrent and related operations yielding cumulative and progressive results. There is a method, then, where there are distinct operations, where each operation is related to the others, where the set of relations forms a pattern, where the pattern is described as the right way of doing the job, where operations in accord with the pattern may be repeated indefinitely, and where the fruits of such repetition are, not repetitious, but cumulative and progressive.

So in the natural sciences method inculcates a spirit of inquiry and inquiries recur. It insists on accurate observation and description: both observations and descriptions recur. Above all, it praises discovery, and discoveries recur. It demands the formulation of discoveries in hypotheses, and hypotheses recur. It

4

requires the deduction of the implications of hypotheses, and deductions recur. It keeps urging that experiments be devised and performed to check the implications of hypotheses against observable fact, and such processes of experimentation recur.

These distinct and recurrent operations are related. Inquiry transforms mere experiencing into the scrutiny of observation. What is observed, is pinned down by description. Contrasting descriptions give rise to problems, and problems are solved by discoveries. What is discovered is expressed in a hypothesis. From the hypothesis are deduced its implications, and these suggest experiments to be performed. So the many operations are related; the relations form a pattern; and the pattern defines the right way of going about a scientific investigation.

Finally, the results of investigations are cumulative and progressive. For the process of experimentation yields new data, new observations, new descriptions that may or may not confirm the hypothesis that is being tested. In so far as they are confirmatory, they reveal that the investigation is not altogether on the wrong track. In so far as they are not confirmatory, they lead to a modification of the hypothesis and, in the limit, to new discovery, new hypothesis, new deduction, and new experiments. The wheel of method not only turns but also rolls along. The field of observed data keeps broadening. New discoveries are added to old. New hypotheses and theories express not only the new insights but also all that was valid in the old, to give method its cumulative character and to engender the conviction that, however remote may still be the goal of the complete explanation of all phenomena, at least we now are nearer to it than we were.

Such, very summarily, is method in the natural sciences. The account is far indeed from being sufficiently detailed to guide the natural scientist in his work. At the same time it is too specific to be transposed to other disciplines. But at least it illustrates a preliminary notion of method as *a normative pattern of recurrent and related operations yielding cumulative and progressive results.*

A few observations are in order.

First, method is often conceived as a set of rules that, even when followed blindly by anyone, none the less yield satisfactory results. I should grant that method, so conceived, is possible when the same result is produced over and over, as in the assembly line or "The New Method Laundry". But it will not do, if progressive and cumulative results are expected. Results are progressive only if there is a sustained succession of discoveries; they are cumulative only if there is effected a synthesis of each new insight with all previous, valid insights. But neither discovery nor synthesis is at the beck and call of any set of rules. Their occurrence follows statistical laws; they can be made more probable; they cannot be assured by a set of prescriptions.

Next, our preliminary notion conceives method not as a set of rules but as a prior, normative pattern of operations from which the rules may be derived. Further, the operations envisaged are not limited to strictly logical operations, that is, to operations on propositions, terms, relations. It includes such operations, of course, for it speaks of describing, of formulating problems and hypotheses, of deducing implications. But it does not hesitate to move outside this group and to speak of inquiry, observation, discovery, experiment, synthesis, verification.

Thirdly, what precisely these non-logical operations are, will concern us in the next section. But at once it may be noted that modern science derives its distinctive character from this grouping together of logical and non-logical operations. The logical tend to consolidate what has been achieved. The non-logical keep all achievement open to further advance. The conjunction of the two results in an open, ongoing, progressive and cumulative process. This process contrasts sharply not only with the static fixity that resulted from Aristotle's concentration on the necessary and immutable but also with Hegel's dialectic which is a movement enclosed within a complete system.

2. THE BASIC PATTERN OF OPERATIONS

Operations in the pattern are seeing, hearing, touching, smelling, tasting, inquiring, imagining, understanding, conceiving, formulating, reflecting, marshalling and weighing the evidence, judging, deliberating, evaluating, deciding, speaking, writing.

It will be assumed that everyone is familiar with some at least of these operations and that he has some notion of what the other terms mean. Our purpose is to bring to light the pattern within which these operations occur and, it happens, we cannot succeed without an exceptional amount of exertion and activity on the part of the reader. He will have to familiarize himself with our terminology. He will have to evoke the relevant operations in his own consciousness. He will have to discover in his own experience the dynamic relationships leading from one operation to the next. Otherwise he will find not merely this chapter but the whole book about as illuminating as a blind man finds a lecture on color.[2]

First, then, the operations in the list are transitive. They have objects. They are transitive not merely in the grammatical sense that they are denoted by transitive verbs but also in the psychological sense that by the operation one becomes aware of the object. This psychological sense is what is meant by the verb, intend, the adjective, intentional, the noun, intentionality. To say that the operations intend objects is to refer to such facts as that by seeing there becomes present what is seen, by hearing there becomes present what is heard, by imagining there becomes present what is imagined, and so on, where in each case the presence in question is a psychological event.

Secondly, the operations in the list are operations of an operator, and the operator is named the subject. The operator is subject not merely in the grammatical sense that he is denoted by a noun that is subject of the verbs that in the active voice refer to the operations. He also is subject in the psychological sense that he operates consciously. In fact, none of the operations in the list

[2] I have presented this pattern of operations at length in the book, *Insight* (London and New York), 1957, and more compendiously in an article, "Cognitional Structure", *Continuum* 2 (1964), 530–542, reprinted in *Collection*, Papers by Bernard Lonergan edited by F. E. Crowe (New York and London), 1967. But the matter is so crucial for the present enterprise that some summary must be included here. Please observe that I am offering only a summary, that the summary can do no more than present a general idea, that the process of self-appropriation occurs only slowly, and, usually, only through a struggle with some such book as *Insight*.

are to be performed in dreamless sleep or in a coma. Again, whenever any of the operations are performed, the subject is aware of himself operating, present to himself operating, experiencing himself operating. Moreover, as will appear presently, the quality of consciousness changes as the subject performs different operations.

The operations then not only intend objects. There is to them a further psychological dimension. They occur consciously and by them the operating subject is conscious. Just as operations by their intentionality make objects present to the subject, so also by consciousness they make the operating subject present to himself.

I have used the adjective, present, both of the object and of the subject. But I have used it ambiguously, for the presence of the object is quite different from the presence of the subject. The object is present as what is gazed upon, attended to, intended. But the presence of the subject resides in the gazing, the attending, the intending. For this reason the subject can be conscious, as attending, and yet give his whole attention to the object as attended to.

Again, I spoke of the subject experiencing himself operating. But do not suppose that this experiencing is another operation to be added to the list, for this experiencing is not intending but being conscious. It is not another operation over and above the operation that is experienced. It is that very operation which, besides being intrinsically intentional, also is intrinsically conscious.

Thirdly, there is the word, introspection, which is misleading inasmuch as it suggests an inward inspection. Inward inspection is just myth. Its origin lies in the mistaken analogy that all cognitional events are to be conceived on the analogy of ocular vision; consciousness is some sort of cognitional event; therefore, consciousness is to be conceived on the analogy of ocular vision; and since it does not inspect outwardly, it must be an inward inspection.

However, "introspection" may be understood to mean, not consciousness itself but the process of objectifying the contents of consciousness. Just as we move from the data of sense through

8

inquiry, insight, reflection, judgment, to statements about sensible things, so too we move from the data of consciousness through inquiry, understanding, reflection, judgment, to statements about conscious subjects and their operations. That, of course, is just what we are doing and inviting the reader to do at the present time. But the reader will do it, not by looking inwardly, but by recognizing in our expressions the objectification of his subjective experience.

Fourthly, different levels of consciousness and intentionality have to be distinguished. In our dream states consciousness and intentionality commonly are fragmentary and incoherent. When we awake, they take on a different hue to expand on four successive, related, but qualitatively different levels. There is the *empirical* level on which we sense, perceive, imagine, feel, speak, move. There is an *intellectual* level on which we inquire, come to understand, express what we have understood, work out the presuppositions and implications of our expression. There is the *rational* level on which we reflect, marshal the evidence, pass judgment on the truth or falsity, certainty or probability, of a statement. There is the *responsible* level on which we are concerned with ourselves, our own operations, our goals, and so deliberate about possible courses of action, evaluate them, decide, and carry out our decisions.

All the operations on these four levels are intentional and conscious. Still, intentionality and consciousness differ from level to level, and within each level the many operations involve further differences. Our consciousness expands in a new dimension when from mere experiencing we turn to the effort to understand what we have experienced. A third dimension of rationality emerges when the content of our acts of understanding is regarded as, of itself, a mere bright idea and we endeavor to settle what really is so. A fourth dimension comes to the fore when judgment on the facts is followed by deliberation on what we are to do about them. On all four levels, we are aware of ourselves but, as we mount from level to level, it is a fuller self of which we are aware and the awareness itself is different.

As empirically conscious, we do not seem to differ from the

higher animals. But in us empirical consciousness and intentionality are only a substratum for further activities. The data of sense provoke inquiry, inquiry leads to understanding, understanding expresses itself in language. Without the data there would be nothing for us to inquire about and nothing to be understood. Yet what is sought by inquiry is never just another datum but the idea or form, the intelligible unity or relatedness, that organizes data into intelligible wholes. Again, without the effort to understand and its conflicting results, we would have no occasion to judge. But such occasions are recurrent, and then the intelligent center of experiencing reveals his reflective and critical rationality. Once more there is a fuller self of which we become aware, and once more the awareness itself is different. As intelligent, the subject seeks insight and, as insights accumulate, he reveals them in his behavior, his speech, his grasp of situations, his mastery of theoretic domains. But as reflectively and critically conscious, he incarnates detachment and disinterestedness, gives himself over to criteria of truth and certitude, makes his sole concern the determination of what is or is not so; and now, as the self, so also the awareness of self resides in that incarnation, that self-surrender, that single-minded concern for truth. There is a still further dimension to being human, and there we emerge as persons, meet one another in a common concern for values, seek to abolish the organization of human living on the basis of competing egoisms and to replace it by an organization on the basis of man's perceptiveness and intelligence, his reasonableness, and his responsible exercise of freedom.

Fifthly, as different operations yield qualitatively different modes of being conscious subjects, so too they yield qualitatively different modes of intending. The intending of our senses is an attending; it normally is selective but not creative. The intending of our imaginations may be representative or creative. What is grasped in insight, is neither an actually given datum of sense nor a creation of the imagination but an intelligible organization that may or may not be relevant to data. The intending that is conception puts together both the content of the insight and as much of the image as is essential to the occurrence of the insight;

the result is the intending of any concrete being selected by an incompletely determinate (and, in that sense, abstract) content.

However, the most fundamental difference in modes of intending lies between the categorial and the transcendental. Categories are determinations. They have a limited denotation. They vary with cultural variations. They may be illustrated by the type of classification associated with totemism and recently argued to be essentially a classification by homology.[3] They may be reflectively known as categories, as were the Aristotelian *substance, quantity, quality, relation, action, passion, place, time, posture, habit.* They need not be called categories, as were the four causes, *end, agent, matter, form,* or the logical distinctions of *genus, difference, species, property, accident.* They may be the fine products of scientific achievement as the concepts of modern physics, the chemist's periodic table, the biologist's evolutionary tree.

In contrast, the transcendentals are comprehensive in connotation, unrestricted in denotation, invariant over cultural change. While categories are needed to put determinate questions and give determinate answers, the transcendentals are contained in questions prior to the answers. They are the radical intending that moves us from ignorance to knowledge. They are *a priori* because they go beyond what we know to seek what we do not know yet. They are unrestricted because answers are never complete and so only give rise to still further questions. They are comprehensive because they intend the unknown whole or totality of which our answers reveal only part. So intelligence takes us beyond experiencing to ask what and why and how and what for. Reasonableness takes us beyond the answers of intelligence to ask whether the answers are true and whether what they mean really is so. Responsibility goes beyond fact and desire and possibility to discern between what truly is good and what only apparently is good. So if we objectify the content of intelligent intending, we form the transcendental concept of the intelligible. If we objectify the content of reasonable intending,

---

[3] Claude Levi-Strauss, *La pensée sauvage*, Paris: Plon, 1962. E.T., *The Savage Mind*, London: Weidenfeld and Nicolson, 1966.

we form the transcendental concepts of the true and the real. If we objectify the content of responsible intending, we get the transcendental concept of value, of the truly good. But quite distinct from such transcendental concepts, which can be misconceived and often are, there are the prior transcendental notions that constitute the very dynamism of our conscious intending, promoting us from mere experiencing towards understanding, from mere understanding towards truth and reality, from factual knowledge to responsible action. That dynamism, so far from being a product of cultural advance, is the condition of its possibility; and any ignorance or error, any negligence or malice, that misrepresents or blocks that dynamism is obscurantism in its most radical form.

Sixthly, we began by speaking of operations intending objects. Now we must distinguish between elementary and compound objects, elementary and compound knowing. By elementary knowing is meant any cognitional operation, such as seeing, hearing, understanding, and so on. By the elementary object is meant what is intended in elementary knowing. By compound knowing is meant the conjunction of several instances of elementary knowing into a single knowing. By the compound object is meant the object constructed by uniting several elementary objects.

Now the process of compounding is the work of the transcendental notions which, from the beginning, intend the unknown that, gradually, becomes better known. In virtue of this intending, what is experienced can be the same as what is understood; what is experienced and understood can be the same as what is conceived, what is experienced and understood and conceived, can be the same as what is affirmed to be real; what is experienced, understood, conceived, affirmed, can be the same as what is approved as truly good. So the many elementary objects are constructed into a single compound object, and in turn the many compound objects will be ordered in a single universe.

Seventhly, we have distinguished many conscious and intentional operations and arranged them in a succession of different levels of consciousness. But as the many elementary objects are constructed into larger wholes, as the many operations are conjoined in a single compound knowing, so too the many levels of consciousness are just successive stages in the unfolding of a single thrust, the eros of the human spirit. To know the good, it must know the real; to know the real, it must know the true; to know the true, it must know the intelligible; to know the intelligible, it must attend to the data. So from slumber, we awake to attend. Observing lets intelligence be puzzled, and we inquire. Inquiry leads to the delight of insight, but insights are a dime a dozen, so critical reasonableness doubts, checks, makes sure. Alternative courses of action present themselves and we wonder whether the more attractive is truly good. Indeed, so intimate is the relation between the successive transcendental notions, that it is only by a specialized differentiation of consciousness that we withdraw from more ordinary ways of living to devote ourselves to a moral pursuit of goodness, a philosophic pursuit of truth, a scientific pursuit of understanding, an artistic pursuit of beauty.

Finally, to conclude this section, we note that the basic pattern of conscious and intentional operations is dynamic. It is dynamic materially inasmuch as it is a pattern of operations, just as a dance is a pattern of bodily movements, or a melody is a pattern of sounds. But it also is dynamic formally, inasmuch as it calls forth and assembles the appropriate operations at each stage of the process, just as a growing organism puts forth its own organs and lives by their functioning. Finally, this doubly dynamic pattern is not blind but open-eyed; it is attentive, intelligent, reasonable, responsible; it is a conscious intending, ever going beyond what happens to be given or known, ever striving for a fuller and richer apprehension of the yet unknown or incompletely known totality, whole, universe.

3. TRANSCENDENTAL METHOD[4]

What we have been describing as the basic pattern of operations is transcendental method. It is a method, for it is a normative

---

[4] In his book, *The Transcendental Method*, New York: Herder and Herder, 1968, Otto Muck works out a generalized notion of transcendental method by

pattern of recurrent and related operations yielding cumulative and progressive results. It is a transcendental method, for the results envisaged are not confined categorically to some particular field or subject, but regard any result that could be intended by the completely open transcendental notions. Where other methods aim at meeting the exigences and exploiting the opportunities proper to particular fields, transcendental method is concerned with meeting the exigences and exploiting the opportunities presented by the human mind itself. It is a concern that is both foundational and universally significant and relevant.

Now in a sense everyone knows and observes transcendental method. Everyone does so, precisely in the measure that he is attentive, intelligent, reasonable, responsible. But in another sense it is quite difficult to be at home in transcendental method, for that is not to be achieved by reading books or listening to lectures or analyzing language. It is a matter of heightening one's consciousness by objectifying it, and that is something that each one, ultimately, has to do in himself and for himself.

In what does this objectification consist? It is a matter of applying the operations as intentional to the operations as conscious. Thus, if for brevity's sake we denote the various operations on the four levels by the principal occurrence on that level, we may speak of the operations as experiencing, understanding, judging, and deciding. These operations are both conscious and intentional. But what is conscious, can be intended. To apply the operations as intentional to the operations as conscious is a fourfold matter of (1) experiencing one's experiencing,

---

determining the common features in the work of those that employ the method. While I have no objection to this procedure, I do not consider it very pertinent to an understanding of my own intentions. I conceive method concretely. I conceive it, not in terms of principles and rules, but as a normative pattern of operations with cumulative and progressive results. I distinguish the methods appropriate to particular fields and, on the other hand, their common core and ground, which I name transcendental method. Here, the word, transcendental, is employed in a sense analogous to Scholastic usage, for it is opposed to the categorial (or predicamental). But my actual procedure also is transcendental in the Kantian sense, inasmuch as it brings to light the conditions of the possibility of knowing an object in so far as that knowledge is *a priori*.

understanding, judging, and deciding, (2) understanding the unity and relations of one's experienced experiencing, understanding, judging, deciding, (3) affirming the reality of one's experienced and understood experiencing, understanding, judging, deciding and (4) deciding to operate in accord with the norms immanent in the spontaneous relatedness of one's experienced, understood, affirmed experiencing, understanding, judging, and deciding.

First, then, there are to be experienced one's experiencing, understanding, judging, deciding. But this fourfold experience is just consciousness. We have it every time we experience, or understand, or judge, or decide. But our attention is apt to be focused on the object, while our conscious operating remains peripheral. We must, then, enlarge our interest, recall that one and the same operation not only intends an object but also reveals an intending subject, discover in our own experience the concrete truth of that general statement. That discovery, of course, is not a matter of looking, inspecting, gazing upon. It is an awareness, not of what is intended, but of the intending. It is finding in oneself the conscious occurrence, seeing, whenever an object is seen, the conscious occurrence, hearing, whenever an object is heard, and so forth.

Since sensations can be produced or removed at will, it is a fairly simple matter to advert to them and become familiar with them. On the other hand, not a little forethought and ingenuity are needed when one is out to heighten one's consciousness of inquiry, insight, formulation, critical reflection, weighing the evidence, judging, deliberating, deciding. One has to know the precise meaning of each of these words. One has to produce in oneself the corresponding operation. One has to keep producing it until one gets beyond the object intended to the consciously operating subject. One has to do all this within the appropriate context, which is a matter not of inward inspection but of inquiry, enlarged interest, discernment, comparison, distinction, identification, naming.

The operations are to be experienced not only singly but in their relations, for there are not merely conscious operations but also conscious processes. Where sensitive perception does not reveal intelligible relations so that, as Hume contended, we perceive not causality but succession, our own consciousness is a different matter. On the empirical level, it is true, process is spontaneous sensitivity; it is intelligible only in the sense that it is understood. But with inquiry the intelligent subject emerges, and process becomes intelligent; it is not merely an intelligible that can be understood, but the active correlative of intelligibility, the intelligence that intelligently seeks understanding, comes to understand, and operates in the light of having understood. When inquiry comes to a term, or an impasse, intelligence intelligently yields place to critical reflection; as critically reflective, the subject stands in conscious relation to an absolute—the absolute that makes us regard the positive content of the sciences not as true and certain but only as probable. Finally, the rational subject, having achieved knowledge of what is and could be, rationally gives way to conscious freedom and conscientious responsibility.

The operations, then, stand within a process that is formally dynamic, that calls forth and assembles its own components, that does so intelligently, rationally, responsibly. Such, then, is the unity and relatedness of the several operations. It is a unity and relatedness that exists and functions before we manage to advert to it explicitly, understand it, objectify it. It is a unity and relatedness quite different from the intelligible unities and relations by which we organize the data of sense, for they are merely intelligible, while the unity and relatedness of conscious process is intelligent, reasonable, responsible.

We have considered, first, experiencing the operations and, secondly, understanding their unity and relatedness. There arises the question for reflection. Do these operations occur? Do they occur in the described pattern? Is not that pattern just hypothetical, sooner or later due for revision and, when revised, sooner or later due for still further revision?

First, the operations exist and occur. Despite the doubts and denials of positivists and behaviorists, no one, unless some of his organs are deficient, is going to say that never in his life did he have the experience of seeing or of hearing, of touching or smelling or tasting, of imagining or perceiving, of feeling or moving; or that if he appeared to have such experience, still it was mere appearance, since all his life long he has gone about like a somnambulist without any awareness of his own activities. Again, how rare is the man that will preface his lectures by repeating his conviction that never did he have even a fleeting experience of intellectual curiosity, of inquiry, of striving and coming to understand, of expressing what he has grasped by understanding. Rare too is the man that begins his contributions to periodical literature by reminding his potential readers that never in his life did he experience anything that might be called critical reflection, that he never paused about the truth or falsity of any statement, that if ever he seemed to exercise his rationality by passing judgment strictly in accord with the available evidence, then that must be counted mere appearance for he is totally unaware of any such event or even any such tendency. Few finally are those that place at the beginning of their books the warning that they have no notion of what might be meant by responsibility, that never in their lives did they have the experience of acting responsibly, and that least of all in composing the books they are offering the public. In brief, conscious and intentional operations exist and anyone that cares to deny their existence is merely disqualifying himself as a non-responsible, non-reasonable, non-intelligent somnambulist.

Next, do the operations occur in the pattern that has been sketched here and presented more fully in the book, *Insight*? The answer to this, of course, is that we do not experience the operations in isolation and then, by a process of inquiry and discovery, arrive at the pattern of relations that link them together. On the contrary, the unity of consciousness is itself given; the pattern of the operations is part of the experience of the operations; and inquiry and discovery are needed, not to effect the synthesis of a manifold that, as given, is unrelated, but to analyze a functional and functioning unity. Without analysis, it is true, we cannot discern and distinguish the several operations; and until the operations have been distinguished, we cannot formulate the relations that link them together. But the point to the statement that the pattern itself is conscious is that, once the relations are formulated, they are not found to express surprising novelties but simply prove to be objectifications of the routines of our conscious living and doing. Before inquiry brings the pattern to light, before the methodologist issues his precepts, the pattern is already conscious and operative. Spontaneously we move from experiencing to the effort to understand; and the spontaneity is not unconscious or blind; on the contrary, it is constitutive of our conscious intelligence, just as the absence of the effort to understand is constitutive of stupidity. Spontaneously we move from understanding with its manifold and conflicting expressions to critical reflection; again, the spontaneity is not unconscious or blind; it is constitutive of our critical rationality, of the demand within us for sufficient reason, a demand that operates prior to any formulation of a principle of sufficient reason; and it is the neglect or absence of this demand that constitutes silliness. Spontaneously we move from judgments of fact or possibility to judgments of value and to the deliberateness of decision and commitment; and that spontaneity is not unconscious or blind; it constitutes us as conscientious, as responsible persons, and its absence would leave us psychopaths. In various detailed manners, method will bid us be attentive, intelligent, reasonable, responsible. The details of its prescriptions will be derived from the work in hand and will vary with it. But the normative force of its imperatives will reside, not just in its claims to authority, not just in the probability that what succeeded in the past will succeed in the future, but at root in the native spontaneities and inevitabilities of our consciousness which assembles its own constituent parts and unites them in a rounded whole in a manner we cannot set aside without, as it were, amputating our own moral personality, our own reasonableness, our own intelligence, our own sensitivity.

But is this pattern not just a hypothesis that can be expected to undergo revision after revision as man's self-knowledge keeps developing?

A distinction must be drawn between the normative pattern

immanent in our conscious and intentional operations and, on the other hand, objectifications of that pattern in concepts, propositions, words. Obviously, revision can affect nothing but objectifications. It cannot change the dynamic structure of human consciousness. All it can do is bring about a more adequate account of that structure.

Moreover, for it to be possible for a revision to take place certain conditions must be fulfilled. For, in the first place, any possible revision will appeal to data which the opinion under review either overlooked or misapprehended, and so any possible revision must presuppose at least an empirical level of operations. Secondly, any possible revision will offer a better explanation of the data, and so any possible revision must presuppose an intellectual level of operations. Thirdly, any possible revision will claim that the better explanation is more probable, and so any possible revision must presuppose a rational level of operations. Fourthly, a revision is not a mere possibility but an accomplished fact only as the result of a judgment of value and a decision. One undertakes the labor with all its risks of failure and frustration only because one holds, not only in theory but also in practice, that it is worth while to get things straight, to know with exactitude, to contribute to the advancement of science. So at the root of all method there has to be presupposed a level of operations on which we evaluate and choose responsibly at least the method of our operations.

It follows that there is a sense in which the objectification of the normative pattern of our conscious and intentional operations does not admit revision. The sense in question is that the activity of revising consists in such operations in accord with such a pattern, so that a revision rejecting the pattern would be rejecting itself.

There is then a rock on which one can build. But let me repeat the precise character of the rock.[5] Any theory, description, account of our conscious and intentional operations is bound to be incomplete and to admit further clarifications and extensions.

[5] It will become evident in Chapter Four that the more important part of the rock has not yet been uncovered.

But all such clarifications and extensions are to be derived from the conscious and intentional operations themselves. They as given in consciousness are the rock; they confirm every exact account; they refute every inexact or incomplete account. The rock, then, is the subject in his conscious, unobjectified attentiveness, intelligence, reasonableness, responsibility. The point to the labor of objectifying the subject and his conscious operations is that thereby one begins to learn what these are and that they are.

4. THE FUNCTIONS OF TRANSCENDENTAL METHOD

We have been inviting the reader to discover in himself the original normative pattern of recurrent and related operations that yield cumulative and progressive results. We have now to consider what uses or functions are served by that basic method.

First, then, there is the normative function. All special methods consist in making specific the transcendental precepts, Be attentive, Be intelligent, Be reasonable, Be responsible. But before they are ever formulated in concepts and expressed in words, those precepts have a prior existence and reality in the spontaneous, structured dynamism of human consciousness. Moreover, just as the transcendental precepts rest simply on a study of the operations themselves, so specific categorial precepts rest on a study of the mind operating in a given field. The ultimate basis of both transcendental and categorial precepts will be advertence to the difference between attention and inattention, intelligence and stupidity, reasonableness and unreasonableness, responsibility and irresponsibility.

Secondly, there is the critical function. The scandal still continues that men, while they tend to agree on scientific questions, tend to disagree in the most outrageous fashion on basic philosophic issues. So they disagree about the activities named knowing about the relation of those activities to reality, and about reality itself. However, differences on the third, reality, can be reduced to differences about the first and second, knowledge and objectivity. Differences on the second, objectivity, can be reduced to differences on the first, cognitional theory. Finally, differences in cognitional theory can be resolved by bringing to light the contradiction between a mistaken cognitional theory and the actual performance of the mistaken theorist.[6] To take the simplest instance, Hume thought the human mind to be a matter of impressions linked together by custom. But Hume's own mind was quite original. Therefore, Hume's own mind was not what Hume considered the human mind to be.

Thirdly, there is the dialectical function. For the critical use of transcendental method can be applied to every mistaken cognitional theory, whether expressed with philosophic generality or presupposed by a method of hermeneutics, of historical investigation, of theology, or demythologization. Moreover, these applications can be extended to concomitant views on epistemology and metaphysics. In this fashion one can determine the dialectical series of basic positions, which criticism confirms, and of basic counter-positions, which criticism confounds.

Fourthly, there is the systematic function. For in the measure that transcendental method is objectified, there are determined a set of basic terms and relations, namely, the terms that refer to the operations of cognitional process, and the relations that link these operations to one another. Such terms and relations are the substance of cognitional theory. They reveal the ground for epistemology. They are found to be isomorphic[7] with the terms and relations denoting the ontological structure of any reality proportionate to human cognitional process.

Fifthly, the foregoing systematic function assures continuity without imposing rigidity. Continuity is assured by the source of the basic terms and relations, for that source is human cognitional process in its concrete reality. Rigidity is not imposed, for a fuller and more exact knowledge of human cognitional process is by no means excluded and, in the measure it is attained, there will follow a fuller and more exact determination of basic terms and relations. Finally, the exclusion of rigidity is not a

[6] In greater detail, *Insight*, pp. 387 ff. *Collection*, pp. 203 ff.

[7] This isomorphism rests on the fact that one and the same process constructs both elementary acts of knowing into a compound knowing and elementary objects of knowing into the compound object.

menace to continuity for, as we have seen, the conditions of the possibility of revision set limits to the possibility of revising cognitional theory, and the more elaborate the revision, the stricter and more detailed these limits will be.

Sixthly, there is the heuristic function. Every inquiry aims at transforming some unknown into a known. Inquiry itself, then, is something between ignorance and knowledge. It is less than knowledge, else there would be no need to inquire. It is more than sheer ignorance, for it makes ignorance manifest and strives to replace it with knowledge. This intermediary between ignorance and knowing is an intending, and what is intended is an unknown that is to be known.

Now fundamentally all method is the exploitation of such intending, for it outlines the steps to be taken if one is to proceed from the initial intending of the question to the eventual knowing of what has been intended all along. Moreover, within method the use of heuristic devices is fundamental. They consist in designating and naming the intended unknown, in setting down at once all that can be affirmed about it, and in using this explicit knowledge as a guide, a criterion, and/or a premiss in the effort to arrive at a fuller knowledge. Such is the function in algebra of the unknown, x, in the solution of problems. Such is the function in physics of indeterminate or generic functions and of the classes of functions specified by differential equations.

Now transcendental method fulfils a heuristic function. It reveals the very nature of that function by bringing to light the activity of intending and its correlative, the intended that, though unknown, at least is intended. Moreover, inasmuch as the systematic function has provided sets of basic terms and relations, there are to hand basic determinations that may be set down at once whenever the unknown is a human subject or an object proportionate to human cognitional process, i.e. an object to be known by experiencing, understanding, and judging.

Seventhly, there is the foundational function. Special methods derive their proper norms from the accumulated experience of investigators in their several fields. But besides the proper norms there are also common norms. Besides the tasks in each field there are interdisciplinary problems. Underneath the consent of men as scientists, there is their dissent on matters of ultimate significance and concern. It is in the measure that special methods acknowledge their common core in transcendental method, that norms common to all the sciences will be acknowledged, that a secure basis will be attained for attacking interdisciplinary problems, and that the sciences will be mobilized within a higher unity of vocabulary, thought, and orientation, in which they will be able to make their quite significant contribution to the solution of fundamental problems.

Eighthly, transcendental method is relevant to theology. This relevance, of course, is mediated by the special method proper to theology and developed through the reflection of theologians on the successes and failures of their efforts past and present. But this special method, while it has its own special classes and combinations of operations, none the less is the work of human minds performing the same basic operations in the same basic relations as are found in other special methods. In other words, transcendental method is a constituent part of the special method proper to theology, just as it is a constituent part in the special methods proper to the natural and to the human sciences. However true it is that one attends, understands, judges, decides differently in the natural sciences, in the human sciences, and in theology, still these differences in no way imply or suggest a transition from attention to inattention, from intelligence to stupidity, from reasonableness to silliness, from responsibility to irresponsibility.

Ninthly, the objects of theology do not lie outside the transcendental field. For that field is unrestricted, and so outside it there is nothing at all. Moreover, it is not unrestricted in the sense that the transcendental notions are abstract, least in connotation and greatest in denotation; for the transcendental notions are not abstract but comprehensive; they intend everything about everything. So far from being abstract, it is by them that we intend the concrete, i.e., all that is to be known about a thing. Finally, while it is, of course, true that human knowing is limited, still the transcendental notions are not a matter of knowing but of intending; they intended all that each of us has managed to learn, and they now intend all that as yet remains unknown. In other words, the transcendental field is defined not by what man knows, not by what he can know, but by what he can ask about; and it is only because we can ask more questions than we can answer that we know about the limitations of our knowledge.

Tenthly, to assign to transcendental method a role in theology adds no new resource to theology but simply draws attention to a resource that has always been used. For transcendental method is the concrete and dynamic unfolding of human attentiveness, intelligence, reasonableness, and responsibility. That unfolding occurs whenever anyone uses his mind in an appropriate fashion. Hence, to introduce transcendental method introduces no new resource into theology, for theologians always have had minds and always have used them. However, while transcendental method will introduce no new resource, it does add considerable light and precision to the performance of theological tasks, and this, I trust, will become manifest in due course.

In the eleventh place, transcendental method offers a key to unified science. The immobility of the Aristotelian ideal conflicts with developing natural science, developing human science, developing dogma, and developing theology. In harmony with all development is the human mind itself which effects the developments. In unity with all fields, however disparate, is again the human mind that operates in all fields and in radically the same fashion in each. Through the self-knowledge, the self-appropriation, the self-possession that result from making explicit the basic normative pattern of the recurrent and related operations of human cognitional process, it becomes possible to envisage a future in which all workers in all fields can find in transcendental method common norms, foundations, systematics, and common critical, dialectical, and heuristic procedures.

In the twelfth place, the introduction of transcendental method abrogates the old metaphor that describes philosophy as the handmaid of theology and replaces it by a very precise fact. Transcendental method is not the intrusion into theology of alien matter from an alien source. Its function is to advert to the fact that theologies are produced by theologians, that theologians have minds and use them, that their doing so should not be ignored or passed over but explicitly acknowledged in itself and in its implications. Again, transcendental method is coincident with a notable part of what has been considered philosophy, but it is not any philosophy or all philosophy. Very precisely, it is a heightening of consciousness that brings to light our conscious and intentional operations and thereby leads to the answers to three basic questions. What am I doing when I am knowing? Why is doing that knowing? What do I know when I do it? The first answer is a cognitional theory. The second is an epistemology. The third is a metaphysics where, however, the metaphysics is transcendental, an integration of heuristic structures, and not some categorial speculation that reveals that all is water, or matter, or spirit, or process, or what have you.

It remains, however, that transcendental method is only a part of theological method. It supplies the basic anthropological component. It does not supply the specifically religious component. Accordingly, to advance from transcendental to theological method, it is necessary to add a consideration of religion. And before we can speak of religion, we first must say something about the human good and about human meaning.

2

THE HUMAN GOOD

WHAT is good, always is concrete. But definitions are abstract. Hence, if one attempts to define the good, one runs the risk of misleading one's readers. The present chapter, then, aims at assembling the various components that enter into the human good. So it will speak of skills, feelings, values, beliefs, cooperation, progress, and decline.

1. SKILLS

Jean Piaget analyzed the acquisition of a skill into elements. Each new element consisted in an adaptation to some new object or situation. In each adaptation there were distinguished two parts, assimilation and adjustment. Assimilation brought into play the spontaneous or the previously learned operations employed successfully on somewhat similar objects or in somewhat similar situations. Adjustment by a process of trial and error gradually modified and supplemented previously learned operations.

As adaptation to ever more objects and situations occurs, there goes forward a twofold process. There is an increasing differentiation of operations so that more and more different operations are in one's repertory. There also is an ever greater multiplication of different combinations of differentiated operations. So the baby gradually develops oral, visual, manual, bodily skills, and he increasingly combines them in ever varying manners.

Skill begets mastery and, to define it, Piaget invoked the mathematical notion of group. The principal characteristic of the group of operations is that every operation in the group is matched by an opposite operation and every combination of operations is matched by an opposite combination. Hence, inasmuch as operations are grouped, the operator can always return to his starting-point and, when he can do so unhesitatingly, he has reached mastery at some level of development. It was by distinguishing and defining different groups of operations and successive grouping of groups that Piaget was able to mark off stages in child development and to predict what operations school children of various ages would be able or unable to perform.

Finally, there is the notion of mediation. Operations are said to be immediate when their objects are present. So seeing is immediate to what is being seen, hearing to what is being heard, touch to what is being touched. But by imagination, language, symbols, we operate in a compound manner; immediately with respect to the image, word, symbol; mediately with respect to what is represented or signified. In this fashion we come to operate not only with respect to the present and actual but also with respect to the absent, the past, the future, the merely possible or ideal or normative or fantastic. As the child learns to speak, he moves out of the world of his immediate surroundings towards the far larger world revealed through the memories of other men, through the common sense of community, through the pages of literature, through the labors of scholars, through the investigations of scientists, through the experience of saints, through the meditations of philosophers and theologians.

This distinction between immediate and mediate operations has quite a broad relevance. It sets off the world of immediacy of the infant against the vastly larger world mediated by meaning. Further, it provides a basis for a distinction between lower and higher cultures. The lower regards a world mediated by meaning but it lacks controls over meaning and so easily indulges in magic and myth. The higher culture develops reflexive techniques that operate on the mediate operations themselves in an effort to safeguard meaning. So alphabets replace vocal with visual signs, dictionaries fix the meanings of words, grammars control their inflections and combinations, logics promote the clarity, coherence, and rigor of discourse, hermeneutics studies the varying relationships between meaning and meant, and philosophies explore the more basic differences between worlds mediated by meaning. Finally, among high cultures one may distinguish classical and modern by the general type of their controls: the classical thinks of the control as a universal fixed for all time; the modern thinks of the controls as themselves involved in an ongoing process.

Corresponding to different degrees of development and different worlds mediated by meaning, there are similar differences in the differentiation of consciousness. It is only in the process of development that the subject becomes aware of himself and of his distinction from his world. As his apprehension of his world and as his conduct in it develop, he begins to move through different patterns of experience. When children imitate or play, they are living in a world mediated by their own meanings; it is not for "real" but just for fun. When their elders shift from the world mediated by meaning to the reflexive techniques in which they operate on the mediating operations, they are moving from "real" life to a world of theory or, as many say, of abstractions that, despite the rare atmosphere, has a mysterious relevance to successful performance in the "real" world. When they listen to music, gaze upon a tree or landscape, are stopped by beauty of any kind, they are freeing their sensitivity from the routines imposed by development and allowing it to follow fresher and deeper rhythms of apprehension and feeling. When finally the mystic withdraws into the *ultima solitudo*, he drops the constructs of culture and the whole complicated mass of mediating operations to return to a new, mediated immediacy of his subjectivity reaching for God.[1]

The relevance, then, of Piaget's analysis goes far beyond the field of educational psychology. It enables one to distinguish

[1] On patterns of experience, see *Insight*, pp. 181 ff. On peak experiences, A. H. Maslow, *Toward a Psychology of Being*, Princeton, N.J., 1962; A Reza Aresteh, *Final Integration in the Adult Personality*, Leiden: E. J. Brill, 1965; William Johnston, *The Mysticism of the Cloud of Unknowing*, New York, Rome, Paris, Tournai: Desclée, 1967; *Christian Zen*, New York: Harper and Row, 1971; A. H. Maslow, *Religions, Values, and Peak Experiences*, New York: Viking Press, 1970.

stages in cultural development and to characterize man's breaking loose from it in play, in the climax of making love, in aesthetic experience, and in contemplative prayer. Moreover, any technical proficiency can be analyzed as a group of combinations of differentiated operations. That does not define the concert pianist's ability to project a sonata, but it does say in what his technical skill consists. Again, it does not reveal the grand plan of Aquinas' *Contra Gentiles*. But if one reads a series of successive chapters, one finds the same arguments recurring over and over in ever slightly different forms; what was going forward when the *Contra Gentiles* was being written, was the differentiation of operations and their conjunction in ever fresh combinations. Finally, as there is the technical proficiency of the individual, so too there is the technical proficiency of a team whether of players or artists or skilled workers, the possibility of their learning new operations, and of the coach, the impresario, the entrepreneur bringing them together in new combinations to new ends.

2. FEELINGS

Distinct from operational development is the development of feeling. On this topic I would draw on Dietrich von Hildebrand and distinguish non-intentional states and trends from intentional responses. The former may be illustrated by such states as fatigue, irritability, bad humor, anxiety, and the latter by such trends or urges as hunger, thirst, sexual discomfort. The states have causes. The trends have goals. But the relation of the feeling to the cause or goal is simply that of effect to cause, of trend to goal. The feeling itself does not presuppose and arise out of perceiving, imagining, representing the cause or goal. Rather, one first feels tired and, perhaps belatedly, one discovers that what one needs is a rest. Or first one feels hungry and then one diagnoses the trouble as a lack of food.

Intentional responses, on the other hand, answer to what is intended, apprehended, represented. The feeling relates us, not just to a cause or an end, but to an object. Such feeling gives intentional consciousness its mass, momentum, drive, power. Without these feelings our knowing and deciding would be paper thin. Because of our feelings, our desires and our fears, our hope or despair, our joys and sorrows, our enthusiasm and indignation, our esteem and contempt, our trust and distrust, our love and hatred, our tenderness and wrath, our admiration, veneration, reverence, our dread, horror, terror, we are oriented massively and dynamically in a world mediated by meaning. We have feelings about other persons, we feel for them, we feel with them. We have feelings about our respective situations, about the past, about the future, about evils to be lamented or remedied, about the good that can, might, must be accomplished.[2]

Feelings that are intentional responses regard two main classes of objects: on the one hand, the agreeable or disagreeable, the satisfying or dissatisfying; on the other hand, values, whether the ontic value of persons or the qualitative value of beauty, understanding, truth, virtuous acts, noble deeds. In general, response to value both carries us towards self-transcendence and selects an object for the sake of whom or of which we transcend ourselves. In contrast, response to the agreeable or disagreeable is ambiguous. What is agreeable may very well be what also is a true good. But it also happens that what is a true good may be disagreeable. Most good men have to accept unpleasant work, privations, pain, and their virtue is a matter of doing so without excessive self-centered lamentation.[3]

Not only do feelings respond to values. They do so in accord with some scale of preference. So we may distinguish vital, social, cultural, personal, and religious values in an ascending order. Vital values, such as health and strength, grace and vigor, normally are preferred to avoiding the work, privations, pains involved in acquiring, maintaining, restoring them. Social values, such as the good of order which conditions the vital values of the whole community, have to be preferred to the vital values

[2] A wealth of analysis of feelings is to be had in Dietrich von Hildebrand's *Christian Ethics*, New York: David McKay, 1953. See also Manfred Frings, *Max Scheler*, Pittsburgh: Duquesne University Press, 1965.

[3] The next two sections of this chapter will endeavor to clarify both the notion of value and judgments of value.

of individual members of the community. Cultural values do not exist without the underpinning of vital and social values, but none the less they rank higher. Not on bread alone doth man live. Over and above mere living and operating, men have to find a meaning and value in their living and operating. It is the function of culture to discover, express, validate, criticize, correct, develop, improve such meaning and value. Personal value is the person in his self-transcendence, as loving and being loved, as originator of values in himself and in his milieu, as an inspiration and invitation to others to do likewise. Religious values, finally, are at the heart of the meaning and value of man's living and man's world, but to this topic we return in Chapter Four.

No less than of skills, there is a development of feelings. It is true, of course, that fundamentally feelings are spontaneous. They do not lie under the command of decision as do the motions of our hands. But, once they have arisen, they may be reinforced by advertence and approval, and they may be curtailed by disapproval and distraction. Such reinforcement and curtailment not only will encourage some feelings and discourage others but also will modify one's spontaneous scale of preferences. Again, feelings are enriched and refined by attentive study of the wealth and variety of the objects that arouse them, and so no small part of education lies in fostering and developing a climate of discernment and taste, of discriminating praise and carefully worded disapproval, that will conspire with the pupil's or student's own capacities and tendencies, enlarge and deepen his apprehension of values, and help him towards self-transcendence.

I have been conceiving feelings as intentional responses but I must add that they are not merely transient, limited to the time that we are apprehending a value or its opposite, and vanishing the moment our attention shifts. There are, of course, feelings that easily are aroused and easily pass away. There are too the feelings that have been snapped off by repression to lead thereafter an unhappy subterranean life. But there are in full consciousness feelings so deep and strong, especially when deliberately reinforced, that they channel attention, shape one's horizon, direct one's life. Here the supreme illustration is loving. A man or woman that falls in love is engaged in loving not only when attending to the beloved but at all times. Besides particular acts of loving, there is the prior state of being in love, and that prior state is, as it were, the fount of all one's actions. So mutual love is the intertwining of two lives. It transforms an "I" and "thou" into a "we" so intimate, so secure, so permanent, that each attends, imagines, thinks, plans, feels, speaks, acts in concern for both.

As there is a development of feelings, so too there are aberrations. Perhaps the most notable is what has been named "ressentiment", a loan-word from the French that was introduced into philosophy by Friedrich Nietzsche and later in a revised form employed by Max Scheler.[4] According to Scheler, ressentiment is a re-feeling of a specific clash with someone else's value-qualities. The someone else is one's superior physically or intellectually or morally or spiritually. The re-feeling is not active or aggressive but extends over time, even a life-time. It is a feeling of hostility, anger, indignation that is neither repudiated nor directly expressed. What it attacks is the value-quality that the superior person possessed and the inferior not only lacked but also feels unequal to acquiring. The attack amounts to a continuous belittling of the value in question, and it can extend to hatred and even violence against those that possess that value-quality. But perhaps its worst feature is that its rejection of one value involves a distortion of the whole scale of values and that this distortion can spread through a whole social class, a whole people, a whole epoch. So the analysis of ressentiment can turn out to be a tool of ethical, social, and historical criticism.

More generally, it is much better to take full cognizance of one's feelings, however deplorable they may be, than to brush them aside, overrule them, ignore them. To take cognizance of them makes it possible for one to know oneself, to uncover the inattention, obtuseness, silliness, irresponsibility that gave rise to the feeling one does not want, and to correct the aberrant attitude.

[4] On various applications of the analysis of ressentiment, see Manfred Frings, *Max Scheler*, Chapter Five, Pittsburgh: Duquesne University Press, and Louvain: Nauwelaerts, 1965.

On the other hand, not to take cognizance of them is to leave them in the twilight of what is conscious but not objectified.[5] In the long run there results a conflict between the self as conscious and, on the other hand, the self as objectified. This alienation from oneself leads to the adoption of misguided remedies, and they in their turn to still further mistakes until, in desperation, the neurotic turns to the analyst or counsellor.[6]

3. THE NOTION OF VALUE

Value is a transcendental notion. It is what is intended in questions for deliberation, just as the intelligible is what is intended in questions for intelligence, and just as truth and being are what are intended in questions for reflection. Such intending is not knowing. When I ask what, or why, or how, or what for, I do not know the answers, but already I am intending what would be known if I knew the answers. When I ask whether this or that is so, I do not as yet know whether or not either is so, but already I am intending what would be known if I did know the answers. So when I ask whether this is truly and not merely apparently good, whether that is or is not worth while, I do not yet know value but I am intending value.

The transcendental notions are the dynamism of conscious intentionality. They promote the subject from lower to higher levels of consciousness, from the experiential to the intellectual,

---

[5] This twilight of what is conscious but not objectified seems to be the meaning of what some psychiatrists call the unconscious. See Karen Horney, *The Neurotic Personality of Our Time*, New York: W. W. Norton, 1937, pp. 68 f. *Neurosis and Human Growth*, New York: W. W. Norton, 1950, pp. 162 f. Raymond Hostie, *Religion and the Psychology of Jung*, New York: Sheed and Ward, 1957, p. 72. Wilhelm Stekel, *Compulsion and Doubt*, New York: Grosset and Dunlap, 1962, pp. 252, 256.

[6] On the development of the malady, Karen Horney, *Neurosis and Human Growth*, New York: W. W. Norton, 1950. On the therapeutic process, Carl Rogers, *On Becoming a Person*, Boston: Houghton Mifflin, 1961. Just as transcendental method rests on a self-appropriation, on attending to, inquiring about, understanding, conceiving, affirming one's attending, inquiring, understanding, conceiving, affirming, so too therapy is an appropriation of one's own feelings. As the former task is blocked by misconceptions of human knowing, so too the latter is blocked by misconceptions of what one spontaneously is.

from the intellectual to the rational, from the rational to the existential. Again, with respect to objects, they are the intermediaries between ignorance and knowledge; indeed, they refer to objects immediately and directly, while answers refer to objects only mediately, only because they are answers to the questions that intend the objects.

Not only do the transcendental notions promote the subject to full consciousness and direct him to his goals. They also provide the criteria that reveal whether the goals are being reached. The drive to understand is satisfied when understanding is reached but it is dissatisfied with every incomplete attainment and so it is the source of ever further questions. The drive to truth compels rationality to assent when evidence is sufficient but refuses assent and demands doubt whenever evidence is insufficient.[7] The drive to value rewards success in self-transcendence with a happy conscience and saddens failures with an unhappy conscience.

Self-transcendence is the achievement of conscious intentionality, and as the latter has many parts and a long development, so too has the former. There is a first step in attending to the data of sense and of consciousness. Next, inquiry and understanding yield an apprehension of a hypothetical world mediated by meaning. Thirdly, reflection and judgment reach an absolute: through them we acknowledge what really is so, what is independent of us and our thinking. Fourthly, by deliberation, evaluation, decision, action, we can know and do, not just what pleases us, but what truly is good, worth while. Then we can be principles of benevolence and beneficence, capable of genuine collaboration and of true love. But it is one thing to do this occasionally, by fits and starts. It is another to do it regularly, easily, spontaneously. It is, finally, only by reaching the sustained self-transcendence of the virtuous man that one becomes a good judge, not on this or that human act, but on the whole range of human goodness.[8]

[7] On the precise meaning of sufficient and insufficient evidence, see *Insight*, Chapters Ten and Eleven.

[8] To this point we return in the next section on judgments of value.

Finally, while the transcendental notions are broader than any category, it would be a mistake to infer that they were more abstract. On the contrary, they are utterly concrete. For the concrete is the real not under this or that aspect but under its every aspect in its every instance. But the transcendental notions are the fount not only of initial questions but also of further questions. Moreover, though the further questions come only one at a time, still they keep coming. There are ever further questions for intelligence pushing up towards a fuller understanding and ever further doubts urging us to a fuller truth. The only limit to the process is at the point where no further questions arise, and that point would be reached only when we correctly understood everything about everything, only when we knew reality in its every aspect and every instance.

Similarly, by the good is never meant some abstraction. Only the concrete is good. Again, as the transcendental notions of the intelligible, the true, the real head for a complete intelligibility, all truth, the real in its every part and aspect, so the transcendental notion of the good heads for a goodness that is beyond criticism. For that notion is our raising questions for deliberation. It is our being stopped with the disenchantment that asks whether what we are doing is worth while. That disenchantment brings to light the limitation in every finite achievement, the stain in every flawed perfection, the irony of soaring ambition and faltering performance. It plunges us into the height and depth of love, but it also keeps us aware of how much our loving falls short of its aim. In brief, the transcendental notion of the good so invites, presses, harries us, that we could rest only in an encounter with a goodness completely beyond its powers of criticism.

4. JUDGMENTS OF VALUE

Judgments of value are simple or comparative. They affirm or deny that some x is truly or only apparently good. Or they compare distinct instances of the truly good to affirm or deny that one is better or more important, or more urgent than the other.

Such judgments are objective or merely subjective inasmuch as they proceed or do not proceed from a self-transcending subject. Their truth or falsity, accordingly, has its criterion in the authenticity or the lack of authenticity of the subject's being. But the criterion is one thing and the meaning of the judgment is another. To say that an affirmative judgment of value is true is to say what objectively is or would be good or better. To say that an affirmative judgment of value is false is to say what objectively is not or would not be good or better.

Judgments of value differ in content but not in structure from judgments of fact. They differ in content, for one can approve of what does not exist, and one can disapprove of what does. They do not differ in structure, inasmuch as in both there is the distinction between criterion and meaning. In both, the criterion is the self-transcendence of the subject, which, however, is only cognitive in judgments of fact but is heading towards moral self-transcendence in judgments of value. In both, the meaning is or claims to be independent of the subject: judgments of fact state or purport to state what is or is not so; judgments of value state or purport to state what is or is not truly good or really better.

True judgments of value go beyond merely intentional self-transcendence without reaching the fulness of moral self-transcendence. That fulness is not merely knowing but also doing, and man can know what is right without doing it. Still, if he knows and does not perform, either he must be humble enough to acknowledge himself to be a sinner, or else he will start destroying his moral being by rationalizing, by making out that what truly is good really is not good at all. The judgment of value, then, is itself a reality in the moral order. By it the subject moves beyond pure and simple knowing. By it the subject is constituting himself as proximately capable of moral self-transcendence, of benevolence and beneficence, of true loving.

Intermediate between judgments of fact and judgments in value lie apprehensions of value. Such apprehensions are given of feelings. The feelings in question are not the already described non-intentional states, trends, urges, that are related to efficient and final causes but not to objects. Again, they are not intentional responses to such objects as the agreeable or disagreeable, the pleasant or painful, the satisfying or dissatisfying. For, while these are objects, still they are ambiguous objects that may prove to be truly good or bad or only apparently good or bad. Apprehensions of value occur in a further category of intentional response which greets either the ontic value of a person or the qualitative value of beauty, of understanding, of truth, of noble deeds, of virtuous acts, of great achievements. For we are so endowed that we not only ask questions leading to self-transcendence, not only can recognize correct answers constitutive of intentional self-transcendence, but also respond with the stirring of our very being when we glimpse the possibility or the actuality of moral self-transcendence.[9]

In the judgment of value, then, three components unite. First, there is knowledge of reality and especially of human reality. Secondly, there are intentional responses to values. Thirdly, there is the initial thrust towards moral self-transcendence constituted by the judgment of value itself. The judgment of value presupposes knowledge of human life, of human possibilities proximate and remote, of the probable consequences of projected courses of action. When knowledge is deficient, then fine feelings are apt to be expressed in what is called moral idealism, i.e. lovely proposals that don't work out and often do more harm than good. But knowledge alone is not enough and, while everyone has some measure of moral feeling for, as the saying is, there is honor among thieves, still moral feelings have to be cultivated, enlightened, strengthened, refined, criticized and pruned of oddities. Finally, the development of knowledge and the development of moral feeling head to the existential discovery, the discovery of oneself as a moral being, the realization that one not only chooses between courses of action but also thereby makes oneself an authentic human being or an unauthentic one. With that discovery, there emerges in consciousness the significance of personal value and the meaning of personal responsibility.

[9] On values, scales of preference, feelings and their development, see above, pp. 31 and 37.

One's judgments of value are revealed as the door to one's fulfilment or to one's loss. Experience, especially repeated experience, of one's frailty or wickedness raises the question of one's salvation and, on a more fundamental level, there arises the question of God.

The fact of development and the possibility of failure imply that judgments of value occur in different contexts. There is the context of growth, in which one's knowledge of human living and operating is increasing in extent, precision, refinement, and in which one's responses are advancing from the agreeable to vital values, from vital to social, from social to cultural, from cultural to personal, from personal to religious. Then there prevails an openness to ever further achievement.[10] Past gains are organized and consolidated but they are not rounded off into a closed system but remain incomplete and so open to still further discoveries and developments. The free thrust of the subject into new areas is recurrent and, as yet, there is no supreme value that entails all others. But at the summit of the ascent from the initial infantile bundle of needs and clamors and gratifications, there are to be found the deep-set joy and solid peace, the power and the vigor, of being in love with God. In the measure that that summit is reached, then the supreme value is God, and other values are God's expression of his love in this world, in its aspirations, and in its goal. In the measure that one's love of God is complete, then values are whatever one loves, and evils are whatever one hates so that, in Augustine's phrase, if one loves God, one may do as one pleases, *Ama Deum et fac quod vis.* Then affectivity is of a single piece. Further developments only fill out previous achievement. Lapses from grace are rarer and more quickly amended.

But continuous growth seems to be rare.[11] There are the deviations occasioned by neurotic need. There are the refusals to keep on taking the plunge from settled routines to an as yet

[10] On growth, growth motivation, and neurotic needs, see A. Maslow, *Towards a Psychology of Being*, Princeton, N.J.: Van Nostrand, 1962.
[11] Prof. Maslow (op. cit., p. 190) finds self-actualization in less than one per cent of the adult population.

unexperienced but richer mode of living. There are the mistaken endeavors to quieten an uneasy conscience by ignoring, belittling, denying, rejecting higher values. Preference scales become distorted. Feelings soured. Bias creeps into one's outlook, rationalization into one's morals, ideology into one's thought. So one may come to hate the truly good, and love the really evil. Nor is that calamity limited to individuals. It can happen to groups, to nations, to blocks of nations, to mankind.[12] It can take different, opposed, belligerent forms to divide mankind and to menace civilization with destruction. Such is the monster that has stood forth in our day.

In his thorough and penetrating study of human action, Joseph de Finance distinguished between horizontal and vertical liberty.[13] Horizontal liberty is the exercise of liberty within a determinate horizon and from the basis of a corresponding existential stance. Vertical liberty is the exercise of liberty that selects that stance and the corresponding horizon. Such vertical liberty may be implicit: it occurs in responding to the motives that lead one to ever fuller authenticity, or in ignoring such motives and drifting into an ever less authentic selfhood. But it also can be explicit. Then one is responding to the transcendental notion of value, by determining what it would be worth while for one to make of oneself, and what it would be worth while for one to do for one's fellow men. One works out an ideal of human reality and achievement, and to that ideal one dedicates oneself. As one's knowledge increases, as one's experience is enriched, as one's reach is strengthened or weakened, one's ideal may be revised and the revision may recur many times.

In such vertical liberty, whether implicit or explicit, are to be found the foundations of the judgments of value that occur. Such judgments are felt to be true or false in so far as they generate a peaceful or uneasy conscience. But they attain their proper context, their clarity and refinement, only through

[12] On ressentiment and the distortion of preference scales, see Manfred Frings, *Max Scheler*, Pittsburgh and Louvain, 1965, Chapter Five.

[13] J. de Finance, *Essai sur l'agir humain*, Rome: Presses de l'Université Grégorienne, 1962, pp. 287 ff.

man's historical development and the individual's personal appropriation of his social, cultural, and religious heritage. It is by
the transcendental notion of value and its expression in a good
and an uneasy conscience that man can develop morally. But
a rounded moral judgment is ever the work of a fully developed self-transcending subject or, as Aristotle would put it, of
a virtuous man.[14]

5. BELIEFS[15]

To appropriate one's social, cultural, religious heritage is
largely a matter of belief. There is, of course, much that one
finds out for oneself, that one knows simply in virtue of one's
own inner and outer experience, one's own insights, one's own
judgments of fact and of value. But such immanently generated
knowledge is but a small fraction of what any civilized man
considers himself to know. His immediate experience is filled
out by an enormous context constituted by reports of the experience of other men at other places and times. His understanding
rests not only on his own but also on the experience of others,
and its development owes little indeed to his personal originality,
much to his repeating in himself the acts of understanding first
made by others, and most of all to presuppositions that he has
taken for granted because they commonly are assumed and, in

[14] While Aristotle spoke not of values but of virtues, still his account of
virtue presupposes the existence of virtuous men, as my account of value presupposes the existence of self-transcending subjects. See Aristotle, *Nicomachean
Ethics*, II, iii, 4; 1105b 5–8: "Actions, then, are called just and temperate when
they are such as the just and temperate man would do; but it is not the man
who does these that is just and temperate, but the man who also does them *as*
just and temperate men do them." Similarly, ibid., II, vi, 15; 1106b 36 ff.:
"Virtue, then, is a state of character concerned with choice, lying in a mean, i.e.
the mean relative to us, this being determined by a rational principle, and by that
principle by which the man of practical wisdom would determine it." Translation by W. D. Ross in R. McKeon's *The Basic Works of Aristotle*, New York:
Random House, 1941, pp. 956, 959.
[15] I have treated the topic of belief more fully in *Insight*, pp. 703–718. The
same facts are treated by sociologists under the heading of the sociology of
knowledge.

any case, he has neither the time nor the inclination nor, perhaps, the ability to investigate for himself. Finally, the judgments, by which he assents to truths of fact and of value, only rarely depend exclusively on his immanently generated knowledge, for such knowledge stands not by itself in some separate compartment but in symbiotic fusion with a far larger context of beliefs.

Thus, one knows the relative positions of the major cities in the United States. After all, one has examined maps and seen their names plainly printed beside small circles representing their positions. But is the map accurate? That one does not know but believes. Nor does the map-maker know for, in all probability, his map was just a compilation of the many maps of much smaller areas made by surveyors that had been over the terrain. Knowledge, then, of the accuracy of the map is divided up; part is in the mind of each surveyor; but the accuracy of the whole is a matter not of knowledge but of belief, of the surveyors believing one another and the rest of us believing the surveyors. It may be urged, however, that the accuracy of maps is verified in countless manners. It is on the basis of maps that planes fly and ships sail, that highways are built and cities are laid out, that people travel about and that property is bought and sold. Over and over in myriad ways transactions based on maps prove to be successful. But only a minute fraction of such verifications is a matter of one's own immanently generated knowledge. It is only by belief that one can invoke to one's support the cloud of witnesses who also have found maps satisfactory. It is that belief, that dependence on countless others, that is the real basis of one's confidence in maps.

Science is often contrasted with belief, but the fact of the matter is that belief plays as large a role in science as in most other areas of human activity. A scientist's original contributions to his subject are not belief but knowledge. Again, when he repeats another's observations and experiments, when he works out for himself the theorems needed to formulate the hypothesis, its presuppositions, and its implications, when he grasps the evidence for excluding alternative views, then he does not believe but knows. But it would be a mistake to fancy that scientists spend their lives repeating one another's work. They do not suffer from a pointless mania to attain immanently generated knowledge of their fields. On the contrary, the aim of the scientist is the advancement of science, and the attainment of that goal is by a division of labor. New results, if not disputed, tend to be assumed in further work. If the further work prospers, they begin to be regarded with confidence. If the further work runs into difficulties, they will come under suspicion, be submitted to scrutiny, tested at this or that apparently weak point. Moreover, this indirect process of verification and falsification is far more important than the initial direct process. For the indirect process is continuous and cumulative. It regards the hypothesis in all its suppositions and consequences. It recurs every time any of these is presupposed. It constitutes an ever increasing body of evidence that the hypothesis is satisfactory. And, like the evidence for the accuracy of maps, it is operative only slightly as immanently generated knowledge but overwhelmingly as belief.

I have been pointing to the social character of human knowledge and I now must invite attention to its historical character. The division of labor not only is among those inquiring today but also extends down the ages. There is a progress in knowledge from primitives to moderns only because successive generations began where their predecessors left off. But successive generations could do so, only because they were ready to believe. Without belief, relying solely on their own individual experience, their own insights, their own judgment, they would have ever been beginning afresh, and either the attainments of primitives would never be surpassed or, if they were, then the benefits would not be transmitted.

Human knowledge, then, is not some individual possession but rather a common fund, from which each may draw by believing, to which each may contribute in the measure that he performs his cognitional operations properly and reports their results accurately. A man does not learn without the use of his own senses, his own mind, his own heart, yet not exclusively by these. He learns from others, not solely by repeating the operations they have performed but, for the most part, by taking their word for the results. Through communication and belief there are generated common sense, common knowledge, common science, common values, a common climate of opinion. No doubt, this public fund may suffer from blindspots, oversights, errors, bias. But it is what we have got, and the remedy for its short-comings is not the rejection of belief and so a return to primitivism, but the critical and selfless stance that, in this as in other matters, promotes progress and offsets decline.

One promotes progress by being attentive, intelligent, reasonable, responsible not only in all one's cognitional operations but also in all one's speech and writing. One offsets decline by following through on one's discoveries. For when one makes a discovery, when one comes to know what one did not know before, often enough one is advancing not merely from ignorance to truth but from error to truth. To follow up on such discovery is to scrutinize the error, to uncover other connected views that in one way or another supported or confirmed it. These associates of the error may themselves be errors. They will bear examination. In the measure they come under suspicion and prove to be erroneous, one can move on to their associates, and so make the discovery of one error the occasion of purging many. It is not enough, however, simply to reject errors. Besides the false beliefs there is the false believer. One has to look into the manner in which one happened to have accepted erroneous beliefs and one has to try to discover and correct the carelessness, the credulity, the bias that led one to mistake the false for the true. Finally, it is not enough to remove mistaken beliefs and to reform the mistaken believer. One has to replace as well as remove, to build up as well as tear down. Mere hunting for errors can leave one a personal and cultural wreck without convictions or commitments. By far the healthier procedure is primarily positive and constructive, so that what is true more and more fills out one's mind, and what is false falls away without leaving a gap or scar.

Such, in general, is belief and now we must turn to an outline of the process of coming to believe. The process is possible because what is true is of itself not private but public, not something to be confined to the mind that grasps it, but something independent of that mind and so in a sense detachable and communicable. This independence is, as already we have emphasized, the cognitional self-transcendence involved in the true judgment of fact and the moral self-transcendence involved in the true judgment of value. I cannot give another my eyes for him to see with, but I can truly report what I see, and he can believe. I cannot give another my understanding, but I can truly report what I have come to understand to be so, and he can believe. I cannot transfer to another my powers of judgment, but I can report what I affirm and what I deny, and he can believe me. Such is the first step. It is taken, not by the person that believes, but by the person whom he believes.

The second step is a general judgment of value. It approves man's division of labor in the acquisition of knowledge both in its historical and in its social dimensions. The approval is not uncritical. It is fully aware of the fallibility of believing. But it finds it obvious that error would increase rather than diminish by a regression to primitivism. So it enters into man's collaboration in the development of knowledge, determined to promote truth and to combat error.

The third step is a particular judgment of value. It regards the trustworthiness of a witness, a source, a report, the competence of an expert, the soundness of judgment of a teacher, a counsellor, a leader, a statesman, an authority. The point at issue in each case is whether one's source was critical of his sources, whether he reached cognitional self-transcendence in his judgments of fact and moral self-transcendence in his judgments of value, whether he was truthful and accurate in his statements. Commonly such questions cannot be answered by direct methods and recourse must be had to indirect. Thus, there may be more than one source, expert, authority; they may be independent and yet concur. Again, the source, expert, authority, may speak on several occasions: his or her statements may be inherently probable, consistent with one another and with all one knows from other sources, experts, authorities. Further, other inquirers may have frequently appealed to the same source, expert, authority, and have concluded to the trustworthiness of the source, the competence of the expert, the sound judgment of the authority. Finally, when everything favors belief except the intrinsic probability of the statement to be believed, one can ask oneself whether the fault is not in oneself, whether it is not the limitation of one's own horizon that prevents one from grasping the intrinsic probability of the statement in question.

The fourth step is the decision to believe. It is a choice that follows upon the general and particular judgments of value. Already one has judged that critically controlled belief is essential to the human good; it has its risks but it is unquestionably better than regression to primitivism. Just now one has judged that such and such a statement is credible, that it can be believed by a reasonable and responsible person. The combination of the general and the particular judgment yields the conclusion that the statement ought to be believed for, if believing is a good thing, then what can be believed should be believed. Finally, what should be so, actually becomes so, through a decision or choice.

The fifth step is the act of believing. I, in my own mind, judge to be true the communicated judgment of fact or of value. I do so, not because of my own immanently generated knowledge, for that I do not possess in the matter in question, but because of the immanently generated knowledge of others. Moreover, my knowledge of the immanently generated knowledge of others, as is clear from the third step, is not exclusively a matter of my immanently generated knowledge; as in most human knowledge it, too, depends to a notable extent on further acts of belief.

Now analysis can be misleading. Without a concrete illustration it may arouse suspicion and even make people feel that they should never believe anything. Think, then, of the engineer who whips out his slide rule and in a few moments performs a long and difficult calculation. He knows precisely what he is doing. He can explain just why the movements of the slide yield the results. Still the results are not exclusively the fruit of the engineer's immanently generated knowledge. For the markings on the rule represent logarithmic and trigonometric tables. The engineer never worked out for himself such a set of tables. He does not know but believes that such tables are correct. Again, the engineer never checked the markings on his rule against a set of tables. He has no doubt about their correspondence, but the absence of doubt is due not to immanently generated knowledge but to belief. Is he acting unintelligently, unreasonably, irresponsibly? Is anyone willing to defend the thesis that all engineers using slide rules should desist until each one for himself has acquired immanently generated knowledge of the accuracy of logarithmic and trigonometric tables and of the correspondence of the markings on their rules with the tables they have worked out each for himself?

The reader may find our account of belief quite novel. He may be surprised both by the extent of belief in human knowledge and by the value we attribute to it. But if notwithstanding he agrees with our position, his agreement may mark an advance not from ignorance but from error to truth. In that case, he should ask whether the error was a mistaken belief, whether it was associated with other beliefs, whether they too were mistaken and, if they were, whether they were associated with still further mistaken beliefs. As the reader will observe, this critical procedure does not attack belief in general; it does not ask you to believe that your beliefs are mistaken; it takes its start from a belief you have discovered to be mistaken and it proceeds along the lines that link beliefs together to determine how far the contagion has spread.

6. THE STRUCTURE OF THE HUMAN GOOD

The human good is at once individual and social, and some account of the way the two aspects combine has now to be attempted. This will be done by selecting some eighteen terms and gradually relating them to one another.

Our eighteen terms regard (1) individuals in their potentialities and actuations, (2) cooperating groups, and (3) ends. A threefold division of ends is allowed to impose a threefold division in the other categories to yield the following scheme.

| Individual | | Social | Ends |
Potentiality	Actuation		
capacity, need	operation	cooperation	particular good
plasticity, perfectibility	development, skill	institution, role, task	good of order
liberty	orientation, conversion	personal relations	terminal value

A first step will relate four terms from the first line: capacity, operation, particular good, and need. Individuals, then, have capacities for operating. By operating they procure themselves instances of the particular good. By such an instance is meant any entity, whether object or action, that meets a need of a particular individual at a given place and time. Needs are to be understood in the broadest sense; they are not to be restricted to necessities but rather to be stretched to include wants of every kind.

Next are related four terms from the third column: cooperation, institution, role, and task. Individuals, then, live in groups. To a notable extent their operating is cooperating. It follows some settled pattern, and this pattern is fixed by a role to be fulfilled or a task to be performed within an institutional frame-work. Such frame-works are the family and manners (mores), society and education, the state and the law, the economy and technology, the church or sect. They constitute the commonly understood and already accepted basis and mode of cooperation. They tend to change only slowly for change, as distinct from breakdown, involves a new common understanding and a new common consent.

Thirdly, there are to be related the remaining terms in the second row: plasticity, perfectibility, development, skill, and the good of order. The capacities of individuals, then, for the performance of operations, because they are plastic and perfectible, admit the development of skills and, indeed, of the very skills demanded by institutional roles and tasks. But besides the

48

institutional basis of cooperation, there is also the concrete manner in which copoeration is working out. The same economic set-up is compatible with prosperity and with recession. The same constitutional and legal arrangements admit wide differences in political life and in the administration of justice. Similar rules for marriage and the family in one case generate domestic bliss and in another misery.

This concrete manner, in which cooperation actually is working out, is what is meant by the good of order. It is distinct from instances of the particular good but it is not separate from them. It regards them, however, not singly and as related to the individual they satisfy, but all together and as recurrent. My dinner today is for me an instance of the particular good. But dinner every day for all members of the group that earn it is part of the good of order. Again, my education was for me a particular good. But education for everyone that wants it is another part of the good of order.

The good of order, however, is not merely a sustained succession of recurring instances of types of the particular good. Besides that recurrent manifold, there is the order that sustains it. This consists basically (1) in the ordering of operations so that they are cooperations and ensure the recurrence of all effectively desired instances of the particular good, and (2) the interdependence of effective desires or decisions with the appropriate performance by cooperating individuals.[16]

It is to be insisted that the good of order is not some design for utopia, some theoretic ideal, some set of ethical precepts, some code of laws, or some super-institution. It is quite concrete. It is the actually functioning or malfunctioning set of "if—then" relationships guiding operators and coordinating operations. It is the ground whence recur or fail to recur whatever instances of the particular good are recurring or failing to recur. It has a basis in institutions but it is a product of much more, of all the skill and know-how, all the industry and resourcefulness, all the ambition and fellow-feeling of a whole people, adapting to each

[16] For the general case of such relationships, see *Insight* on emergent probability, pp. 115–128.

change of circumstance, meeting each new emergency, struggling against every tendency to disorder.[17]

There remains the third row of terms: liberty, orientation, conversion, personal relations, and terminal values. Liberty means, of course, not indeterminism but self-determination. Any course of individual or group action is only a finite good and, because only finite, it is open to criticism. It has its alternatives, its limitations, its risks, its drawbacks. Accordingly, the process of deliberation and evaluation is not itself decisive, and so we experience our liberty as the active thrust of the subject terminating the process of deliberation by settling on one of the possible courses of action and proceeding to execute it. Now in so far as that thrust of the self regularly opts, not for the merely apparent good, but for the true good, the self thereby is achieving moral self-transcendence; he is existing authentically; he is constituting himself as an originating value, and he is bringing about terminal values, namely a good of order that is truly good and instances of the particular good that are truly good. On the other hand, in so far as one's decisions have their principal motives, not in the values at stake, but in a calculus of the pleasures and pains involved one is failing in self-transcendence, in authentic human existence, in the origination of value in oneself and in one's society.

Liberty is exercised within a matrix of personal relations. In the cooperating community persons are bound together by their needs and by the common good of order that meets their needs. They are related by the commitments that they have freely undertaken and by the expectations aroused in others by the commitments, by the roles they have assumed and by the tasks that they meet to perform. These relationships normally are alive with feeling. There are common or opposed feelings about qualitative values and scales of preference. There are mutual feelings in which one responds to another as an ontic value or as just a source of satisfactions. Beyond feelings there is the sub-substance of community. People are joined by common experience, by common or complementary insights, by similar

[17] For a fuller presentation, *Insight*, on the good of order, p. 596, on common sense, pp. 173-181, 207-216, on belief, pp. 703-718, and on bias, pp. 218-242.

judgments of fact and of value, by parallel orientations in life. They are separated, estranged, rendered hostile, when they have got out of touch, when they misunderstand one another, when they judge in opposed fashions, opt for contrary social goals. So personal relations vary from intimacy to ignorance, from love to exploitation, from respect to contempt, from friendliness to enmity. They bind a community together, or divide it into factions, or tear it apart.[18]

Terminal values are the values that are chosen; true instances of the particular good, a true good of order, a true scale of preferences regarding values and satisfactions. Correlative to terminal values are the originating values that do the choosing: they are authentic persons achieving self-transcendence by their good choices. Since man can know and choose authenticity and self-transcendence, originating and terminal values can coincide. When each member of the community both wills authenticity in himself and, inasmuch as he can, promotes it in others, then the originating values that choose and the terminal values that are chosen overlap and interlace.

Presently we shall have to speak of the orientation of the community as a whole. But for the moment our concern is with the orientation of the individual within the orientated community. At its root this consists in the transcendental notions that both enable us and require us to advance in understanding, to judge truthfully, to respond to values. Still, this possibility and exigence become effective only through development. One has to acquire the skills and learning of a competent human being in some walk of life. One has to grow in sensitivity and responsiveness to values if one's humanity is to be authentic. But development is not inevitable, and so results vary. There are human failures.

[18] On interpersonal relations as ongoing processes, there is in Hegel's *Phäno-menologie* the dialectic of master and slave, and in Gaston Fessard's *De l'actualité historique*, Paris: Desclée de Brouwer, 1960, Vol. I, a parallel dialectic of Jew and Greek. Far more concrete is Rosemary Haughton's *The Transformation of Man: A Study of Conversion and Community*, London: G. Chapman, and Springfield, Ill.: Templegate, 1967. Description, technique and some theory in Carl Rogers' *On Becoming a Person*, Boston: Houghton Mifflin, 1961.

There are mediocrities. There are those that keep developing and growing throughout a long life-time, and their achievement varies with their initial background, with their opportunities, with their luck in avoiding pitfalls and setbacks, and with the pace of their advance.[19]

As orientation is, so to speak, the direction of development, so conversion is a change of direction and, indeed, a change for the better. One frees oneself from the unauthentic. One grows in authenticity. Harmful, dangerous, misleading satisfactions are dropped. Fears of discomfort, pain, privation have less power to deflect one from one's course. Values are apprehended where before they were overlooked. Scales of preference shift. Errors, rationalizations, ideologies fall and shatter to leave one open to things as they are and to man as he should be.

The human good then is at once individual and social. Individuals do not just operate to meet their needs but cooperate to meet one another's needs. As the community develops its institutions to facilitate cooperation, so individuals develop skills to fulfil the roles and perform the tasks set by the institutional framework. Though the roles are fulfilled and the tasks are performed that the needs be met, still all is done not blindly but knowingly, not necessarily but freely. The process is not merely the service of man; it is above all the making of man, his advance in authenticity, the fulfilment of his affectivity, and the direction of his work to the particular goods and a good of order that are worth while.

7. PROGRESS AND DECLINE

Our account of the structure of the human good is compatible with any stage of technological, economic, political, cultural, religious development. But as individuals not only develop but also suffer breakdowns, so too do societies. Accordingly, we have to add a sketch of social progress and of social decline and, indeed, one that will be relevant to an account of the social function of religion.

[19] On various aspects of growth, see A. H. Maslow, *Towards a Psychology of Being*, Princeton, N.J.: Van Nostrand, 1962.

Progress proceeds from originating value, from subjects being their true selves by observing the transcendental precepts, Be attentive, Be intelligent, Be reasonable, Be responsible. Being attentive includes attention to human affairs. Being intelligent includes a grasp of hitherto unnoticed or unrealized possibilities. Being reasonable includes the rejection of what probably would not work but also the acknowledgment of what probably would. Being responsible includes basing one's decisions and choices on an unbiased evaluation of short-term and long-term costs and benefits to oneself, to one's group, to other groups.

Progress, of course, is not some single improvement but a continuous flow of them. But the transcendental precepts are permanent. Attention, intelligence, reasonableness, and responsibility are to be exercised not only with respect to the existing situation but also with respect to the subsequent, changed situation. It spots the inadequacies and repercussions of the previous venture to improve what is good and remedy what is defective. More generally, the simple fact of change of itself makes it likely that new possibilities will have arisen and old possibilities will have advanced in probability. So change begets further change and the sustained observance of the transcendental precepts makes these cumulative changes an instance of progress.

But precepts may be violated. Evaluation may be biased by an egoistic disregard of others, by a loyalty to one's own group matched by hostility to other groups, by concentrating on short-term benefits and overlooking long-term costs.[20] Moreover, such aberrations are easy to maintain and difficult to correct. Egoists do not turn into altruists overnight. Hostile groups do not easily forget their grievances, drop their resentments, overcome their fears and suspicions. Common sense commonly feels itself omnicompetent in practical affairs, commonly is blind to long-term consequences of policies and courses of action, commonly is unaware of the admixture of common nonsense in its more cherished convictions and slogans.

The extent of such aberration is, of course, a variable. But the

---

[20] I have elaborated these points in *Insight*, pp. 218–242.

greater it is, the more rapidly it will distort the process of cumulative change and bring to birth a host of social and cultural problems. Egoism is in conflict with the good of order. Up to a point it can be countered by the law, the police, the judiciary, the prisons. But there is a limit to the proportion of the population that can be kept in prison and, when egoism passes that limit, the agents of the law and ultimately the law itself have to become more tolerant and indulgent. So the good of order deteriorates. Not only is it less efficient but also there is the difficulty of exercising even-handed justice in deciding which injustices are to be winked at. The practical question is apt to be whose social sins are to be forgiven, and whose are to be punished, and then the law is compromised. It is no longer coincident with justice. In all likelihood it becomes to a greater or less extent the instrument of a class.

For besides the egoism of the individual there is the egoism of the group. While the individual egoist has to put up with the public censure of his ways, group egoism not merely directs development to its own aggrandizement but also provides a market for opinions, doctrines, theories that will justify its ways and, at the same time, reveal the misfortunes of other groups to be due to their depravity. Of course, as long as the successful group continues to succeed, as long as it meets each new challenge with a creative response, it feels itself the child of destiny and it provokes more admiration and emulation than resentment and opposition. But development, guided by group egoism, is bound to be one-sided. It divides the body social not merely into those that have and those that have not but also makes the former the representatives of the cultural flower of the age to leave the latter apparent survivals from a forgotten era. Finally, in the measure that the group encouraged and accepted an ideology to rationalize its own behavior, in the same measure it will be blind to the real situation, and it will be bewildered by the emergence of a contrary ideology that will call to consciousness an opposed group egoism.

Decline has a still deeper level. Not only does it compromise and distort progress. Not only do inattention, obtuseness, unreasonableness, irresponsibility produce objectively absurd situations. Not only do ideologies corrupt minds. But compromise and distortion discredit progress. Objectively absurd situations do not yield to treatment. Corrupt minds have a flair for picking the mistaken solution and insisting that it alone is intelligent, reasonable, good. Imperceptibly the corruption spreads from the harsh sphere of material advantage and power to the mass media, the stylish journals, the literary movements, the educational process, the reigning philosophies. A civilization in decline digs its own grave with a relentless consistency. It cannot be argued out of its self-destructive ways, for argument has a theoretical major premiss, theoretical premisses are asked to conform to matters of fact, and the facts in the situation produced by decline more and more are the absurdities that proceed from inattention, oversight, unreasonableness and irresponsibility.

The term, alienation, is used in many different senses. But on the present analysis the basic form of alienation is man's disregard of the transcendental precepts, Be attentive, Be intelligent, Be reasonable, Be responsible. Again, the basic form of ideology is a doctrine that justifies such alienation. From these basic forms, all others can be derived. For the basic forms corrupt the social good. As self-transcendence promotes progress, so the refusal of self-transcendence turns progress into cumulative decline.

Finally, we may note that a religion that promotes self-transcendence to the point, not merely of justice, but of self-sacrificing love, will have a redemptive role in human society inasmuch as such love can undo the mischief of decline and restore the cumulative process of progress.[21]

[21] I have elaborated this point in Chapter Twenty of my book, *Insight*. The practical problem of deciding who is and who is not alienated comes up in this book in the chapter on *Dialectic*.

3

MEANING

MEANING is embodied or carried in human intersubjectivity, in art, in symbols, in language, and in the lives and deeds of persons. It can be clarified by a reduction to its elements. It fulfils various functions in human living. It opens upon quite different realms. Its techniques vary in the successive stages of man's historical development. To say something on each of these topics not only will prepare the way for an account of such functional specialties as interpretation, history, systematics, and communications, but also will yield some insight into the diversity of the expressions of religious experience.

I. INTERSUBJECTIVITY

Prior to the "we" that results from the mutual love of an "I" and a "thou", there is the earlier "we" that precedes the distinction of subjects and survives its oblivion. This prior "we" is vital and functional. Just as one spontaneously raises one's arm to ward off a blow against one's head, so with the same spontaneity one reaches out to save another from falling. Perception, feeling, and bodily movement are involved, but the help given another is not deliberate but spontaneous. One adverts to it not before it occurs but while it is occurring. It is as if "we" were members of one another prior to our distinctions of each from the others.

Intersubjectivity appears not only in spontaneous mutual aid but also in some of the ways in which feelings are communicated. Here we shall be reporting Max Scheler who distinguished community of feeling, fellow-feeling, psychic contagion, and emotional identification.[1]

[1] See Manfred Frings, *Max Scheler*, Pittsburgh and Louvain, 1965, pp. 56–66.

Both community of feeling and fellow-feeling are intentional responses that presuppose the apprehension of objects that arouse feeling. In community of feeling two or more persons respond in parallel fashion to the same object. In fellow-feeling a first person responds to an object, and a second responds to the manifested feeling of the first. So community of feeling would be illustrated by the sorrow felt by both parents for their dead child, but fellow-feeling would be felt by a third party moved by their sorrow. Again, in community worship, there is community of feeling inasmuch as worshippers are similarly concerned with God, but there is fellow-feeling inasmuch as some are moved to devotion by the prayerful attitude of others.

In contrast, psychic contagion and emotional identification have a vital rather than an intentional basis. Psychic contagion is a matter of sharing another's emotion without adverting to the object of the emotion. One grins when others are laughing although one does not know what they find funny. One becomes sorrowful when others are weeping although one does not know the cause of their grief. An on-looker, without undergoing another's ills, is caught up in the feeling of extreme pain expressed on the face of the sufferer. Such contagion seems to be the mechanism of mass-excitement in panics, revolutions, revolts, demonstrations, strikes, where in general there is a disappearance of personal responsibility, a domination of drives over thinking, a decrease of the intelligence level, and a readiness for submission to a leader. Needless to say, such contagion can be deliberately provoked, built up, exploited by political activists, by the entertainment industry, by religious and especially pseudo-religious leaders.

In emotional identification either personal differentiation is as yet undeveloped or else there is a retreat from personal differentiation to vital unity. Undeveloped differentiation has its basic illustration in the emotional identification of mother and infant. But it also appears in the identifications of primitive mentality and, again, in the earnestness of a little girl's play with her doll; she identifies herself with her mother and at the same time projects herself into the doll. Retreat from differentiation is illustrated by Scheler in various ways. It is his account of hypnosis. It occurs in sexual intercourse when both partners undergo a suspension of individuality and fall back into a single stream of life. In the group mind members identify with their leader and spectators with their team; in both cases the group coalesces in a single stream of instinct and feeling. In the ancient mysteries the mystic in a state of ecstasy became divine; and, in the writings of later mystics, experiences with a pantheist implication are not infrequently described.

2. INTERSUBJECTIVE MEANING

Besides the intersubjectivity of action and of feeling, there also are intersubjective communications of meaning. This I propose to illustrate by borrowing a phenomenology of a smile proximately from my notebook but remotely from sources I have been unable to trace.

First, then, a smile does have a meaning. It is not just a certain combination of movements of lips, facial muscles, eyes. It is a combination with a meaning. Because that meaning is different from the meaning of a frown, a scowl, a stare, a glare, a snicker, a laugh, it is named a smile. Because we all know that that meaning exists, we do not go about the streets smiling at everyone we meet. We know we should be misunderstood.

Next, a smile is highly perceptible. For our perceiving is not just a function of the impressions made on our senses. It has an orientation of its own and it selects, out of a myriad of others, just those impressions that can be constructed into a pattern with a meaning. So one can converse with a friend on a noisy street, disregard the meaningless surrounding tumult, and pick out the band of sound waves that has a meaning. So, too, a smile, because of its meaning, is easily perceived. Smiles occur in an enormous range of variations of facial movements, of lighting, of angle of vision. But even an incipient, suppressed smile is not missed, for the smile is a *Gestalt*, a patterned set of variable movements, and it is recognized as a whole.

Both the meaning of the smile and the act of smiling are natural and spontaneous. We do not learn to smile as we learn to walk, to talk, to swim, to skate. Commonly we do not think of smiling and then do it. We just do it. Again, we do not learn the meaning of smiling as we learn the meaning of words. The meaning of the smile is a discovery we make on our own, and that meaning does not seem to vary from culture to culture, as does the meaning of gestures.

There is something irreducible to the smile. It cannot be explained by causes outside meaning. It cannot be elucidated by other types of meaning. Some illustration of this will be had by comparing the meaning of the smile with that of language.

Linguistic meaning tends to be univocal, but smiles have a wide variety of different meanings. There are smiles of recognition, of welcome, of friendliness, of friendship, of love, of joy, of delight, of contentment, of satisfaction, of amusement, of refusal, of contempt. Smiles may be ironic, sardonic, enigmatic, glad or sad, fresh or weary, eager or resigned.

Linguistic meaning may be true in two ways: true as opposed to mendacious and true as opposed to false. A smile may be simulated and so it may be true as opposed to mendacious, but it cannot be true as opposed to false.

Linguistic meaning contains distinctions between what we feel, what we desire, what we fear, what we think, what we know, what we wish, what we command, what we intend. The meaning of a smile is global; it expresses what one person means to another; it has the meaning of a fact and not the meaning of a proposition.

Linguistic meaning is objective. It expresses what has been objectified. But the meaning of the smile is intersubjective. It supposes the interpersonal situation with its antecedents in previous encounters. It is a recognition and an acknowledgment of that situation and, at the same time, a determinant of the situation, an element in the situation as process, a meaning with its significance in the context of antecedent and subsequent meanings. Moreover, that meaning is not about some object. Rather it reveals or even betrays the subject, and the revelation is immediate. It is not the basis of some inference, but rather in the smile one incarnate subject is transparent or, again, hidden to another, and that transparency or hiddenness antedates all subsequent analysis that speaks of body and soul, or of sign and signified.

From smiles one might go on to all the facial or bodily movements or pauses, to all the variations of voice in tone, pitch, volume, and in silence, to all the ways in which our feelings are revealed or betrayed by ourselves or are depicted by actors on the stage. But our purpose is not to exhaust the topic but rather to point to the existence of a special carrier or embodiment of meaning, namely, human intersubjectivity.

3. ART

Here I borrow from Suzanne Langer's *Feeling and Form* where art is defined as the objectification of a purely experiential pattern, and each term in this definition is carefully explained.

A pattern may be abstract or concrete. There is an abstract pattern in a musical score or in the indentation in the grooves of a gramophone record. But there is a concrete pattern in these colors, these tones, these volumes, these movements. The concrete pattern consists in the internal relations of colors, tones, volumes, movements. It does not consist in, say, the colors as unrelated and it does not consist in the colors as representative of something else.

Now the pattern of the perceived is also the pattern of the perceiving, and the pattern of the perceiving is an experiential pattern. But all perceiving is a selecting and organizing. Precisely because the perceived is patterned, it is easily perceived. So one can repeat a tune or melody but not a succession of street noises. So verse makes information memorable. Decoration makes a surface visible. Patterns achieve, perhaps, a special perceptibility by drawing on organic analogies. The movement is from root through trunk to branches, leaves, and flowers. It is repeated with varying variations. Complexity mounts and yet the multiplicity is organized into a whole.

A pattern is said to be pure inasmuch as it excludes alien patterns that instrumentalize experience. One's senses can become merely an apparatus for receiving and transmitting signals. At the red light the brake goes on and at the green the accelerator is pressed down. So there results the behavior of the ready-made subject in his ready-made world. Again, sense may function simply in the service of scientific intelligence. It submits to the alien pattern of conceptual genera and species, of theoretical schemes and models, of judgmental concern for evidence that confirms or opposes an opinion. Finally, sense may be reshaped by an *a priori* theory of experience. Instead of having its own proper life, sense is subordinated to some view drawn from physics, physiology, or psychology. It is divided by an epistemology that thinks of impressions as objective and of their pattern as subjective. It is alienated by a utilitarianism that attends to objects just in the measure there is something in them for me to get out of them.

Not only are alien patterns to be excluded but also the pattern must be purely experiential. It is of the colors that are visible and not of the stereotypes that are anticipated. It is of shapes as visible and so in perspective and not of shapes as really constructed, as known perhaps to touch but not to sight. So too it is of the sounds in their actual tone, pitch, and volume, their overtones, harmonics, dissonances. To them accrue their retinue of associations, affects, emotions, incipient tendencies. Out of them may rise a lesson, but into them a lesson may not be intruded in the manner of didacticism, moralism, or social realism. To them also there accrues the experiencing subject with his capacity for wonder, for awe and fascination, with his openness to adventure, daring, greatness, goodness, majesty.

The required purity of the existential pattern aims not at impoverishment but at enrichment. It curtails what is alien to let experiencing find its full complement of feeling. It lets experiencing fall into its own proper patterns and take its own line of expansion, development, organization, fulfilment. So experiencing becomes rhythmic, one movement necessitating another and the other in turn necessitating the first. Tensions are built up to be resolved; variations multiply and grow in complexity yet remain within an organic unity that eventually rounds itself off.

Meaning, when fully developed, intends something meant.

But the meaning of an experiential pattern is elemental. It is the conscious performing of a transformed subject in his transformed world. That world may be regarded as illusion, but it also may be regarded as more true and more real. We are transported from the space in which we move to the space within the picture, from the time of sleeping and waking, working and resting, to the time of the music, from the pressures and determinisms of home and office, of economics and politics to the powers depicted in the dance, from conversational and media use of language to the vocal tools that focus, mould, grow with consciousness. As his world, so too the subject is transformed. He has been liberated from being a replaceable part adjusted to a ready-made world and integrated within it. He has ceased to be a responsible inquirer investigating some aspect of the universe or seeking a view of the whole. He has become just himself: emergent, ecstatic, originating freedom.

It is possible to set within the conceptual field this elemental meaning of the transformed subject in his transformed world. But this procedure reflects without reproducing the elemental meaning. Art criticism and art history are like the thermodynamic equations, which guide our control of heat but, of themselves, cannot make us feel warmer or cooler.

The proper expression of the elemental meaning is the work of art itself. That meaning lies within the consciouness of the artist but, at first, it is only implicit, folded up, veiled, unrevealed, unobjectified. Aware of it, the artist has yet to get hold of it; he is impelled to behold, inspect, dissect, enjoy, repeat it; and this means objectifying, unfolding, making explicit, unveiling, revealing.

The process of objectifying involves psychic distance. Where the elemental meaning is just experiencing, its expression involves detachment, distinction, separation from experience. While the smile or frown expresses intersubjectively the feeling as it is felt, artistic composition recollects emotion in tanquillity. It is a matter of insight into the elemental meaning, a grasp of the commanding form that has to be expanded, worked out, developed, and the subsequent process of working out, adjusting, correcting, completing the initial insight. There results an idealization of the original experiential pattern. Art is not autobiography. It is not telling one's tale to the psychiatrist. It is grasping what is or seems significant, of moment, concern, import, to man. It is truer than experience, leaner, more effective, more to the point. It is the central moment with its proper implications, and they unfold without the distortions, interferences, accidental intrusions of the original pattern.

As the proper expression of the elemental meaning is the work of art itself, so too the proper apprehension and appreciation of the work of art is not any conceptual clarification or judicial weighing of conceptualized evidence. The work of art is an invitation to participate, to try it, to see for oneself. As the mathematician withdraws from the sciences that verify to explore possibilities of organizing data, so the work of art invites one to withdraw from practical living and to explore possibilities of fuller living in a richer world.[2]

4. SYMBOLS

A symbol is an image of a real or imaginary object that evokes a feeling or is evoked by a feeling.

Feelings are related to objects, to one another, and to their subject. They are related to objects: one desires food, fears pain, enjoys a meal, regrets a friend's illness. They are related to one another through changes in the object: one desires the good that is absent, hopes for the good that is sought, enjoys the good that is present; one fears absent evil, becomes disheartened at its approach, sad in its presence. Again, feelings are related to one another through personal relationships: so love, gentleness, tenderness, intimacy, union go together; similarly, alienation, hatred, harshness, violence, cruelty form a group; so too there

[2] Again, let me stress that I am not attempting to be exhaustive. For an application of the above analysis to different art forms in drawing and painting, statuary and architecture, music and dance, epic, lyric, and dramatic poetry, the reader must go to S. K. Langer, *Feeling and Form*, New York, 1953. The point I am concerned to make is that there exist quite distinct carriers or embodiments of meaning.

are such sequences as offense, contumacy, judgment, punishment and, again, offense, repentance, apology, forgiveness. Further, feelings may conflict yet come together: one may desire despite fear, hope against hope, mix joy with sadness, love with hate, gentleness with harshness, tenderness with violence, intimacy with cruelty, union with alienation. Finally, feelings are related to their subject: they are the mass and momentum and power of his conscious living, the actuation of his affective capacities, dispositions, habits, the effective orientation of his being.

The same objects need not evoke the same feelings in different subjects and, inversely, the same feelings need not evoke the same symbolic images. This difference in affective response may be accounted for by differences in age, sex, education, state of life, temperament, existential concern. But, more fundamentally, there is in the human being an affective development that may suffer aberrations. It is the history of that process that terminates in the person with a determinate orientation in life and with determinate affective capacities, dispositions, and habits. What such affective capacities, dispositions, habits are in a given individual can be specified by the symbols that awaken determinate affects and, inversely, by the affects that evoke determinate symbols. Again, from assumptions about normality one can go on to conclude that the responses of a given individual are normal or not.

Symbols of the same affective orientation and disposition are affectively undifferentiated. Hence, they are interchangeable and they may be combined to increase their intensity and reduce their ambiguity. Such combination and organization reveal the difference between the aesthetic and the symbolic; the monsters of mythology are just bizarre. Further, compound affects call for compound symbols, and each member of the compound may be a conglomeration of undifferentiated or only slightly differentiated symbols. So St. George and the Dragon present at once all the values of ascensional symbolism and all the disvalues of its opposite. St. George is seated yet high on his horse; he is in the light and is free to use his arms; one hand guides the horse and the other manipulates the spear. But he could fall, be pressed down by the scaly monster, blinded by its smoke, burnt by its fire, crunched by its teeth, devoured in its maw.

Affective development, or aberration, involves a transvaluation and transformation of symbols. What before was moving no longer moves; what before did not move now is moving. So the symbols themselves change to express the new affective capacities and dispositions. So the conquest of terror can relegate the Dragon to insignificant fancy, but now it brings forth the meaning of Jonah's whale: a monster that swallowed a drowning man and three days later vomited him unharmed upon the shore. Inversely, symbols that do not submit to transvaluation and transformation seem to point to a block in development. It is one thing for a child, another for a man, to be afraid of the dark.

Symbols obey the laws not of logic but of image and feeling. For the logical class the symbol uses a representative figure. For univocity it substitutes a wealth of multiple meanings. It does not prove but it overwhelms with a manifold of images that converge in meaning. It does not bow to the principle of excluded middle but admits the *coincidentia oppositorum*, of love and hate, of courage and fear, and so on. It does not negate but overcomes what it rejects by heaping up all that is opposite to it. It does not move on some single track or on some single level, but condenses into a bizarre unity all its present concerns.

The symbol, then, has the power of recognizing and expressing what logical discourse abhors: the existence of internal tensions, incompatibilities, conflicts, struggles, destructions. A dialectical or methodical viewpoint can embrace, of course, what is concrete, contradictory, and dynamic. But the symbol did this before either logic or dialectic were conceived. It does this for those unfamiliar with logic and dialectic. Finally, it does it in a way that complements and fills out logic and dialectic, for it meets a need that these refinements cannot meet.

This need is for internal communication. Organic and psychic vitality have to reveal themselves to intentional consciousness and, inversely, intentional consciousness has to secure the collaboration of organism and psyche. Again, our apprehensions of values occur in intentional responses, in feelings: here too it is necessary for feelings to reveal their objects and, inversely, for objects to awaken feelings. It is through symbols that mind and body, mind and heart, heart and body communicate.

In that communication symbols have their proper meaning. It is an elemental meaning, not yet objectified, as the meaning of the smile prior to a phenomenology of the smile, or the meaning in the purely experiential pattern prior to its expression in a work of art. It is a meaning that fulfils its function in the imagining or perceiving subject as his conscious intentionality develops or goes astray or both, as he takes his stance to nature, with his fellow men, and before God. It is a meaning that has its proper context in the process of internal communication in which it occurs, and it is to that context with its associated images and feelings, memories and tendencies that the interpreter has to appeal if he would explain the symbol.

To explain the symbol, of course, is to go beyond the symbol. It is to effect the transition from an elemental meaning in an image or percept to a linguistic meaning. Moreover, it is to use the context of the linguistic meaning as an arsenal of possible relations, clues, suggestions in the construction of the elemental context of the symbol. However, such interpretative contexts are many and, perhaps, this multiplicity only reflects the many ways in which human beings can develop and suffer deviation.

There are, then, the three original interpretative systems: the psychoanalysis of Freud, the individual psychology of Adler, the analytic psychology of Jung. But the initial rigidities and oppositions are less and less maintained by their successors.[3] Charles Baudouin has introduced a psychagogy that considers Freud and Jung to be not opposed but complementary: he uses Freud in reverting to causal objects and Jung in attending to subjective

[3] There are, of course, notable exceptions. I mention only Antoine Vergote who follows Freud's genetic psychology quite strictly though he does not accept Freud's philosophical speculations. See Winfrid Huber, Herman Piron, et Antoine Vergote, *La psychanalyse, science de l'homme*, Bruxelles: Dessart, 1964.

development;[4] and this complementarity would seem to be supported by Paul Ricoeur's long study that concludes Freudian thought to be an archeology of the subject that necessarily implies but does not explicitly acknowledge a forward-moving teleology.[5] Again, there are marked tendencies among therapists to develop their own systems of interpretation[6] or to treat interpretation as an art to be learnt.[7] Finally, there are those that feel that therapeutic goals can be more effectively attained by pretty well withdrawing from the interpretation of symbols. So Carl Rogers makes it his aim to provide his client with an interpersonal situation in which the client can gradually come to self-discovery.[8] At an opposite pole Frank Lake gets his theory from Pavlov and administers *LSD 25* to clients thereby enabled to recall and confront traumata suffered in infancy.[9]

Concomitant with the foregoing movement there has been a parallel development outside the therapeutic context.[10] Freud proposed not merely a method of therapy but also highly speculative accounts of man's inner structure and of the nature of civilization and of religion. But this extension of the therapeutic context over the whole of human concern has been met by the erection of non-therapeutic contexts in which symbols are studied

[4] Charles Baudouin, *L'oeuvre de Jung*, Paris: Payot, 1963. Gilberte Aigrisse, "Efficacité du symbole en psychothérapie," *Cahiers internationaux de symbolisme*, no. 14, pp. 3–24.

[5] Paul Ricoeur, *De l'interpretation, Essai sur Freud*, Paris: du Seuil, 1965.

[6] Karen Horney's books exhibit a cumulative development. *The Neurotic Personality of our Time*, 1937; *New Ways in Psychoanalysis*, 1939; *Self-analysis*, 1942; *Our Inner Conflicts*, 1945; *Neurosis and Human Growth*, 1950. Published by W. W. Norton, New York.

[7] Erich Fromm, *The Forgotten Language*, Chapter Six, The Art of Dream Interpretation, New York: Grove Press, 1957.

[8] Carl Rogers, *On Becoming a Person*, Boston: Houghton, Mifflin, 1961.

[9] Frank Lake, *Clinical Theology*, London: Darton Longman & Todd 1966. In similar vein but without any use of drugs Arthur Janov encourages his clients to free themselves of their tensions by accepting consciousness of the pains hitherto they have repressed. See his *The Primal Scream*, New York: Putman, 1970.

[10] Varying viewpoints in Irwin G. Sarason, editor, *Science and Theory in Psychoanalysis*, Princeton, N.J.: Van Nostrand, 1965.

and interpreted. Gilbert Durand has proceeded from a physiological basis in three dominant reflexes, maintaining one's balance, swallowing food, and mating, to organize vast masses of symbolic data, to balance the organization with a contrary organization, and to effect synthesis by alternation of the two.[11] In a great number of works Mircéa Eliade has collected, compared, integrated, explained the symbols of primitive religions.[12] Northrop Frye has appealed to the cycles of day and night, the four seasons, and the course of an organism's growth and decline to construct a matrix from which might be derived the symbolic narratives of literature.[13] Psychologists have turned from the sick to the well, indeed, to those that keep growing over a long lifetime,[14] and there has even been raised the question whether mental illness really pertains to a merely medical context, whether the trouble is real guilt and not merely mistaken feelings of guilt.[15] Finally, and most significant from a basic viewpoint, there is the existential approach that thinks of the dream, not as the twilight of life, but as its dawn, the beginning of the transition from impersonal existence to presence in the world, to constitution of one's self in one's world.[16]

---

[11] Gilbert Durand, *Les structures anthropologiques de l'imaginaire*, Introduction à l'archétypologie générale, 2nd edition, Paris: Presses Universitaires de France, 1963.

[12] Mircéa Eliade, "Methodological Remarks on the Study of Religious Symbolism," in Mircéa Eliade and Joseph Kitagawa, editors, *The History of Religions, Essays in Methodology*, Chicago: University of Chicago Press, 1959, ²1962.

[13] Northrop Frye, *Fables of Identity*, Studies in Poetic Mythology, New York: Harcourt, Bruce & World, 1963.

[14] There exists what is named a "Third Force" in psychology. It is described by A. Maslow, *Toward a Psychology of Being*, Princeton, N.J.: Van Nostrand, 1962, p. *vi*.

[15] O. H. Mowrer, *The Crisis in Psychiatry and Religion*, Princeton, N.J.: Van Nostrand, 1961.

[16] Ludwig Binswanger, *Le rêve et l'existence*, Desclée, 1954, Introduction (128 pp.) et notes de Michel Foucault. Rollo May, Ernest Angel, Henri F. Ellenberger, editors, *Existence*, A New Dimension in Psychiatry and Psychology, New York: Basic Books, 1958. Rollo May, editor, *Existential Psychology*, Random

5. LINGUISTIC MEANING

By its embodiment in language, in a set of conventional signs, meaning finds its greatest liberation. For conventional signs can be multiplied almost indefinitely. They can be differentiated and specialized to the utmost refinement. They can be used reflexively in the analysis and control of linguistic meaning itself. In contrast intersubjective and symbolic meanings seem restricted to the spontaneities of people living together and, while the visual and aural arts can develop conventions, still the conventions themselves are limited by the materials in which colors and shapes, solid forms and structures, sounds and movements are embodied.

The moment of language in human development is most strikingly illustrated by the story of Helen Keller's discovery that the successive touches made on her hand by her teacher conveyed names of objects. The moment when she first caught on was marked by the expression of profound emotion and, in turn, the emotion bore fruit in so powerful an interest that she signified her desire to learn and did learn the names of about twenty objects in a very short time. It was the beginning of an incredible career of learning.

In Helen Keller's emotion and interest one can surmise the reason why ancient civilizations prized names so highly. It was not, as sometimes is said, that for them the name was the essence of the thing named. Concern with essences is a later Socratic concern seeking universal definitions. Prizing names is prizing the human achievement of bringing conscious intentionality into sharp focus and, thereby, setting about the double task of both ordering one's world and orientating oneself within it. Just as the dream at daybreak may be said to be the beginning of the process from an impersonal existence to the presence of a person in his world, so listening and speaking are a major part in the achievement of that presence.

House, 1961. Rollo May, "The Significance of Symbols," in *Symbolism in Religion and Literature*, New York: Braziller, 1961. V. E. Frankl, *The Doctor and the Soul*, New York: Knopf, 1955. *Man's Search for Meaning*, New York: Washington Square Press, 1959, 1963. *The Will to Meaning*, Cleveland: World, 1969. V. E. Frankl with others, *Psychotherapy and Existentialism*, New York: Washington Square Press, 1967.

So it is that conscious intentionality develops in and is moulded by its mother tongue. It is not merely that we learn the names of what we see but also that we can attend to and talk about the things we can name. The available language, then, takes the lead. It picks out the aspects of things that are pushed into the foreground, the relations between things that are stressed, the movements and changes that demand attention. So different languages develop in different manners and the best of translations can express, not the exact meaning of the original, but the closest approximation possible in another tongue.

The action is reciprocal. Not only does language mould developing consciousness but also it structures the world about the subject. Spatial adverbs and adjectives relate places to the place of the speaker. The tenses of verbs relate times to his present. Moods correspond to his intention to wish, or exhort, or command, or declare. Voices make verbs now active and now passive and, at the same time, shift subjects to objects and objects to subjects. Grammar almost gives us Aristotle's categories of substance, quantity, quality, relation, action, passion, place, time, posture, habit, while Aristotle's logic and theory of science are deeply rooted in the grammatical function of predication.[17]

As language develops there emerges a distinction between ordinary, technical, and literary language. Ordinary language is the vehicle in which the human community conducts its collaboration in the day-to-day pursuit of the human good. It is the language of home and school, of industry and commerce, of enjoyment and misfortune, of the mass media and casual conversation. Such language is transient; it expresses the thought of the moment at the moment for the moment. It is elliptical. It knows that a wink is as good as a nod, that full statement is superfluous and would only irritate. Its basis is common sense, where by common sense is meant a nucleus of habitual insights such that the addition of one or two more will bring one to the

[17] In mathematical logic predication yields place to propositional combination. Elsewhere I have argued that the form of inference is the "if—then" relation between propositions. *Collection.* Papers by Bernard Lonergan. Edited by F. E. Crowe (London and New York), 1967.

understanding of any of an open series of concrete situations. By that understanding one will grasp how to behave, what to say, how to say it, what to do, how to do it, in the currently emerging situation. Such a nucleus of insights is centered in the subject: it regards his world as related to him, as the field of his behavior, influence, action, as colored by his desires, hopes, fears, joys, sorrows. When such a nucleus of insights is shared by a group, it is the common sense of the group; when it is just personal, it is thought odd; when it pertains to the common sense of a different group, it is considered strange.[18]

The commonsense development of human intelligence yields not only common but also complementary results. Primitive fruit gatherers differentiate into gardeners, hunters, and fishers. New groups and ends and tasks and tools call forth new words. The division of labor continues and, with it, the specialization of language. Eventually there arises a distinction between words in common use that refer to what is generally known about particular tasks and, on the other hand, the technical words employed by craftsmen, or experts, or specialists, when they speak among themselves. This process is carried much further, when human intelligence shifts from commonsense to theoretical development, when inquiry is pursued for its own sake, when logic and methods are formulated, when a tradition of learning is established, different branches are distinguished, and specialties multiply.

Literary language is a third genus. While ordinary language is transient, literary is permanent: it is the vehicle of a work, a *poïema*, to be learnt by heart or to be written out. While ordinary language is elliptical, content to supplement the common understanding and common feeling already guiding common living, literary language not only aims at fuller statement but also attempts to make up for the lack of mutual presence. It would have the listener or reader not only understand but also feel. So where the technical treatise aims at conforming to the laws of logic and the precepts of method, literary language tends to float somewhere in between logic and symbol. When it is analyzed by a logical mind, it is found to be full of what are termed figures

18 On common sense, *Insight*, Chapters Six and Seven.

of speech. But it is only the intrusion of non-literary criteria into the study of literature that makes figures of speech smack of artifice. For the expression of feeling is symbolic and, if words owe a debt to logic, symbols follow the laws of image and affect. With Giambattista Vico, then, we hold for the priority of poetry. Literal meaning literally expressed is a later ideal and only with enormous effort and care can it be realized, as the tireless labors of linguistic analysts seem to show.

6. INCARNATE MEANING

Cor ad cor loquitur. Incarnate meaning combines all or at least many of the other carriers of meaning. It can be at once inter-subjective, artistic, symbolic, linguistic. It is the meaning of a person, of his way of life, of his words, or of his deeds. It may be his meaning for just one other person, or for a small group, or for a whole national, or social, or cultural, or religious tradition.

Such meaning may attach to a group achievement, to a Thermophylae or Marathon, to the Christian martyrs, to a glorious revolution. It may be transposed to a character or characters in a story or a play, to a Hamlet or Tartuffe or Don Juan. It may emanate from the whole personality and the total performance of an orator or a demagogue.

Finally, as meaning can be incarnate, so too can be the meaning-less, the vacant, the empty, the vapid, the insipid, the dull.

7. ELEMENTS OF MEANING

Distinguish (1) sources, (2) acts, and (3) terms of meaning.

Sources of meaning are all conscious acts and all intended contents, whether in the dream state or on any of the four levels of waking consciousness. The principal division of sources is into transcendental and categorial. The transcendental are the very dynamism of intentional consciousness, a capacity that consciously and unceasingly both heads for and recognizes data, intelligibility, truth, reality, and value. The categorial are the determinations reached through experiencing, understanding, judging, deciding. The transcendental notions ground questioning. Answers develop categorial determinations.

Acts of meaning are (1) potential, (2) formal, (3) full, (4) constitutive or effective, and (5) instrumental. In the potential act meaning is elemental. There has not yet been reached the distinction between meaning and meant. Such is the meaning of the smile that acts simply as an intersubjective determinant, the meaning of the work of art prior to its interpretation by a critic, the meaning of the symbol performing its office of internal communication without help from the therapist. Again, acts of sensing and of understanding of themselves have only potential meaning. As Aristotle put it, the sensible in act and the sense in act are one and the same. Thus, sounding and hearing are an identity: without ears there can be longitudinal waves in the atmosphere but there cannot be sound. Similarly, data are potentially intelligible, but their intelligibility in act coincides with an intelligence in act.

The formal act of meaning is an act of conceiving, thinking, considering, defining, supposing, formulating. There has emerged the distinction between meaning and meant, for the meant is what is conceived, thought, considered, defined, supposed, formulated. However, the precise nature of this distinction has not as yet been clarified. One is meaning precisely what one is thinking about, but one has yet to determine whether the object of one's thought is merely an object of thought or something more than that.

The full act of meaning is an act of judging. One settles the status of the object of thought, that it is merely an object of thought, or a mathematical entity, or a real thing lying in the world of human experience, or a transcendent reality beyond that world.

Active meanings come with judgments of value, decisions, actions. This is a topic to which we revert when we treat, in a later section, the effective and constitutive functions of meaning in the individual and the community.

Instrumental acts of meaning are expressions. They externalize and exhibit for interpretation by others the potential, formal, full, constitutive, or effective acts of meaning of the subject.[19] As the expression and the interpretation may be adequate or faulty, instrumental acts of meaning provide the materials for a special chapter on hermeneutics.

A term of meaning is what is meant. In potential acts of meaning, meaning and meant are not yet sorted out. In formal acts, the distinction has emerged but the exact status of the term remains indeterminate. In full acts of meaning there occurs the probable or certain determination of the status of the term; one settles whether or not A is, or whether or not A is B. In constitutive or effective acts of meaning one settles one's attitude to A, what one will do for B, whether one will endeavor to bring about C.

With regard to full terms of meaning one has to distinguish different spheres of being. We say that the moon exists. We also say that there exists the logarithm of the square root of minus one. In both cases we use the same verb, exist. But we do not mean that the moon is just a conclusion that can be deduced from suitable mathematical postulates, and we do not mean that the logarithm in question can be inspected sailing around the sky. A distinction, accordingly, has to be drawn between a sphere of real being and other restricted spheres such as the mathematical, the hypothetical, the logical, and so on. While these spheres differ enormously from one another, they are not simply disparate. The contents of each sphere are rationally affirmed. The affirmation is rational because it proceeds from an act of reflective understanding in which is grasped the virtually unconditioned, that is, a conditioned whose conditions are fulfilled.[20] But the spheres differ so vastly because the conditions to be fulfilled differ. The fulfilling conditions for affirming real being are appropriate data of sense or consciousness, but the fulfilling condition for proposing an hypothesis is a possible relevance to a correct understanding of data, while the fulfilling conditions for

---

[19] Performative meaning is constitutive or effective meaning linguistically expressed. It has been studied by the analysts, notably by Donald Evans, *The Logic of Self-involvement*, London: SCM Press, 1963.

[20] On the virtually unconditioned, *Insight*, Chapter Ten.

correct mathematical statement do not explicitly include even a possible relevance to data. Finally, beyond restricted spheres and the real sphere there is the transcendent sphere of being; transcendent being is the being that, while known by us through grasping the virtually unconditioned, is itself without any conditions whatever; it is formally unconditioned, absolute.

The foregoing, of course, is the realist account of full terms of meaning. To transpose to the empiricist position, one disregards the virtually unconditioned and identifies the real with what is exhibited in ostensive gestures. What is a dog? Well, here you are, take a look. To move from empiricism to idealism, one draws attention to the empiricist's failure to note all the structuring elements that are constitutive of human knowing yet not given to sense. However, while the idealist is correct in rejecting the empiricist's account of human knowledge, he is mistaken in accepting the empiricist notion of reality and so in concluding that the object of human knowledge is not the real but the ideal. Accordingly, to move beyond idealism to realism, one has to discover that man's intellectual and rational operations involve a transcendence of the operating subject, that the real is what we come to know through a grasp of a certain type of virtually unconditioned.

8. FUNCTIONS OF MEANING[21]

A first function of meaning is cognitive. It takes us out of the infant's world of immediacy, and places us in the adult's world, which is a world mediated by meaning. The world of the infant is no bigger than the nursery. It is the world of what is felt, touched, grasped, sucked, seen, heard. It is a world of immediate experience, of the given as given, of image and affect without any perceptible intrusion from insight or concept, reflection or judgment, deliberation or choice. It is the world of pleasure and pain, hunger and thirst, food and drink, rage and satisfaction and sleep.

However, as the command and use of language develop, one's world expands enormously. For words denote not only what is

---

[21] I have treated this topic in the last two chapters of *Collection*.

present but also what is absent or past or future, not only what is factual but also the possible, the ideal, the normative. Again, words express not merely what we have found out for ourselves but also all we care to learn from the memories of other men, from the common sense of the community, from the pages of literature, from the labors of scholars, from the investigations of scientists, from the experience of saints, from the meditations of philosophers and theologians.

This larger world, mediated by meaning, does not lie within anyone's immediate experience. It is not even the sum, the integral, of the totality of all worlds of immediate experience. For meaning is an act that does not merely repeat but goes beyond experiencing. For what is meant, is what is intended in questioning and is determined not only by experience but also by understanding and, commonly, by judgment as well. This addition of understanding and judgment is what makes possible the world mediated by meaning, what gives it its structure and unity, what arranges it in an orderly whole of almost endless differences partly known and familiar, partly in a surrounding penumbra of things we know about but have never examined or explored, partly an unmeasured region of what we do not know at all.

In this larger world we live out our lives. To it we refer when we speak of the real world. But because it is mediated by meaning, because meaning can go astray, because there is myth as well as science, fiction as well as fact, deceit as well as honesty, error as well as truth, that larger real world is insecure.

Besides the immediate world of the infant and the adult's world mediated by meaning, there is the mediation of immediacy by meaning when one objectifies cognitional process in transcendental method and when one discovers, identifies, accepts one's submerged feelings in psychotherapy. Finally, there is a withdrawal from objectification and a mediated return to immediacy in the mating of lovers and in the prayerful mystic's cloud of unknowing.

A second function of meaning is efficient. Men work. But their work is not mindless. What we make, we first intend. We imagine, we plan, we investigate possibilities, we weigh pro's and con's, we enter into contracts, we have countless orders given and executed. From the beginning to the end of the process, we are engaged in acts of meaning; and without them the process would not occur or the end be achieved. The pioneers on this continent found shore and heartland, mountains and plains, but they have covered it with cities, laced it with roads, exploited it with industries, till the world man has made stands between us and nature. The whole of that added, man-made, artificial world is the cumulative, now planned, now chaoitc, product of human acts of meaning.

3 A third function of meaning is constitutive. Just as language is constituted by articulate sound and meaning, so social institutions and human cultures have meanings as intrinsic components. Religions and art-forms, languages and literatures, sciences, philosophies, histories, all are inextricably involved in acts of meaning. What is true of cultural achievements, no less is true of social institutions. The family, the state, the law, the economy are not fixed and immutable entities. They adapt to changing circumstances; they can be reconceived in the light of new ideas; they can be subjected to revolutionary change. But all such change involves change of meaning—a change of idea or concept, a change of judgment or evaluation, a change of the order or request. The state can be changed by rewriting its constitution. More subtly but no less effectively it can be changed by reinterpreting the consitution or, again, by working on men's minds and hearts to change the objects that command their respect, hold their allegiance, fire their loyalty.

A fourth function of meaning is communicative. What one man means is communicated to another intersubjectively, artistically, symbolically, linguistically, incarnately. So individual meaning becomes common meaning. But a rich store of common meaning is not the work of isolated individuals or even of single generations. Common meanings have histories. They originate in single minds. They become common only through successful and widespread communication. They are transmitted to successive generations only through training and education. Slowly and gradually they are clarified, expressed, formulated, defined, only to be enriched and deepened and transformed, and no less often to be impoverished, emptied out, and deformed.

The conjunction of both the constitutive and communicative functions of meaning yield the three key notions of community, existence, and history.

A community is not just a number of men within a geographical frontier. It is an achievement of common meaning, and there are kinds and degrees of achievement. Common meaning is potential when there is a common field of experience, and to withdraw from that common field is to get out of touch. Common meaning is formal when there is common understanding, and one withdraws from that common understanding by misunderstanding, by incomprehension, by mutual incomprehension. Common meaning is actual inasmuch as there are common judgments, areas in which all affirm and deny in the same manner; and one withdraws from that common judgment when one disagrees, when one considers true what others hold false and false what they think true. Common meaning is realized by decisions and choices, especially by permanent dedication, in the love that makes families, in the loyalty that makes states, in the faith that makes religions. Community coheres or divides, begins or ends, just where the common field of experience, common understanding, common judgment, common commitments begin and end. So communities are of many kinds: linguistic, religious, cultural, social, political, domestic. They vary in extent, in age, in cohesiveness, in their oppositions to one another.

As it is only within communities that men are conceived and born and reared, so too it is only with respect to the available common meanings that the individual grows in experience, understanding, judgment, and so comes to find out for himself that he has to decide for himself what to make of himself. This process for the schoolmaster is education, for the sociologist is socialization, for the cultural anthropologist is acculturation. But for the individual in the process it is his coming to be a man, his existing as a man in the fuller sense of the name.

Such existing may be authentic or unauthentic, and this may

occur in two different ways. There is the minor authenticity or unauthenticity of the subject with respect to the tradition that nourishes him. There is the major authenticity that justifies or condemns the tradition itself. In the first case there is passed a human judgment on subjects. In the second case history and, ultimately, divine providence pass judgment on traditions.

As Kierkegaard asked whether he was a Christian, so divers men can ask themselves whether or not they are genuine Catholics or Protestants, Muslims or Buddhists, Platonists or Aristotelians, Kantians or Hegelians, artists or scientists, and so forth. Now they may answer that they are, and their answers may be correct. But they can also answer affirmatively and still be mistaken. In that case there will exist a series of points in which they are what the ideals of the tradition demand, but there will be another series in which there is a greater or less divergence. These points of divergence are overlooked from a selective inattention, or from a failure to understand, or from an undetected rationalization. What I am is one thing, what a genuine Christian or Buddhist is, is another, and I am unaware of the difference. My unawareness is unexpressed. I have no language to express what I am, so I use the language of the tradition I unauthentically appropriate, and thereby I devaluate, distort, water down, corrupt that language.

Such devaluation, distortion, corruption may occur only in scattered individuals. But it may occur on a more massive scale, and then the words are repeated, but the meaning is gone. The chair was still the chair of Moses, but it was occupied by the scribes and Pharisees. The theology was still scholastic, but the scholasticism was decadent. The religious order still read out the rules, but one wonders whether the home fires were still burning. The sacred name of science may still be invoked but, as Edmund Husserl has argued, all significant scientific ideals can vanish to be replaced by the conventions of a clique. So the unauthenticity of individuals becomes the unauthenticity of a tradition. Then, in the measure a subject takes the tradition, as it exists, for his standard, in that measure he can do no more than authentically realize unauthenticity.

History, then, differs radically from nature. Nature unfolds in accord with law. But the shape and form of human knowledge, work, social organization, cultural achievement, communication, community, personal development, are involved in meaning. Meaning has its invariant structures and elements but the contents in the structures are subject to cumulative development and cumulative decline. So it is that man stands outside the rest of nature, that he is a historical being, that each man shapes his own life but does so only in interaction with the traditions of the communities in which he happens to have been born and, in turn, these traditions themselves are but the deposit left him by the lives of his predecessors.

So, finally, it follows that hermeneutics and the study of history are basic to all human science. Meaning enters into the very fabric of human living but varies from place to place and from one age to another.

9. REALMS OF MEANING

Different exigences give rise to different modes of conscious and intentional operation, and different modes of such operation give rise to different realms of meaning.

There is a systematic exigence that separates the realm of common sense from the realm of theory. Both of these realms, by and large, regard the same real objects. But the objects are viewed from such different standpoints that they can be related only by shifting from one standpoint to the other. The realm of common sense is the realm of persons and things in their relations to us. It is the visible universe peopled by relatives, friends, acquaintances, fellow citizens, and the rest of humanity. We come to know it, not by applying some scientific method, but by a self-correcting process of learning, in which insights gradually accumulate, coalesce, qualify and correct one another, until a point is reached where we are able to meet situations as they arise, size them up by adding a few more insights to the acquired store, and so deal with them in an appropriate fashion. Of the objects in this realm we speak in everyday language, in which words have the function, not of naming the intrinsic properties of things, but of completing the focusing of our conscious intentionality on the things, of crystallizing our attitudes, expectations, intentions, of guiding all our actions.

The intrusion of the systematic exigence into the realm of common sense is beautifully illustrated by Plato's early dialogues. Socrates would ask for the definition of this or that virtue. No one could afford to admit that he had no idea of what was meant by courage or temperance or justice. No one could deny that such common names must possess some common meaning found in each instance of courage, or temperance, or justice. And no one, not even Socrates, was able to pin down just what that common meaning was. If from Plato's dialogues one shifts to Aristotle's *Nicomachean Ethics*, one can find definitions worked out both for virtue and vice in general and for a series of virtues each flanked by two opposite vices, one sinning by excess, and the other by defect. But these answers to Socrates' questions have now ceased to be the single objective. The systematic exigence not merely raises questions that common sense cannot answer but also demands a context for its answers, a context that common sense cannot supply or comprehend. This context is theory, and the objects to which it refers are in the realm of theory. To these objects one can ascend from commonsense starting-points, but they are properly known, not by this ascent, but by their internal relations, their congruences, and differences, the functions they fulfil in their interactions. As one may approach theoretical objects from a commonsense starting-point, so too one can invoke common sense to correct theory. But the correction will not be effected in commonsense language but in theoretical language, and its implications will be the consequences, not of the commonsense facts that were invoked, but of the theoretical correction that was made.

My illustration was from Plato and Aristotle, but any number of others could be added. Mass, temperature, the electromagnetic field are not objects in the world of common sense. Mass is neither weight nor momentum. A metal object will feel colder than a wooden one beside it, but both will be of the same temperature. Maxwell's equations for the electromagnetic field are magnificent in their abstruseness. If a biologist takes his young son to the zoo and both pause to look at a giraffe, the boy will wonder whether it bites or kicks, but the father will see another manner in which skeletal, locomotive, digestive, vascular, and nervous systems combine and interlock.

There are then a realm of common sense and a realm of theory. We use different languages to speak of them. The difference in the languages involves social differences: specialists can speak to their wives about many things but not about their specialties. Finally, what gives rise to these quite different standpoints, methods of coming to know, languages, communities, is the systematic exigence.

However, to meet fully the systematic exigence only reinforces the critical exigence. Is common sense just primitive ignorance to be brushed aside with an acclaim to science as the dawn of intelligence and reason? Or is science of merely pragmatic value, teaching us how to control nature, but failing to reveal what nature is? Or, for that matter, is there any such thing as human knowing? So man is confronted with the three basic questions: What am I doing when I am knowing? Why is doing that knowing? What do I know when I do it? With these questions one turns from the outer realms of common sense and theory to the appropriation of one's own interiority, one's subjectivity, one's operations, their structure, their norms, their potentialities. Such appropriation, in its technical expression, resembles theory. But in itself it is a heightening of intentional consciousness, an attending not merely to objects but also to the intending subject and his acts. And as this heightened consciousness constitutes the evidence for one's account of knowledge, such an account by the proximity of the evidence differs from all other expression.

The withdrawal into interiority is not an end in itself. From it one returns to the realms of common sense and theory with the ability to meet the methodical exigence. For self-appropriation of itself is a grasp of transcendental method, and that grasp provides one with the tools not only for an analysis of common-sense procedures but also for the differentiation of the sciences and the construction of their methods.

Finally, there is the transcendent exigence. There is to human inquiry an unrestricted demand for intelligibility. There is to human judgment a demand for the unconditioned. There is to human deliberation a criterion that criticizes every finite good. So it is—as we shall attempt to show in the next chapter—that man can reach basic fulfilment, peace, joy, only by moving beyond the realms of common sense, theory, and interiority and into the realm in which God is known and loved.

It is, of course, only in a rather highly developed consciousness that the distinction between the realms of meaning is to be carried out. Undifferentiated consciousness uses indiscriminately the procedures of common sense, and so its explanations, its self-knowledge, its religion are rudimentary. Classical consciousness is theoretical as well as common sense, but the theory is not sufficiently advanced for the sharp opposition between the two realms of meaning to be adequately grasped. Troubled consciousness emerges when an Eddington contrasts his two tables: the bulky, solid, colored desk at which he worked, and the manifold of colorless "wavicles" so minute that the desk was mostly empty space. Differentiated consciousness appears when the critical exigence turns attention upon interiority, when self-appropriation is achieved, when the subject relates his different procedures to the several realms, relates the several realms to one another, and consciously shifts from one realm to another by consciously changing his procedures.

The unity, then, of differentiated consciousness is, not the homogeneity of undifferentiated consciousness, but the self-knowledge that understands the different realms and knows how to shift from any one to any other. It remains, however, that what is easy for differentiated consciousness appears very mysterious to undifferentiated consciousness or to troubled consciousness. Undifferentiated consciousness insists on homogeneity. If the procedures of common sense are correct, then theory must be wrong. If theory is correct, then common sense must be just an antiquated relic from a pre-scientific age. If the transition from the undifferentiated to troubled consciousness cannot be avoided when it is clear that common sense and theory, though disparate, must both be accepted, an entirely different set of procedures has to be learnt before interiority can be revealed and the self-appropriation of differentiated consciousness achieved.

No doubt, we have all to begin from undifferentiated consciousness, from commonsense cognitional procedures, from some one of the multitudinous "ordinary languages" in which the endless varieties of common sense express themselves. No doubt, it is only by a humble and docile process of learning that anyone can move beyond his original ordinary language and its common sense and come to understand other ordinary languages and their varieties of common sense. It is only by knowledge making its bloody entrance that one can move out of the realm of ordinary languages into the realm of theory and the totally different scientific apprehension of reality. It is only through the long and confused twilight of philosophic initiation that one can find one's way into interiority and achieve through self-appropriation a basis, a foundation, that is distinct from common sense and theory, that acknowledges their disparateness, that accounts for both and critically grounds them both.

10. STAGES OF MEANING

The stages in question are ideal constructs, and the key to the constructing is undifferentiation or differentiation of consciousness. In the main we have in mind the Western tradition and we distinguish three stages. In the first stage conscious and intentional operations follow the mode of common sense. In a second stage besides the mode of common sense there is also the mode of theory, where the theory is controlled by a logic. In a third stage the modes of common sense and theory remain, science asserts its autonomy from philosophy, and there occur philosophies that leave theory to science and take their stand on interiority.

Such is the theoretical division. It is temporal in the sense that one has to be in the first stage to advance to the second and one has to be in the second to advance to the third. But it is not chronological: large segments of the population may have undifferentiated consciousness though a culture is in the second or third stage; and many learned people may remain in the second stage when a culture has reached the third.

4

Accordingly, our treatment will not follow the theoretical division. On the first stage there will be two sections, namely, *Early Language* and *The Greek Discovery of Mind*. A third section will treat of the second and third stages together. A fourth will regard undifferentiated consciousness in the second and third stages.

10.1. EARLY LANGUAGE

In the first stage there occurs the development of language. But if we have referred to language as an instrumental act of meaning and contrasted it with potential, formal, full, and active acts, still this must not be taken to imply that language is some optional adjunct that may or may not accompany the other acts. On the contrary, some sensible expression is intrinsic to the pattern of our conscious and intentional operations. Just as inquiry supposes sensible data, just as insight occurs with respect to some schematic image, just as the reflective act of understanding occurs with respect to a convincing summation of the relevant evidence, so inversely the interior acts of conceiving, of judging, and of deciding demand the sensible and proportionate substrate we call expression. Indeed, so rigorous is this demand that Ernst Cassirer has been able to put together a pathology of symbolic consciousness: motor disturbances that result in aphasia are accompanied with disturbances in perception, in thought, and in action.[22]

The development of proportionate expression involves three key steps. The first is the discovery of indicative signification. For instance, one tries to grasp but fails. But the failure at least points. When pointing is understood as pointing, then one no longer tries to grasp.[23] One just points. The second step is generalization. Not only does insight rise upon the basis of a schematic image, it also can use the pattern discerned in the image to guide bodily movements including vocal articulation.[24] Such movements may be mere imitation of another's movements,

[22] Ernst Cassirer, *The Philosophy of Symbolic Forms*, three volumes, New Haven, 1953, 1955, 1957, III, pp. 205–277.

[23] Ibid., I, 181 f. More adequately in Gibson Winter, *Elements for a Social Ethic*, New York: Macmillan, 1968, pp. 99 ff., cf. 17 ff.

[24] Ibid., I, 12–15.

but mimesis may be employed to signify, and then it means the other's movements. From mimesis one may advance to analogy: one repeats the pattern but the movements that embody it are quite different; and as mimesis may be used to signify what is imitated, so analogy may be used to signify its original.[25] The third step is the development of language. It is the work of the community that has common insights into common needs and common tasks, and, of course, already is in communication through intersubjective, indicative, mimetic, and analogical expression. Just as its members understand one another's smiles and frowns, their gestures, mimesis, and analogies, so too they can come to endow vocal sounds with signification. So words come to refer to data of experience, sentences to the insights that shape the experience, while the mood of the sentence varies to express assertions, commands, and wishes.

This account of the genesis of language has the advantage of explaining both the strength and the weakness of early language.[26] For gestures occur with respect to perceptual presentations and imaginative representations. So it is that early language has little difficulty in expressing all that can be pointed out or directly perceived or directly represented. But the generic cannot be pointed out, or directly perceived, or directly represented. So in Homer there were words for such specific activities as glancing, peering, staring, but no generic word for seeing.[27] Again, in various American Indian languages one cannot simply say that the man is sick; one also has to retail whether he is near or far, whether he can or cannot be seen; and often the form of the sentence will also reveal his place, position, and posture.[28] Again, since time involves a synthesis that orders all events in a single continuum of earlier and later, it cannot be directly perceived, and it can be represented only by a highly sophisticated geometrical image. So early language may have an abundance of

[25] Ibid., I, 186 ff.

[26] Ibid., I, 198–277; II, 71–151.

[27] J. Russo and B. Simon, "Homeric Psychology and the Oral Epic Tradition", *Journal of the History of Ideas*, 29 (1968), p. 484.

[28] E. Cassirer, op. cit. I, p. 199 ff.

tenses, but they are found to express different kinds or modes of action, and not a synthesis of temporal relationships.[29] Further, the subject and his inner experience are on the side, not of the perceived, but of the perceiving. To point to oneself is to point to one's head or neck or chest or stomach or arms or legs or feet or hands or whole body. So there is no reason for surprise that possessive pronouns, that refer to visible possessions develop before personal pronouns.[30] Again, in Homer, inner mental processes are represented by personified interchanges. Where we would expect an account of the hero's thoughts and feelings, Homer has him converse with a god or goddess, with his horse or a river, or with some part of himself such as his heart or his temper.[31] Again, among the Hebrews, moral defect was first experienced as defilement, then conceived as the people's violation of its covenant with God, and finally felt as personal guilt before God, where, however, each later stage did not eliminate the earlier but took it over to correct it and to complement it.[32] Finally, the divine is the objective of the transcendental notions in their unrestricted and absolute aspects. It cannot be perceived and it cannot be imagined. But it can be associated with the object or event, the ritual or recitation, that occasions religious experience;[33] and so there arise the hierophanies.[34]

[29] Ibid., I, p. 215 ff.

[30] Ibid., I, p. 215.

[31] Russo and Simon, op. cit., p. 487.

[32] Paul Ricoeur, *Finitudé et culpabilité*, II, *La symbolique du mal*, Paris: Aubier, 1960.

[33] See Ernst Benz on Shintoism as a living, ever developing polytheism in his essay "On Understanding Non-Christian Religions", in *The History of Religions, Essays in Methodology*, edited by M. Eliade and J. Kitagawa, Chicago: Chicago University Press, 1959, 1962, pp. 121–124. Also in the same collection, M. Eliade, "Methodological Remarks on the Study of Religious Symbolism". On the apprehension of divinity in the patriarchs of the Old Testament, N. Lohfink, *Bibelauslegung im Wandel*, Frankfurt a. M.: Knecht, 1967, pp. 107–128.

[34] Note that here we are touching on the nature of projection, i.e. the transfer of subjective experience into the field of the perceived or imagined. The transfer occurs to make insight into the experience possible. At a higher level of linguistic development, the possibility of insight is achieved by linguistic feed-back, by expressing the subjective experience in words and as subjective.

Even in its first stage meaning fulfils its four functions: it is communicative, constitutive, efficient, cognitive. However, these functions are not clearly apprehended, sharply defined, carefully delimited. Insights into gestures and percepts easily generate the names of different plants and animals. Insights into human relationships bring about the constitution of tribes and clans and other groupings; but to name the groups which are not perceptibly different from one another, calls for a certain ingenuity. As American sportswriters name teams Bruins and Hawks and Seals, Bears and Colts and Lions, so too primitive groups are associated with the names of plants and animals.

As the constitutive, so too the cognitive function of meaning is exercised. Man moves from the infant's world of immediacy into a world mediated by meaning. However, the mediating meaning is not purely cognitive. It blends insensibly with the constitutive, and the result is myth. Man constitutes not only his social institutions and their cultural significance but also the story of the world's shape and origin and destiny.

As the constitutive function of meaning intrudes into the field of "speculative" knowledge, so the efficient intrudes into that of "practical" knowledge. The result is magic. Words bring about results not only by directing human action but also by a power of their own which myth explains.

As Malinowski has insisted, while myth and magic envelop and penetrate the whole fabric of primitive living, they do not prevent a thorough understanding of the practical tasks of daily life.[35] Moreover, it is the development of practical understanding that takes man beyond fruit-collecting, hunting, fishing, gardening to large-scale argiculture with the social organization of the temple states and later of the empires of the ancient high civilizations in Egypt, Mesopotamia, Crete, the valleys of the Indus and the Hoang-ho, Mexico and Peru. There there emerged great works of irrigation, vast structures of stone or brick, armies and navies, complicated processes of book-keeping, the beginnings of geometry, arithmetic, astronomy. But if the poverty and

[35] B. Malinowski, *Magic, Science and Religion*, New York: Doubleday, Anchor, 1954, pp. 17 ff.

weakness of the primitive were replaced by the wealth and power of great states, if the area over which man exercised practical intelligence increased enormously, the whole achievement stood upon the cosmological myth that depicted as continuous and solidary the order of society, the order of the cosmos, and the divine being.[36]

10.2. THE GREEK DISCOVERY OF MIND

As technique advances, it reveals by contrast the inefficacy of magic and turns man in his weakness from magical incantation to religious supplication. However, if myth is to be broken, more is needed. Man must discover mind. He has to sort out and somehow detach from one another feeling and doing, knowing and deciding. He has to clarify just what it is to know and, in the light of that clarification, keep the cognitive function of meaning apart from its constitutive and efficient functions and from its role in the communication of feeling.

How the Greeks discovered mind, has been told by Bruno Snell. On a first level there was the literary revelation of man to himself. Homeric simile drew on the characteristics of inanimate nature and of plants and animals to illuminate and objectify and distinguish the varied springs of action in the epic heroes. The lyric poets worked out expressions of personal human feeling. The tragedians exhibited human decisions, their conflicts and interplay, and their consequences.[37]

Within the literary tradition there occurred reflection on knowledge.[38] For Homer, knowledge comes by perception or by hearsay. Man's knowledge is always partial and incomplete. But the Muses are omnipresent. They perceive everything. They are the ones that enable the bard to sing as if he had been present or as if he had heard the tale from an eyewitness. But for Hesiod

---

[36] On cosmological symbolism, see Eric Voegelin, *Order and History*, I. *Israel and Revelation*, Louisiana State University Press, 1956. A definition of the symbolism is to be found on p. 27, its distribution on p. 14. See also F. H. Borsch, *The Son of Man in Myth and History*, London: SCM, 1967.

[37] B. Snell, *The Discovery of the Mind*, New York: Harper Torchbook, 1960. Chapters One, Three, Five, and Nine.

[38] Ibid., Chapter Seven.

the Muses do not inspire but teach; and they are far less trust-worthy than Homer claimed. They may teach the truth but they also may teach plausible falsehood. They singled Hesiod out on Mount Helicon and taught him not to repeat the folly and the lies of his predecessors but to tell the truth about the struggle in which man ekes out his livelihood.

Xenophanes was still more critical. He rejected the multitude of anthropomorphic gods; for him, god was unity, perfect in wisdom, operating without toil, merely by the thought of his mind. In contrast, human wisdom was imperfect, caught in semblance, but still the best of the virtues and, indeed, to be attained by long seeking. Similarly, for Hecataeus, the stories of the Greeks were many and foolish. Man's knowledge is not the gift of the gods; stories of the past are to be judged by everyday experience; one advances in knowledge by inquiry and search, and the search is not just accidental, as it was in Odysseus, but deliberate and planned.

This empirical interest lived on in Herodotus, in the physicians, and in the physicists. But a new turn emerged with Heraclitus. He maintained that the mere amassing of information did not make one grow in intelligence. Where his predecessors were opposed to ignorance, he was opposed to folly. He prized eyes and ears but thought them bad witnesses for men with barbarian souls. There is an intelligence, a *logos*, that steers through all things. It is found in god and man and beast, the same in all though in different degrees. To know it, is widsom.

Where Heraclitus emphasized process, Parmenides denied both multiplicity and motion. Though his expression revived the myth of revelation, his position at its heart was a set of arguments. While he could not be expected to formulate the principles of excluded middle and of identity, he reached analogous con-clusions. For he denied the possibility of "becoming" as an intermediary between being and nothing; and he denied a distinction between "being" and "being" and so precluded any multiplicity of beings. While his specific achievement was only a mistake, still it provided a carrier for a breakthrough. Linguistic argument had emerged as an independent power that could dare to challenge the evidence of the senses.[39] The distinction between sense and intellect was established. The way lay open for Zeno's paradoxes, for the eloquence and scepticism of the Sophists, for Socrates' demand for definition, for Plato's distinction between eristic and dialectic, and for the Aristotelian *Organon*.

Earlier we had occasion to speak of the limitation of early language. Because the development of thought and language depends upon insights, because insights occur with respect to sensible presentations and representations, early language can come to dominate the spatial field yet remain unable to handle adequately the generic, the temporal, the subjective, the divine. But these limitations recede in the measure that linguistic explanations and statements provide the sensible presentations for the insights that effect further developments of thought and language. Moreover, such advance for a time can occur exponentially: the more language develops, the more it can develop still more. Eventually, there begins the reflex movement in which language comes to mediate and objectify and examine the linguistic process itself. Alphabets make words visible. Dictionaries collect their meanings. Grammars study their inflections and syntax. Literary criticism interprets and evaluates compositions. Logics promote clarity, coherence, and rigor. Hermeneutics studies the varying relations of acts of meaning to terms of meaning. Philosophers reflect on the world of immediacy and the many worlds mediated by meaning.

To grasp the significance of this superstructure, one must return to the limitations of mythic consciousness. As Ernst Cassirer states, it lacks any clear dividing line between mere "representation" and "real" perception, between wish and fulfilment, between image and thing. He goes on immediately to mention the continuity of dream and waking consciousness and, later, he adds that no less than the image, the name tends to merge with the thing.[40] It would seem, despite his later retraction, to be the same absence of distinction that Lucien Lévy-Bruhl

---

[39] See F. Copleston, *A History of Philosophy*, Volume I, Chapter Six, London: Burns, Oates & Washbourne, 1946. There are many editions.

[40] E. Cassirer, op. cit., II, pp. 36 and 40 f.

wished to describe when he spoke of a law of participation governing the common representations and the institutions of primitives, a participation that made the content of their representations appear mystical while it made relations between representations largely tolerant of contradictions.[41]

Now these characteristics of the primitive mind seem very mysterious. But one is not to conclude that they argue any lack of intelligence or reasonableness on the part of primitives. For, after all, to draw distinctions is not a simple matter, and to acknowledge the import of the distinctions, once they are drawn, is not a simple matter. What is a distinction? Let us say that A and B are distinct, if it is true that A is not B. Let us add that A and B may stand either for mere words, or for the meaning of words, or for the realities meant by words, so that distinctions may be merely verbal, or notional, or real. Let us note that the reality in question is the reality that becomes known, not by sense alone, but by sense and understanding and rational judgment.

10.3. THE SECOND AND THIRD STAGES

The discovery of mind marks the transition from the first stage of meaning to the second. In the first stage the world mediated by meaning is just the world of common sense. In the second stage the world mediated by meaning splits into the realm of common sense and the realm of theory. Corresponding to this division and grounding it, there is a differentiation of consciousness. In the first stage the subject, in his pursuit of the concrete good, also attends, understands, judges. But he does not make a specialty of these activities. He does not formulate a theoretical ideal in terms of knowledge, truth, reality, causality. He does not formulate linguistically a set of norms for the pursuit of that ideal goal. He does not initiate a distinct economic and social and cultural context within which the pursuit of the ideal goal could be carried out by human animals. But in the second stage of meaning the subject continues to operate in the

[41] L. Lévy-Bruhl, *Les fonctions mentales dans les sociétés inférieures*, Paris: P.U.F., [9]1951, pp. 78 ff. E. E. Evans-Pritchard, *Theories of Primitive Religion*, Oxford: Clarendon, 1965, pp. 78–99, discusses the value of Lévy-Bruhl's work.

commonsense manner in all his dealings with the particular and concrete, but along with this mode of operation he also has another, the theoretical. In the theoretical mode the good that is pursued is the truth and, while this pursuit is willed, still the pursuit itself consists only in operations on the first three levels of intentional consciousness: it is the specialization of attending, understanding, and judging.

Now just as the second stage comes out of developments occurring in the first, so the third stage comes out of developments occurring in the second. Accordingly, it will help clarify what is proper to the second stage if at once we characterize the third. In the third stage, then, the sciences have become ongoing processes. Instead of stating the truth about this or that kind of reality, their aim is an ever better approximation towards the truth, and this is attained by an ever fuller and exacter understanding of all relevant data. In the second stage, theory was a specialty for the attainment of truth; in the third stage scientific theory has become a specialty for the advance of understanding. Further, the sciences are autonomous. They consider questions scientific if and only if they can be settled by an appeal to sensible data. As they have evolved, they have developed ever more effective ways of using this criterion in settling issues. In other words, they have worked out their respective methods, and there is no higher discipline that could discover their proper methods for them. Finally, since they are ongoing processes, their unification has to be an ongoing process; it cannot be some single well-ordered formulation; it has to be a succession of different formulations; in other words, unification will be the achievement not of logic but of method.

Now the emergence of the autonomous sciences has repercussions on philosophy. Since the sciences between them undertake the explanation of all sensible data, one may conclude with the positivists that the function of philosophy is to announce that philosophy has nothing to say. Since philosophy has no theoretic function, one may conclude with the linguistic analysts that the function of philosophy is to work out a hermeneutics for the clarification of the local variety of everyday language.

But there remains the possibility—and it is our option—that philosophy is neither a theory in the manner of science nor a somewhat technical form of common sense, nor even a reversal to Presocratic wisdom. Philosophy finds its proper data in intentional consciousness. Its primary function is to promote the self-appropriation that cuts to the root of philosophic differences and incomprehensions. It has further, secondary functions in distinguishing, relating, grounding the several realms of meaning and, no less, in grounding the methods of the sciences and so promoting their unification.

But what in the third stage are differentiated, specialized, moving towards an integration, in the second stage are more or less undifferentiated. We have spoken of the world mediated by meaning splitting into a world of theory and a world of common sense. At a certain stage in Plato's thought there seem to be asserted two really distinct worlds, a transcendent world of eternal Forms, and a transient world of appearance.[42] In Aristotle, there are not two sets of objects but two approaches to one set. Theory is concerned with what is prior in itself but posterior for us; but everyday human knowledge is concerned with what is prior for us though posterior in itself. But, though Aristotle by beguilingly simple analogies could set up a properly systematic metaphysics, his contrast was not between theory and common sense as we understand these terms but between *epistēmē* and *doxa*, between *sophia* and *phronēsis*, between necessity and contingence.

Again, in Aristotle the sciences are conceived not as autonomous but as prolongations of philosophy and as further determinations of the basic concepts philosophy provides.[43] So it is that, while Aristotelian psychology is not without profound insight into human sensibility and intelligence, still its basic concepts are derived not from intentional consciousness but from metaphysics. Thus "soul" does not mean "subject" but

[42] For a careful statement of this very complex issue, see F. Copleston, op. cit., Chapter Twenty.

[43] See Aristotle, *Metaphysics*, Theta, 6, 1048 a 25 ff. Aquinas, *In IX Metaphys.*, lect. 5, # 1828 ff. *Insight*, p. 432, gives the basis for the generality of the terms, potency, form, act.

"the first act of an organic body" whether of a plant, an animal, or a man.[44] Similarly, the notion of "object" is not derived from a consideration of intentional acts; on the contrary, just as potencies are to be conceived by considering their acts, so acts are to be conceived by considering their objects, i.e. their efficient or final causes.[45] As in psychology, so too in physics, the basic concepts are metaphysical. As an agent is principle of movement in the mover, so a nature is principle of movement in the moved. But agent is agent because it is in act. The nature is matter or form and rather form than matter. Matter is pure potency. Movement is incomplete act, the act of what is in potency still.

This continuity of philosophy and science has often been the object of nostalgic admiration. But if it had the merit of meeting the systematic exigence and habituating the human mind to theoretical pursuits, it could be no more than a transitional phase. Modern science had to develop its own proper basic concepts and thereby achieve its autonomy. In doing so it gave a new form to the opposition between the world of theory and the world of common sense. This new form, in turn, evoked a series of new philosophies: Galileo's primary qualities, which admitted geometrization and so were real, and his refractory secondary qualities, which were pronounced merely apparent; Descartes' imnd in a machine; Spinoza's two known attributes; Kant's *a priori* forms and *a posteriori* filling of the sensibility.[46] But Kant's Copernican revolution marks a dividing line. Hegel turned from substance to the subject. Historians and philologists worked out their autonomous methods for human studies. Will and decision, actions and results, came up for emphasis in Kierkegaard, Schopenhauer, Nietzsche, Blondel, the pragmatists. Brentano inspired Husserl, and intentionality analysis routed faculty psychology. The second stage of meaning is vanishing, and a third is about to take its place.

---

[44] Aristotle, *De Anima*, II, 1, 412b, pp. 4 ff.

[45] Ibid., II, 4, 415a, pp. 14–20. Aquinas, *In II de Anima*, lect. 6, # 305.

[46] The interaction of science and philosophy has been studied in detail by Ernst Cassirer, *Das Erkenntnisproblem in der Philosophie und Wissenschaft der neueren Zeit*, three volumes, Berlin, 1906, 1907, 1920.

10.4. UNDIFFERENTIATED CONSCIOUSNESS IN
THE LATER STAGES

Our outline of the development and the eclipse of the second stage would be very incomplete if no mention were made of the mode of survival of undifferentiated consciousness in the later stages. For it is not the philosophic or scientific theorist that does the world's work, conducts its business, governs its cities and states, teaches most of its classes and runs all of its schools. As before the emergence of theory, so too afterwards all such activities are conducted in the commonsense mode of intellectual operation, in the mode in which conscious and intentional operations occur in accord with their own immanent and spontaneous norms. However, if the mode and much of the scope of commonsense operation remain the same, the very existence of another mode is bound to shift concerns and emphases.

It was on a rising tide of linguistic feed-back that logic and philosophy and early science emerged. But such technical achievements may repel rather than impress. One may be content to marvel at the fact of language, the fact that makes man unique among the animals. One may with Isocrates trace cities and laws, arts and skills and, indeed, all aspects of culture to man's powers of speech and persuasion. One may go on to urge one's fellow townsmen to seek eloquence through education and thereby to excel among men in the very respect in which man excels among the animals. So to be educated linguistically and to become human are found to be interchangeable. So there emerged one strand of humanism that spread from Greece to Rome and from antiquity to the late middle ages.[47]

Another strand was moral, and its name was *philanthropia*. It was respect and devotion to man as man. It rested not on kinship, or noble blood, or common citizenship and laws, or even on education, but on the fact that another, particularly a sufferer, was a human being. Practice of *philanthropia* could, of course, be quite modest: credit for it was given conquerors that showed some restraint in plundering and enslaving the vanquished. But, at least, it was an ideal that inspired education and fostered the

[47] Bruno Snell, op. cit., Chapter Eleven.

gracious urbanity, the ease and affability, the charm and taste exhibited in Menander's comedies and their Latin counterparts in Plautus and Terence.

A third strand came from the world of theory. For if creative thought in philosophy and science is too austere for general consumption, creative thinkers are usually rare. They have their brief day, only to be followed by the commentators, the teachers, the popularizers that illuminate, complete, transpose, simplify. So the worlds of theory and of common sense partly interpenetrate and partly merge. The results are ambivalent. It will happen that the exaggerations of philosophic error are abandoned, while the profundities of philosophic truth find a vehicle that compensates for the loss of the discredited myths. But it will also happen that theory fuses more with common nonsense than with common sense, to make the nonsense pretentious and, because it is common, dangerous and even disastrous.

Finally, literature moved into a quite different phase. Bruno Snell has contrasted the pre-philosophical with the post-philosophical poets.[48] The earlier poetry, he remarked, was ever intent to stake out new areas of the mind. The epic sagas opened the way to history, the cosmogonies to Ionian speculation on the first principle, the lyric to Heraclitus, the drama to Socrates and Plato.[49] The later poetry is acquainted with the literary critics and with theories of poetry. Poets have to select their genre, style, tone. They can be content, as was Callimachus, to be playful and artistic or, with Virgil in his Eclogues, to express a complex civilization's nostalgia for earlier times and simpler living.[50]

That simpler living, of course, continues. The humanism we have been describing belongs to an educated class. In a people united by common language, common loyalties, common moral and religious traditions as well as by economic interdependence,

[48] Bruno Snell, op. cit., pp. 266 ff.

[49] Science was foreshadowed by the similes in Empedocles' hexameters, e.g. "the light of the sun was thrown back by the moon like an echo; the moon revolves about the earth like the felloe of a wheel about the axle ..." ibid., p. 217.

[50] Ibid., Chapters Twelve and Thirteen.

the culture of the educated may affect many of the uneducated, much as theory affected pre-theoretical common sense. So by successive adaptations the innovations of theory can penetrate in ever weaker forms through all layers of a society to give it some approximation to the homogeneity necessary for mutual comprehension.

But such ideal conditions need not obtain. Discontinuities may arise. The better educated become a class closed in upon themselves with no task proportionate to their training. They become effete. The less educated and the uneducated find themselves with a tradition that is beyond their means. They cannot maintain it. They lack the genius to transform it into some simpler vital and intelligible whole. It degenerates. The meaning and values of human living are impoverished. The will to achieve both slackens and narrows. Where once there were joys and sorrows, now there are just pleasures and pains. The culture has become a slum.

Just as philosophic theory begot humanism of common sense, so too modern science has its progeny. As a form of knowledge, it pertains to man's development and grounds a new and fuller humanism. As a rigorous form of knowledge, it calls forth teachers and popularizers and even the fantasy of science fiction. But it also is a principle of action, and so it overflows into applied science, engineering, technology, industrialism. It is an acknowledged source of wealth and power, and the power is not merely material. It is the power of the mass media to write for, speak to, be seen by all men. It is the power of an educational system to fashion the nation's youth in the image of the wise man or in the image of a fool, in the image of a free man or in the image prescribed for the Peoples' Democracies.

In its third stage, then, meaning not merely differentiates into the realms of common sense, theory, and interiority, but also acquires the universal immediacy of the mass media and the moulding power of universal education. Never has adequately differentiated consciousness been more difficult to achieve. Never has the need to speak effectively to undifferentiated consciousness been greater.

Some of this chapter—
good for Readings.
Orientation to G
the Ques. of G

4

RELIGION

I. THE QUESTION OF GOD

THE facts of good and evil, of progress and decline, raise questions about the character of our universe. Such questions have been put in very many ways, and the answers given have been even more numerous. But behind this multiplicity there is a basic unity that comes to light in the exercise of transcendental method. We can inquire into the possibility of fruitful inquiry. We can reflect on the nature of reflection. We can deliberate whether our deliberating is worth while. In each case, there arises the question of God.

The possibility of inquiry on the side of the subject lies in his intelligence, in his drive to know what, why, how, and in his ability to reach intellectually satisfying answers. But why should the answers that satisfy the intelligence of the subject yield anything more than a subjective satisfaction? Why should they be supposed to possess any relevance to knowledge of the universe? Of course, we assume that they do. We can point to the fact that our assumption is confirmed by its fruits. So implicitly we grant that the universe is intelligible and, once that is granted, there arises the question whether the universe could be intelligible without having an intelligent ground. But that is the question about God.

Again, to reflect on reflection is to ask just what happens when we marshal and weigh the evidence for pronouncing that this probably is so and that probably is not so. To what do these metaphors of marshalling and weighing refer? Elsewhere I have worked out an answer to this question and here I can do no more than summarily repeat my conclusion.[1] Judgment proceeds rationally from a grasp of a virtually unconditioned. By an unconditioned is meant any "x" that has no conditions. By a virtually unconditioned is meant any "x" that has no unfulfilled conditions. In other words, a virtually unconditioned is a conditioned whose conditions are all fulfilled. To marshal the evidence is to ascertain whether all the conditions are fulfilled. To weigh the evidence is to ascertain whether the fulfillment of the conditions certainly or probably involves the existence or occurrence of the conditioned.

Now this account of judgment implicitly contains a further element. If we are to speak of a virtually unconditioned, we must first speak of an unconditioned. The virtually unconditioned has no unfulfilled conditions. The strictly unconditioned has no conditions whatever. In traditional terms, the former is a contingent being, and the latter is a necessary being. In more contemporary terms the former pertains to this world, to the world of possible experience, while the latter transcends this world in the sense that its reality is of a totally different order. But in either case we come to the question of God. Does a necessary being exist? Does there exist a reality that transcends the reality of this world?

To deliberate about "x" is to ask whether "x" is worth while. To deliberate about deliberating is to ask whether any deliberating is worth while. Has "worth while" any ultimate meaning? Is moral enterprise consonant with this world? We praise the developing subject ever more capable of attention, insight, reasonableness, responsibility. We praise progress and denounce every manifestation of decline. But is the universe on our side, or are we just gamblers and, if we are gamblers, are we not perhaps fools, individually struggling for authenticity and collectively endeavoring to snatch progress from the ever mounting welter of decline? The questions arise and, clearly, our attitudes and our resoluteness may be profoundly affected by the answers. Does there or does there not necessarily exist a transcendent,

[1] *Insight*, Chapters Nine, Ten, and Eleven.

intelligent ground of the universe? Is that ground or are we the primary instance of moral consciousness? Are cosmogenesis, biological evolution, historical process basically cognate to us as moral beings or are they indifferent and so alien to us?

Such is the question of God. It is not a matter of image or feeling, of concept or judgment. They pertain to answers. It is a question. It rises out of our conscious intentionality, out of the *a priori* structured drive that promotes us from experiencing to the effort to understand, from understanding to the effort to judge truly, from judging to the effort to choose rightly. In the measure that we advert to our own questioning and proceed to question it, there arises the question of God.

It is a question that will be manifested differently in the different stages of man's historical development and in the many varieties of his culture. But such differences of manifestation and expression are secondary. They may introduce alien elements that overlay, obscure, distort the pure question, the question that questions questioning itself. None the less, the obscurity and the distortion presuppose what they obscure and distort. It follows that, however much religious or irreligious answers differ, however much there differ the questions they explicitly raise, still at their root there is the same transcendental tendency of the human spirit that questions, that questions without restriction, that questions the significance of its own questioning, and so comes to the question of God.

The question of God, then, lies within man's horizon. Man's transcendental subjectivity is mutilated or abolished, unless he is stretching forth towards the intelligible, the unconditioned, the good of value. The reach, not of his attainment, but of his intending is unrestricted. There lies within his horizon a region for the divine, a shrine for ultimate holiness. It cannot be ignored. The atheist may pronounce it empty. The agnostic may urge that he finds his investigation has been inconclusive. The contemporary humanist will refuse to allow the question to arise. But their negations presuppose the spark in our clod, our native orientation to the divine.

2. SELF-TRANSCENDENCE

Man achieves authenticity in self-transcendence.

One can live in a world, have a horizon, just in the measure that one is not locked up in oneself. A first step towards this liberation is the sensitivity we share with the higher animals. But they are confined to a habitat, while man lives in a universe. Beyond sensitivity man asks questions, and his questioning is unrestricted.

First, there are questions for intelligence. We ask what and why and how and what for. Our answers unify and relate, classify and construct, serialize and generalize. From the narrow strip of space-time accessible to immediate experience we move towards the construction of a world-view and towards the exploration of what we ourselves could be and could do.

On questions for intelligence follow questions for reflection. We move beyond imagination and guess-work, idea and hypothesis, theory and system, to ask whether or not this really is so or that really could be. Now self-transcendence takes on a new meaning. Not only does it go beyond the subject but also it seeks what is independent of the subject. For a judgment that this or that is so reports, not what appears to me, not what I imagine, not what I think, not what I wish, not what I would be inclined to say, not what seems to me, but what is so.

Still such self-transcendence is only cognitive. It is in the order not of doing but only of knowing. But on the final level of questions for deliberation, self-transcendence becomes moral. When we ask whether this or that is worth while, whether it is not just apparently good but truly good, then we are inquiring, not about pleasure or pain, not about comfort or ill ease, not about sensitive spontaneity, not about individual or group advantage, but about objective value. Because we can ask such questions, and answer them, and live by the answers, we can effect in our living a moral self-transcendence. That moral self-transcendence is the possibility of benevolence and beneficence, of honest collaboration and of true love, of swinging completely out of the habitat of an animal and of becoming a person in a human society.

The transcendental notions, that is, our questions for intelligence, for reflection, and for deliberation, constitute our capacity for self-transcendence. That capacity becomes an actuality when one falls in love. Then one's being becomes being-in-love. Such being-in-love has its antecedents, its causes, its conditions, its occasions. But once it has blossomed forth and as long as it lasts, it takes over. It is the first principle. From it flow one's desires and fears, one's joys and sorrows, one's discernment of values, one's decisions and deeds.

Being-in-love is of different kinds. There is the love of intimacy, of husband and wife, of parents and children. There is the love of one's fellow men with its fruit in the achievement of human welfare. There is the love of God with one's whole heart and whole soul, with all one's mind and all one's strength (Mk. 12, 30). It is God's love flooding our hearts through the Holy Spirit given to us (Rom. 5, 5). It grounds the conviction of St. Paul that "there is nothing in death or life, in the realm of spirits or superhuman powers, in the world as it is or the world as it shall be, in the forces of the universe, in heights or depths—nothing in all creation that can separate us from the love of God in Christ Jesus our Lord" (Rom. 8, 38 f.).

As the question of God is implicit in all our questioning, so being in love with God is the basic fulfilment of our conscious intentionality. That fulfilment brings a deep-set joy that can remain despite humiliation, failure, privation, pain, betrayal, desertion. That fulfilment brings a radical peace, the peace that the world cannot give. That fulfilment bears fruit in a love of one's neighbor that strives mightily to bring about the kingdom of God on this earth. On the other hand, the absence of that fulfilment opens the way to the trivialization of human life in the pursuit of fun, to the harshness of human life arising from the ruthless exercise of power, to despair about human welfare springing from the conviction that the universe is absurd.

3. RELIGIOUS EXPERIENCE

Being in love with God, as experienced, is being in love in an unrestricted fashion. All love is self-surrender, but being in love with God is being in love without limits or qualifications or conditions or reservations. Just as unrestricted questioning is our capacity for self-transcendence, so being in love in an unrestricted fashion is the proper fulfilment of that capacity.

That fulfilment is not the product of our knowledge and choice. On the contrary, it dismantles and abolishes the horizon in which our knowing and choosing went on and it sets up a new horizon in which the love of God will transvalue our values and the eyes of that love will transform our knowing.

Though not the product of our knowing and choosing, it is a conscious dynamic state of love, joy, peace, that manifests itself in acts of kindness, goodness, fidelity, gentleness, and self-control (Gal. 5, 22).

To say that this dynamic state is conscious is not to say that it is known. For consciousness is just experience, but knowledge is a compound of experience, understanding, and judging. Because the dynamic state is conscious without being known, it is an experience of mystery. Because it is being in love, the mystery is not merely attractive but fascinating; to it one belongs; by it one is possessed. Because it is an unmeasured love, the mystery evokes awe. Of itself, then, inasmuch as it is conscious without being known, the gift of God's love is an experience of the holy, of Rudolf Otto's *mysterium fascinans et tremendum*.[2] It is what Paul Tillich named a being grasped by ultimate concern.[3] It corresponds to St. Ignatius Loyola's consolation that has no cause, as expounded by Karl Rahner.[4]

It is conscious on the fourth level of intentional consciousness. It is not the consciousness that accompanies acts of seeing, hearing, smelling, tasting, touching. It is not the consciousness that accompanies acts of inquiry, insight, formulating, speaking.

[2] Rudolf Otto, *The Idea of the Holy*, London: Oxford, 1923. Note that the meaning of *tremendum* varies with the stage of one's religious development.

[3] D. M. Brown, *Ultimate Concern: Tillich in Dialogue*, New York: Harper & Row, 1965.

[4] Karl Rahner, *The Dynamic Element in the Church*, Quaestiones disputatae 12, Montreal: Palm Publishers, 1964, pp. 131 ff. Fr. Rahner takes "consolation without a cause" to mean "consolation with a content but without an object".

It is not the consciousness that accompanies acts of reflecting, marshalling and weighing the evidence, making judgments of fact or possibility. It is the type of consciousness that deliberates, makes judgments of value, decides, acts responsibly and freely. But it is this consciousness as brought to a fulfilment, as having undergone a conversion, as possessing a basis that may be broadened and deepened and heightened and enriched but not superseded, as ready to deliberate and judge and decide and act with the easy freedom of those that do all good because they are in love. So the gift of God's love occupies the ground and root of the fourth and highest level of man's intentional consciousness. It takes over the peak of the soul, the *apex animae*.

This gift we have been describing really is sanctifying grace but notionally differs from it. The notional difference arises from different stages of meaning. To speak of sanctifying grace pertains to the stage of meaning when the world of theory and the world of common sense are distinct but, as yet, have not been explicitly distinguished from and grounded in the world of interiority. To speak of the dynamic state of being in love with God pertains to the stage of meaning when the world of interiority has been made the explicit ground of the worlds of theory and of common sense. It follows that in this stage of meaning the gift of God's love first is described as an experience and only consequently is objectified in theoretical categories.

Finally, it may be noted that the dynamic state of itself is operative grace, but the same state as principle of acts of love, hope, faith, repentance, and so on, is grace as cooperative. It may be added that, lest conversion be too violent a change and disrupt psychological continuity, the dynamic state may be preceded by similar transient dispositions that also are both operative and cooperative. Again, once the dynamic state has been established, it is filled out and developed by still further additional graces.[5]

---

[5] See my *Grace and Freedom in Aquinas*, London: Darton, Longman, & Todd, and New York: Herder & Herder, 1971. This puts in book form articles first published by *Theological Studies* 2(1941), 289–324; 3(1942), 69–88; 375–402; 533–578.

4. EXPRESSIONS OF RELIGIOUS EXPERIENCE

Religious experience spontaneously manifests itself in changed attitudes, in that harvest of the Spirit that is love, joy, peace, kindness, goodness, fidelity, gentleness, and self-control. But it also is concerned with its base and focus in the *mysterium fascinans et tremendum*, and the expression of this concern varies greatly as one moves from earlier to later stages of meaning.

In the earliest stage, expression results from insight into sensible presentations and representations. There easily is pointed out the spatial but not the temporal, the specific but not the generic, the external but not the internal, the human but not the divine. Only in so far as the temporal, generic, internal, divine can somehow be associated with or—in the language of the naive realist—"projected" upon the spatial, specific, external, human, can an insight be had and expression result. So it is by associating religious experience with its outward occasion that the experience becomes expressed and thereby something determinate and distinct for human consciousness.

Such outward occasions are called hierophanies, and they are many. When each of the many is something distinct and unrelated to the others, the hierophanies reveal the so-called gods of the moment. When they are many but recognized as possessing a family resemblance, then there is a living polytheism represented today by the 800,000 gods of Shintoism.[6] When distinct religious experiences are associated with a single place, there arises the god of this or that place. When they are the experiences of a single person and united by the unity of that person, then there is the god of the person, such as was the god of Jacob or of Laban.[7] Finally, when the unification is social, there result the god(s) of the group.

There is, I suppose, no clear-cut evidence to show that such religious experience conforms to the model I have set forth,

[6] See Ernst Benz, "On Understanding Non-Christian Religions," *The History of Religions* edited by M. Eliade and J. Kitagawa, Chicago: Chicago University Press, 1959, especially pp. 120 ff.

[7] On local and personal apprehensions of God in the bible, see N. Lohfink, *Bibelauslegung im Wandel*, Frankfurt-am-Main: Knecht, 1967.

apart from the antecedent probability established by the fact that God is good and gives to all men sufficient grace for salvation. But there is at least one scholar on whom one may call for an explicit statement on the areas common to such world religions as Christianity, Judaism, Islam, Zoroastrian Mazdaism, Hinduism, Buddhism, Taoism. For Friedrich Heiler has described at some length seven such common areas.[8] While I cannot reproduce here the rich texture of his thought, I must, at least, give a list of the topics he treats: that there is a transcendent reality; that he is immanent in human hearts; that he is supreme beauty, truth, righteousness, goodness; that he is love, mercy, compassion; that the way to him is repentance, self-denial, prayer; that the way is love of one's neighbor, even of one's enemies; that the way is love of God, so that bliss is conceived as knowledge of God, union with him, or dissolution into him.

Now it is not, I think, difficult to see how these seven common features of the world religions are implicit in the experience of being in love in an unrestricted manner. To be in love is to be in love with someone. To be in love without qualifications or conditions or reservations or limits is to be in love with someone transcendent. When someone transcendent is my beloved, he is in my heart, real to me from within me. When that love is the fulfilment of my unrestricted thrust to self-transcendence through intelligence and truth and responsibility, the one that fulfils that thrust must be supreme in intelligence, truth, goodness. Since he chooses to come to me by a gift of love for him, he himself must be love. Since loving him is my transcending myself, it also is a denial of the self to be transcended. Since loving him means loving attention to him, it is prayer, meditation, contemplation. Since love of him is fruitful, it overflows into love of all those that he loves or might love. Finally, from an experience of love focused on mystery there wells forth a longing for knowledge, while love itself is a longing for union; so for the lover of the unknown beloved the concept of bliss is knowledge of him and union with him, however they may be achieved.

[8] F. Heiler, "The History of Religions as a Preparation for the Cooperation of Religions", *The History of Religions* as above note 6, pp. 142–153.

5. RELIGIOUS DEVELOPMENT DIALECTICAL

Religious development is not simply the unfolding in all its consequences of a dynamic state of being in love in an unrestricted manner. For that love is the utmost in self-transcendence, and man's self-transcendence is ever precarious. Of itself, self-transcendence involves tension between the self as transcending and the self as transcended. So human authenticity is never some pure and serene and secure possession. It is ever a withdrawal from unauthenticity, and every successful withdrawal only brings to light the need for still further withdrawals. Our advance in understanding is also the elimination of oversights and misunderstandings. Our advance in truth is also the correction of mistakes and errors. Our moral development is through repentance for our sins. Genuine religion is discovered and realized by redemption from the many traps of religious aberration. So we are bid to watch and pray, to make our way in fear and trembling. And it is the greatest saints that proclaim themselves the greatest sinners, though their sins seem slight indeed to less holy folk that lack their discernment and their love.

This dialectical character of religious development implies that the seven common areas or features listed above will be matched in the history of religions by their opposites. Being in love, we said, is being in love with someone. It has a personal dimension. But this can be overlooked in a school of prayer and asceticism that stresses the orientation of religious experience to transcendent mystery. The transcendent is nothing in this world. Mystery is the unknown. Without a transcendental notion of being as the to-be-known, transcendent mystery can come to be named nothing at all.[9]

Again, at a far earlier stage, transcendence can be over-emphasized and immanence overlooked. Then God becomes remote, irrelevant, almost forgotten.[10] Inversely, immanence can

---

[9] On Buddhism see E. Benz, op. cit., p. 120 and F. Heiler, op. cit., p. 139.

[10] See F. M. Bergounioux and J. Goetz, *Prehistoric and Primitive Religions*, Faith and Fact Books 146, London: Burns and Oates, 1965, pp. 82–91.

be over-emphasized and transcendence overlooked. Then the loss of reference to the transcendent will rob symbol, ritual, recital of their proper meaning to leave them merely idol and magic and myth.[11] Then too the divine may be identified with life as universal process, of which the individual and the group are part and in which they participate.[12]

I have conceived being in love with God as an ultimate fulfilment of man's capacity for self-transcendence; and this view of religion is sustained when God is conceived as the supreme fulfilment of the transcendental notions, as supreme intelligence, truth, reality, righteousness, goodness. Inversely, when the love of God is not strictly associated with self-transcendence, then easily indeed it is reinforced by the erotic, the sexual, the orgiastic.[13] On the other hand, the love of God also is penetrated with awe. God's thoughts and God's ways are very different from man's and by that difference God is terrifying. Unless religion is totally directed to what is good, to genuine love of one's neighbor and to a self-denial that is subordinated to a fuller goodness in oneself, then the cult of a God that is terrifying can slip over into the demonic, into an exultant destructiveness of oneself and of others.[14]

Such, then, is what is meant by saying that religious development is dialectical. It is not a struggle between any opposites whatever but the very precise opposition between authenticity and unauthenticity, between the self as transcending and the self as transcended. It is not just as opposition between contrary propositions but an opposition within the human reality of individuals and of groups. It is not be to defined simply by some *a priori* construction of categories but also to be discovered *a posteriori* by a discerning study of history. It is not confined to the oppositions we have sketched but down the ages it ranges through the endless variety of institutional, cultural, personal,

[11] A. Vergote, *Psychologie religieuse*, Bruxelles: Dessart, 1966, p. 55.

[12] Bergounioux and Goetz, op. cit., pp. 117–126.

[13] A. Vergote, op. cit., p. 56.

[14] Ibid., p. 57. Cf. Rollo May, *Love and Will*, New York: Norton, 1969, Chapters Five and Six.

and religious development, decline, and recovery. To it we return when we come to treat the functional specialty, dialectic.

6. THE WORD

By the word is meant any expression of religious meaning or of religious value. Its carrier may be intersubjectivity, or art, or symbol, or language, or the remembered and portrayed lives or deeds or achievements of individuals or classes or groups. Normally all modes of expression are employed but, since language is the vehicle in which meaning becomes most fully articulated, the spoken and written word are of special importance in the development and the clarification of religion.

By its word, religion enters the world mediated by meaning and regulated by value. It endows that world with its deepest meaning and its highest value. It sets itself in a context of other meanings and other values. Within that context it comes to understand itself, to relate itself to the object of ultimate concern, to draw on the power of ultimate concern to pursue the objectives of proximate concern all the more fairly and all the more efficaciously.

Before it enters the world mediated by meaning, religion is the prior word God speaks to us by flooding our hearts with his love. That prior word pertains, not to the world mediated by meaning, but to the world of immediacy, to the unmediated experience of the mystery of love and awe. The outwardly spoken word is historically conditioned: its meaning depends upon the human context in which it is uttered, and such contexts vary from place to place and from one generation to another. But the prior word in its immediacy, though it differs in intensity, though it resonates differently in different temperaments and in different stages of religious development, withdraws man from the diversity of history by moving out of the world mediated by meaning and towards a world of immediacy in which image and symbol, thought and word, lose their relevance and even disappear.

One must not conclude that the outward word is something incidental. For it has a constitutive role. When a man and a woman love each other but do not avow their love, they are not yet in love. Their very silence means that their love has not reached the point of self-surrender and self-donation. It is the love that each freely and fully reveals to the other that brings about the radically new situation of being in love and that begins the unfolding of its life-long implications.[15]

What holds for the love of a man and a woman, also holds in its own way for the love of God and man. Ordinarily the experience of the mystery of love and awe is not objectified. It remains within subjectivity as a vector, an undertow, a fateful call to a dreaded holiness. Perhaps after years of sustained prayerfulness and self-denial, immersion in the world mediated by meaning will become less total and experience of the mystery become clear and distinct enough to awaken attention, wonder, inquiry. Even then in the individual case there are not certain answers. All one can do is let be what is, let happen what in any case keeps recurring. But then, as much as ever, one needs the word—the word of tradition that has accumulated religious wisdom, the word of fellowship that unites those that share the gift of God's love, the word of the gospel that announces that God has loved us first and, in the fulness of time, has revealed that love in Christ crucified, dead, and risen.

The word, then, is personal. *Cor ad cor loquitur:* love speaks to love, and its speech is powerful. The religious leader, the prophet, the Christ, the apostle, the priest, the preacher announces in signs and symbols what is congruent with the gift of love that God works within us. The word, too, is social: it brings into a single fold the scattered sheep that belong together because at the depth of their hearts they respond to the same mystery of love and awe. The word, finally, is historical. It is meaning outwardly expressed. It has to find its place in the context of

[15] See A. Vergote, "La liberté religieuse comme pouvoir de symbolisation", in *L'Herméneutique de la liberté religieuse,* edited by E. Castelli, Paris: Aubier, 1968, pp. 383 ff. The presence of another person takes one out of a purely epistemological context. The words he speaks introduce a new dimension to meaning. See also Gibson Winter, *Elements for a Social Ethic,* New York: Macmillan pb., 1968, pp. 99 ff. on the social origins of meaning.

other, non-religious meanings. It has to borrow and adapt a language that more easily speaks of this world than of transcendence. But such languages and contexts vary with time and place to give words changing meanings and statements changing implications.

It follows that religious expression will move through the stages of meaning and speak in its different realms. When the realms of common sense, of theory, of interiority, and of transcendence are distinguished and related, one easily understands the diversity of religious utterance. For its source and core is in the experience of the mystery of love and awe, and that pertains to the realm of transcendence. Its foundations, its basic terms and relationships, its method are derived from the realm of interiority. Its technical unfolding is in the realm of theory. Its preaching and teaching are in the realm of common sense.

Once these realms are distinguished and their relations are understood, it is easy enough to understand the broad lines of earlier stages and diverse developments. Eastern religion stressed religious experience. Semitic religion stressed prophetic monotheism. Western religion cultivated the realm of transcendence through its churches and liturgies, its celibate clergy, its religious orders, congregations, confraternities. It moved into the realm of theory by its dogmas, its theology, its juridical structures and enactments. It has to construct the common basis of theory and of common sense that is to be found in interiority and it has to use that basis to link the experience of the trancendent with the world mediated by meaning.

But if hindsight is easy, foresight is difficult indeed. When expression is confined to the realm of common sense, it can succeed only by drawing upon the power of symbols and figures to suggest or evoke what cannot adequately be said. When the realm of theory becomes explicit, religion may take advantage of it to bring about a clearer and firmer delineation of itself, its objectives, and its aims. But in so far as intellectual conversion is lacking, there arise controversies. Even where that conversion obtains, there emerge the strange contrast and tension between the old commonsense apprehension instinct with feeling and the new theoretical apprehension devoid of feeling and bristling with definitions and theorems. So the God of Abraham, Isaac, and Jacob is set against the God of the philosophers and theologians. Honoring the Trinity and feeling compunction are set against learned discourse on the Trinity and against defining compunction. Nor can this contrast be understood or the tension removed within the realms of common sense and of theory. One must go behind them to the realm of interiority. For only through the realm of interiority can differentiated consciousness understand itself and so explain the nature and the complementary purposes of different patterns of cognitional activity.

7. FAITH

Faith is the knowledge born of religious love.

First, then, there is a knowledge born of love. Of it Pascal spoke when he remarked that the heart has reasons which reason does not know. Here by reason I would understand the compound of the activities on the first three levels of cognitional activity, namely, of experiencing, of understanding, and of judging. By the heart's reasons I would understand feelings that are intentional responses to values; and I would recall the two aspects of such responses, the absolute aspect that is a recognition of value, and the relative aspect that is a preference of one value over another. Finally, by the heart I understand the subject on the fourth, existential level of intentional consciousness and in the dynamic state of being in love. The meaning, then, of Pascal's remark would be that, besides the factual knowledge reached by experiencing, understanding, and verifying, there is another kind of knowledge reached through the discernment of value and the judgments of value of a person in love.

Faith, accordingly, is such further knowledge when the love is God's love flooding our hearts. To our apprehension of vital, social, cultural, and personal values, there is added an apprehension of transcendent value. This apprehension consists in the experienced fulfilment of our unrestricted thrust to self-transcendence, in our actuated orientation towards the mystery of love and awe. Since that thrust is of intelligence to the intelligible, of reasonableness to the true and the real, of freedom and responsibility to the truly good, the experienced fulfilment of that thrust in its unrestrictedness may be objectified as a clouded revelation of absolute intelligence and intelligibility, absolute truth and reality, absolute goodness and holiness. With that objectification there recurs the question of God in a new form. For now it is primarily a question of decision. Will I love him in return, or will I refuse? Will I live out the gift of his love, or will I hold back, turn away, withdraw? Only secondarily do there arise the questions of God's existence and nature, and they are the questions either of the lover seeking to know him or of the unbeliever seeking to escape him. Such is the basic option of the existential subject once called by God.

As other apprehensions of value, so too faith has a relative as well as an absolute aspect. It places all other values in the light and the shadow of transcendent value. In the shadow, for transcendent value is supreme and incomparable. In the light, for transcendent value links itself to all other values to transform, magnify, glorify them. Without faith the originating value is man and the terminal value is the human good man brings about. But in the light of faith, originating value is divine light and love, while terminal value is the whole universe. So the human good becomes absorbed in an all-encompassing good. Where before an account of the human good related men to one another and to nature, now human concern reaches beyond man's world to God and to God's world. Men meet not only to be together and to settle human affairs but also to worship. Human development is not only in skills and virtues but also in holiness. The power of God's love brings forth a new energy and efficacy in all goodness, and the limit of human expectation ceases to be the grave.

To conceive God as originating value and the world as terminal value implies that God too is self-transcending and that the world is the fruit of his self-transcendence, the expression and manifestation of his benevolence and beneficence, his glory. As the excellence of the son is the glory of his father, so too the excellence of mankind is the glory of God. To say that God created the world for his glory is to say that he created it not for his sake but for ours.[16] He made us in his image, for our authenticity consists in being like him, in self-transcending, in being origins of value, in true love.

Without faith, without the eye of love, the world is too evil for God to be good, for a good God to exist. But faith recognizes that God grants men their freedom, that he wills them to be persons and not just his automata, that he calls them to the higher authenticity that overcomes evil with good. So faith is linked with human progress and it has to meet the challenge of human decline. For faith and progress have a common root in man's cognitional and moral self-transcendence. To promote either is to promote the other indirectly. Faith places human efforts in a friendly universe; it reveals an ultimate significance in human achievement; it strengthens new undertakings with confidence. Inversely, progress realizes the potentialities of man and of nature; it reveals that man exists to bring about an ever fuller achievement in this world; and that achievement because it is man's good also is God's glory. Most of all, faith has the power of undoing decline. Decline disrupts a culture with conflicting ideologies. It inflicts on individuals the social, economic, and psychological pressures that for human frailty amount to determinism. It multiplies and heaps up the abuses and absurdities that breed resentment, hatred, anger, violence. It is not propaganda and it is not argument but religious faith that will liberate human reasonableness from its ideological prisons. It is not the promises of men but religious hope that can enable men to resist the vast pressures of social decay. If passions are to quiet down, if wrongs are to be not exacerbated, not ignored, not merely palliated, but acknowledged and removed, then human possessiveness and human pride have to be replaced by religious charity, by the charity of the suffering servant, by self-sacrificing love. Men are sinners. If human progress is not to be ever distorted and destroyed by the inattention, oversights, irrationality, irresponsibility of decline, men have to be reminded of their sinfulness. They have to acknowledge their real guilt and amend their

[16] "... Deus suam gloriam non quaerit propter se sed propter nos." Aquinas, *Sum. Theol.*, II–II, q. 132, a. 1 ad 1m.

ways. They have to learn with humility that religious development is dialectical, that the task of repentance and conversion is life-long.

8. RELIGIOUS BELIEF

Among the values that faith discerns is the value of believing the word of religion, of accepting the judgments of fact and the judgments of value that the religion proposes. Such belief and acceptance have the same structure as other belief already described in Chapter Two. But now the structure rests on a different basis, and that basis is faith.

For however personal and intimate is religious experience, still it is not solitary. The same gift can be given to many, and the many can recognize in one another a common orientation in their living and feeling, in their criteria and their goals. From a common communion with God, there springs a religious community.

Community invites expression, and the expression may vary. It may be imperative, commanding the love of God above all things and the love of one's neighbor as of oneself. It may be narrative, the story of the community's origins and development. It may be ascetic and mystical, teaching the way to total otherwordly love and warning against pitfalls on the journey. It may be theoretical, teaching the wisdom, the goodness, the power of God, and manifesting his intentions and his purposes. It may be a compound of all four or of any two or three of these. The compound may fuse the components into a single balanced synthesis, or it may take some one as basic and use it to interpret and manifest the others. It may remain unchanged for ages, and it may periodically develop and adapt to different social and cultural conditions.

Communities endure. As new members replace old, expression becomes traditional. The religion becomes historical in the general sense that it exists over time and that it provides basic components in the ongoing process of personal development, social organization, cultural meaning and value.

But there is a further and far deeper sense in which a religion may be named historical. The dynamic state of being in love has the character of a response. It is an answer to a divine initiative. The divine initiative is not just creation. It is not just God's gift of his love. There is a personal entrance of God himself into history, a communication of God to his people, the advent of God's word into the world of religious expression. Such was the religion of Israel. Such has been Christianity.

Then not only the inner word that is God's gift of his love but also the outer word of the religious tradition comes from God. God's gift of his love is matched by his command to love unrestrictedly, with all one's heart and all one's soul and all one's mind and all one's strength. The narrative of religious origins is the narrative of God's encounter with his people. Religious effort towards authenticity through prayer and penance and religious love of all men shown in good deeds become an apostolate, for "... you will recognize them by their fruits" (Mt. 7, 20). Finally, the word of religious expression is not just the objectification of the gift of God's love; in a privileged area it also is specific meaning, the word of God himself.

So we come to questions that are not methodological but theological, questions concerning revelation and inspiration, scripture and tradition, development and authority, schisms and heresies. To the theologians we must leave them, though something will be said on the method of resolving them in our later chapters on *Dialectic* and on *Foundations*.

We may note, however, that by distinguishing faith and belief we have secured a basis both for ecumenical encounter and for an encounter between all religions with a basis in religious experience. For in the measure that experience is genuine, it is orientated to the mystery of love and awe; it has the power of unrestricted love to reveal and uphold all that is truly good; it remains the bond that unites the religious community, that directs their common judgments, that purifies their beliefs. Beliefs do differ, but behind this difference there is a deeper unity. For beliefs result from judgments of value, and the judgments of value relevant for religious belief come from faith, the eye of religious love, an eye that can discern God's self-disclosures.

9. A TECHNICAL NOTE

Where we distinguish four realms of meaning, namely, common sense, theory, interiority, and transcendence, an older theology distinguished only two, common sense and theory, under the Aristotelian designation of the *priora quoad nos* and *priora quoad se*. Hence, the older theology, when it spoke of inner experience or of God, either did so within the realm of common sense—and then its speech was shot through with figure and symbol—or else it did so in the realm of theory—and then its speech was basically metaphysical. One consequence of this difference has already been noted. The older theology conceived sanctifying grace as an entitative habit, absolutely supernatural, infused into the essence of the soul. On the other hand, because we acknowledge interiority as a distinct realm of meaning, we can begin with a description of religious experience, acknowledge a dynamic state of being in love without restrictions, and later identify this state with the state of sanctifying grace.

But there are other consequences. Because its account of interiority was basically metaphysical, the older theology distinguished sensitive and intellectual, apprehensive and appetitive potencies. There followed complex questions on their mutual interactions. There were disputes about the priority of intellect over will or of will over intellect, of speculative over practical intellect or of practical over speculative. In contrast, we describe interiority in terms of intentional and conscious acts on the four levels of experiencing, understanding, judging, and deciding. The lower levels are presupposed and complemented by the higher. The higher sublate the lower. If one wishes to transpose this analysis into metaphysical terms, then the active potencies are the transcendental notions revealed in questions for intelligence, questions for reflection, questions for deliberation. The passive potencies are the lower levels as presupposed and complemented by the higher. While these relationships are fixed, still they do not settle questions of initiative or precedence. Significant change on any level calls for adjustments on other levels, and the order in which the adjustments take place depends mostly on the readiness with which they can be effected.

The fourth level, which presupposes, complements, and sublates the other three, is the level of freedom and responsibility, of moral self-transcendence and in that sense of existence, of self-direction and self-control. Its failure to function properly is the uneasy or the bad conscience. Its success is marked by the satisfying feeling that one's duty has been done.

As the fourth level is the principle of self-control, it is responsible for proper functioning on the first three levels. It fulfils its responsibility or fails to do so in the measure that we are attentive or inattentive in experiencing, that we are intelligent or unintelligent in our investigations, that we are reasonable or unreasonable in our judgments. Therewith vanish two notions: the notion of pure intellect or pure reason that operates on its own without guidance or control from responsible decision; and the notion of will as an arbitrary power indifferently choosing between good and evil.

In fact, the emergence of the fourth level of deliberation, evaluation, choice is a slow process that occurs between the ages of three and six. Then the child's earlier affective symbiosis with the mother is complemented by relations with the father who recognizes in the child a potential person, tells him or her what he or she may and may not do, sets before him or her a model of human conduct, and promises to good behavior the later rewards of the self-determining adult. So the child gradually enters the world mediated by meaning and regulated by values and, by the age of seven years, is thought to have attained the use of reason.[17] Still this is only the beginning of human authenticity. One has to have passed well beyond the turmoil of puberty before becoming fully responsible in the eyes of the law. One has to have found out for oneself that one has to decide for oneself what one is to make of oneself; one has to have proved oneself equal to that moment of existential decision; and one has to have kept on proving it in all subsequent decisions, if one is to be an authentic human person. It is this highly complex business of authenticity and unauthenticity that has to replace the overly

[17] A. Vergote, *Psychologie religieuse*, Bruxelles: Dessart, 1966, pp. 192 ff.

simple notion of will as arbitrary power. Arbitrariness is just another name for unauthenticity. To think of will as arbitrary power is to assume that authenticity never exists or occurs.

Again, what gives plausibility to the notion of pure intellect or pure reason is the fact that cognitional self-transcendence is much easier than moral self-transcendence. But this does not mean that cognitional self-transcendence is easy. Primitive peoples live under a regime of myth and magic. Only slowly and reluctantly do the young master grammar, logic, method. Only through deliberate decision do people dedicate themselves to lives of scholarship or science, and only through the continuous renewal of that dedication do they achieve the goals they have set themselves. A life of pure intellect or pure reason without the control of deliberation, evaluation, responsible choice is something less than the life of a psychopath.

Let us now turn to a further aspect of the matter. It used to be said, *Nihil amatum nisi praecognitum*, Knowledge precedes love. The truth of this tag is the fact that ordinarily operations on the fourth level of intentional consciousness presuppose and complement corresponding operations on the other three. There is a minor exception to this rule inasmuch as people do fall in love, and that falling in love is something disproportionate to its causes, conditions, occasions, antecedents. For falling in love is a new beginning, an exercise of vertical liberty in which one's world undergoes a new organization. But the major exception to the Latin tag is God's gift of his love flooding our hearts. Then we are in the dynamic state of being in love.[18] But who it is we love, is neither given nor as yet understood. Our capacity for moral self-transcendence has found a fulfilment that brings deep joy and profound peace. Our love reveals to us values we had not appreciated, values of prayer and worship, or repentance and belief. But if we would know what is going on within us, if we would learn to integrate it with the rest of our living, we have

---

[18] For equivalent but differing accounts of this being in love, see: Alan Richardson, *Religion in Contemporary Debate*, London: SCM, 1966, pp. 113 ff.; Oliver Rabut, *L'expérience religieuse fondamentale*, Tournai: Castermann, 1969, p. 168.

to inquire, investigate, seek counsel. So it is that in religious matters love precedes knowledge and, as that love is God's gift, the very beginning of faith is due to God's grace.

On this showing, not only is the ancient problem of the salvation of non-Christians greatly reduced, but also the true nature of Christian apologetic is clarified. The apologist's task is neither to produce in others nor to justify for them God's gift to his love. Only God can give that gift, and the gift itself is self-justifying. People in love have not reasoned themselves into being in love. The apologist's task is to aid others in integrating God's gift with the rest of their living. Any significant event on any level of consciousness calls for adjustments elsewhere. Religious conversion is an extremely significant event and the adjustments it calls for may be both large and numerous. For some, one consults friends. For others, one seeks a spiritual director. For commonly needed information, interpretation, the formulation of new and the dropping of mistaken judgments of fact and of value, one reads the apologists. They cannot be efficacious, for they do not bestow God's grace. They must be accurate, illuminating, cogent. Otherwise they offer a stone to one asking for bread, and a serpent to one asking for fish.

A final remark is terminological. We have distinguished between faith and religious beliefs. We have done so as a consequence of our view that there is a realm in which love precedes knowledge. Also we have done so because this manner of speech facilitates ecumenical discourse. But while we consider our grounds to be valid and our purposes legitimate, we must acknowledge the existence of an older and more authoritative tradition in which faith and religious belief are identified. We make this acknowledgment all the more readily because we are departing, not from the older doctrine, but only from the older manner of speech. We are not departing from the older doctrine, for in acknowledging religious beliefs we are acknowledging what also was termed faith, and in acknowledging a faith that grounds belief we are acknowledging what would have been termed the *lumen gratiae* or *lumen fidei* or infused wisdom. Finally, while a classicist would maintain that one should never depart from an accepted terminology, I must contend that classicism is no more than the mistaken view of conceiving culture normatively and of concluding that there is just one human culture. The modern fact is that culture has to be conceived empirically, that there are many cultures, and that new distinctions are legitimate when the reasons for them are explained and the older truths are retained.

5

FUNCTIONAL SPECIALTIES

To put method in theology is to conceive theology as a set of related and recurrent operations cumulatively advancing towards an ideal goal. However, contemporary theology is specialized, and so it is to be conceived, not as a single set of related operations, but as a series of interdependent sets. To formulate this conception of theology, first, we shall distinguish field, subject, and functional specializations. Next, we shall describe the eight functional specializations in theology, set forth the grounds for this division, and give some account of its utility. Finally, we shall indicate the dynamic unity linking the functional specialties to religion and to one another.

I. THREE TYPES OF SPECIALIZATION

Specialties may be distinguished in three manners, namely (1) by dividing and subdividing the field of data, (2) by classifying the results of investigations, and (3) by distinguishing and separating stages of the process from data to results.

Field specialization is the most easily understood. As time passes, as centers of learning increase, as periodicals multiply and monographs follow on one another ever more closely, it becomes increasingly difficult for scholars to keep abreast with the whole movement in their field. For good or ill a division of labor has to be accepted, and this is brought about by dividing and then subdividing the field of relevant data. So scriptural, patristic, medieval, reformation studies become genera to be divided into species and subspecies, to make the specialist one who knows more and more about less and less.

Department and subject specialization is the most familiar type, for everyone has followed courses on subjects in a department. Now what is divided is no longer the field of data to be investigated but the results of investigations to be communicated. Again, where before the division was into material parts, now it is a conceptual classification that distinguishes the departments of a faculty and the subjects taught in a department. Thus, where field specialization would divide the Old Testament into the Law, the Prophets, and the Writings, subject specialization would distinguish semitic languages, Hebrew history, the religions of the ancient Near East, and Christian theology.

Functional specialization distinguishes and separates successive stages in the process from data to results. Thus, textual criticism aims at determining what was written. The interpreter or commentator takes over where the textual critic leaves off; his aim is to determine what was meant. The historian moves in on a third level; he assembles interpreted texts and endeavors to construct a single narrative or view.

Again, to take a quite different instance, experimental physicists alone have the knowledge and skills needed to handle a cyclotron. But only theoretical physicists are able to tell what experiments are worth trying and, when they are tried, what is the significance of the results. Once more a single process of investigation is divided into successive stages, and each stage becomes a distinct specialty.

It is to be noted that such functional specialties are intrinsically related to one another. They are successive parts of one and the same process. The earlier parts are incomplete without the later. The later presuppose the earlier and complement them. In brief, functional specialties are functionally interdependent.

Such interdependence is of the greatest methodological interest. First, without any prejudice to unity, it divides and clarifies the process from data to results. Secondly, it provides an orderly link between field specialization, based on the division of data, and subject specialization, based on a classification of results. Thirdly, the unity of functional specialties will be found, I think, to overcome or, at least, counter-balance the endless divisions of field specialization.

2. AN EIGHTFOLD DIVISION

In this section we propose to describe briefly eight functional specialties in theology, namely, (1) research, (2) interpretation, (3) history, (4) dialectic, (5) foundations, (6) doctrines, (7) systematics, and (8) communications. Later we shall attempt to state the grounds for the foregoing division, its precise meaning, and its implications. For the moment, however, we aim at no more than a preliminary indication of the material meaning of functional specialization in theology.

(1) Research makes available the data relevant to theological investigation. It is either general or special. Special research is concerned with assembling the data relevant to some particular question or problem, such as the doctrine of Mr. X on the question Y. Such special research operates all the more rapidly and effectively the more familiar it is with the tools made available by general research. General research locates, excavates, and maps ancient cities. It fills museums and reproduces or copies inscriptions, symbols, pictures, statues. It deciphers unknown scripts and languages. It collects and catalogues manuscripts, and prepares critical editions of texts. It composes indices, tables, repertories, bibliographies, abstracts, bulletins, handbooks, dictionaries, encyclopedias. Some day, perhaps, it will give us a complete information-retrieval system.

(2) While research makes available what was written, interpretation understands what was meant. It grasps that meaning in its proper historical context, in accord with its proper mode and level of thought and expression, in the light of the circumstances and intention of the writer. Its product is the commentary or monograph. It is an enterprise replete with pitfalls and today it is further complicated by the importation of the problems of cognitional theory, epistemology, and metaphysics. To it we return when later we speak of hermeneutics.

(3) History is basic, special, or general.

Basic history tells where (places, territories) and when (dates, periods) who (persons, peoples) did what (public life, external acts) to enjoy what success, suffer what reverses, exert what influence. So it makes as specific and precise as possible the more easily recognized and acknowledged features of human activities in their geographical distribution and temporal succession.

Special histories tell of movements whether cultural (language, art, literature, religion), institutional (family, mores, society, education, state, law, church, sect, economy, technology), or doctrinal (mathematics, natural science, human science, philosophy, history, theology).

General history is, perhaps, just an ideal. It would be basic history illuminated and completed by the special histories. It would offer the total view or some approximation to it. It would express the historian's information, understanding, judgment, and evaluation with regard to the sum of cultural, institutional, and doctrinal movements in their concrete setting.

History, as a functional specialty within theology, is concerned in different degrees and manners with basic, special, and general history. In the main it has to presuppose basic history. Its substantial concern is the doctrinal history of Christian theology with its antecedents and consequents in the cultural and institutional histories of the Christian religion and the Christian churches and sects. Finally, it cannot remain aloof from general history, for it is only within the full view that can be grasped the differences between the Christian churches and sects, the relations between different religions, and the role of Christianity in world history.

But to history we return later. No less than hermeneutics, contemporary historical thought and criticism, over and above their specific tasks, have become involved in the basic philosophic problems of our time.

(4) Our fourth functional specialty is dialectic. While that

name has been employed in many ways, the sense we intend is simple enough. Dialectic has to do with the concrete, the dynamic, and the contradictory, and so it finds abundant materials in the history of Christian movements. For all movements are at once concrete and dynamic, while Christian movements have been marked with external and internal conflict, whether one considers Christianity as a whole or even this or that larger church or communion.

The materials of dialectic, then, are primarily the conflicts centering in Christian movements. But to these must be added the secondary conflicts in historical accounts and theological interpretations of the movements.

Besides the materials of dialectic, there is its aim. This is high and distant. As empirical science aims at a complete explanation of all phenomena, so dialectic aims at a comprehensive viewpoint. It seeks some single base or some single set of related bases from which it can proceed to an understanding of the character, the oppositions, and the relations of the many viewpoints exhibited in conflicting Christian movements, their conflicting histories, and their conflicting interpretations.

Besides the conflicts of Christians and the distant goal of a comprehensive viewpoint, there is also the past and the present fact of the many diverging viewpoints that result in the conflicts. Such viewpoints are manifested in confessions of faith and learned works of apologists. But they also are manifested, often in a more vital manner, in the unnoticed assumptions and oversights, in the predilections and aversions, in the quiet but determined decisions of scholars, writers, preachers, and the men and women in the pews.

Now the study of these viewpoints takes one beyond the fact to the reasons for conflict. Comparing them will bring to light just where differences are irreducible, where they are complementary and could be brought together within a larger whole, where finally they can be regarded as successive stages in a single process of development.

Besides comparison there is criticism. Not every viewpoint is coherent, and those that are not can be invited to advance to a consistent position. Not every reason is a sound reason, and Christianity has nothing to lose from a purge of unsound reasons, of *ad hoc* explanations, of the stereotypes that body forth suspicions, resentments, hatreds, malice. Not every irreducible difference is a serious difference, and those that are not can be put in second or third or fourth place so that attention, study, analysis can be devoted to differences that are serious and profound.

By dialectic, then, is understood a generalized apologetic conducted in an ecumenical spirit, aiming ultimately at a comprehensive viewpoint, and proceeding towards that goal by acknowledging differences, seeking their grounds real and apparent, and eliminating superfluous oppositions.

(5) As conversion is basic to Christian living, so an objectification of conversion provides theology with its foundations.

By conversion is understood a transformation of the subject and his world. Normally it is a prolonged process though its explicit acknowledgment may be concentrated in a few momentous judgments and decisions. Still it is not just a development or even a series of developments. Rather it is a resultant change of course and direction. It is as if one's eyes were opened and one's former world faded and fell away. There emerges something new that fructifies in inter-locking, cumulative sequences of developments on all levels and in all departments of human living.

Conversion is existential, intensely personal, utterly intimate. But it is not so private as to be solitary. It can happen to many, and they can form a community to sustain one another in their self-transformation and to help one another in working out the implications and fulfilling the promise of their new life. Finally, what can become communal, can become historical. It can pass from generation to generation. It can spread from one cultural milieu to another. It can adapt to changing circumstances, confront new situations, survive into a different age, flourish in another period or epoch.

Conversion, as lived, affects all of a man's conscious and intentional operations. It directs his gaze, pervades his imagination, releases the symbols that penetrate to the depths of his psyche. It enriches his understanding, guides his judgments, reinforces his decisions. But as communal and historical, as a movement with its own cultural, institutional, and doctrinal dimensions, conversion calls forth a reflection that makes the movement thematic, that explicitly explores its origins, developments, purposes, achievements, and failures.

Inasmuch as conversion itself is made thematic and explicitly objectified, there emerges the fifth functional specialty, foundations. Such foundations differ from the old fundamental theology in two respects. First, fundamental theology was a theological first; it did not follow on four other specialties named research, interpretation, history, and dialectic. Secondly, fundamental theology was a set of doctrines, *de vera religione, de legato divino, de ecclesia, de inspiratione scripturae, de locis theologicis*. In contrast, foundations present, not doctrines, but the horizon within which the meaning of doctrines can be apprehended. Just as in religious living "a man who is unspiritual refuses what belongs to the Spirit of God; it is folly to him; he cannot grasp it" (1 Cor. 2, 14), so in theological reflection on religious living there have to be distinguished the horizons within which religious doctrines can or cannot be apprehended; and this distinction is foundational.

In due course we shall have to ask how horizon is to be understood and defined and how one horizon may differ from another. At once, however, we may note that as conversion may be authentic or unauthentic, so there may be many Christian horizons and not all of them need represent authentic conversion. Further, while it may be possible to conceive authentic conversion in more than one manner, still the number of possible manners would seem to be far fewer than the number of possible horizons. It follows that our foundations contain a promise both of an elucidation of the conflicts revealed in dialectic and of a selective principle that will guide the remaining specialties concerned with doctrines, systematics, and communications.

(6) Doctrines express judgments of fact and judgments of value. They are concerned, then, with the affirmations and negations not only of dogmatic theology but also of moral, ascetical, mystical, pastoral, and any similar branch.

Such doctrines stand within the horizon of foundations. They have their precise definition from dialectic, their positive wealth of clarification and development from history, their grounds in the interpretation of the data proper to theology.

(7) The facts and values affirmed in doctrines give rise to further questions. For doctrinal expression may be figurative or symbolic. It may be descriptive and based ultimately on the meaning of words rather than on an understanding of realities. It may, if pressed, quickly become vague and indefinite. It may seem, when examined, to be involved in inconsistency or fallacy.

The functional specialty, systematics, attempts to meet these issues. It is concerned to work out appropriate systems of conceptualization, to remove apparent inconsistencies, to move towards some grasp of spiritual matters both from their own inner coherence and from the analogies offered by more familiar human experience.

(8) Communications is concerned with theology in its external relations. These are of three kinds. There are interdisciplinary relations with art, language, literature, and other religions, with the natural and the human sciences, with philosophy and history. Further, there are the transpositions that theological thought has to develop if religion

is to retain its identity and yet at the same time find access into the minds and hearts of men of all cultures and classes. Finally, there are the adaptations needed to make full and proper use of the diverse media of communication that are available at any place and time.

3. GROUNDS OF THE DIVISION

We have indicated in summary fashion eight functional specialties. We have now to explain where this list of eight comes from and what are the principles to be invoked in further clarifications of meaning and delimitations of function.

The first principle of the division is that theological operations occur in two basic phases. If one is to harken to the word, one must also bear witness to it. If one engages in *lectio divina*, there come to mind *quaestiones*. If one assimilates tradition, one learns that one should pass it on. If one encounters the past, one also has to take one's stand toward the future. In brief, there is a theology *in oratione obliqua* that tells what Paul and John, Augustine and Aquinas, and anyone else had to say about God and the economy of salvation. But there is also a theology *in oratione recta* in which the theologian, enlightened by the past, confronts the problems of his own day.

The second principle of division is derived from the fact that our conscious and intentional operations occur on four distinct levels and that each level has its own proper achievement and end. So the proper achievement and end of the first level, experiencing, is the apprehension of data; that of the second level, understanding, is insight into the apprehended data; that of the third level, judgment, is the acceptance or rejection of the hypotheses and theories put forward by understanding to account for the data; that of the fourth level, decision, the acknowledgment of values and the selection of the methods or other means that lead to their realization.

Now in everyday, commonsense performance, all four levels are employed continuously without any explicit distinction between them. In that case no functional specialization arises, for what is sought is not the end of any particular level but the cumulative, composite resultant of the ends of all four levels. But in a scientific investigation the ends proper to particular levels may become the objective sought by operations on all four levels. So the textual critic will select the method (level of decision) that he feels will lead to the discovery (level of understanding) of what one may reasonably affirm (level of judgment) was written in the original text (level of experience). The textual critic, then, operates on all four levels, but his goal is the end proper to the first level, namely, to ascertain the data. The interpreter, however, pursues a different goal. He wishes to understand the text, and so he selects a different method. Moreover, he cannot confine his operations to the second level, understanding, and to the fourth, a selective decision. He must apprehend the text accurately before he can hope to understand it, and so he has to operate on the first level; and he has to judge whether or not his understanding is correct, for otherwise he will fail to distinguish between understanding and misunderstanding.

Functional specializations arise, then, inasmuch as one operates on all four levels to achieve the end proper to some particular level. But there are four levels and so four proper ends. It follows that the very structure of human inquiry results in four functional specializations and, since in theology there are two distinct phases we are led to expect eight functional specializations in theology. In the first phase of theology *in oratione obliqua* there are research, interpretation, history, and dialectic. In the second phase of theology *in oratione recta* there are foundations, doctrines, systematics, and communications.

So in assimilating the past, first, there is research that uncovers and makes available the data, secondly, there is interpretation that understands their meaning, thirdly, there is history that judges and narrates what occurred and, fourthly, there is dialectic that endeavors to unravel the conflicts concerning values, facts, meanings, and experiences. The first four functional specialties, then, seek the ends proper respectively to experiencing, understanding, judging, and deciding; and, of course, each one does so by employing not some one but all four of the levels of conscious and intentional operations.

This fourfold specialization corresponds to the four dimensions of the Christian message and the Christian tradition. For that message and tradition, first of all, are a range of data. Secondly, the data purport to convey not the phenomena of things, as in the natural sciences, but the meanings entertained and communicated by minds, as in the human sciences. Thirdly, these meanings were uttered at given times and places and transmitted through determinate channels and under sundry vicissitudes. Fourthly, the utterance and the transmission were the work of persons bearing witness to Christ Jesus and, by their words and deeds, bringing about the present religious situation.

Research, then, interpretation, history, and dialectic reveal the religious situation. They mediate an encounter with persons witnessing to Christ. They challenge to a decision: in what manner or measure am I to carry to burden of continuity or to risk the initiative of change? That decision, however, is primarily not a theological but a religious event; it pertains to the prior more spontaneous level on which theology reflects and which it illuminates and objectifies; it enters explicitly into theology only as reflected on and objectified in the fifth specialty, foundations.

With such a decision, however, there is effected the transition from the first to the second phase. The first phase is mediating theology. It is research, interpretation, history, dialectic that introduce us to knowledge of the Body of Christ. But the second phase is mediated theology. It is knowledge of God and of all things as ordered to God, not indeed as God is known immediately (1 Cor. 13, 12), nor as he is known mediately through created nature, but as he is known mediately through the whole Christ, Head and members.

In the second phase the specialties have been named in inverse order. Like dialectic, foundations is on the level of decision. Like history, doctrines is on the level of judgment. Like interpretation, systematics aims at understanding. Finally, as research tabulates the data from the past, so communications produces data in the present and for the future.

The reason for the inverted order is simple enough. In the first phase one begins from the data and moves through meanings and facts towards personal encounter. In the second phase one begins from reflection on authentic conversion, employs it as the horizon within which doctrines are to be apprehended and an understanding of their content sought, and finally moves to a creative exploration of communications differentiated according to media, according to classes of men, and according to common cultural interests.

4. THE NEED FOR DIVISION

The need for some division is clear enough from the divisions that already exist and are recognized. Thus, our divisions of the second phase—foundations, doctrines, systematics, and communications—correspond roughly to the already familiar distinctions between fundamental, dogmatic, speculative, and pastoral or practical theology. Nor can the specialties of the first phase—research, interpretation, history, and dialectic—be described as sheer novelties. Textual criticism and other types of research are pursued for their own sakes. Commentaries and interpretative monographs are a well-known genre. To church history, the history of dogmas, and the history of theology there has recently been added salvation history. Dialectic, finally, is an ecumenical variant on the long-standing controversial and apologetic types of theology.

What, however, is new is the conception of these branches of theological activity as functional specialties, as distinct and separable stages in a single process from data to ultimate results. Accordingly, what has to be explained is the need for this conception of the many existing branches of theology and for the reorganization that this conception brings in its train.

First, then, the need is not simply a matter of convenience. One can justify field specialization by urging that the relevant data are too extensive to be investigated by a single mind. One can defend subject specialization on the ground that the matter is too broad to be taught successfully by a single professor. But functional specialization is essentially not a distinction of specialists but a distinction of specialties. It arises, not to divide the same sort of task among many hands, but to distinguish different tasks and to prevent them from being confused. Different ends are pursued by employing different means, different means are used in different manners, different manners are ruled by different methodical precepts.

Secondly, there exist the different tasks. For once theology reaches a certain stage of development, there becomes apparent the radical difference between the two phases, and in each of the phases the four ends that correspond to the four levels of conscious and intentional operations. If these eight ends exist, then there are eight different tasks to be performed, and eight different sets of methodical precepts that have to be distinguished. Without such distinctions, investigators will not have clear and distinct ideas about what precisely they are doing, how their operations are related to their immediate ends, and how such immediate ends are related to the total end of the subject of their inquiry.

Thirdly, the distinction and division are needed to curb one-sided totalitarian ambitions. Each of the eight has its proper excellence. None can stand without the other seven. But the man with the blind-spot is fond of concluding that his specialty is to be pursued because of its excellence and the other seven are to be derided because by themselves they are insufficient. From such one-sidedness theology has suffered gravely from the middle ages to the present day. Only a well-reasoned total view can guard against its continuance in the present and its recurrence in the future.

Fourthly, the distinction and division are needed to resist excessive demands. If all of the eight are needed for the complete process from data to results, still a serious contribution to one of the eight is as much as can be demanded of a single piece of work.

What is such a contribution? It includes, I should say, two parts. The major part is to produce the type of evidence proper to the specialty. So the exegete does exegesis on exegetical principles. The historian does history on historical principles. The doctrinal theologian ascertains doctrine on doctrinal principles. The systematic theologian clarifies, reconciles, unifies on systematic principles. But there is, besides this major and principal part, also a minor part. Each of the specialties is functionally related to the others. Especially until such time as a method in theology is generally recognized, it will serve to preclude misunderstanding, misinterpretation, and misrepresentation, if the specialist draws attention to the fact of specialization and gives some indication of his awareness of what is to be added to his statements in the light of the evidence available to other, distinct specialties.

5. A DYNAMIC UNITY

The unity of a subject in process of development is dynamic. For as long as further advance is possible, the perfection of complete immobility has not yet been attained, and, for that reason, there cannot yet be reached the logical ideal of fixed terms, accurately and immutably formulated axioms, and absolutely rigorous deduction of all possible conclusions. The absence, however, of static unity does not preclude the presence of dynamic unity, and what this can mean we must now consider.

Development, then, seems to be from an initial state of undifferentiation through a process of differentiation and specialization towards a goal in which the differentiated specialties function as an integrated unity.

So initially the Christian religion and Christian theology were not distinguished. Tradition was assimilated. Efforts were made to penetrate its meaning and recast it for apostolic or apologetic ends. Not all were happy. Innovators formed schools that splintered off in various directions and by their very separation and diversity emphasized a main, unchanging tradition. The main tradition itself was confronted with ever deeper issues. Painfully it learnt from Nicea the necessity of going beyond scriptural language to formulate what was considered scriptural truth. Painfully it learnt from Chalcedon the necessity of employing terms in senses unknown both to scripture and to the earlier patristic tradition. But it is in reflection on such developments, as in Byzantine Scholasticism, and in the extension of such reflective consideration to the whole of Christian thought, as in medieval Scholasticism, that theology became an academic subject, at once intimately connected with the Christian religion and manifestly distinct from it.

The validity of this first differentiation is, of course, questioned today. Is not such academic theology merely a cultural super-structure, divorced from real life, and thereby inimical to it? A distinction, I feel, must be made. For primitives and, generally, for undifferentiated consciousness any academic development is not merely useless but also impossible. The differentiation of operations and objects necessitates a differentiation in the con‑sciousness of the operating subject. So for undifferentiated con-sciousness all that is academic is essentially alien, and any effort to impose it not only is an intolerable and deadening intrusion but also is doomed to failure. Still this is not the whole story. For once consciousness is differentiated, a corresponding develop-ment in the expression and presentation of religion becomes necessary. So in an educated and alert consciousness a childish apprehension of religious truth either must be sublated within an educated apprehension or else it will simply be dropped as outmoded and outworn. To return, then, to the common objec-tion, one must, I should say, ask whose "real life" is in question. If concern is expressed for the real life of primitives and other instances of undifferentiated consciousness, then manifestly an academic theology is utterly irrelevant. But if concern is for the real life of differentiated consciousness, then in the measure that consciousness is differentiated an academic theology is a necessity.

If I have been attending to the individual aspect of the matter, I am by no means denying its social and historical aspects. As we have seen, the principal part of human living is constituted by meaning, and so the principal part of human movements is concerned with meaning. It follows more or less inevitably that the further any movement spreads and the longer it lasts, the more it is forced to reflect on its own proper meaning, to distinguish itself from other meanings, to guard itself against aberration. Moreover, as rivals come and go, as circumstances and problems change, as issues are driven back to their presuppositions and decisions to their ultimate consequences, there emerges that shift towards system, which was named by Georg Simmel, *die Wendung zur Idee*. But what is true of movements generally, also is true of Christianity. The mirror in which it reflects itself is theology.

So religion and theology become distinct and separate in the very measure that religion itself develops and adherents to religion move easily from one pattern of consciousness to another. Still this withdrawal must not be without a compensating return. Development is through specialization but it must end in integration. Nor is integration to be achieved by mere regression. To identify theology with religion, with liturgy, with prayer, with preaching, no doubt is to revert to the earliest period of Christianity. But it is also to overlook the fact that the conditions of the earliest period have long since ceased to exist. There are real theological problems, real issues that, if burked, threaten the very existence of Christianity. There are real problems of communication in the twentieth century, and they are not solved by preaching to ancient Antioch, Corinth, or Rome. So it is that we have been led to the conclusion of acknowledging a distinction between the Christian religion and Christian theology and, at the same time, of demanding an eighth functional specialty, communications.

Such is our first instance of differentiation and dynamic unity. Religion and theology become distinct and separate. But the separateness of theology is a withdrawal that always intends and in its ultimate stage effects a return.

Our second instance of differentiation and dynamic unity regards the major divisions within theology itself. These are the two phases each containing four functional specialties. For it is within these eight specialties that all theological operations occur, and so field specialization on the one hand and subject specialization on the other turn out to be subdivisions of the eight specialties.

In fact, field specialization subdivides the materials on which the specialties of the first phase operate, while subject specialization classifies the results obtained by the specialties of the second phase.

The subdivisions effected by field specialization vary with the task to be performed. Special research takes a narrow strip of the data, while general research cuts a broad swath. Interpretation will confine itself to some single work of an author or to some aspect of all his works, while history arises only from an array of general and special researches, of monographs and commentaries.

Dialectic finally finds its units in the metamorphoses of what is basically the same conflict, now on the level of religious living, now in opposed histories of the prior events, now in opposed theological interpretations.

The unity of this first phase is manifestly not static but dynamic. The four specialties stand to one another, not in some logical relationship of premiss to conclusion, of particular to universal, or anything of the sort, but as successive partial objects in the cumulative process that inquiry promotes from experiencing to understanding, that reflection promotes from understanding to judging, that deliberation promotes from judging to deciding. Such a structure is essentially open. Experience is open to further data. Understanding to a fuller and more penetrating grasp. Judgment to acknowledgment of new and more adequate perspectives, of more nuanced pronouncements, of more detailed information. Decision, finally, is reached only partially by dialectic, which tends to eliminate evidently foolish oppositions and so narrows down issues, but is not to be expected to go to the roots of all conflict for, ultimately, conflicts have their ground in the heart of man.

Interdependence is reciprocal dependence. Not only does interpretation depend upon research but also research depends on interpretation. Not only does history depend upon both research and interpretation, but no less history supplies the context and perspectives within which research and interpretation operate. Not only does dialectic depend on history, interpretation, and research, but inversely in so far as dialectic is transcendentally grounded it is able, as we shall see, to provide interpretation and history with heuristic structures, much as mathematics provides the natural sciences with such structures.

Such reciprocal dependence is most easily achieved when the four specialties are performed by a single specialist. For, within the confines of a single mind, the interdependence of experience, understanding, judgment, and decision is achieved spontaneously and without effort. It remains, however, that the more the specialties develop, the more their techniques are refined, the more delicate the operations they perform, the less will it be possible for the single specialist to master all four specialties. Then recourse must be had to team-work. The different specialists must understand the relevance of one another's work for their own. They must be familiar with what already has been achieved and so able to grasp each new development. Finally, they must be in easy and rapid communication, so that all may profit at once from the advances made by anyone, and each may be able to set forth at once the problems and difficulties that arise in his own specialty from the changes proposed in another.

As the first phase rises from the almost endless multiplicity of data first to an interpretative, then to a narrative, and then to a dialectical unity, the second phase descends from the unity of a grounding horizon towards the almost endlessly varied sensibilities, mentalities, interests, and tastes of mankind.

This descent is, not properly a deduction, but rather a succession of transpositions to ever more determinate contexts. Foundations provides a basic orientation. This orientation, when applied to the conflicts of dialectic and to the ambiguities of history, becomes a principle of selection of doctrines. But doctrines tend to be regarded as mere verbal formulae, unless their ultimate meaning is worked out and their possible coherence revealed by systematics. Nor is such ultimate clarification enough. It fixes the substance of what there is to be communicated. But there remains both the problem of creative use of the available media and the task of finding the appropriate approach and procedure to convey the message to people of different classes and cultures.

I have spoken of foundations selecting doctrines, of doctrines setting the problems of systematics, of systematics fixing the kernel of the message to be communicated in many different ways. But there is not to be overlooked the fact of dependence in the opposite direction. Questions for systematics can arise from communications. Systematic modes of conceptualization can be employed in doctrines. The conversion, formulated as horizon in foundations, will possess not only personal but also social and doctrinal dimensions.

There is, then, reciprocal dependence within each of the two phases, and this was only to be expected since the four levels of conscious and intentional operations (which determine the four specialties in each phase) are themselves interdependent. Further there is dependence of the second phase on the first, for the second confronts the present and future in the light of what has been assimilated from the past. It will be asked, however, whether there is a reciprocal dependence between the first and the second phases, whether the first depends on the second, as the second on the first.

To this question, the answer must be qualified. There is, perhaps inevitably, a dependence of the first phase on the second. But the greatest care must be taken that this influence from the second phase does not destroy either the proper openness of the first phase to all relevant data or its proper function of reaching its results by an appeal to the data.[1] Just what is to be understood by proper openness and proper function is a matter to be clarified in due course. But the point to be made at once is that a second phase, which interferes with the proper functioning of the first, by that very fact is cutting itself off from its own proper source and ground and blocking the way to its own vital development.

Within the limits of this qualification, however, there is to be acknowledged an interdependence of doctrine and doctrinal history and, as well, of foundations and dialectic. Thus, if one attempted to write a history of mathematics, or of chemistry, or of medicine, without a thorough grasp of these subjects, one's work would be foredoomed to failure. One would ever tend to overlook significant events and to set great store by minor matters. One's language would be inaccurate or out of date, one's emphases mistaken, one's perspectives distorted, one's omissions intolerable. What is true of mathematics, chemistry, medicine, also is true of religion and theology. It is a commonplace today that to understand a doctrine one had best study its history. It is

---

[1] Only concrete instances can convey what is meant by the phrase, "its proper function of reaching its results by an appeal to the data". So I beg any reader not familiar with my meaning to read Stephen Neill, *The Interpretation of the New Testament, 1861–1961*, London: Oxford University Press, 1964, pp. 36–59, on J. B. Lightfoot's refutation of C. C. Baur's dating of the New Testament writings.

no less true that to write the history one has to understand the doctrine.

There is a somewhat similar affinity between dialectic and foundations. Foundations objectifies conversion. They bring to light the opposite poles of a conflict in personal history. Though we may not hope for a single and uniform account of authentic conversion, still any plausible account will add a dimension of depth and seriousness to the analyses reached by dialectic. That depth and seriousness, in turn, will reinforce the ecumenical spirit of dialectic and, at the same time, weaken its merely polemical tendencies.

Finally, from the foregoing instances of interdependence there follows a general, if indirect, interdependence of the first and second phases. For the four specialties of the first phase are interdependent. Similarly, the four specialties of the second phase are interdependent. So the interdependence of dialectic and foundations and of history and doctrines involves all eight specialties in, at least, an indirect interdependence.

Such, then, is in outline the dynamic unity of theology. It is a unity of interdependent parts, each adjusting to changes in the others, and the whole developing as a result of such changes and adjustments. Further, this internal process and interaction has its external relations. For theology as a whole functions within the larger context of Christian living, and Christian living within the still larger process of human history.

6. CONCLUSION

Christian theology has been conceived as *die Wendung zur Idee*, the shift towards system, occurring within Christianity. It makes thematic what already is a part of Christian living. Such differentiation and development within Christian living is followed by further differentiations and developments within theology itself. For theology divides into a mediating phase, that encounters the past, and a mediated phase, that confronts the future. Each of the phases subdivides into four functional specialties. These interact with one another as theology endeavors to make its contribution towards meeting the needs of Christian living, actuating its potentialities, and taking advantage of the opportunities offered by world history.

As this conception of theology starts from the notion of functional specialization, so other conceptions rest on the notions of subject or of field specialization. Subject specialization is presupposed in the Aristotelian division of sciences by their formal objects, and it is in this context that theology in the past has been defined as the science of God and of all things in their relations to God, conducted under the light of revelation and faith. On the other hand, field specialization is dominant in contemporary thought concerned with biblical theology, patristic theology, medieval theology, renaissance theology, modern theology.

I am not, perhaps, unjust in pointing out that the subject approach tended to emphasize the mediated phase and neglect the mediating phase, while the field approach tends to emphasize the mediating phase and over-simplify the mediated phase. If this is correct, the functional approach must be credited with giving full attention to both phases and, as well, showing how they can possess a dynamic interdependence and unity.

PART TWO
FOREGROUND

6

RESEARCH

In the preceding chapter there were outlined some of the chief
characteristics of the first functional specialty, research. In this
chapter the reader may be expecting to find a set of precise
instructions on the way to do research. But, perhaps unfortunately,
research is an enormously diversified category and doing research
is much more a matter of practice than of theory. If one's intention is general research, then one should find out who and where
are the masters in the area in which one wishes to work. To them
one must go and with them one must work until one is familiar
with all the tools they employ and has come to understand
precisely why they make their each and every move. On the
other hand, if one's intention is special research, one has to select
the further functional specialty one's research is to serve. Again,
one has to find out who and where there is a master that works
in that further specialty on the basis of his research. To him one
must go, join in his seminar, do a doctoral dissertation under his
direction. For doing research, whether general or special, is
always a concrete task that is guided not by abstract generalities
but by the practical intelligence generated by the self-correcting
process of learning by which also we acquire what we call
common sense.

But if we do not propose to give instruction on the procedures
of research, we may be expected to indicate the areas that theological research is to investigate. Such an indication we are
prepared to offer, but it will settle not theological but only
methodical issues.

Let us begin by distinguishing human studies, religious studies,

Christian studies, Roman Catholic studies. All four are concerned with man. Each of the four differs from the others inasmuch as it recognizes a broader or narrower field of data as relevant to its research. Now the areas proper to human studies and to religious studies need not occupy us here.[1] Our concern is to find a way of dealing with the varying views of Christians on the data relevant to Christian theology.

The issue is not new. Is theology to be based on scripture alone, or on scripture and tradition? Is the tradition just the explicit teaching of the apostles, or is it the ongoing teaching of the church? Is it the ongoing teaching of the church up to Nicea, or up to A.D. 1054, or up to the reception of Scholastic doctrines, or up to the council of Trent, or up to the days of Pius IX, or forever?

Not all answers can be correct. But to ascertain the correct answer will not occur until the sixth functional specialty, doctrines, is reached. But how can the sixth specialty be reached, if one does not know which are the areas relevant to theological research, and how each area is to be weighted?

My answer is to let Christian theologians begin from where they already stand. Each will consider one or more areas relevant to theological research. Let him work there. He will find that the method is designed to take care of the matter.

After all, Christian theologians disagree not only on the areas relevant to theological research but also on the interpretation of texts, on the occurrence of events, on the significance of movements. Such differences can have quite different grounds. Some may be eliminated by further progress in research, interpretation, history, and they can be left to the healing office of time. Some may result from developmental pluralism: there exist disparate cultures and diverse differentiations of consciousness; and such differences are to be bridged by working out the suitable transposition from one culture to another or from one differentiation of consciousness to another. Others, finally, arise because intellectual or moral or religious conversion has not occurred, and

---

[1] In the final chapter on *Communications* something will be said on the relation of theology to religious studies and to human studies.

our chapters on *Dialectic* and on *Foundations* will attempt to indicate how these differences can be brought out into the open so that men of good will can discover one another.

Finally, of course, the method is not just a one-way street. The various specialties interact. If in doctrines a theologian changes his mind about the areas relevant to theological research, he will be led also to change his practice in research.

7

INTERPRETATION

OUR concern is with interpretation as a functional specialty. It is related to research, history, dialectic, foundations, doctrines, systematics, and communications. It depends on them and they depend on it. None the less, it has its own proper end and its specific mode of operating. It can be treated separately.[1]

I shall follow a common enough terminology and understand by "hermeneutics" principles of interpretation and by "exegesis" the application of the principles to a given task. The task to be envisaged will be the interpretation of a text, but the presentation will be so general that it can be applied to any exegetical task.

First, then, not every text stands in need of exegesis. In general, the more a text is systematic in conception and execution, the less does it stand in need of any exegesis. So Euclid's *Elements* were composed about twenty-three centuries ago. One has to study to come to understand them, and that labor may be greatly reduced by a competent teacher. But while there is a task of coming to understand Euclid, there is no task of interpreting Euclid. The correct understanding is unique; incorrect

[1] One of the advantages of the notion of functional specialty is precisely this possibility of separate treatment of issues that otherwise become enormously complex. See, for example, such monumental works as Emilio Betti's *Teoria generale della interpretazione*, Milano: Giuffrè, 1955, and Hans-Georg Gadamer's *Wahrheit und Methode*, Tübingen: Mohr, 1960. Or see my own discussion of the truth of an interpretation in *Insight*, pp. 562–594, and observe how ideas presented there recur here in quite different functional specialties. For instance, what there is termed a universal viewpoint, here is realized by advocating a distinct functional specialty named dialectic.

On the historical background of contemporary hermeneutical thought, see H. G. Gadamer, op. cit., pp. 162–250.

understanding can be shown to be mistaken; and so, while there have been endless commentators on the clear and simple gospels, there exists little or no exegetical literature on Euclid.

However, besides the systematic mode of cognitional operations, there is also the commonsense mode. Moreover, there are very many brands of common sense. Common sense is common, not to all men of all places and times, but to the members of a community successfully in communication with one another. Among them one's commonsense statements have a perfectly obvious meaning and stand in no need of any exegesis. But statements may be transported to other communities distant in place or in time. Horizons, values, interests, intellectual development, experience may differ. Expression may have intersubjective, artistic, symbolic components that appear strange. Then there arises the question, What is meant by the sentence, the paragraph, the chapter, the book? Many answers seem possible, and none seems quite satisfactory.

Such in general is the problem of interpretation. But at the present time four factors have combined to heighten it enormously. The first is the emergence of world consciousness and historical consciousness: we are aware of many very different cultures existing at the present time, and we are aware of the great differences that separate present from past cultures. The second is the pursuit of the human sciences, in which meaning is a fundamental category and, consequently, interpretation a fundamental task. The third is the confusion that reigns in cognitional theory and epistemology: interpretation is just a particular case of knowing, namely, knowing what is meant; it follows that confusion about knowing leads to confusion about interpreting. The fourth factor, finally, is modernity: modern man has been busy creating his modern world, freeing himself from reliance on tradition and authority, working out his own world-view, and so re-interpreting the views held in the past. So the Greek and Latin classical authors have been removed from the context of Christian humanism and revealed as pagans. So the Law has been removed from the context of Christian morality and theology to be placed in the context of some post-Christian philosophy and attitude to life. So the Scriptures have been removed from the context of Christian doctrinal development and restored to the pre-dogmatic context of the history of religions.

Embedded in the problem of hermeneutics, then, there are quite different and far profounder problems. They are to be met neither by wholesale rejection of modernity nor by wholesale acceptance of modernity. In my opinion, they can be met only by the development and application of theological method. Only in that fashion can one distinguish and keep separate problems of hermeneutics and problems in history, dialectic, foundations, doctrines, systematics, and communications. In fact the most striking feature of much contemporary discussion of hermeneutics is that it attempts to treat all these issues as if they were hermeneutical. They are not.

1. BASIC EXEGETICAL OPERATIONS

There are three basic exegetical operations: (1) understanding the text; (2) judging how correct one's understanding of the text is; and (3) stating what one judges to be the correct understanding of the text.

Understanding the text has four main aspects. One understands the object to which the text refers. One understands the words employed in the text. One understands the author that employed the words. One arrives at such understanding through a process of learning and even at times as a result of a conversion. Needless to say, the four aspects are aspects of a single coming to understand.

To judge the correctness of one's understanding of a text raises the problem of context, of the hermeneutical circle, of the relativity of the totality of relevant data, of the possible relevance of more remote inquiries, of the limitations to be placed on the scope of one's interpretation.

To state what one judges to be the correct understanding of the text raises the question of the precise task of the exegete, of the categories he is to employ, of the language he is to speak.

2. UNDERSTANDING THE OBJECT

A distinction has to be drawn between the exegete and the student. Both learn, but what they learn is different. The student reads a text to learn about objects that as yet he does not know. He is required to have learnt the meanings of words and to know about similar or analogous objects that he can use as starting-points in constructing the objects he is to learn about. On the other hand, the exegete may already know all about the objects treated in a text, yet his whole task remains to be performed; for that task is not to know about objects; it is not to know whether or not the text reveals adequate knowledge of the objects; it is simply to know what happened to be the objects, real or imaginary, intended by the author of the text.

In practice, of course, the foregoing distinction will imply not a rigid separation of the roles of student and of exegete but rather a difference of emphasis. The student also is something of an interpreter of texts, and the exegete also learns from texts something that otherwise he would not know. However, though the distinction in practice is only of emphasis, it remains that our present concern is theory and, indeed, not the general learning theory that regards students but the special learning theory that regards exegesis.

I have said that the whole exegetical task remains to be performed even though the exegete already knows all about the objects treated in a text. I must now add that the more the exegete does know about such objects, the better. For he cannot begin to interpret the text unless he knows the language in which it is written and, if he knows that language, then he also knows the objects to which the words in that language refer. Such knowledge, of course, is general and potential. Reading the text, when its meaning is obvious, makes that general knowledge more particular and that potential knowledge actual. On the other hand, when the meaning of the text is not obvious because of this or that defect, still the greater the exegete's resources, the greater the likelihood that he will be able to enumerate all possible interpretations and assign to each its proper measure of probability.

Now the foregoing amounts to a rejection of what may be named the *Principle of the Empty Head*. According to this principle, if one is not to "read into" the text what is not there, if one is not to settle in *a priori* fashion what the text must mean no matter what it says, if one is not to drag in one's own notions and opinions, then one must just drop all preconceptions of every kind, attend simply to the text, see all that is there and nothing that is not there, let the author speak for himself, let the author interpret himself. In brief, the less one knows, the better an exegete one will be.

These contentions, I should say, are both right and wrong. They are right in decrying a well-known evil: interpreters tend to impute to authors opinions that the authors did not express. They are wrong in the remedy they propose, for they take it for granted that all an interpreter has to do is to look at a text and see what is there. That is quite mistaken.

The principle of the empty head rests on a naive intuitionism. So far from tackling the complex task of, first, understanding the object, the words, the author, oneself, secondly, of judging just how correct one's understanding is and, thirdly, of adverting to the problems in expressing one's understanding and judgment, the principle of the empty head bids the interpreter forget his own views, look at which is out there, let the author interpret himself. In fact, what is out there? There is just a series of signs. Anything over and above a re-issue of the same signs in the same order will be mediated by the experience, intelligence, and judgment of the interpreter. The less that experience, the less cultivated that intelligence, the less formed that judgment, the greater the likelihood that the interpreter will impute to the author an opinion that the author never entertained. On the other hand, the wider the interpreter's experience, the deeper and fuller the development of his understanding, the better balanced his judgment, the greater the likelihood that he will discover just what the author meant. Interpretation is not just a matter of looking at signs. That is imperative. But it is no less imperative that, guided by the signs, one proceed from one's habitual general knowledge to actual and more particular knowledge; and the greater the habitual knowledge one possesses, the greater the likelihood that one will be guided by the signs themselves and not by personal preferences and by guess-work.[2]

3. UNDERSTANDING THE WORDS

Understanding the object accounts for the plain meaning of the text, the meaning that is obvious because both author and interpreter understand the same thing in the same way. However, as in conversation, so too in reading, the author may be speaking of P and the reader may be thinking of Q. In that case, sooner or later, there will arise difficulty. Not everything true of P will also be true of Q, and so the author will appear to the interpreter to be saying what is false and even absurd.

At this point there comes to light the difference between the interpreter and the controversialist. On his mistaken assumption that the author is speaking of Q, the controversialist sets about his triumphant demonstration of the author's errors and absurdities. But the interpreter considers the possibility that he himself is at fault. He reads further. He rereads. Eventually he stumbles on the possibility that the author was thinking, not of Q, but of P, and with that correction the meaning of the text becomes plain.

Now this process can occur any number of times. It is the

[2] In this connection, Rudolf Bultmann has written: "Nothing is sillier than the requirement that an interpreter must silence his subjectivity, extinguish his individuality, if he is to attain objective knowledge. That requirement makes good sense only in so far as it is taken to mean that the interpreter has to silence his personal wishes with regard to the outcome of the interpretation. ... For the rest, unfortunately, the requirement overlooks the very essence of genuine understanding. Such understanding presupposes precisely the utmost liveliness of the understanding subject and the richest possible development of his individuality." From an article entitled "Das Problem der Hermeneutik", *Zschr. f. Theol. u. Kirche*, 47(1950), 64. Reprinted in *Glauben und Verstehen*, II, 230.

With this view I agree as far as it goes. However, I sharply distinguish between understanding and judgment, between the development of the one and the development of the other. Bultmann stands in the Kantian tradition in which *Verstand* is thought to be the faculty of judgment.

self-correcting process of learning. It is the manner in which we acquire and develop common sense. It heads towards a limit in which we possess a habitual core of insights that enables us to deal with any situation, or any text of a group, by adding one or two more insights relevant to the situation or text in hand.

Such commonsense understanding is preconceptual. It is not to be confused with one's formulation of the meaning of the text that one has come to understand. And this formulation itself is not to be confused with the judgments one makes on the truth of the understanding and formulation. One has to understand if one is to formulate what one has understood. One has to understand and formulate if one is to pass judgment in any explicit fashion.

Moreover, it is understanding that surmounts the hermeneutic circle. The meaning of a text is an intentional entity. It is a unity that is unfolded through parts, sections, chapters, paragraphs, sentences, words. We can grasp the unity, the whole, only through the parts. At the same time the parts are determined in their meaning by the whole which each part partially reveals. Such is the hermeneutic circle. Logically it is a circle. But coming to understand is not a logical deduction. It is a self-correcting process of learning that spirals into the meaning of the whole by using each new part to fill out and qualify and correct the understanding reached in reading the earlier parts.

Rules of hermeneutics or exegesis list the points worth considering in one's efforts to arrive at an understanding of the text. Such are an analysis of the composition of the text, the determination of the author's purpose, knowledge of the people for whom he wrote, of the occasion on which he wrote, of the nature of the linguistic, grammatical, stylistic means he employed. However, the main point about all such rules is that one does not understand the text because one has observed the rules but, on the contrary, one observes the rules in order to arrive at an understanding of the text. Observing the rules can be no more than mere pedantry that leads to an understanding of nothing of any moment or to missing the point entirely. The essential observance is to note one's every failure to understand clearly and exactly and to sustain one's reading and rereading until one's inventiveness or good luck have eliminated one's failures in comprehension.

4. UNDERSTANDING THE AUTHOR

When the meaning of a text is plain, then with the *author* by his *words* we understand the object to which his words refer. When a simple misunderstanding arises, as when the author thought of P but the reader of Q, then its correction is the relatively simple matter of sustained rereading and inventiveness. But there can arise the need for a long and arduous use of the self-correcting process of learning. Then a first reading yields a little understanding and a host of puzzles, and a second reading yields only slightly more understanding but far more puzzles. The problem, now, is a matter not of understanding the object or the words but of understanding the author himself, his nation, language, time, culture, way of life, and cast of mind.

Now the self-correcting process of learning is, not only the way in which we acquire our own common sense, but also the way in which we acquire an understanding of other people's common sense. Even with our contemporaries with the same language, culture, and station in life, we not only understand things with them but also understand things in our own way and, at the same time, their different way of understanding the same things. We can remark that a phrase or an action is "just like you". By that we mean that the phrase or action fits in with the way we understand your way of understanding and going about things. But just as we can come to an understanding of our fellows' understanding, a commonsense grasp of the ways in which we understand not with them but them, so the same process can be pushed to a far fuller development, and then the self-correcting process of learning will bring us to an understanding of the common sense of another place, time, culture, and cast of mind. This is, however, the enormous labor of becoming a scholar.

The phrase, understanding another's common sense, must not be misunderstood. It is not a matter of understanding what common sense is: that is the task of the cognitional theorist. It is not making another's common sense one's own, so that one would go about speaking and acting like a fifth-century Athenian or a first-century Christian. But, just as common sense itself is a matter of understanding what to say and what to do in any of a series of situations that commonly arise, so understanding another's common sense is a matter of understanding what he would say and what he would do in any of the situations that commonly arose in his place and time.

5. UNDERSTANDING ONESELF

The major texts, the classics, in religion, letters, philosophy, theology, not only are beyond the initial horizon of their interpreters but also may demand an intellectual, moral, religious conversion of the interpreter over and above the broadening of his horizon.

In this case the interpreter's initial knowledge of the object is just inadequate. He will come to know it only in so far as he pushes the self-correcting process of learning to a revolution in his own outlook. He can succeed in acquiring that habitual understanding of an author that spontaneously finds his wavelength and locks on to it, only after he has effected a radical change in himself.

This is the existential dimension of the problem of hermeneutics. It lies at the very root of the perennial divisions of mankind in their views on reality, morality, and religion. Moreover, in so far as conversion is only the basic step, in so far as there remains the labor of thinking out everything from the new and profounder viewpoint, there results the characteristic of the classic set forth by Friedrich Schlegel: "A classic is a writing that is never fully understood. But those that are educated and educate themselves must always want to learn more from it."[3]

From this existential dimension there follows another basic component in the task of hermeneutics. The classics ground a tradition. They create the milieu in which they are studied and

[3] Quoted by H. G. Gadamer, *Wahrheit und Methode*, Tübingen: Mohr, 1960, p. 274, n. 2.

interpreted. They produce in the reader through the cultural tradition the mentality, the *Vorverständnis*, from which they will be read, studied, interpreted. Now such a tradition may be genuine, authentic, a long accumulation of insights, adjustments, re-interpretations, that repeats the original message afresh for each age. In that case the reader will exclaim, as did the disciples on the way to Emmaus: "Did not our hearts burn within us, when he spoke on the way and opened to us the scriptures?" (Lk. 24, 32). On the other hand, the tradition may be unauthentic. It may consist in a watering-down of the original message, in recasting it into terms and meanings that fit into the assumptions and convictions of those that have dodged the issue of radical conversion. In that case a genuine interpretation will be met with incredulity and ridicule, as was St. Paul when he preached in Rome and was led to quote Isaiah: "Go to this people and say: you will hear and hear but never understand; you will look and look, but never see" (Acts 28, 26).

At this point one moves from the functional specialty, interpretation, to the functional specialties, history, dialectic, and foundations. If the interpreter is to know, not merely what his author meant, but also what is so, then he has to be critical not merely of his author but also of the tradition that has formed his own mind. With that step he is propelled beyond writing history to making history.

6. JUDGING THE CORRECTNESS OF ONE'S INTERPRETATION

Such a judgment has the same criterion as any judgment on the correctness of commonsense insights.[4] The criterion is whether or not one's insights are invulnerable, whether or not they hit the bull's eye, whether or not they meet *all* relevant questions so that there are no further questions that can lead to further insights and so complement, qualify, correct the insights already possessed.

The relevant questions usually are not the questions that inspire the investigation. One begins from one's own *Fragestellung*, from

[4] On commonsense judgments, see *Insight*, pp. 283–299.

the viewpoint, interests, concerns one had prior to studying the text. But the study of the text is a process of learning. As one learns, one discovers more and more the questions that concerned the author, the issues that confronted him, the problems he was trying to solve, the material and methodical resources at his disposal for solving them. So one comes to set aside one's own initial interests and concerns, to share those of the author, to reconstruct the context of his thought and speech.[5]

But what precisely is meant by the word, context? There are two meanings. There is the heuristic meaning the word has at the beginning of an investigation, and it tells one where to look to find the context. There is the actual meaning the word acquires as one moves out of one's initial horizon and moves to a fuller horizon that includes a significant part of the author's.

Heuristically, then, the context of the word is the sentence. The context of the sentence is the paragraph. The context of the paragraph is the chapter. The context of the chapter is the book. The context of the book is the author's *opera omnia*, his life and times, the state of the question in his day, his problems, prospective readers, scope and aim.

Actually, context is the interweaving of questions and answers in limited groups. To answer any one question will give rise to further questions. To answer them will give rise to still more. But, while this process can recur a number of times, while it might go on indefinitely if one keeps changing the topic, still it does not go on indefinitely on one and the same topic. So context is a nest of interlocked or interwoven questions and answers; it is limited inasmuch as all the questions and answers have a bearing, direct or indirect, on a single topic; and because it is limited, there comes a point in an investigation when no further relevant questions arise, and then the possibility of judgment has emerged. When there are no further relevant questions, there are

---

[5] My own experience of this change was in writing my doctoral dissertation. I had been brought up a Molinist. I was studying St. Thomas' Thought on *Gratia Operans*, a study later published in *Theological Studies*, 1941–1942. Within a month or so it was completely evident to me that Molinism had no contribution to make to an understanding of Aquinas.

no further insights to complement, correct, qualify those that have been reached.

Still, what is this single topic that limits the set of relevant questions and answers? As the distinction between the heuristic and the actual meanings of the word, context, makes plain, the single topic is something to be discovered in the course of the investigation. By persistence or good luck or both one hits upon some element in the interwoven set of questions and answers. One follows up one's discovery by further questions. Sooner or later one hits upon another element, then several more. There is a period in which insights multiply at a great rate, when one's perspectives are constantly being reviewed, enlarged, qualified, refined. One reaches a point when the overall view emerges, when other components fit into the picture in a subordinate manner, when further questions yield ever diminishing returns, when one can say just what was going forward and back it up with the convergence of multitudinous evidence.

The single topic, then, is something that can be indicated generally in a phrase or two yet unfolded in an often enormously complex set of subordinate and interconnected questions and answers. One reaches that set by striving persistently to understand the object, understand the words, understand the author and, if need be, understand oneself. The key to success is to keep adverting to what has not yet been understood, for that is the source of further questions, and to hit upon the questions directs attention to the parts or aspects of the text where answers may be found. So R. G. Collingwood has praised "... the famous advice of Lord Acton, 'study problems, not periods' ".[6] So H. G. Gadamer has praised Collingwood's insistence that knowledge consists, not just in propositions, but in answers to questions, so that to understand the answers one has to know the questions as well.[7] But my present point is not merely the significance of questions as well as answers—though, of course, that is in full

[6] R. G. Collingwood, *Autobiography*, London: Oxford University Press, [1]1939, [5]1967, p. 130. See also *The Idea of History*, Oxford: Clarendon, 1946, p. 281.
[7] H. G. Gadamer, op. cit., p. 352.

accord with my cognitional theory—but also regards the inter-locking of questions and answers and the eventual enclosure of the interrelated multiplicity within a higher limited unity. For it is the emergence of that enclosure that enables one to recognize the task as completed and to pronounce one's interpretation as probable, highly probable, in some respects, perhaps, certain.

7. A CLARIFICATION

A few contrasts may add clarity to what I have been saying. Collingwood has conceived history as re-enacting the past. Schleiermacher has contended that the interpreter will under-stand the text better than the author did. There is something in these statements but they are not quite accurate and so may be misleading. To clear things up let me take a concrete example. Thomas Aquinas effected a remarkable development in the theology of grace. He did so not at a single stroke but in a series of writings over a period of a dozen years or more. Now, while there is no doubt that Aquinas was quite conscious of what he was doing on each of the occasions on which he returned to the topic, still on none of the earlier occasions was he aware of what he would be doing on the later occasions, and there is just no evidence that after the last occasion he went back over all his writings on the matter, observed each of the long and compli-cated series of steps in which the development was effected, grasped their interrelations, saw just what moved him forward and, perhaps, what held him back in each of the steps. But such a reconstruction of the whole process is precisely what the interpreter does. His overall view, his nest of questions and answers, is precisely a grasp of this array of interconnections and interdependences constitutive of a single development.

What I find true, then, in Schleiermacher's contention is that the interpreter may understand very fully and accurately some-thing that the author knew about only in a very vague and general fashion. Moreover, this precise knowledge will be of enormous value in interpreting the text. But it does not follow that the interpreter will understand the text better than the author did for, while the interpreter can have a firm grasp of all that was going forward, it is rare indeed that he will have access to sources and circumstances that have to be known if the many accidentals in the text are to be accounted for. Again, with respect to Collingwood, it is true that the interpreter or historian reconstructs but it is not true that in thought he reproduces the past. In our example, what Aquinas was doing, was developing the doctrine of grace. What the interpreter was doing, was building up the evidence for an element in the history of the theology of grace and, while he can arrive at a grasp of the main movement and an understanding of many details, he rarely achieves and never needs an understanding of every detail. Judgment rests on the absence of further *relevant* questions.

The reader may feel, however, that I have been arguing from a very special case, from which general conclusions should not be drawn. Certainly, I have not been arguing about a case that is universal, for I have already affirmed that there are cases in which the hermeneutical problem is slight or non-existent. The question, accordingly, is how general are the main lines of the instance from which I have argued.

First, then, my instance was from the history of ideas. It is quite a broad field and of major interest to theological method. But it is uncluttered by the complexities involved in interpreting instances of intersubjective, artistic, symbolic, or incarnate meaning. In these cases understanding the author is inadequate unless the interpreter has some capacity to feel what the author felt and to respect the values that the author respected. But this is re-enactment, not in understanding and thought, but in feeling and value-judgments.

Secondly, even within the history of ideas, the selected instance was exceptionally clear-cut. But while the same clarity is not to be had in other types of instance, the points that here are clear either recur in other instances or possess different features that compensate. In the first place there is always the distinction between the author's consciousness of his activities and his knowledge of them. Authors are always conscious of their intentional operations but to reach knowledge of them there must be added introspective attention, inquiry and understanding, reflection and judgment. Further, this process from consciousness to knowledge, if more than general and vague, is arduous and time-consuming; it leads into the impasse of scrutinizing the self-scrutinizing self and into the oddity of the author who writes about himself writing; such authors are exceptional. Finally, the selected example was a slow development that can be documented. But any notable development occurs slowly. The insight that provokes the cry, Eureka, is just the last insight in a long series of slowly accumulating insights. This process can be documented if the author writes steadily while it is going forward. On the other hand, if he does not write until the development is completed, his presentation will approximate logical or even systematic form, and this form will reveal the nest of relevant questions and answers.

So much for judging the correctness of an interpretation. We have concentrated on the possibility of this judgment. On actual judgment little can be said. It depends on many factors and, in a general discussion, these factors can be no more than hypothetical. Let us suppose that an exegete has grasped with great accuracy just what was going forward and that his understanding of the text can be confirmed by multitudinous details. Now, if really there are no further questions, his interpretation will be certain. But there may be further relevant questions that he has overlooked and, on this account, he will speak modestly. Again, there may be further relevant questions to which he adverts, but he is unable to uncover the evidence that would lead to a solution. Such further questions may be many or few, of major or minor importance. It is this range of possibilities that leads exegetes to speak with greater or less confidence or diffidence and with many careful distinctions between the more probable and the less probable elements in their interpretations.

8. STATING THE MEANING OF THE TEXT

Our concern is with the statement to be made by the exegete *qua* exegete. As in the other functional specialties, so too in interpretation the exegete experiences, understands, judges, and decides. But he does so for a specific purpose. His principal concern is to understand, and the understanding he seeks is, not the understanding of objects, which pertains to the systematics of the second phase, but the understanding of texts, which pertains to the first phase of theology, to theology not as speaking to the present but as listening, as coming to listen to the past.

It is true, of course, that texts are understood in the seven other functional specialties. They are understood in research but, then, the aim of the textual critic is to settle, not what was meant, but just what was written. They are understood in history but, then, the aim of the historian is to settle, not what one author was intending, but what was going forward in a group or community. They are understood in dialectic but, then, the aim is confrontation: interpreters and historians disagree; their disagreement will not be eliminated by further study of the data because it arises from the personal stance and horizon of the interpreters and historians; the purpose of dialectic is to invite the reader to an encounter, a personal encounter, with the originating and traditional and interpreting and history-writing persons of the past in their divergences. As understanding texts is relevant to the dialectic that invites or challenges the theologian to conversion, so too it is relevant to the foundations that objectify the conversion though, of course, objectifying a conversion is one thing and understanding a text is quite another. No less, understanding texts has its importance for the specialty, doctrines, but there the theologian's concern is the relation between the community's origins and the decisions it reached in its successive identity-crises. In like manner, a systematic understanding of objects is something quite different from a commonsense understanding of texts, even though one learns about the objects from the texts. Finally, all this listening to the past and transposing it into the present have no purpose unless one is ready to tell people of today just what it implies for them; and so we have the eighth functional specialty, communications, concerned with the effective presentation—to every individual in every class and culture through all media—of the message deciphered by the exegete.

Now I have not the slightest objection to the existence of highly gifted individuals that can perform and do so superbly in all eight of these functional specialties. My only concern is that there be recognized that the eight performances consist of eight different sets of operations directed to eight interdependent but distinct ends. This concern is, of course, a concern for method, a concern to obstruct the blind imperialism that selects some of the ends, insists on their importance, and neglects the rest.

Accordingly, when I ask about the expression of the meaning of a text by an exegete *qua* exegete, I am in no wise impugning or deprecating the occurrence or the importance of many other modes of expression. H. G. Gadamer has contended that one really grasps the meaning of a text only when one brings its implications to bear upon contemporary living.[8] This, of course, is paralleled by Reinhold Niebuhr's insistence that history is understood in the effort to change it.[9] I have no intention of disputing such views, for they seem to me straight-forward applications of Newman's distinction between notional and real apprehension. All I wish to say is that there are distinct theological tasks performed in quite different manners, that the kind of work outlined in the preceding sections only leads to an understanding of the meaning of a text, and that quite distinct operations are to be performed before entering upon the specialty, communications, and telling people just what the meaning of the text implies in their lives.

Again, Rudolf Bultmann has employed categories derived from the philosophy of Martin Heidegger to express his apprehension of the theology of the New Testament. His procedure imitates that of St. Thomas Aquinas who used Aristotelian categories in his scripture commentaries. I have not the slightest doubt about the propriety of a systematic theology, but the procedures to be employed in developing one are not outlined in an account of hermeneutics as a functional specialty. Similarly, I hold for a doctrinal theology, but I refuse to conclude that the language of exegete *qua* exegete is to be that of Denzinger's

8 H. G. Gadamer, op. cit., pp. 290–324.

9 I am relying on C. R. Stinnette, Jr., "Reflection and Transformation," *The Dialogue between Theology and Psychology, Studies in Divinity No. 3*, The University of Chicago Press, 1968, p. 100.

Enchiridion or of theological textbooks. Finally, I believe in a theology of encounter, but would not confuse theology and religion. Theology reflects on the religion; it promotes the religion; but it does not constitute religious events. I consider religious conversion a presupposition of moving from the first phase to the second but I hold that that conversion occurs, not in the context of doing theology, but in the context of becoming religious. I point out to the exegete that coming to understand himself may be the condition of his understanding the author, his words, and what the author meant. None the less, I conceive that coming to understand himself, not as part of his job as an exegete but as an event of a higher order, an event in his own personal development.

The exegete *qua* exegete expresses his interpretations to his colleagues technically in notes, articles, monographs, commentaries. The expression is technical in the sense that it puts to full use the instruments for investigation provided by research: grammars, lexicons, comparative linguistics, maps, chronologies, handbooks, bibliographies, encyclopedias, etc. The expression, again, is technical inasmuch as it is functionally related to previous work in the field, summarizing what has been done and has become accepted, bringing to light the grounds for raising further questions, integrating results with previous achievement.

The exegete also speaks to his pupils, and he must speak to them in a different manner. For notes, articles, monographs, commentaries fail to reveal the kind of work and the amount of work that went into writing them. That revelation only comes in the seminar. It can come to a great degree by working with a director on some project that he has still in process. But I think there is much to be said for the value of a seminar that repeats previous discovery. This is done by selecting some complex and basically convincing monograph, finding in the original sources the clues and trails that led the author to his discoveries, assigning one's students tasks based on these clues and trails so that they may repeat his discoveries. Even though it is only rediscovery, it is an exhilarating experience for students, and also it is well for them in one of their seminars to have been confronted with a finished piece of work and to have understood why and in what sense it was finished.

However, the exegete has to speak not only to his colleagues in his own field and to his pupils but also to the theological community, to exegetes in other fields and to those engaged principally in other functional specialties. Here there are, I suggest, two procedures, one basic and the other supplementary.

The basic procedure I derive from a description of Albert Descamps of the biblical theologian *qua* exegete. He argued that biblical theology must be as multiple and diverse as are, for the alert exegete, the innumerable biblical authors. So there will be as many biblical theologies as there were inspired authors, and the exegete will aim above all to respect the originality of each of them.

He will appear to be happy to proceed slowly, and often he will follow the ways of beginners. His descriptions will convey a feeling for things long past; they will give the reader an impression of the foreign, the strange, the archaic; his care for genuineness will appear in the choice of a vocabulary as biblical as possible; and he will be careful to avoid any premature transposition to later language, even though that language is approved by a theological tradition.

Any general presentation will have to be based on the chronology and the literary history of the biblical books. If possible, it will be genetic in structure; and for this reason questions of date and authenticity, which might be thought secondary in biblical theology, really have a decisive importance.

Further, general presentations will not be very general. If they regard the whole bible, they will be limited to some very precise topic. If their object is more complex, they will be confined to some single writing or group of writings. If a biblical theology were to aim at presenting the whole or a very large part of the bible, it could do so only by being content to be as manifold and internally differentiated as some "general history" of Europe or of the world.

It is true, Bishop Descamps admits, that there are those that dream of some sort of short-cut, of a presentation of the divine plan running through the history of the two testaments; and many of them would claim that this is almost the proper function of biblical theology. But he himself is of a contrary opinion. A sketch of the divine plan pertains to biblical theology only in the measure that a historian can feel at home with it; not even the believer reaches the divine plan except through the manifold intentions of the many inspired writers.[10]

The foregoing account of the expression proper to an exegete speaking to the theological community seems to me eminently relevant, sane, and solid. Many perhaps will hesitate to agree with the rejection of general presentations of the divine plan running through scriptural history. But they too will come around, I think, when a distinction is drawn; such general expositions are highly important in the functional specialty, communications; but they are not the vehicle by which the exegete communicates his results to the theological community.

It remains, however, that the basic mode of expression, just described, has to be supplemented. While every theologian has to have some training in exegesis, he cannot become a specialist in all fields; and while the exegete of ancient texts very properly gives an impression of the foreign, the strange, the archaic, his readers cannot be content to leave it at that. This need would seem to be at the root of efforts to portray the Hebrew mind, Hellenism, the spirit of Scholasticism, and so on. But these portraits too easily lead to the emergence of mere occult entities. Unless one oneself is a specialist in the field, one does not know how to qualify their generalities, to correct their simplifications, to avoid mistaken inferences. What is needed is not mere description but explanation. If people were shown how to find in their own experience elements of meaning, how these elements can be assembled into ancient modes of meaning, why in antiquity the elements were assembled in that manner, then they would find themselves in possession of a very precise tool, they would know it in all its suppositions and implications, they

[10] Albert Descamps, "Réflexions sur la méthode en théologie biblique," *Sacra Pagina*, I, 142 f., Paris: Gabalda, and Gembloux: Duculot, 1959.

could form for themselves an exact notion and they could check just how well it accounted for the foreign, strange, archaic things presented by the exegetes.

Is this a possible project? Might I suggest that the section on stages of meaning in Chapter Three offers a beginning? If transcendental method coupled with a few books by Cassirer and Snell could make this beginning, why might not transcendental method coupled with the at once extensive and precise knowledge of many exegetes in many fields not yield far more? The benefits would be enormous; not only would the achievements of exegetes be better known and appreciated but also theology as a whole would be rid of the occult entities generated by an inadequately methodical type of investigation and thought.

8

HISTORY

THE word, history, is employed in two senses. There is history (1) that is written about, and there is history (2) that is written. History (2) aims at expressing knowledge of history (1).

The precise object of historical inquiry and the precise nature of historical investigation are matters of not a little obscurity. This is not because there are no good historians. It is not because good historians have not by and large learnt what to do. It is mainly because historical knowledge is an instance of knowledge, and few people are in possession of a satisfactory cognitional theory.[1]

I. NATURE AND HISTORY

A first step will be to set forth the basic differences between history and natural science, and we shall begin from a few reflections on time.

[1] A similar view has been expressed by Gerhard Ebeling. He considers it unquestionable that modern historical science is still a long way from being able to offer a theoretically unobjectionable account of the critical historical method, and that it needs the cooperation of philosophy to reach that goal. *Word and Faith*, London: SCM, 1963, p. 49. Originally, "Die Bedeutung der historisch-kritischen Methode," *Zschr. f. Theol. u. Kirche*, 47(1950), 34.

A more concrete illustration of the matter may be had by reading the *Epilegomena* in R. G. Collingwood, *The Idea of History*, Oxford: Clarendon, 1946. The first three sections on Nature and History, The Historical Imagination, and Historical Evidence, are right on the point. The fourth on History as Re-enactment is complicated by the problems of idealism. See ibid., Editor's Preface, pp. vii–xx. See also Alan Donagan, *The Later Philosophy of R. G. Collingwood*, Oxford: Clarendon, 1962.

One can think of time in connection with such questions as what is the time, what is the date, how soon, how long ago. On that basis one arrives at the Aristotelian definition that time is the number or measure determined by the successive equal stages of a local movement. It is a number when one answers three o'clock or January 26, 1969. It is a measure when one answers three hours or 1969 years. One can push this line of thought further by asking whether there is just one time for the universe or, on the other hand, there are as many distinct times as there are distinct local movements. Now on the Ptolemaic system there did exist a single standard time for the universe, since the outmost of the celestial spheres, the *primum mobile*, contained the material universe and was the first source of all local movement. With the acceptance of the Copernican theory, there vanished the *primum mobile*, but there remained a single standard time, a survival Newton explained by distinguishing true and apparent motion and by conceiving true motion as relative to absolute space and absolute time. Finally, with Einstein, Newton's absolute time vanished, and there emerged as many standard times as there are inertial reference frames that are in relative motion.[2]

Now the foregoing notion of time certainly is of great importance to the historian, for he has to date his events. It is not, however, an adequate account of what time is, for it is limited to counting, measuring, and relating to one another in a comprehensive view all possible instances of such counting and measuring. Moreover, it is this aspect of time that suggests the image of time as a raceway of indivisible instants, an image that little accords with our experience of time.

Fortunately, besides questions about time that are answered by numbers and measurements, there is a further different set concerned with "now". Aristotle asked whether there is a succession of "now's" or just a single "now". He answered with a comparison. Just as "time" is the measure of the movement, so the "now" corresponds to the body that is moving. In so far as there is

---

[2] More on this topic in *Insight*, pp. 155–158.

succession, there is difference in the "now". But underpinning such differences is the identity of the substratum.[3]

Now this advertence to the identity of the substratum, to the body that is moving, removes from one's notion of time the total extrinsicism of each moment from the next. No doubt, each successive moment is different, but in the difference there is also an identity.

With this clue we may advance to our experience of time. There is succession in the flow of conscious and intentional acts; there is identity in the conscious subject of the acts; there may be either identity or succession in the object intended by the acts. Analysis may reveal that what actually is visible is a succession of different profiles; but experience reveals that what is perceived is the synthesis (*Gestalt*) of the profiles into a single object. Analysis may reveal that the sounds produced are a succession of notes and chords; but experience reveals that what is heard is their synthesis into a melody. There results what is called the psychological present, which is not an instant, a mathematical point, but a time-span, so that our experience of time is, not of a raceway of instants, but a now leisurely, a now rapid succession of overlapping time-spans. The time of experience is slow and dull, when the objects of experience change slowly and in expected ways. But time becomes a whirligig, when the objects of experience change rapidly and in novel and unexpected ways.

Whether slow and broad or rapid and short, the psychological present reaches into its past by memories and into its future by anticipations. Anticipations are not merely of the prospective objects of our fears and our desires but also the shrewd estimate of the man of experience or the rigorously calculated forecast of applied science. Again, besides the memories of each individual, there are the pooled memories of the group, their celebration in song and story, their preservation in written narratives, in coins and monuments and every other trace of the group's words and deeds left to posterity. Such is the field of historical investigation.

Now the peculiarity of this field resides in the nature of individual and group action. It has both a conscious and an

[3] Aristotle, *Physics*, V, II, 219b 12.

unconscious side. Apart from neurosis and psychosis the conscious side is in control. But the conscious side consists in the flow of conscious and intentional acts that we have been speaking of since our first chapter. What differentiates each of these acts from the others lies in the manifold meanings of meaning set forth in Chapter Three. Meaning, then, is a constitutive element in the conscious flow that is the normally controlling side of human action. It is this constitutive role of meaning in the controlling side of human action that grounds the peculiarity of the historical field of investigation.

Now meaning may regard the general or the universal, but most human thought and speech and action are concerned with the particular and the concrete. Again, there are structural and material invariants to meaning, but there also are changes that affect the manner in which the carriers of meaning are employed, the elements of meaning are combined, the functions of meaning are distinguished and developed, the realms of meaning are extended, the stages of meaning blossom forth, meet resistance, compromise, collapse. Finally, there are the further vicissitudes of meaning as common meaning. For meaning is common in the measure that community exists and functions, in the measure that there is a common field of experience, common and complementary understanding, common judgments or at least an agreement to disagree, common and complementary commitments. But people can get out of touch, misunderstand one another, hold radically opposed views, commit themselves to conflicting goals. Then common meaning contracts, becomes confined to banalities, moves towards ideological warfare.

It is in this field of meaningful speech and action that the historian is engaged. It is not, of course, the historian's but the exegete's task to determine what was meant. The historian envisages a quite different object. He is not content to understand what people meant. He wants to grasp what was going forward in particular groups at particular places and times. By "going forward" I mean to exclude the mere repetition of a routine. I mean the change that originated the routine and its dissemination. I mean process and development but, no less, decline and collapse. When things turn out unexpectedly, pious people say, "Man proposes but God disposes". The historian is concerned to see how God disposed the matter, not by theological speculation, not by some world-historical dialectic, but through particular human agents. In literary terms history is concerned with the drama of life, with what results through the characters, their decisions, their actions, and not only because of them but also because of their defects, their oversights, their failures to act. In military terms history is concerned, not just with the opposing commanders' plans of the battle, not just with the experiences of the battle had by each soldier and officer, but with the actual course of the battle as the resultant of conflicting plans now successfully and now unsuccessfully executed. In brief, where exegesis is concerned to determine what a particular person meant, history is concerned to determine what, in most cases, contemporaries do not know. For, in most cases, contemporaries do not know what is going forward, first, because experience is individual while the data for history lie in the experiences of many, secondly, because the actual course of events results not only from what people intend but also from their oversights, mistakes, failures to act, thirdly, because history does not predict what will happen but reaches its conclusions from what has happened and, fourthly, because history is not merely a matter of gathering and testing all available evidence but also involves a number of interlocking discoveries that bring to light the significant issues and operative factors.

So the study of history differs from the study of physical, chemical, biological nature. There is a difference in their objects, for the objects of physics, chemistry, biology are not in part constituted by acts of meaning. There is similarity inasmuch as both types of study consist in an ongoing process of cumulative discoveries, that is, of original insights, of original acts of understanding, where by "insight", "act of understanding" is meant a prepropositional, preverbal, preconceptual event, in the sense that propositions, words, concepts express the content of the event and so do not precede it but follow from it. There is, however, a difference in the expression of the respective sets of discoveries. The discoveries of physics, chemistry, biology are expressed in universal systems and are refuted if they are found to be incompatible with a relevant particular instance. But the discoveries of the historian are expressed in narratives and descriptions that regard particular persons, places, and times. They have no claim to universality: they could, of course, be relevant to the understanding of other persons, places, times; but whether in fact they are relevant, and just how relevant they are, can be settled only by a historical investigation of the other persons, places, and times. Finally, because they have no claim to universality, the discoveries of the historians are not verifiable in the fashion proper to the natural sciences; in history verification is parallel to the procedures by which an interpretation is judged correct.

Let us now turn to such human sciences as psychology and sociology. Two cases arise. These sciences may be modelled on the procedures of the natural sciences. In so far as this approach is carried out rigorously, meaning in human speech and action is ignored, and the science regards only the unconscious side of human process. In this case the relations between history and human science are much the same as the relations between history and natural science. However, there is much psychology and sociology that does recognize meaning as a constitutive and normally controlling element in human action. To their study the historian leaves all that is the repetition of routine in human speech and action and all that is universal in the genesis, development, breakdown of routines. Moreover, the more psychology and sociology the historian knows, the more he will increase his interpretative powers. Conversely, the greater the achievements of historians, the broader will be the field of evidence on human speech and action that has been opened up for psychological and sociological investigation.[4]

---

[4] For an extensive anthology and a twenty-page bibliography on the foregoing and related topics, see Patrick Gardiner, editor, *Theories of History*, New York: Free Press, and London: Collier Macmillan, 1959. Where authors there diverge from the present approach, I think the reader will find the root difference to lie in cognitional theory.

2. HISTORICAL EXPERIENCE AND
HISTORICAL KNOWLEDGE

I conceive human knowing to be, not just experiencing, but a compound of experiencing, understanding, and judging. Hence if there is historical knowledge, there must be historical experience, historical understanding, and historical judging. Our present aim is to say something about historical experience and then something about the thought process from historical experience to written history.

Already there has been described the subject in time. He is identical, ever himself. But his conscious and intentional acts keep shifting in one way or another to make his "now" slip out of the past and into the future, while the field of objects that engage his attention may change greatly or slightly, rapidly or slowly. Not only is the subject's psychological present not an instant but a time-span but in it the subject may be reaching into the past by memories, stories, history and into the future by anticipations, estimates, forecasts.

Now it is sometimes said that man is a historical being. The meaning of the statement may be grasped most vividly by a thought experiment. Suppose a man suffers total amnesia. He no longer knows who he is, fails to recognize relatives and friends, does not recall his commitments or his lawful expectations, does not know where he works or how he makes his living, and has lost even the information needed to perform his once customary tasks. Obviously, if he is to live, either the amnesia has to be cured, or else he must start all over. For our pasts have made us whatever we are and on that capital we have to live or else we must begin afresh. Not only is the individual an historical entity, living off his past, but the same holds for the group. For, if we suppose that all members in the group suffer total amnesia, there will be as total a collapse of all group functioning as there is in each individual in the group. Groups too live on their past, and their past, so to speak, lives on in them. The present functioning of the good of order is what it is mostly because of past functioning and only slightly because of the minor efforts now needed to keep things going and, when possible, improve them. To start completely afresh would be to revert to a very distant age.

Now I am not offering a medical account of amnesia. I am simply attempting to portray the significance of the past in the present, and, thereby, to communicate what is meant by saying that man is a historical being. But being historical is the history that is written about. It may be named, if considered interiorly, an existential history—the living tradition which formed us and thereby brought us to the point where we began forming ourselves.[5] This tradition includes at least individual and group memories of the past, stories of exploits and legends about heroes, in brief, enough of history for the group to have an identity as a group and for individuals to make their several contributions towards maintaining and promoting the common good of order. But from this rudimentary history, contained in any existential history, any living tradition, we must now attempt to indicate the series of steps by which one may, in thought, move towards the notion of scientific history.[6]

In general it is a process of objectification, and we shall begin from the simpler instances of autobiography and biography before going on to the more complex matter of history which regards groups.

Towards an autobiography, a first step is a diary. Day by day one records, not every event that occurred—one has other things to do—but what seems important, significant, exceptional, new. So one selects, abbreviates, sketches, alludes. One omits most of what is too familiar to be noticed, too obvious to be mentioned, too recurrent to be thought worth recording.

Now as the years pass and the diary swells, retrospect lengthens. What once were merely remote possibilities, now have been realized. Earlier events, thought insignificant, prove to have been quite important, while others, thought important, turn out to

[5] For a contemporary reaction against the destructive aspects of the Enlightenment and a rehabilitation of tradition as the condition of the possibility of an interpretation, see H. G. Gadamer, *Wahrheit und Methode*, pp. 250-290.

[6] It is from the *vécu* to the *thématique*, from the *existenziell* to the *existenzial*, from *exercite* to *signate*, from the fragmentarily experienced to the methodically known.

have been quite minor. Omitted earlier events have to be recalled and inserted both to supply the omitted context of the earlier period and to make later events more intelligible. Earlier judgments, finally, have to be complemented, qualified, corrected. But if all this is attempted, one has shifted from keeping a diary to writing one's memoirs. One enlarges one's sources from the diary to add to the diary all the letters and other material one can acquire. One ransacks one's memory. One asks questions and to meet them one starts reconstructing one's past in one's imagination, depicting to oneself now this now that former *Sitz im Leben*, to find answers and then ask the further questions that arise from these answers. As in interpretation, so here too there gradually are built up contexts, limited nests of questions and answers, each bearing on some multi-faceted but determinate topic. In this fashion the old, day-by-day, organization of the diary becomes quite irrelevant. Much that had been overlooked now has been restored. What had merely been juxtaposed now is connected. What had been dimly felt and remembered now stands in sharp relief within perhaps hitherto unsuspected perspectives. There has emerged a new organization that distinguishes periods by broad differences in one's mode of living, in one's dominant concern, in one's tasks and problems, and in each period distinguishes contexts, that is, nests of questions and answers bearing on distinct but related topics. The periods determine the sections, the topics determine the chapters of one's autobiography.

Biography aims at much the same goal but has to follow a different route. The autobiographer recounts what "I saw, heard, remembered, anticipated, imagined, felt, gathered, judged, decided, did. ..." In the biography, statements shift to the third person. Instead of stating what is remembered or has been recalled, the biographer has to do research, gather evidence, reconstruct in imagination each successive *Sitz im Leben*, ask determinate concrete questions, and so build up his set of periods each containing a larger or smaller set of related contexts. In the main there are three main differences between autobiography and biography. The biographer is free from the embarrassment that may trouble an autobiographer in his self-revelation. The biographer may appeal to later events that put in a new light the judgments, decisions, deeds of his subject, to reveal him to be more or less profound, wise, far-sighted, astute than one otherwise would have thought. Finally, since the biographer has to make his subject intelligible to a later generation, he has to write not just a "life" but rather a "life and times".

While in biography the "times" are a subordinate clarification of the "life", in history this perspective is reversed. Attention is centered on the common field that, in part, is explored in each of the biographies that are or might be written. Still this common field is not just an area in which biographies might overlap. There is social and cultural process. It is not just a sum of individual words and deeds. There exists a developing and/or deteriorating unity constituted by cooperations, by institutions, by personal relations, by a functioning and/or malfunctioning good of order, by a communal realization of originating and terminal values and disvalues. Within such processes we live out our lives. About them each of us ordinarily is content to learn enough to attend to his own affairs and perform his public duties. To seek a view of the actual functioning of the whole or of a notable part over a significant period of time is the task of the historian.

As the biographer, so too the historian proceeds (1) from the data made available by research, (2) through imaginative reconstruction and cumulative questioning and answering, (3) towards related sets of limited contexts. But now the material basis is far larger in extent, far more complex, more roundabout in relevance. The center of interest has shifted from the individual to the group, from private to public life, from the course of a single life to the course of the affairs of a community. The range of relevant topics has increased enormously and, on many, specialized knowledge may be a necessary prerequisite to undertaking historical investigation. Finally, history itself becomes a specialty; historians become a professional class; the field of historical investigation is divided and subdivided; and the results of investigations are communicated in congresses and accumulated in periodicals and books.

3. CRITICAL HISTORY

A first step towards understanding critical history lies in an account of precritical history. For it, then, the community is the conspicuous community, one's own. Its vehicle is narrative, an ordered recital of events. It recounts who did what, when, where, under what circumstances, from what motives, with what results. Its function is practical: a group can function as a group only by possessing an identity, knowing itself and devoting itself to the cause, at worst, of its survival, at best, of its betterment. The function of precritical history is to promote such knowledge and devotion. So it is never just a narrative of bald facts. It is *artistic*: it selects, orders, describes; it would awaken the reader's interest and sustain it; it would persuade and convince. Again, it is *ethical*: it not only narrates but also apportions praise and blame. It is *explanatory*: it accounts for existing institutions by telling of of their origins and development and by contrasting them with alternative institutions found in other lands. It is *apologetic*, correcting false or tendentious accounts of the people's past, and refuting the calumnies of neighboring peoples. Finally, it is *prophetic*: to hindsight about the past there is joined foresight on the future and there are added the recommendations of a man of wide reading and modest wisdom.

Now such precritical history, even purged of its defects, though it might well meet very real needs in the functional specialty, communications, at least does not qualify as the functional specialty, history. For that specialty, while it operates on the four levels of experiencing, understanding, judging, and deciding, still operates on the other three with a principal concern for judging, for settling matters of fact. It is not concerned with the highly important educational task of communicating to fellow citizens or fellow churchmen a proper appreciation of their heritage and a proper devotion to its preservation, development, dissemination. It is concerned to set forth what really happened or, in Ranke's perpetually quoted phrase, *wie es eigentlich gewesen*. Finally, unless this work is done in detachment, quite apart from political or apologetic aims, it is attempting to serve two masters and usually suffers the evangelical consequences.[7]

Next, this work is not just a matter of finding testimonies, checking them for credibility, and stringing together what has been found credible. It is not just that, because historical experience is one thing and historical knowledge is quite another. The string of credible testimonies merely re-edits historical experience. It does not advance to historical knowledge which grasps what was going forward, what, for the most part, contemporaries did not know. Many early Christians may have had a fragmentary experience of the manner in which the elements in the synoptic gospels were formed; but Rudolf Bultmann was concerned to set forth the process as a whole and, while he found his evidence in the synoptic gospels, still that evidence did not presuppose belief in the truth of the evangelists' statements.[8]

Thirdly, only a series of discoveries can advance the historian from the fragmentary experiences, that are the source of his data, to knowledge of a process as a whole. Like a detective confronted with a set of clues that at first leave him baffled, the historian has to discover in the clues, piece by piece, the evidence that will yield a convincing account of what happened.

Since the evidence has to be discovered, a distinction has to be drawn between potential, formal, and actual evidence. Potential evidence is any datum, here and now perceptible. Formal evidence is such a datum in so far as it is used in asking and answering a question for historical intelligence. Actual evidence is a formal evidence invoked in arriving at a historical judgment. In other words, data as perceptible are potential evidence; data as perceptible and understood are formal evidence; data as perceptible, as understood, and as grounding a reasonable judgment are actual evidence.

---

[7] See, for example, G. P. Gooch, *History and Historians in the Nineteenth Century*, London: Longmans, [1]1913, [2]1952, Chapter Eight on the Prussian School.

[8] R. Bultmann, *Geschichte der synoptischen Tradition*, Göttingen: Vandenhoeck & Ruprecht, [4]1958. The first edition was in 1921. On the same topic, I. de la Potterie, (ed.) *De Jésus aux Évangiles*, Gembloux: Duculot, 1967, where *Formgeschichte* plays an intermediate role between *Traditionsgeschichte* and *Redaktionsgeschichte*.

What starts the process is the question for historical intelligence. With regard to some defined situation in the past one wants to understand what was going forward. Clearly, any such question presupposes some historical knowledge. Without it, one would not know of the situation in question, nor would one know what was meant by "going forward". History, then, grows out of history. Critical history was a leap forward from precritical history. Precritical history was a leap forward from stories and legends. Inversely, the more history one knows, the more data lie in one's purview, the more questions one can ask, and the more intelligently one can ask them.

The question for historical intelligence is put in the light of previous knowledge and with respect to some particular datum. It may or may not lead to an insight into that datum. If it does not, one moves on to a different question. If it does, the insight is expressed in a surmise, the surmise is represented imaginatively, and the image leads to a further related question. This process may or may not be recurrent. If it is not, one has come to a dead end and must try another approach. If it is recurrent, and all one attains is a series of surmises, then one is following a false trail and once more must try another approach. But if one's surmises are coincident with further data or approximate to them, one is on the right track. The data are ceasing to be merely potential evidence; they are becoming formal evidence; one is discovering what the evidence might be.

Now if one is on the right track long enough, there occurs a shift in the manner of one's questioning for, more and more, the further questions come from the data rather than from images based on surmises. One still has to do the questioning. One still has to be alert. But one has moved out of the assumptions and perspectives one had prior to one's investigation. One has attained sufficient insight into the object of one's inquiry to grasp something of the assumptions and perspectives proper to that object. And this grasp makes one's approach to further data so much more congenial that the further data suggest the further questions to be put. To describe this feature of historical investigation, let us say that the cumulative process of datum, question, insight, surmise, image, formal evidence, is ecstatic. It is not the hot ecstasy of the devotee but the cool one of growing insight. It takes one out of oneself. It sets aside earlier assumptions and perspectives by bringing to light the assumptions and perspectives proper to the object under investigation.

The same process is selective, constructive, and critical. It is selective: not all data are promoted from the status of potential evidence to the status of formal evidence. It is constructive: for the selected data are related to one another through an interconnected set of questions and answers or, expressed alternatively, by a series of insights that complement one another, correct one another, and eventually coalesce into a single view of a whole. Finally, it is critical: for insights not only are direct but also inverse. By direct insight one grasps how things fit together, and one murmurs one's "Eureka". By inverse insight one is prompted to exclaim, How could I have been so stupid as to take for granted. ... One sees that things are not going to fit and, eventually, by a direct insight one grasps that some item fits not in this context but in some other. So a text is discovered to have been interpolated or mutilated. So the pseudo-Dionysius is extradited from the first century and relocated at the end of the fifth: he quoted Proclus. So an esteemed writer comes under suspicion: the source of his information has been discovered; in whole or in part, without independent confirmation, he is used not as evidence for what he narrates but in the roundabout fashion that rests on his narrating—his intentions, readers, methods, omissions, mistakes.[9]

Now I have been attributing to a single process of developing understanding a whole series of different functions. It is *heuristic*, for it brings to light the relevant data. It is *ecstatic*, for it leads the inquirer out of his original perspectives and into the perspectives

---

[9] Note that the word, critical, has two quite different meanings. In precritical history it means that one has tested the credibility of one's authorities before believing them. In critical history it means that one has shifted data from one field of relevance to another. On this topic R. G. Collingwood is brilliant and convincing. See his two studies, "The Historical Imagination" and "Historical Evidence", in *The Idea of History*, Oxford: Clarendon, 1946, pp. 231–282.

proper to his object. It is *selective*, for out of a totality of data it selects those relevant to the understanding achieved. It is *critical*, for it removes from one use or context to another the data that might otherwise be thought relevant to present tasks. It is *constructive*, for the data that are selected are knotted together by the vast and intricate web of interconnecting links that cumulatively came to light as one's understanding progressed.

Now it is the distinguishing mark of critical history that this process occurs twice. In the first instance one is coming to understand one's sources. In the second instance one is using one's understood sources intelligently to come to understand the object to which they are relevant. In both cases the development of understanding is heuristic, ecstatic, selective, critical, constructive. But in the first case one is identifying authors, locating them and their work in place and time, studying the milieu, ascertaining their purposes in writing and their prospective readers, investigating their sources of information and the use they made of them. In a previous section on *Interpretation* we spoke of understanding the author, but there the ulterior aim was to understand what he meant. In history we also seek to understand the authors of sources, but now the ulterior aim is to understand what they were up to and how they did it. It is this understanding that grounds the critical use of sources, the fine discrimination that distinguishes an author's strength and weaknesses and uses him accordingly. Once this is achieved, one is able to shift one's attention to one's main objective, namely, to understanding the process referred to in one's sources. Where before one's developing understanding was heuristic, ecstatic, selective, critical, constructive in determining what authors were up to, now it is heuristic, ecstatic, selective, critical, and constructive in determining what was going forward in the community.

Needless to say, the two developments are interdependent. Not only does understanding the authors contribute to understanding the historical events, but in coming to understand the events there arise questions that may lead to a revision of one's understanding of the authors and, consequently, to a revision of one's use of them.

Again, while each new insight uncovers evidence, moves one away from previous perspectives, selects or rejects data as relevant or irrelevant, and adds to the picture that is being constructed, still what gains attention is, not each single insight, but the final insight in each cumulative series. It is such final insights that are called discoveries. With them the full force of the cumulative series breaks forth and, as the cumulation has a specific direction and meaning, discoveries now are of the new evidence, now of a new perspective, now of a different selection or critical rejection in the data, now of ever more complicated structures.

So far we have been thinking of structuring as the intelligible pattern grasped in the data and relating the data to one another. But there is a further aspect to the matter. For what is grasped by understanding in data, also is expressed by understanding in concepts and words. So from the intelligible pattern grasped in the data, one moves to the intelligible pattern expressed in the narrative. At first, the narrative is simply the inquirer mumbling his surmises to himself. As surmises less and less are mere surmises, as more and more they lead to the uncovering of further evidence, there begin to emerge trails, linkages, interconnected wholes. As the spirit of inquiry catches every failure to understand, as it brings to attention what is not yet understood and, as a result, is so easily overlooked, one of the interconnected wholes will advance to the role of a dominant theme running through other interconnected wholes that thereby become subordinate themes. As the investigation progresses and the field of data coming under control broadens, not only will the organization in terms of dominant and subordinate themes keep extending, but also there will emerge ever higher levels of organization. So among dominant themes there will emerge dominant topics to leave other dominant themes just subordinate topics; and the fate of dominant themes awaits most of the dominant topics, as the process of organization keeps moving, not only over more territory, but up to ever higher levels of organization. It is not to be thought that this process of advancing organization is a single uniform progress. There occur discoveries that complement and correct previous discoveries and so, as understanding changes, the organization also must change. Themes and topics become more exactly conceived and more happily expressed. The range of their dominance may be extended or curtailed. Items once thought of major interest can slip back to less prominent roles, and, inversely, other items can mount from relative obscurity to notable significance.

The exact conception and happy expression of themes and topics are matters of no small moment. For they shape the further questions that one will ask and it is those further questions that lead to further discoveries. Nor is this all. Part by part, historical investigations come to a term. They do so when there have been reached the set of insights that hit all nails squarely on the head. They are known to do so when the stream of further questions on a determinate theme or topic gradually diminishes and finally dries up. The danger of inaccurate or unhappy conception and formulation is that either the stream of questions may dry up prematurely or else that it may keep flowing when really there are no further relevant questions.

It follows that the cumulative process of developing understanding not only is heuristic, ecstatic, selective, critical, and constructive but also is reflective and judicial. The understanding that has been achieved on a determinate point can be complemented, corrected, revised, only if further discoveries on that very point can be made. Such discoveries can be made only if further relevant questions arise. If, in fact, there are no further relevant questions then, in fact, a certain judgment would be true. If, in the light of the historian's knowledge, there are no further relevant questions, then the historian can say that, as far as he knows, the question is closed.

There is, then, a criterion for historical judgment, and so there is a point where formal evidence becomes actual evidence. Such judgments occur repeatedly throughout an investigation, as each minor and then each major portion of the work is completed. But as in natural science, so too in critical history the positive content of judgment aspires to be no more than the best available opinion. This is evident as long as an historical investigation is in process, for later discoveries may force a correction and revision of earlier ones. But what is true of investigations in process, has to be extended to investigations that to all intents and purposes are completed.

For, in the first place, one cannot exclude the possibility that new sources of information will be uncovered and that they will affect subsequent understanding and judgment. So archeological investigations of the ancient Near East complement Old Testament study, the caves of Qumran have yielded documents with a bearing on New Testament studies, while the unpublished writings found at Kenoboskion restrain pronouncements on Gnosticism.

But there is, as well, another source of revision. It is the occurrence of later events that place earlier events in a new perspective. The outcome of a battle fixes the perspective in which the successive stages of the battle are viewed; military victory in a war reveals the significance of the successive battles that were fought; the social and cultural consequences of the victory and the defeat are the measure of the effects of the war. So, in general, history is an ongoing process. As the process advances, the context within which events are to be understood keeps enlarging. As the context enlarges, perspectives shift.

However, neither of these sources of revision will simply invalidate earlier work competently done. New documents fill out the picture; they illuminate what before was obscure; they shift perspectives; they refute what was venturesome or speculative; they do not simply dissolve the whole network of questions and answers that made the original set of data massive evidence for the earlier account. Again, history is an ongoing process, and so the historical context keeps enlarging. But the effects of this enlargement are neither universal nor uniform. For persons and events have their place in history through one or more contexts, and these contexts may be narrow and brief or broad and enduring with any variety of intermediates. Only inasmuch as a context is still open, or can be opened or extended, do later events throw new light on earlier persons, events, processes. As Karl Heussi put it, it is easier to understand Frederick William III of Prussia than to understand Schleiermacher and, while Nero will always be Nero, we cannot as yet say the same for Luther.[10]

Besides the judgments reached by a historian in his investigation, there are the judgments passed upon his work by his peers and his successors. Such judgments constitute critical history at the second degree. For they are not mere wholesale judgments of belief or disbelief. They are based on an understanding of how the work was done. Just as the historian, first, with respect to his sources and, then, with respect to the object of his inquiry, undergoes a development of understanding that at once is heuristic, ecstatic, selective, critical, constructive and, in the limit, judicial, so the critics of a historical work undergo a similar development with respect to the work itself. They do so all the more easily and all the more competently, the more the historian has been at pains not to conceal his tracks but to lay all his cards on the table, and the more the critics already are familiar with the field or, at least, with neighboring fields.

The result of such critical understanding of a critical history is, of course, that one can make an intelligent and discriminating use of the criticized historian. One learns where he has worked well. One has spotted his limitations and his weaknesses. One can say where, to the best of present knowledge, he can be relied on, where he must be revised, where he may have to be revised. Just as historians make an intelligent and discriminating use of their sources, so too the professional historical community makes a discriminating use of the works of its own historians.

Early in this section we noted that asking historical questions presupposed historical knowledge and, the greater that knowledge, the more the data in one's purview, the more questions one could ask, and the more intelligently one could ask them. Our consideration has now come full circle, for we have arrived at an account of that presupposed historical knowledge. It is critical history of the second degree. It consists basically in the cumulative works of historians. But it consists actually, not in mere belief in those works, but in a critical appreciation of them. Such critical appreciation is generated by critical book reviews,

10 Karl Heussi, *Die Krisis des Historismus*, Tübingen: Mohr, 1932, p. 58.

by the critiques that professors communicate to their students and justify by their explanations and arguments, by informal discussions in common rooms and more formal discussions at congresses.

Critical history of the second degree is a compound. At its base are historical articles and books. On a second level there are critical writings that compare and evaluate the historical writings: these may vary from brief reviews to long studies right up to such a history of the historiography of an issue as Herbert Butterfield's *George III & the Historians*.[11] Finally, there are the considered opinions of professional historians on historians and their critics —opinions that influence their teaching, their remarks in discussions, their procedures in writing on related topics.

Before concluding this section it will be well to recall what precisely has been our aim and concern. Explicitly, it has been limited to the functional specialty, history. There has been excluded all that pertains to the functional specialty, communications. I have no doubt that historical knowledge has to be communicated, not merely to professional historians, but in some measure to all members of the historical community. But before that need can be met, historical knowledge has to be acquired and kept up to date. The present section has been concerned with the prior task. It has been concerned to indicate what set and sequence of operations secure the fulfilment of that task. If it is commonly thought that such a task is all the more likely to be performed well if one comes to it without an axe to grind, at least that has not been my main reason for distinguishing between the functional specialties, history and communications. My main reason has been that they name different tasks performed in quite different manners and, unless their distinction is acknowledged and maintained, there is just no possibility of arriving at an exact understanding of either task.

[11] London: Collins, 1957. For a variety of views on the history of historiography, see Carl Becker, "What is Historiography?" *The American Historical Review*, 44(1938), 20–28; reprinted in Phil. L. Snyder (ed.), *Detachment and the Writing of History, Essays and Letters of Carl L. Becker*, Cornell University Press, 1958.

Again, it is a commonplace for theorists of history to struggle with the problems of historical relativism, to note the influence exerted on historical writing by the historian's views on possibility, by his value-judgments, by his *Weltanschauung* or *Fragestellung* or *Standpunkt*. I have omitted any consideration of this matter, not because it is not extremely important, but because it is brought under control, not by the techniques of critical history, but by the techniques of our fourth specialty, dialectic.

The concern, then, of the present section has been strictly limited. It presupposed the historian knew how to do his research and how to interpret the meaning of documents. It left to later specialties certain aspects of the problem of relativism and the great task of revealing the bearing of historical knowledge on contemporary policy and action. It was confined to formulating the set of procedures that, *caeteris paribus*, yield historical knowledge, to explaining how that knowledge arises, in what it consists, what are its inherent limitations.

If I have been led to adopt the view that the techniques of critical history are unequal to the task of eliminating historical relativism totally, I affirm all the more strongly that they can and do effect a partial elimination. I have contended that critical history is not a matter of believing credible testimonies but of discovering what hitherto had been experienced but not properly known. In that process of discovery I have recognized not only its heuristic, selective, critical, constructive, and judicial aspects, but also an ecstatic aspect that eliminates previously entertained perspectives and opinions to replace them with the perspectives and views that emerge from the cumulative interplay of data, inquiry, insight, surmise, image, evidence. It is in this manner that critical history of itself moves to objective knowledge of the past, though it may be impeded by such factors as mistaken views on possibility, by mistaken or misleading value-judgments, by an inadequate world-view or standpoint or state of the question.

In brief, this section has been attempting to bring to light the set of procedures that lead historians in various manners to affirm the possibility of objective historical knowledge. Carl

Becker, for instance, agreed he was a relativist in the sense that *Weltanschauung* influences the historian's work, but at the same time maintained that a considerable and indeed increasing body of knowledge was objectively ascertainable.[12] Erich Rothacker correlated *Wahrheit* with *Weltanschauung*, granted that they influenced historical thought, but at the same time affirmed the existence of a correctness (*Richtigkeit*) attached to critical procedures and proper inferences.[13] In a similar vein Karl Heussi held that philosophic views would not affect critical procedures though they might well have an influence on the way the history was composed;[14] and he advanced that while the relatively simple form, in which the historian organizes his materials, resides not in the enormously complex courses of events but only in the historian's mind, still different historians operating from the same standpoint arrive at the same organization.[15] In like manner, Rudolf Bultmann held that, granted a *Fragestellung*, critical method led to univocal results.[16] These writers are speaking in various manners of the same reality. They mean, I believe, that there exist procedures that, *caeteris paribus*, lead to historical knowledge. Our aim and concern in this section has been to indicate the nature of those procedures.

[12] Quoted from Carl Becker, "Review of Maurice Mendelbaum's *The Problem of Historical Knowledge*," *Philosophic Review*, 49(1940), 363, by C. W. Smith, *Carl Becker: On History and the Climate of Opinion*, Cornell University Press, 1956, p. 97.

[13] Erich Rothacker, *Logik und Systematik der Geisteswissenschaften (Handbuch der Philosophie)*, Munich and Berlin, 1927, Bonn, 1947, p. 144.

[14] Karl Heussi, *Die Krisis des Historismus*, Tübingen: Mohr, 1932, p. 63.

[15] Ibid., p. 56.

[16] Rudolf Bultmann, "Das Problem der Hermeneutik", *Zschr. f. Theol. u. Kirche*, 47(1950), 64; also *Glauben und Verstehen, II*, Tübingen: Mohr, 1961, p. 229.

9

HISTORY AND HISTORIANS

NORMALLY historians are content to write history without raising any questions about the nature of historical knowledge.[1] Nor is this surprising. For historical knowledge is reached by an adaptation of the every-day procedures of human understanding and, while the adaptation itself has to be learnt, the underlying procedures are too intimate, too spontaneous, too elusive to be objectified and described without a protracted and, indeed, highly specialized effort.[2] So even a great innovator, such as Leopold von Ranke, explained that his practice arose by a sort of necessity, in its own way, and not from an attempt to imitate the practice of his pioneering predecessor, Barthold Niebuhr.[3]

At times, however, historians are impelled to do more than just write history. They may be teaching it. They may feel obliged to defend their practice against encroaching error. They may be led to state in part or in whole just what they are doing when doing history. Then, whether they wish it or not, they are using some more or less adequate or inadequate cognitional theory, and easily they become involved in some philosophic undertow that they cannot quite master.

This dialectic can be highly instructive provided, of course,

[1] *The Varieties of History: From Voltaire to the Present,* Edited, selected, and introduced by Fritz Stern, New York: Meridian Books, 1956, p. 14.

[2] On commonsense understanding and judgment, see *Insight,* pp. 173–181 and 280–299.

[3] G. P. Gooch, *History and Historians in the Nineteenth Century,* London: Longmans, 1952, p. 75.

that one is not a mere logician testing the clarity of terms, the coherence of statements, the rigor of inferences. For what the historian has to offer is not a coherent cognitional theory but an awareness of the nature of his craft and an ability to describe it in the concrete and lively fashion that only a practitioner can manage.

I. THREE HANDBOOKS

Handbooks on the method of history have gone out of fashion. But in the latter part of the nineteenth century they were common and influential. I shall select three that represent different tendencies, and I shall compare them on a single, but, I believe, significant issue, namely, the relationship between historical facts and their intelligible interconnections, their *Zusammenhang*.

For twenty-five years Johann Gustav Droysen (1808-1884) constantly revised his lectures on the encyclopedia and methodology of history. As well, he composed a *Grundriss der Historik* which appeared as *Manuskriptdruck* in 1858 and 1862 and in full-fledged editions in 1868, 1875, 1882. Interest in his work continues, for an edition combining both the 1882 version of the lectures and the *Grundriss* with all its variants reached a fourth printing in 1960.[4]

Droysen divided the historian's task into four parts. *Heuristic* uncovered the relevant remains, monuments, accounts. *Criticism* evaluated their reliability. *Interpretation* brought to light the realities of history in the fulness of their conditions and the process of their emergence. *Presentation*, finally, made an account of the past a real influence in the present on the future.[5]

Now in one important respect Droysen's division differed from that of his predecessors and his contemporaries. He limited criticism to ascertaining the reliability of sources. They extended it to determining the occurrence of the facts of history. Their

[4] J. G. Droysen, *Historik. Vorlesungen über die Enzyklopädie und Methodologie der Geschichte*, hrsg. von Rudolf Hübner, München, ⁴1960.

[5] For an outline of Droysen's position, see P. Hünermann, *Der Durchbruch geschichtlichen Denkens im 19. Jahrhundert*, Freiburg-Basel-Wien: Herder, 1967, pp. 111-128.

position, Droysen felt, was due to mere inertia. Their model for historical criticism had been the textual criticism of the philologists. But textual criticism is one thing and historical criticism is another. The textual critic ascertains objective facts, namely, the original state of the text. But the facts of history resemble, not a text, but the meaning of a text. They are like battles, councils, rebellions. They are complex unities that result from manifold actions and interactions of individuals. They extend over space and over time. They cannot be singled out and observed in some single act of perception. They have to be put together by assembling a manifold of particular events into a single interpretative unity.[6]

For Droysen, then, the historian does not first determine the facts and then discover their interconnections. On the contrary, facts and interconnections form a single piece, a garment without seam. Together they constitute historical reality in the fulness of its conditions and the process of its emergence. They are discovered in an interpretative process guided by the watchword, *forschend verstehen*, advance through research to understanding. The research was directed to four areas: first, to the course of events, say, in a military campaign; secondly, to the conditions forming the context of the events; thirdly, to the character of the participants; and fourthly, to the purposes and ideas that were being realized.[7] So historical interpretation moves towards historical reality, grasping the series of events, first in their inner connections, next in their dependence on the situation, thirdly in the light of the character or psychology of the agents, and finally, as a realization of purposes and ideas. Only through this fourfold grasp of meaning and significance do the events stand revealed in their proper reality.

Droysen did not prevail. In Ernst Bernheim's monumental *Lehrbuch der historischen Methode und der Geschichtsphilosophie* there may be discerned a similar fourfold division of the historian's task. But now criticism is divided into outer and inner.[8] Outer criticism determines whether *single* sources are reliable historical

[6] Ibid., pp. 112 ff.   [7] Ibid., pp. 118 ff.
[8] E. Bernheim, *Lehrbuch der historischen Methode*, Munich, 1905, p. 294.

witnesses.[9] Inner criticism has to settle the factuality of the events witnessed by *several* sources taken together.[10] So it would seem that the historical facts are settled, before there begins the work of interpretation, which Bernheim names the *Auffassung* and defines as the determination of the interconnections (*Zusammenhang*) of the events.[11]

It remains, however, that if Bernheim assigned to inner criticism the determination of events, still he did not consider this determination to be independent of the way in which historians apprehended interconnections. On the contrary, he taught explicitly that the determination of events and the apprehension of their interconnections are interdependent and inseparable. He even added that, without an objective apprehension of interconnections, one cannot even ascertain in proper fashion the sources relevant to one's inquiry.[12]

Still further removed from Droysen's position is the *Introduction aux études historiques* composed by C. Langlois and C. Seignobos and published in Paris in 1898.[13] This manual is divided into three parts or books. Book I deals with preliminary studies. Book II deals with analytical operations. Book III deals with synthetic operations. The analytical operations divide into external and internal criticism. External criticism yields critical editions of texts, ascertains their authors, and classifies historical sources. Internal criticism proceeds by the analogies of general psychology to reproduce the successive mental states of the document's author. It determines (1) what he meant, (2) whether he believed what he said, and (3) whether his belief was justified.

This last step was considered to bring the document to the point where it resembled the data of the "objective" sciences. Thereby it became the equivalent of an observation, and it was to be utilized in the same manner as were the observations of natural scientists.[14] But in the natural sciences facts are asserted,

---

[9] Ibid., p. 300.   [10] Ibid., p. 429.

[11] Ibid., p. 522.   [12] Ibid., p. 701.

[13] My reference will be to the English translation by G. G. Berry (New York: Henry Holt, 1925).

[14] Langlois and Seignobos, *Introduction*, p. 67.

not as the result of single observations, but only when corroborated by several independent observations. So far from being exempt from this principle, history with its imperfect sources of information must be subjected to it all the more rigorously. There followed the necessity of independent and mutually supporting testimonies for the determination of historical facts.[15]

The implications of such analysis were not overlooked. For it removed the facts from their original context, isolated them from one another, reduced them, as it were, to a powder.[16] Accordingly the analytical operations of Book II had to be complemented by the synthetic operations of Book III. These were described under such rubrics as classifying, question and answer, analogy, grouping, inference, working out general formulae. But all of these risked numerous aberrations, against which warnings were sounded continuously. Indeed, so many were the pitfalls that M. Langlois himself in later life, instead of writing history, was content to reproduce selected documents.[17]

With Langlois and Seignobos, then, there emerges a clear-cut distinction and separation between the determination of historical facts and the determination of their interconnections. This distinction and separation has its ground, it would seem, in notions of natural science current in nineteenth-century positivist and empiricist circles.[18] But in those very circles there were bound to arise the further question. Why add to the facts? Must not any addition that is not obvious to everyone be merely subjective? Why not let the facts speak for themselves?

2. DATA AND FACTS

At this point it may be well to insert a clarification, for data are one thing, and facts are another.

There are the data of sense and the data of consciousness.

---

[15] Ibid., p. 195 f.   [16] Ibid., pp. 211 and 214.

[17] H. I. Marrou, *The Meaning of History*, Baltimore-Dublin: Helicon, 1966, p. 17.

[18] On this movement see Bernheim, *Lehrbuch*, pp. 648–667; Stern, *Varieties*, pp. 16, 20, 120–137, 209–223, 314–328; P. Gardiner, *Theories of History*, New York: Free Press, 1959, excerpts from Buckle, Mill, Comte; B. Mazlish, *The Riddle of History*, New York: Harper & Row, 1966, chapter on Comte.

Common to both is that they are or may be given. They may or may not be attended to, investigated, understood, conceived, invoked as evidence in judgment. If they are not, then they are merely given. But in so far as they are investigated then they are not merely given but also are entering into combination with other components in human cognitional activity.

In contrast, historical facts are known events. The events that are known pertain to the historian's past. The knowledge of the events is in the historian's present. Moreover, this knowledge is human knowledge. It is not some single activity but a compound of activities that occur on three different levels. So a historical fact will have the concreteness of an object of external or internal experience. It will have the precision of an object of understanding and conception. It will have the stubbornness of what has been grasped as (approximating the) virtually unconditioned and so as something (probably) independent of the knowing subject.[19]

Now as an investigation proceeds, insights accumulate and oversights diminish. This ongoing process, while it does not affect data inasmuch as they are or may be given, does affect enormously data inasmuch as they are sought out, attended to, combined now this way and now that in ever larger and more complex structures. On the other hand, it is only as the structures take definite shape, as the process of asking further questions begins to dry up, that there commence to emerge the facts. For the facts emerge, not before the data are understood, but only after they have been understood satisfactorily and thoroughly.

There is a further complication in critical history, for there, there occur two distinct, though interdependent, processes from data to facts. In a first process, the data are here and now perceptible monuments, remains, accounts; from them one endeavors to ascertain the genesis and evaluate the reliability of the information they convey; the facts at which the first process terminates are a series of statements obtained from the sources and marked with an index of greater or less reliability. In so far as they are reliable, they yield information about the past. But the information they

<hr/>

[19] On data, see *Insight*, pp. 73 f.; on fact, ibid., pp. 331, 347, 366, 411 ff.

yield is, as a general rule, not historical knowledge but historical experience. It regards the fragments, the bits and pieces, that have caught the attention of diarists, letter-writers, chroniclers, newsmen, commentators. It is not the rounded view of what was going forward at a given time and place for, in general, contemporaries have not at their disposal the means necessary for forming such a rounded view. It follows that the facts ascertained in the critical process are, not historical facts, but just data for the discovery of historical facts. The critical process has to be followed by an interpretative process, in which the historian pieces together the fragments of information that he has gathered and critically evaluated. Only when this interpretative process of reconstruction is terminated do there emerge what may properly be called the historical facts.

3. THREE HISTORIANS

In a celebrated address, read twice before learned societies in 1926 but published only posthumously, Carl Becker recalled that he had been told by an eminent and honored historian that a historian had nothing to do but "present all the facts and let them speak for themselves". He then proceeded to repeat what he had been teaching for twenty years "that this notion is preposterous; first, because it is impossible to present all the facts; and second, because even if you could present all the facts the miserable things wouldn't say anything, would just say nothing at all".[20]

Becker was not content to attack what he considered one of the fondest illusions of the nineteenth-century historians.[21] Sixteen years previously, in an article in the *Atlantic Monthly* for October, 1910, he had described with considerable skill the process that has to occur if the card cases, containing the results of historical criticism, are to lead the historian to an apprehension of the historical course of events.

"As he goes over his cards, some aspects of the reality recorded there interest him more, others less; some are retained, others forgotten; some

[20] Carl Becker, *Detachment and the Writing of History*, Essays and Letters edited by Phil Snyder, Ithaca N.Y.: Cornell, 1958, p. 54.
[21] Ibid., p. 53.

have power to start a new train of thought; some appear to be causally connected; some logically connected; some are without perceptible connection of any sort. And the reason is simple; some facts strike the mind as interesting or suggestive, have a meaning of some sort, lead to some desirable end, because they associate themselves with ideas already in mind; they fit in somehow to the ordered experience of the historian. This original synthesis—not to be confused with the making of a book for the printer, a very different matter—is only half deliberate. It is accomplished almost automatically. The mind *will* select and discriminate from the very beginning. It is the whole 'apperceiving mass' that does the business, seizing upon this or that new impression and building it up into its own growing content. As new facts are taken in, the old ideas and concepts, it is true, are modified, distinguished, destroyed even; but the modified ideas become new centers of attraction. And so the process is continued, for years it may be. The final synthesis is doubtless composed of facts unique, causally connected, revealing unique change; but the unique fact, selected because of its importance, was in every case selected because of its importance for some idea already in possession of the field.[22]

I have quoted this rather long passage because in it a historian reveals the activities that occur subsequently to the tasks of historical criticism and prior to the work of historical composition. It cannot be claimed that Becker was a successful cognitional theorist: there cannot be assembled from his writings an exact and coherent theory of the genesis of historical knowledge.[23] None the less, he was not a man to be taken in by current clichés, and he was sufficiently alert and articulate to have written a happy description of what I would call the gradual accumulation of insights, each complementing or qualifying or correcting those that went before, until—perhaps years later—the stream of further questions has dried up and the historian's information on past historical experience has been promoted to historical knowledge.

The issues that concerned Carl Becker in the United States also concerned R. G. Collingwood in England. Both insisted on the constructive activities of the historian. Both attacked what above I named the principle of the empty head. But the epitome

22 Ibid., pp. 24 f.
23 The point is made by B. T. Wilkins, *Carl Becker*, Cambridge: M.I.T. and Harvard, 1961, pp. 189–209.

of the position Becker attacked was the view that the historian had merely to present all the facts and then let them speak for themselves. Collingwood attacks the same position under the name of "scissors-and-paste history".[24] It is a naive view of history in terms of memory, testimony, credibility.[25] It gathers statements from sources, decides whether they are to be regarded as true or false, pastes true statements in a scrap-book later to be worked up into a narrative, while it consigns false statements to the waste-basket.[26] It was the type of history alone known in the ancient world and in the middle ages.[27] It has been on the wane since the days of Vico. While Collingwood would not venture to say that it has totally disappeared, he does assert that any history written today on such principles is at least a century out of date.[28]

There has been, then, a Copernican revolution[29] in the study of history inasmuch as history has become both critical and constructive.[30] This process is ascribed to the historical imagination[31] and, again, to a logic in which questions are more fundamental than answers.[32] The two ascriptions are far from incompatible. The historian starts out from statements he finds in his sources. The attempt to represent imaginatively their meaning gives rise to questions that lead on to further statements in the sources. Eventually he will have stretched a web of imaginative construction linking together the fixed points supplied by the statements in the sources.[33] However, these so-called fixed points are fixed not absolutely but relatively.[34] In his present inquiry the historian has decided to assume them as fixed. But, in fact, their being fixed is just the fruit of earlier historical inquiry. If the statements from which the historian proceeds are to be found in Thucydides, still it is historical knowledge that enables the historian to go beyond mere odd marks on paper to

[24] R. G. Collingwood, *The Idea of History*, Oxford, Clarendon, 1946, pp. 257–263, 269 f., 274–282.

[25] Ibid., p. 234.   [26] Ibid., p. 259.   [27] Ibid., p. 258.
[28] Ibid., p. 260.   [29] Ibid., pp. 236, 240.   [30] Ibid., p. 240.
[31] Ibid., pp. 241 ff.   [32] Ibid., pp. 269–274.   [33] Ibid., p. 242.
[34] Ibid., p. 243.

a recognition of the Greek alphabet, to meanings in the Attic dialect, to the authenticity of the passages, to the judgment that on these occasions Thucydides knew what he was talking about and was trying to tell the truth.[35]

It follows that, if history is considered not in this or that work but as a totality, then it is an autonomous discipline. It depends upon data, on the remains of the past perceptible in the present. But it is not a matter of believing authorities, and it is not a matter of inferring from authorities. Critical procedures decide in what manner and measure sources will be used.[36] Constructive procedures arrive at results that may not have been known by the authors of the sources. Hence ". . . so far from relying on an authority other than himself, to whose statements his thought must conform, the historian is his own authority and his thought autonomous, self-authorizing, possessed of a criterion to which his so-called authorities must conform and by reference to which they are criticized".[37]

Such is the Copernican revolution Collingwood recognized in modern history. It is a view that cannot be assimilated on naive realist or empiricist premises. As presented by Collingwood, unfortunately it is contained in an idealist context. But by introducing a satisfactory theory of objectivity and of judgment, the idealism can be removed without dropping the substance of what Collingwood taught about the historical imagination, historical evidence, and the logic of question and answer.

Issues raised in the United States and in England also were raised in France. In 1938 Raymond Aron portrayed the historical thought of Dilthey, Rickert, Simmel, and Max Weber[38] and, as well, in another volume set forth his own developments of German *Verstehen* that in French was named *compréhension*.[39] My present concern, however, is not with theorists of history but with professional historians, and so I turn to Henri-Irénée Marrou who

[35] Ibid., p. 244.   [36] Ibid., p. 238.

[37] Ibid., p. 236; see p. 249; also Marrou, *Meaning of History*, pp. 307–310.

[38] R. Aron, *La philosophie critique de l'histoire*, Paris: Vrin, 1950.

[39] R. Aron, *Introduction à la philosophie de l'histoire*, Paris: Gallimard, 1948.

was invited to occupy the *Chaire Cardinal Mercier* at Louvain in 1953, and used this opportunity to discuss the nature of historical knowledge.

The following year there appeared his *De la connaissance historique*.[40] It is concerned, not with theoretical issues, but rather with making a systematic inventory, a reasonable and balanced synopsis, of conclusions that historians had reached on the nature of their task.[41] The nature of that task, he felt, was as well established as had been the theory of experiment in the days of John Stuart Mill and Claude Bernard.[42] So it is that M. Marrou treated all the general issues of historical investigation and did so both with a grasp of theoretical opinions and with all the sensitivity of a Pieter Geyl to the endless complexity of historical reality.[43]

Out of this abundance, for the moment, we are concerned only with the relationship between fact and theory, analysis and synthesis, criticism and construction. M. Marrou treats the two in successive chapters. His views on criticism, he feels, would make his old positivist teachers turn over in their graves. Where they urged a relentlessly critical spirit, he calls for sympathy and understanding.[44] The negative critical approach, concerned with the honesty, competence, and accuracy of authors, was well adapted to specialist work on the political and ecclesiastical history of western Europe in the middle ages, where there was a rash of second-hand chronicles, forged charters and decretals, and antedated lives of saints.[45] But the historian's task is not limited to eliminating errors and deceptions. Documents can be used in a great variety of manners, and the historian's proper task is to

[40] My references are to the English translation, *The Meaning of History*, Baltimore and Dublin: Helicon, 1966.

[41] Marrou, *Meaning of History*, p. 25.

[42] Later Marrou had to confess that agreement was less than he had anticipated. See the appendix to *Meaning of History*, pp. 301–316.

[43] Complexity is a recurrent theme in Pieter Geyls *Debates with Historians*, New York: Meridian Books, 1965.

[44] Marrou, *Meaning of History*, pp. 103 ff.

[45] Ibid., pp. 112 f.

understand his documents thoroughly, grasp exactly what they reveal directly or indirectly, and so use them intelligently.[46]

As M. Marrou calls for a shift from mere criticism of documents to their comprehension, so too he stresses the continuity and interdependence of coming to understand the relevant documents and coming to understand the course of events. The historian begins by determining a topic, assembling a file of relevant documents, annotating each on its credibility. Still this is a merely abstract scheme. One advances in knowledge along a spiral. As knowledge of events increases, new light is thrown on the character of the documents. The original question is recast. Documents, that seemed irrelevant, now acquire relevance. New facts come to light. So the historian gradually comes to master the area under investigation, to acquire confidence in his grasp of the meaning, scope, worth of his documents, and to apprehend the course of events that the documents once concealed and now reveal.[47]

4. VERSTEHEN

Already I have mentioned Droysen's notion of historical investigation as *forschend verstehen*, and Raymond Aron's introduction of German historical reflection into the French milieu. To that reflection we have now to revert, for it was empirical without being empiricist. It was empirical, for it was closely associated with the work of the German historical school, and that school's charter was its protest against Hegel's *a priori* construction of the meaning of history. It was not empiricist, for it was fully aware that historical knowledge was not just a matter of taking a good look, that, on the contrary, it involved some mysterious, divinatory process in which the historian came to understand.

This need for understanding appeared in two manners. First, there was the hermeneutic circle. For instance, one grasps the meaning of a sentence by understanding the words, but one

[46] Ibid., pp. 113 f. Cf. Collingwood, *Idea of History*, pp. 247, 259 f.; Becker, *Detachment*, pp. 46 f.
[47] Marrou, *Meaning of History*, pp. 131 f.

understands the words properly only in the light of the sentence as a whole. Sentences stand in a similar relationship to paragraphs, paragraphs to chapters, chapters to books, books to an author's situation and intentions. Now this cumulative network of reciprocal dependence is not to be mastered by any conceptual set of procedures. What is needed is the self-correcting process of learning, in which preconceptual insights accumulate to complement, qualify, correct one another.

Secondly, the need for understanding appeared again in the irrelevance of the universal or general. The more creative the artist, the more original the thinker, the greater the genius, the less can his achievement be subsumed under universal principles or general rules. If anything, he is the source of new rules and, while the new rules will be followed by others, still they are not followed in exactly the manner of the master. Even lesser lights have their originality, while servile imitation is the work not of mind but of the machine. Now this high degree of individuality found in artists, thinkers, writers, though beyond the reach of general rules or universal principles, is within easy reach of understanding. For what in the first instance is understood is what is given to sense or consciousness or, again, what is represented in images, words, symbols, signs. What is so given or represented is individual. What is grasped by understanding is the intelligibility of the individual. Apart from failures to control properly one's use of language, generalization is a later step and, in works of interpretation, usually a superfluous step. There is only one *Divina commedia*, only one *Hamlet* by Shakespeare, only one two-part *Faust* by Goethe.

The scope of understanding, the range of its significance, was gradually extended. To the grammatical interpretation of texts, Schleiermacher (1768–1834) added a psychological interpretation that aimed at understanding persons, and especially at divining the basic moment in a creative writer's inspiration.[48] August Boeckh (1785–1867) a pupil of F. Wolf's as well as of F. Schleiermacher's, extended the scope of understanding to the whole

---

[48] H. G. Gadamer, *Wahrheit und Methode*, pp. 172–185; R. E. Palmer, *Hermeneutics*, Evanston: Northwestern, 1969, pp. 84–97.

range of the philological sciences. In his *Enzyklopädie und Methodologie der philologischen Wissenschaften* the idea of philology was conceived as the interpretative reconstruction of the constructions of the human spirit.[49] What Boeckh did for philology, Droysen would do for history. He moved the notion of understanding from a context of aesthetics and psychology to the broader context of history by (1) assigning expression as the object of understanding and (2) noting that not only individuals but also such groups as families, peoples, states, religions express themselves.[50]

With Wilhelm Dilthey (1833–1911) there is a further broadening of the horizon. He discovered that the German historical school, while it appealed to historical fact against *a priori* idealist construction, none the less in its actual procedures was far closer to idealist than to empiricist ideas and norms.[51] With remarkable astuteness he recognized that the success of the historical school, like the earlier success of natural science, constituted a new datum for cognitional theory. On that new datum he proposed to build. Just as Kant had asked how *a priori* universal principles were possible, Dilthey set himself the question of the possibility of historical knowledge and, more generally, of the human sciences conceived as *Geisteswissenschaften*.[52]

Dilthey's basic step may be conceived as a transposition of Hegelian thought from idealist *Geist* to human *Leben*. Hegel's objective spirit returns, but now it is just the integral of the objectification effected in concrete human living. Living expresses itself. In the expression there is present the expressed. So the data of human studies are not just given; by themselves, prior to any interpretation, they are expressions, manifestations, objectifications of human living. Further, when they are understood by an interpreter, there also is understood the living that is expressed, manifested, objectified.[53] Finally, just as an interpretation

---

[49] Hünerman, *Durchbruch*, p. 64; pp. 63–69 outline Boeckk's thought.
[50] Ibid., pp. 106 ff.; Gadamer, *Wahrheit*, pp. 199–205.
[51] Gadamer, *Wahrheit*, p. 205.
[52] Ibid., p. 52; Palmer, *Hermeneutics*, pp. 100 ff.
[53] Gadamer, *Wahrheit*, pp. 211, 214.

expresses and communicates an interpreter's understanding, so too the objectifications of living are living's own interpretation of itself. *Das Leben selbst legt sich aus.*[54]

In the concrete physical, chemical, vital reality of human living, then, there also is meaning. It is at once inward and outward, inward as expressing, outward as expressed. It manifests need and satisfaction. It responds to values. It intends goals. It orders means to ends. It constitutes social systems and endows them with cultural significance. It transforms environing nature.

The many expressions of individual living are linked together by an intelligible web. To reach that intelligible connectedness is not just a matter of assembling all the expressions of a lifetime. Rather, there is a developing whole that is present in the parts, articulating under each new set of circumstances the values it prizes and the goals it pursues, and thereby achieving its own individuality and distinctiveness. Just as human consciousness is not confined to the moment but rises on cumulative memories and proceeds in accord with preference schedules towards its hierarchy of goals, so too its expressions not only together but even singly have the capacity to reveal the direction and momentum of a life.[55]

As there is intelligibility in the life of the individual, so too is there intelligibility in the common meanings, common values, common purposes, common and complementary activities of groups. As these can be common or complementary, so too they can differ, be opposed, conflict. Therewith, in principle, the possibility of historical understanding is reached. For if we can understand singly our own lives and the lives of others, so too we can understand them in their interconnections and interdependence.[56]

Moreover, just as the historian can narrate an intelligible course of events, so too human scientists can proceed to the analysis of

[54] Ibid., p. 213; Palmer, pp. 103–114.

[55] Gadamer, *Wahrheit*, pp. 212 f.

[56] Wilhelm Dilthey, *Pattern and Meaning in History*, edited and introduced by H. P. Rickman, New York: Harper & Row, 1962; London: Allen & Unwin, 1961. Chapters Five and Six.

recurring or developing structures and processes in individual and group living. So far from being opposed, history and the human sciences will be interdependent. The human scientist will have to view his data within their appropriate historical context; and the historian can fully master his materials only if he also masters the relevant human sciences.[57]

It can be said, I think, that Dilthey did much to meet his specific problem. Decisively he drew the distinction between natural science and human studies. Clearly he conceived the possibility of historical knowledge that conformed neither to the *a priori* constructions of idealism nor to the procedures of natural science. However, he did not resolve the more basic problem of getting beyond both empiricist and idealist suppositions. His *Lebensphilosophie* has empiricist leanings. His history and human science based on *Verstehen* cannot be assimilated by an empiricist.[58]

Two advances on Dilthey's position have since developed and may be treated briefly. First, Edmund Husserl (1859–1938) by his painstaking analysis of intentionality made it evident that human thinking and judging are not just psychological events but always and intrinsically intend, refer to, mean objects distinct from themselves.[59] Secondly, where Dilthey conceived expression as manifestation of life, Martin Heidegger (1889–   ) conceives all human projects to be products of understanding; in this fashion *Verstehen* is *Dasein* in so far as the latter is man's ability to be.[60] There follows the universality of hermeneutic structure: just as interpretation proceeds from the understanding of an expression, so this expression itself proceeds from an understanding of what it can be to be a man.

A few comments are now in order. First, our use of the terms, insights, understanding, both is more precise and has a broader range than the connotation and denotation of *Verstehen*. Insight occurs in all human knowledge, in mathematics, natural science,

[57] Ibid., p. 123.
[58] Gadamer, *Wahrheit*, pp. 218–228.
[59] Ibid., p. 230 f.
[60] Gadamer, *Wahrheit*, p. 245.

common sense, philosophy, human science, history, theology. It occurs (1) in response to inquiry, (2) with respect to sensible presentations or representations including words and symbols of all kinds. It consists in a grasp of intelligible unity or relation in the data or image or symbol. It is the active ground whence proceed conception, definition, hypothesis, theory, system. This proceeding, which is not merely intelligible but intelligent, provided the human model for Thomist and Augustinian trinitarian theory.[61] Finally, the simple and clear-cut proof of the preconceptual character of insight is had from the modern reformulation of Euclidean geometry.[62] Euclid's *Elements* depends on insights that were not acknowledged in his definitions, axioms, and postulates, that easily occur, that ground the validity of his conclusions, that cannot be expressed in a strictly Euclidean vocabulary.[63]

Secondly, experience and understanding taken together yield not knowledge but only thought. To advance from thinking to knowing there must be added a reflective grasp of the virtually unconditioned and its rational consequent, judgment. There is an insufficient awareness of this third level of cognitional activity in the authors we have been mentioning and a resultant failure to break away cleanly and coherently from both empiricism and idealism.

Thirdly, over and above a clear-headed grasp of cognitional fact, the break from both empiricism and idealism involves the elimination of cognitional myth. There are notions of knowledge and of reality that are formed in childhood, that are in terms of

---

[61] This is the thesis in my *Verbum: Word and Idea in Aquinas*, London: Darton, Longman & Todd, and Notre Dame: University Press, 1967.

[62] See, for example, H. G. Forder, *The Foundations of Euclidean Geometry*, Cambridge: Cambridge University Press, 1927.

[63] For example, Euclid solves the problem of constructing an equilateral triangle by drawing two circles that intersect; but there is no Euclidean proof that the circles must intersect. Again, he proves the theorem that the exterior angle of a triangle is greater than the interior opposite angle by constructing within the exterior angle an angle equal to the interior opposite; but there is no Euclidean proof that this constructed angle must lie within the exterior angle. However, the *must* can be grasped by an insight that has no Euclidean formulation.

seeing and of what's there to be seen, that down the centuries have provided the unshakable foundations of materialism, empiricism, positivism, sensism, phenomenalism, behaviorism, pragmatism, and that at the same time constitute the notions of knowledge and reality that idealists know to be nonsense.

5. PERSPECTIVISM

In 1932 Karl Heussi published a small book with the title, *Die Krisis des Historismus*. The first twenty-one pages reviewed the various meanings of the term, *Historismus*. Out of many candidates Heussi selected, as the *Historismus* undergoing a crisis, the views on history current among historians about the year 1900. These views involved four main elements: (1) a determinate but simple-minded stand on the nature of objectivity; (2) the interconnectedness of all historical objects; (3) a universal process of development; and (4) the confinement of historical concern to the world of experience.[64]

Of these four elements, it was the first that occasioned the crisis.[65] Around 1900, historians, while they emphasized the danger of subjective bias, assumed that the object of history was stably given and unequivocally structured. Men's opinions about the past may keep changing but the past itself remains what it was. In contrast, Heussi himself held that the structures were only in the minds of men, that similar structures were reached when investigations proceeded from the same standpoint, that historical reality, so far from being unequivocally structured, was rather an inexhaustible incentive to ever fresh historical interpretations.[66]

While this statement has idealist implications, at least Heussi did not wish it to be interpreted too strictly. He immediately added that there are many constants in human living, and that unequivocally determined structures are not rare. What is problematic is the insertion of these constants and structures into larger wholes. The fewer and the narrower the contexts to which a person, a group, a movement belongs, the less the likelihood

---

[64] Karl Heussi, *Die Krisis des Historismus*, Tübingen, 1932, p. 20.
[65] Ibid., pp. 37, 103.   [66] Ibid., p. 56.

that subsequent developments will involve a revision of earlier history.[67] On the other hand, where different world-views and values are involved, one can expect agreement on single incidents and single complexes, but disagreement on larger issues and broader interconnections.[68]

There is, however, a more fundamental qualification to be added. Heussi's basic point is that historical reality is far too complicated for an exhaustively complete description ever to occur. No one is ever going to relate everything that happened at the battle of Leipzig from October 16–19, 1813. Inevitably the historian selects what he thinks of moment and omits what he considers unimportant. This selection to some extent goes forward spontaneously in virtue of some mysterious capacity that can determine what is to be expected, that groups and constructs, that possesses the tact needed to evaluate and refine, that proceeds as though in one's mind there were some governing and controlling law of perspective so that, granted the historian's standpoint, his milieu, his presuppositions, his training, there must result just the structures and the emphases and the selection that do result. Finally, this result cannot be described as a mere rehandling of old materials; it is something new. It does not correspond to the inexhaustible complexity of historical reality. But by selecting what from a given standpoint is significant or important, it does purport to mean and portray historical reality in some incomplete and approximate fashion.[69]

It is this incomplete and approximate character of historical narrative that explains why history is rewritten for each new generation. Historical experience is promoted to historical knowledge only if the historian is asking questions. Questions can be asked only by introducing linguistic categories. Such

---

[67] Ibid., pp. 57 f.   [68] Ibid., p. 58.

[69] Ibid., p. 47 f. The passage is an excellent description of accumulating insights, though Heussi himself is of the opinion (op. cit., p. 60) that *Verstehen* regards only the larger constructive steps and not the basic constitution of historical knowledge. On selection in history see Marrou, *Meaning of History*, p. 200; also Charlotte W. Smith, *Carl Becker: On History and the Climate of Opinion*, Ithaca, N.Y.: Cornell University Press, 1956, pp. 125–130.

categories carry with them their host of presuppositions and implications. They are colored by a retinue of concerns, interests, tastes, feelings, suggestions, evocations. Inevitably the historian operates under the influence of his language, his education, his milieu, and these with the passage of time inevitably change[70] to give rise to a demand for and supply of rewritten history. So excellent historical works, composed in the final decades of the nineteenth century, had lost all appeal by the nineteen-thirties, even among readers that happened to be in full agreement with the religious, theological, political, and social views of the older authors.[71]

The reason why the historian cannot escape his time and place is that the development of historical understanding does not admit systematic objectification. Mathematicians submit to the rigor of formalization to be certain that they are not using unacknowledged insights. Scientists define their terms systematically, formulate their hypotheses precisely, work out rigorously the suppositions and implications of the hypotheses, and carry out elaborate programs of observational or experimental verification. Philosophers can have resort to transcendental method. But the historian finds his way in the complexity of historical reality by the same type and mode of developing understanding, as the rest of us employ in day-to-day living. The starting-point is not some set of postulates or some generally accepted theory but all that the historian already knows and believes. The more intelligent and the more cultivated he is, the broader his experience, the more open he is to all human values, the more competent and rigorous his training, the greater is his capacity to discover the past.[72] When an investigation is succeeding, his insights are so numerous, their coalescence so spontaneous, the manner in which they complement or qualify or correct one another is so immediate and so deft, that the historian can objectify, not every twist and turn in the genesis of his discovery, but only the broad lines of the picture at which eventually he arrives.[73]

[70] Heussi, *Krisis*, pp. 52–56.   [71] Ibid., p. 71.
[72] Marrou, *Meaning of History*, p. 247.
[73] Ibid., pp. 292 f.; cf. Smith, *Carl Becker*, pp. 128, 130.

In saying that the historian cannot escape his background, I am not suggesting that he cannot overcome individual, group, or general bias,[74] or that he cannot undergo intellectual, moral, or religious conversion. Again, I am not retracting in any way what previously I said about the "ecstatic" character of developing historical insight, about the historian's ability to move out of the viewpoint of his place and time and come to understand and appreciate the mentality and the values of another place and time. Finally, I am not implying that historians with different backgrounds cannot come to understand one another and so move on from diverging to converging views on the past.[75]

The point I have been endeavoring to make is what is called perspectivism. Where relativism has lost hope about the attainment of truth, perspectivism stresses the complexity of what the historian is writing about and, as well, the specific difference of historical from mathematical, scientific, and philosophic knowledge. It does not lock historians up in their backgrounds, confine them to their biases, deny them access to development and openness. But it does point out that historians with different backgrounds will rid themselves of biases, undergo conversions, come to understand the quite different mentalities of other places and times, and even move towards understanding one another, each in his own distinctive fashion. They may investigate the same area, but they ask different questions. Where the questions are similar, the implicit, defining contexts of suppositions and implications are not identical. Some may take for granted what others labor to prove. Discoveries can be equivalent, yet approached from different sets of previous questions, expressed in different terms, and so leading to different sequences of further questions. Even where results are much the same, still the reports will be written for different readers, and each historian has to devote special attention to what his readers would easily overlook or misesteem.

Such is perspectivism. In a broad sense the term may be used

[74] On bias, see *Insight*, pp. 218–242.
[75] Marrou, *Meaning of History*, p. 235.

to refer to any case in which different historians treat the same matter differently. But its proper meaning is quite specific. It does not refer to differences arising from human fallibility, from mistaken judgments of possibility, probability, fact or value. It does not refer to differences arising from personal inadequacy, from obtuseness, oversights, a lack of skill or thoroughness. It does not refer to history as an ongoing process, to that gradual conquest that discovers ever new ways to make potential evidence into formal and eventually actual evidence.[76]

In its proper and specific meaning, perspectivism results from three factors. First, the historian is finite; his information is incomplete; his understanding does not master all the data within his reach; not all his judgments are certain. Were his information complete, his understanding all-comprehensive, his every judgment certain, then there would be room neither for selection nor for perspectivism. Then historical reality would be known in its fixity and its unequivocal structures.

Secondly, the historian selects. The process of selecting has its main element in a commonsense, spontaneous development of understanding that can be objectified in its results but not in its actual occurrence. In turn, this process is conditioned by the whole earlier process of the historian's development and attainments; and this development is not an object of complete information and complete explanation. In brief, the process of selection is not subject to objectified controls either in itself or in its initial conditions.

Thirdly, we can expect processes of selection and their initial conditions to be variables. For historians are historical beings, immersed in the ongoing process in which situations change and meanings shift and different individuals respond each in his own way.

In brief, the historical process itself and, within it, the personal development of the historian give rise to a series of different standpoints. The different standpoints give rise to different selective processes. The different selective processes give rise to

---

[76] Collingwood, *Idea of History*, p. 247,; Marrou p. 291.

different histories that are (1) not contradictory, (2) not complete information and not complete explanation, but (3) incomplete and approximate portrayals of an enormously complex reality.

Is then history not a science but an art? Collingwood has pointed out three differences between historical narrative and literary fiction. The historical narrative regards events located in space and dated in time; in a novel places and dates may be and largely are fictitious. Secondly, all historical narratives have to be compatible with one another and tend to form a single view. Thirdly, the historical narrative at every step is justified by evidence; the novel either makes no appeal to evidence or, if it does, the appeal normally is part of the fiction.[77]

On the other hand, history differs from natural science, for its object is in part constituted by meaning and value, while the objects of the natural sciences are not. Again, it differs from both the natural and the human sciences, for its results are descriptions and narratives about particular persons, actions, things, while their results aim at being universally valid. Finally, while it can be said that history is a science in the sense that it is guided by a method, that that method yields univocal answers when identical questions are put, and that the results of historical investigations are cumulative, still it has to be acknowledged that these properties of method are not realized in the same manner in history and in the natural and the human sciences.

All discovery is a cumulation of insights. But in the sciences this cumulation is expressed in some well-defined system, while in history it is expressed in a description and narrative about particulars. The scientific system can be checked in endless different manners, but the description and narrative, while it can come under suspicion in various ways, is really checked only by repeating the initial investigation. Scientific advance is constructing a better system, but historical advance is a fuller and more penetrating understanding of more particulars. Finally, the scientist can aim at a full explanation of all phenomena, because his explanations are laws and structures that can cover countless instances; but the historian that aimed at a full explanation of all

[77] Collingwood, *Idea*, p. 246.

METHOD IN THEOLOGY

history would need more information than is available and then
countless explanations.

Let us now revert, for a moment, to the view of history
commonly entertained at the beginning of this century. From
what has just been said it is plain that its error was not precisely
where Karl Heussi placed it. The past is fixed and its intelligible
structures are unequivocal; but the past that is so fixed and
unequivocal is the enormously complex past that historians
know only incompletely and approximately. It is incomplete
and approximate knowledge of the past that gives rise to
perspectivism.

Finally, to affirm perspectivism is once more to reject the
view that the historian has only to narrate all the facts and let
them speak for themselves. It is once more to deplore the scissors-
and-paste conception of history. It is once more to lament with
M. Marrou the havoc wrought by positivist theories of "scientific"
history.[78] But it also adds a new moment. It reveals that history
speaks not only of the past but also of the present. Historians go
out of fashion only to be rediscovered. The rediscovery finds
them, if anything, more out of date than ever. But the significance
of the rediscovery lies, not in the past that the historian wrote
about, but in the historian's own self-revelation. Now his account
is prized because it incarnates so much of its author's humanity,
because it offers a first-rate witness on the historian, his milieu,
his times.[79]

6. HORIZONS

Sir Lewis Namier has described a historical sense as "an
intuitive understanding of how things do not happen".[80] He
was referring, of course, to the case in which such intuitive
understanding is the fruit of historical study, but our present
concern with horizons directs our attention to the prior understanding that the historian derives not from historical study but
from other sources.

[78] Marrou, *Meaning of History*, pp. 10 f., 23, 54, 138, 161 f., 231.
[79] Ibid., p. 296.   [80] See Stern, *Varieties*, p. 375.

On this matter Carl Becker dwelt in a paper read at Cornell in 1937 and at Princeton in 1938. His topic was Bernheim's rule that a fact can be established by the testimony of at least two independent witnesses not self-deceived. While he went over each term in the rule, his interest centered on the question whether historians considered witnesses to be self-deceived, not because they were known to be excited or emotionally involved or of poor memory, but simply because of the historian's own view on what was possible and what was impossible. His answer was affirmative. When the historian is convinced that an event is impossible, he will always say that the witnesses were self-deceived, whether there were just two or as many as two hundred. In other words, historians have their preconceptions, if not about what must have happened, at least about what could not have happened. Such preconceptions are derived, not from the study of history, but from the climate of opinion in which the historian lives and from which he inadvertently acquires certain fixed convictions about the nature of man and of the world. Once such convictions are established, it is easier for him to believe that any number of witnesses are self-deceived than for him to admit that the impossible has actually occurred.[81]

This open acknowledgment—that historians have preconceived ideas and that these ideas modify their writing of history—is quite in accord, not only with what we have already recounted of Becker's views, but also with what we ourselves have said about horizons and about meaning. Each of us lives in a world mediated by meaning, a world constructed over the years by the sum total of our conscious, intentional activities. Such a world is a matter not merely of details but also of basic options. Once such options are taken and built upon, they have to be maintained, or else one must go back, tear down, reconstruct. So radical a procedure is not easily undertaken; it is not comfortably performed; it is not quickly completed. It can be comparable to major surgery, and most of us grasp the knife gingerly and wield it clumsily.

Now the historian is engaged in extending his world mediated

[81] Smith, *Carl Becker*, pp. 89–90.

by meaning, in enriching it with regard to the human, the past, the particular. His historical questions, in great part, regard matters of detail. But even they can involve questions of principle, issues that set basic options. Can miracles happen? If the historian has constructed his world on the view that miracles are impossible, what is he going to do about witnesses testifying to miracles as matters of fact? Obviously, either he has to go back and reconstruct his world on new lines, or else has to find these witnesses either incompetent or dishonest or self-deceived. Becker was quite right in saying that the latter is the easier course. He was quite right in saying that the number of witnesses is not the issue. The real point is that the witnesses, whether few or many, can exist in that historian's world only if they are pronounced incompetent or dishonest or at least self-deceived.

More than a quarter of a century earlier in his essay on "Detachment and the Writing of History" Becker was fully aware that whatever detachment historians exhibited, they were not detached from the dominant ideas of their own age.[82] They knew quite well that no amount of testimony can establish about the past what is not found in the present.[83] Hume's argument did not really prove that no miracles had ever occurred. Its real thrust was that the historian cannot deal intelligently with the past when the past is permitted to be unintelligible to him.[84] Miracles are excluded because they are contrary to the laws of nature that in his generation are regarded as established; but if scientists come to find a place for them in experience, there will be historians to restore them to history.[85]

What holds for questions of fact, also holds for questions of interpretation. Religion remains in the twentieth century, but it no longer explains medieval asceticism. So monasteries are associated less with the salvation of souls and more with sheltering travelers and reclaiming marsh land. St. Simeon Stylites is not a physical impossibility; he can fit, along with one-eyed monsters and knights-errant, into a child's world; but his motives lie

[82] Becker, *Detachment and the Writing of History*, p. 25.
[83] Ibid., p. 12.   [84] Ibid., p. 13.
[85] Ibid., p. 13 f.

outside current adult experience and so, most conveniently, they are pronounced pathological.[86]

Becker's contention that historians operate in the light of preconceived ideas implies a rejection of the Enlightenment and Romantic ideal of presuppositionless history.[87] That ideal, of course, has the advantage of excluding from the start all the errors that the historian has picked up from his parents and teachers and, as well, all that he has generated by his own lack of attention, his obtuseness, his poor judgments. But the fact remains that, while mathematicians, scientists, and philosophers all operate on presuppositions that they can explicitly acknowledge, the historian operates in the light of his whole personal development, and that development does not admit complete and explicit formulation and acknowledgment.[88] To say that the historian should operate without presuppositions is to assert the principle of the empty head, to urge that the historian should be uneducated, to claim that he should be exempted from the process variously named socialization and acculturation,[89] to strip him of historicity. For the historian's presuppositions are not just his but also the living on in him of developments that human society and culture have slowly accumulated over the centuries.[90]

It was Newman who remarked, apropos of Descartes' methodic doubt, that it would be better to believe everything than to doubt everything. For universal doubt leaves one with no basis for advance, while universal belief may contain some truth that in time may gradually drive out the errors. In somewhat similar vein, I think, we must be content to allow historians to be educated, socialized, acculturated, historical beings, even though this will involve them in some error. We must allow them to write their histories in the light of all they happen to know or

[86] Ibid., p. 22 f.
[87] Cf. Gadamer, *Wahrheit*, pp. 256 ff.
[88] See *Insight*, p. 175.
[89] See P. Berger and T. Luckmann, *The Social Construction of Reality*, Garden City, N.Y.: Doubleday, 1966.
[90] Gadamer, *Wahrheit*, p. 261.

think they know and of all they inadvertently take for granted: they cannot do otherwise and a pluralist society lets them do what they can. But we need not proclaim that they are writing presuppositionless history, when that is something no one can do. We have to recognize that the admission of history written in the light of preconceived ideas may result in different notions of history, different methods of historical investigation, incompatible standpoints, and irreconcilable histories.[91] Finally, we have to seek methods that will help historians from the start to avoid incoherent assumptions and procedures, and we have to develop further methods that will serve to iron out differences once incompatible histories have been written.

But the mere acknowledgment of these needs is all that can be achieved in the present section. To meet them pertains, not to the functional specialty, history, but to the later specialties, dialectic and foundations. For any notable change of horizon is done, not on the basis of that horizon, but by envisaging a quite different and, at first sight, incomprehensible alternative and then undergoing a conversion.

7. HEURISTIC STRUCTURES

Has the historian philosophic commitments? Does he employ analogies, use ideal types, follow some theory of history? Does he explain, investigate causes, determine laws? Is he devoted to social and cultural goals, subject to bias, detached from bias? Is history value-free, or is it concerned with values? Do historians know or do they believe?

Such questions are asked. They not merely regard the historian's notion of history but also have a bearing on his practice of historical investigation and historical writing. Different answers, accordingly, would modify this or that heuristic structure,[92] that is, this or that element in historical method.

First, then, the historian need not concern himself at all with

[91] In contrast, perspectivism (as we understand the term) accounts for different but not for incompatible histories.

[92] On heuristic structures, see *Insight*, Index s.v. Heuristic. Note that heuristic has the same root as Eureka.

philosophy in a common but excessively general sense that denotes the contents of all books and courses purporting to be philosophic. Through that labyrinth there is no reason why a historian should try to find his way.

There is, however, a very real connection between the historian and philosophy, when "philosophy" is understood in an extremely restricted sense, namely, the set of real conditions of the possibility of historical inquiry. Those real conditions are the human race, remains and traces from its past, the community of historians with their traditions and instruments, their conscious and intentional operations especially in so far as they occur in historical investigation. It is to be noted that the relevant conditions are conditions of possibility and not the far larger and quite determinate set that in each instance condition historical investigation.

In brief, then, history is related to philosophy, as historical method is related to transcendental method or, again, as theological method is related to transcendental method. The historian may or may not know of this relationship. If he does, that is all to the good. If he does not, then, he still can be an excellent historian, just as M. Jourdain might speak excellent French without knowing that his talk was prose. But while he can be an excellent historian, it is not likely that he will be able to speak about the proper procedures in historical investigation without falling into the traps that in this chapter we have been illustrating.

Secondly, it is plain that the historian has to employ something like analogy when he proceeds from the present to the past. The trouble is that the term covers quite different procedures from the extremely reliable to the fallacious. Distinctions accordingly must be drawn.

In general, the present and the past are said to be analogous when they are partly similar and partly dissimilar. Again, in general, the past is to be assumed similar to the present, except in so far as there is evidence of dissimilarity. Finally, in so far as evidence is produced for dissimilarity, the historian is talking history; but in so far as he asserts that there must be similarity or that there cannot be dissimilarity, then he is drawing upon the climate of opinion in which he lives or else he is representing some philosophic position.

Next, it is not to be assumed that the present is known completely and in its entirety. On the contrary, we have been arguing all along that the rounded view of a historical period is to be expected not from contemporaries but from historians. Moreover, while the historian has to construct his analogies in the first instance by drawing on his knowledge of the present, still he can learn history in this fashion and then construct further history on the analogy of the known past.

Further, nature is uniform, but social arrangements and cultural interpretations are subject to change. There exist at the present time extremely different societies and cultures. There is available evidence for still more differences to be brought to light by historical methods. One hears at times that the past has to conform to present experience, but on that opinion Collingwood commented quite tartly. The ancient Greeks and Romans controlled the size of their populations by exposing new-born infants. The fact is not rendered doubtful because it lies outside current experience of the contributors to the *Cambridge Ancient History*.[93]

Again, while the possibility and the occurrence of miracles are topics, not for the methodologist, but for the theologian, I may remark that the uniformity of nature is conceived differently at different times. In the nineteenth century natural laws were thought to express necessity, and Laplace's view on the possibility in theory of deducing the whole course of events from some given stage of the process was taken seriously. Now laws of the classical type are considered not necessary but just verified possibilities; they are generalized on the principle that similars are similarly understood; they are a basis for prediction or deduction, not by themselves, but only when combined into schemes of recurrence; such schemes function concretely, not absolutely, but only if other things are equal; and whether other things are equal, is a matter of statistical frequencies.[94] Evidently the scientific case concerning miracles has weakened.

[93] Collingwood, *Idea of History*, p. 240.

[94] For this notion of science, see *Insight*, Chapters Two, Three, and Four.

Finally, while each historian has to work on the analogy of what he knows of the present and has learnt of the past, still the dialectical confrontation of contradictory histories needs a basis that is generally accessible. The basis we would offer would be transcendental method extended into the methods of theology and history by constructs derived from transcendental method itself. In other words, it would be the sort of thing we have been working out in these chapters. No doubt, those with different philosophic positions would propose alternatives. But such alternatives would only serve to clarify further the dialectic of diverging research, interpretation, and history.

Thirdly, do historians use ideal-types? I may note at once that the notion and use of the ideal-type commonly are associated with the name of the German sociologist, Max Weber, but they have been discussed in a strictly historical context, among others, by M. Marrou.

The ideal-type, then, is not a description of reality or a hypothesis about reality. It is a theoretical construct in which possible events are intelligibly related to constitute an internally coherent system. Its utility is both heuristic and expository, that is, it can be useful inasmuch as it suggests and helps formulate hypotheses and, again, when a concrete situation approximates to the theoretical construct, it can guide an analysis of the situation and promote a clear understanding of it.[95]

M. Marrou took Fustel de Coulanges' *La cité antique* as an ideal-type. The city state is conceived as a confederation of the great patriarchal families, assembled in phratries and then in tribes, consolidated by cults regarding ancestors or heroes and practised around a common center. Now such a structure is based, not by selecting what is common to all instances of the ancient city, not by taking what is common to most instances, but by concentrating on the most favorable instances, namely, those offering more intelligibility and explanatory power. The use of such an ideal-type is twofold. In so far as the historical situation satisfies the conditions of the ideal-type, the situation is illuminated. In

[95] Max Weber, *The Methodology of the Social Sciences*, New York: Free Press, 1949, pp. 89 ff.

so far as the historical situation does not satisfy the conditions of the ideal-type, it brings to light precise differences that otherwise would go unnoticed, and it sets questions that otherwise might not be asked.[96]

M. Marrou approves the use of ideal-types in historical investigation, but he issues two warnings. First, they are just theoretical constructs: one must resist the temptation of the enthusiast that mistakes them for descriptions of reality; even when they do hit off main features of a historical reality, one must not easily be content with them, gloss over inadequacies, reduce history to what essentially is an abstract scheme. Secondly, there is the difficulty of working out appropriate ideal-types: the richer and the more illuminating the construct, the greater the difficulty of applying it; the thinner and looser the construct, the less is it able to contribute much to history.[97]

Finally, I would like to suggest that Arnold Toynbee's *Study of History* might be regarded as a source-book of ideal-types. Toynbee himself has granted that his work was not quite as empirical as he once thought it. At the same time so resolute a critic as Pieter Geyl[98] has found the work immensely stimulating and has confessed that such daring and imaginative spirits as Toynbee have an essential function to fulfil.[99] That function is, I suggest, to provide the materials from which carefully formulated ideal-types might be derived.

Fourthly, does the historian follow some theory of history? By a theory of history I do not mean the application to history of a theory established scientifically, philosophically, or theologically. Such theories have their proper mode of validation; they are to be judged on their own merits; they broaden the historian's knowledge and make his apprehensions more precise; they do not constitute historical knowledge but facilitate its development.

By a theory of history I understand a theory that goes beyond

96 Marrou, *Meaning of History*, pp. 167 ff.
97 Ibid., pp. 170 ff.
98 See his criticisms in his *Debates with Historians*.
99 P. Gardiner, *Theories of History*, p. 319.

its scientific, philosophic, or theological basis to make statements about the actual course of human events. Such theories are set forth, for instance, by Bruce Mazlish in his discussion of the great speculators from Vico to Freud.[100] They have to be criticized in the light of their scientific, philosophic, or theological basis. In so far as they survive such criticism, they possess the utility of grand-scale ideal-types,[101] and may be employed under the precautions already indicated for the use of ideal-types. But they never grasp the full complexity of historical reality, and consequently they tend to throw in high relief certain aspects and connections and to disregard others that may be of equal or greater importance. In M. Marrou's phrase ". . . the most ingenious hypothesis . . . underlines in red pencil certain lines lost in a diagram whose thousand curves cross one another in every direction."[102] General hypotheses, though they have their uses, easily become ". . . big anti-comprehension machines."[103]

Fifthly, does the historian explain? On the German distinction between *erklären* and *verstehen*, natural scientists explain but historians only understand. However, this distinction is somewhat artificial. Both scientists and historians understand; both communicate the intelligibility that they grasp. The difference lies in the kind of intelligibility grasped and in the manner in which it develops. Scientific intelligibility aims at being an internally coherent system or structure valid in any of a specified set or series of instances. It is expressed in a technical vocabulary, constantly tested by confronting its every implication with data, and adjusted or superseded when it fails to meet the tests. In contrast, historical intelligibility is like the intelligibility reached by common sense. It is the content of a habitual accumulation of insights that, by themselves, are incomplete; they are never applied in any situation without the pause that grasps how relevant they are and, if need be, adds a few more insights derived from the situation in hand. Such commonsense understanding is like a many purpose adjustable tool, where the number of

[100] In his *The Riddle of History*, New York: Harper & Row, 1966.
[101] See B. Mazlish, op. cit., p. 447.
[102] Marrou, *Meaning of History*, p. 200.　　　[103] Ibid. p. 201.

purposes is enormous, and the adjustment is based on the precise task in hand. Hence, common sense thinks and speaks, proposes and acts, with respect, not to the general, but to the particular and concrete. Its generalities are not principles, relevant to every possible instance, but proverbs saying what may be useful to bear in mind, and commonly rounded out by a contradictory piece of advice. Look before you leap! He who hesitates is lost![104]

Historical explanation is a sophisticated extension of common-sense understanding. Its aim is an intelligent reconstruction of the past, not in its routines, but in each of its departures from the previous routine, in the interlocked consequences of each departure, in the unfolding of a process that theoretically might but in all probability never will be repeated.

Sixthly, does the historian investigate causes and determine laws? The historian does not determine laws, for the determination of laws is the work of the natural or human scientist. Again, the historian does not investigate causes, where "cause" is taken in a technical sense developed through the advance of the sciences. However, if "cause" is understood in the ordinary language meaning of "because", then the historian does investigate causes; for ordinary language is just the language of common sense, and historical explanation is the expression of the common-sense type of developing understanding. Finally, the problems concerning historical explanation that currently are discussed seem to arise from a failure to grasp the differences between scientific and commonsense developments of human intelligence.[105]

Seventhly, is the historian devoted to social and cultural goals, is he subject to bias, is he detached from bias?

The historian may well be devoted to social and cultural goals, but in so far as he is practising the functional specialty, history, his devotion is not proximate but remote. His immediate purpose is to settle what was going forward in the past. If he does his job properly, he will supply the materials which may be

[104] See *Insight*, pp. 173–181.
[105] Mathematical and scientific growth in insight is treated in *Insight*, Chapters One to Five; commonsense growth in Chapters Six and Seven.

employed for promoting social and cultural goals. But he is not likely to do his job properly, if in performing his tasks he is influenced not only by their immanent exigences but also by ulterior motives and purposes.

Accordingly, we are setting up a distinction, parallel in some fashion to Max Weber's distinction between social science and social policy.[106] Social science is an empirical discipline organizing the evidence on group behavior. It has to be pursued in the first instance for its own sake. Only when it has reached its proper term, can it usefully be employed in the construction of effective policies for the attainment of social ends. In somewhat similar fashion our two phases of theology keep apart our encounter with the religious past and, on the other hand, our action in the present on the future.

Next, all men are subject to bias, for a bias is a block or distortion of intellectual development, and such blocks or distortions occur in four principal manners. There is the bias of unconscious motivation brought to light by depth psychology. There is the bias of individual egoism, and the more powerful and blinder bias of group egoism. Finally, there is the general bias of common sense, which is a specialization of intelligence in the particular and concrete, but usually considers itself omnicompetent. On all of these I have expanded elsewhere, and I may not repeat myself here.[107]

Further, the historian should be detached from all bias. Indeed, he has greater need of such detachment than the scientist, for scientific work is adequately objectified and publicly controlled, but the historian's discoveries accumulate in the manner of the development of common sense, and the only adequate positive control is to have another historian go over the same evidence.

Just how one conceives the achievement of such detachment depends on one's theory of knowledge and of morals. Our formula is a continuous and ever more exacting application of the transcendental precepts. Be attentive, Be intelligent, Be reasonable, Be responsible. However, nineteenth-century

[106] Max Weber, *Methodology of the Social Sciences*, pp. 51 ff.
[107] *Insight*, pp. 191–206; pp. 218–244.

empiricists conceived objectivity as a matter of seeing all that's there to be seen and seeing nothing that's not there. Accordingly, they demanded of the historian a pure receptivity that admitted impressions from phenomena but excluded any subjective activity. This is the view that Becker was attacking in his "Detachment and the Writing of History" and again in his "What are Historical Facts?"[108] Later in life, when he had seen relativism at work in its crudest forms, he attacked it and insisted on the pursuit of truth as the primary value.[109] But, as I have noted already, Becker did not work out a complete theory.

Eighthly, is history value-free? History, as a functional specialty, is value-free in the sense already outlined: it is not directly concerned to promote social and cultural goals. It pertains to the first phase of theology which aims at an encounter with the past; the more adequate that encounter, the more fruitful it can prove to be; but one is not pursuing a specialty, when one attempts to do it and something quite different at the same time. Further, social and cultural goals are incarnated values; they are subject to the distortions of bias; and so concern for social and cultural goals can exercise not only a disturbing but even a distorting influence on historical investigation.

Further, history is value-free in the further sense that it is a functional specialty that aims at settling matters of fact by appealing to empirical evidence. Now value-judgments neither settle matters of fact nor constitute empirical evidence. In that respect, then, history once more is value-free.

Finally, history is not value-free in the sense that the historian refrains from all value-judgments. For the functional specialties, while they concentrate on the end proper to one of the four levels of conscious and intentional activity, none the less are the achievement of operations on all four levels. The historian ascertains matters of fact, not by ignoring data, by failing to understand, by omitting judgments of value, but by doing all of these for the purpose of settling matters of fact.[110]

---

[108] Becker, *Detachment*, pp. 3–28; pp. 41–64.

[109] Smith, *Carl Becker*, p. 117.

[110] See Meinecke's essay in Stern, *Varieties*, pp. 267–288.

In fact, the historian's value-judgments are precisely the means that make his work a selection of things that are worth knowing, that, in Meinecke's phrase, enables history to be "the content, the wisdom, and the signposts of our lives."[111] Nor is this influence of value-judgments an intrusion of subjectivity. There are true and there are false value-judgments. The former are objective in the sense that they result from a moral self-transcendence. The latter are subjective in the sense that they represent a failure to effect moral self-transcendence. False value-judgments are an intrusion of subjectivity. True value-judgments are the achievement of a moral objectivity, of an objectivity that, so far from being opposed to the objectivity of true judgments of fact, presupposes them and completes them by adding to mere cognitional self-transcendence a moral self-transcendence.

However, if the historian makes value-judgments, still that is not his specialty. The task of passing judgments on the values and disvalues offered us by the past pertains to the further specialties of dialectic and foundations.

Finally, do historians believe? They do not believe in the sense that critical history is not a compilation of testimonies regarded as credible. But they believe in the sense that they cannot experiment with the past as natural scientists can experiment on natural objects. They believe in the sense that they cannot have before their eyes the realities of which they speak. They believe in the sense that they depend on one another's critically evaluated work and participate in an ongoing collaboration for the advance of knowledge.

8. SCIENCE AND SCHOLARSHIP

I wish to propose a convention. Let the term, science, be reserved for knowledge that is contained in principles and laws and either is verified universally or else is revised. Let the term, scholarship, be employed to denote the learning that consists in a commonsense grasp of the commonsense thought, speech, action of distant places and/or times. Men of letters, linguists,

[111] Ibid., p. 272.

exegetes, historians generally would be named, not scientists, but scholars. It would be understood, however, that a man might be both a scientist and scholar. He might apply contemporary science to an understanding of ancient history, or he might draw on historical knowledge to enrich contemporary theory.

DIALECTIC

DIALECTIC, the fourth of our functional specialties, deals with conflicts. The conflicts may be overt or latent. They may lie in religious sources, in the religious tradition, in the pronouncements of authorities, or in the writings of theologians. They may regard contrary orientations of research, contrary interpretations, contrary histories, contrary styles of evaluation, contrary horizons, contrary doctrines, contrary systems, contrary policies.

Not all opposition is dialectical. There are differences that will be eliminated by uncovering fresh data. There are the differences we have named perspectival, and they merely witness to the complexity of historical reality. But beyond these there are fundamental conflicts stemming from an explicit or implicit cognitional theory, an ethical stance, a religious outlook. They profoundly modify one's mentality. They are to be overcome only through an intellectual, moral, religious conversion. The function of dialectic will be to bring such conflicts to light, and to provide a technique that objectifies subjective differences and promotes conversion.

1. HORIZONS

In its literal sense the word, horizon, denotes the bounding circle, the line at which earth and sky appear to meet. This line is the limit of one's field of vision. As one moves about, it recedes in front and closes in behind so that, for different standpoints, there are different horizons. Moreover, for each different standpoint and horizon, there are different divisions of the totality of visible objects. Beyond the horizon lie the objects that, at least for the moment, cannot be seen. Within the horizon lie the objects that can now be seen.

As our field of vision, so too the scope of our knowledge, and the range of our intersts are bounded. As fields of vision vary with one's standpoint, so too the scope of one's knowledge and the range of one's interests vary with the period in which one lives, one's social background and milieu, one's education and personal development. So there has arisen a metaphorical or perhaps analogous meaning of the word, horizon. In this sense what lies beyond one's horizon is simply outside the range of one's knowledge and interests: one neither knows nor cares. But what lies within one's horizon is in some measure, great or small, an object of interest and of knowledge.

Differences in horizon may be complementary, or genetic, or dialectical. Workers, foremen, supervisors, technicians, engineers, managers, doctors, lawyers, professors have different interests. They live in a sense in different worlds. Each is quite familiar with his own world. But each also knows about the others, and each recognizes the need for the others. So their many horizons in some measure include one another and, for the rest, they complement one another. Singly they are not self-sufficient, and together they represent the motivations and the knowledge needed for the functioning of a communal world. Such horizons are complementary.

Next, horizons may differ genetically. They are related as successive stages in some process of development. Each later stage presupposes earlier stages, partly to include them, and partly to transform them. Precisely because the stages are earlier and later, no two are simultaneous. They are parts, not of a single communal world, but of a single biography or of a single history.

Thirdly, horizons may be opposed dialectically. What in one is found intelligible, in another is unintelligible. What for one is true, for another is false. What for one is good, for another is evil. Each may have some awareness of the other and so each in a manner may include the other. But such inclusion is also negation and rejection. For the other's horizon, at least in part, is attributed to wishful thinking, to an acceptance of myth, to ignorance or fallacy, to blindness or illusion, to backwardness or immaturity, to infidelity, to bad will, to a refusal of God's grace. Such a rejection of the other may be passionate, and then the suggestion that openness is desirable will make one furious. But again rejection may have the firmness of ice without any trace of passion or even any show of feeling, except perhaps a wan smile. Both astrology and genocide are beyond the pale, but the former is ridiculed, the latter is execrated.

Horizons, finally, are the structured resultant of past achievement and, as well, both the condition and the limitation of further development. They are structured. All learning is, not a mere addition to previous learning, but rather an organic growth out of it. So all our intentions, statements, deeds stand within contexts. To such contexts we appeal when we outline the reasons for our goals, when we clarify, amplify, qualify our statements, or when we explain our deeds. Within such contexts must be fitted each new item of knowledge and each new factor in our attitudes. What does not fit, will not be noticed or, if forced on our attention, it will seem irrelevant or unimportant. Horizons then are the sweep of our intersts and of our knowledge; they are the fertile source of further knowledge and care; but they also are the boundaries that limit our capacities for assimilating more than we already have attained.

2. CONVERSIONS AND BREAKDOWNS

Joseph de Finance has drawn a distinction between a horizontal and vertical exercise of freedom. A horizontal exercise is a decision or choice that occurs within an established horizon. A vertical exercise is the set of judgments and decisons by which we move from one horizon to another. Now there may be a sequence of such vertical exercises of freedom, and in each case the new horizon, though notably deeper and broader and richer, none the less is consonant with the old and a development out of its potentialities. But it is also possible that the movement into a new horizon involves an about-face; it comes out of the old by repudiating characteristic features; it begins a new sequence that can keep revealing ever greater depth and breadth and wealth. Such an about-face and new beginning is what is meant by a conversion.

Conversion may be intellectual or moral or religious. While each of the three is connected with the other two, still each is a different type of event and has to be considered in itself before being related to the others.

Intellectual conversion is a radical clarification and, consequently, the elimination of an exceedingly stubborn and misleading myth concerning reality, objectivity, and human knowledge. The myth is that knowing is like looking, that objectivity is seeing what is there to be seen and not seeing what is not there, and that the real is what is out there now to be looked at. Now this myth overlooks the distinction between the world of immediacy, say, the world of the infant and, on the other hand, the world mediated by meaning. The world of immediacy is the sum of what is seen, heard, touched, tasted, smelt, felt. It conforms well enough to the myth's view of reality, objectivity, knowledge. But it is but a tiny fragment of the world mediated by meaning. For the world mediated by meaning is a world known not by the sense experience of an individual but by the external and internal experience of a cultural community, and by the continuously checked and rechecked judgments of the community. Knowing, accordingly, is not just seeing; it is experiencing, understanding, judging, and believing. The criteria of objectivity are not just the criteria of ocular vision; they are the compounded criteria of experiencing, of understanding, of judging, and of believing. The reality known is not just looked at; it is given in experience, organized and extrapolated by understanding, posited by judgment and belief.

The consequences of the myth are various. The naive realist knows the world mediated by meaning but thinks he knows it by looking. The empiricist restricts objective knowledge to sense experience; for him, understanding and conceiving, judging and believing are merely subjective activities. The idealist insists that human knowing always includes understanding as well as sense; but he retains the empiricist's notion of reality, and so he thinks of the world mediated by meaning as not real but ideal. Only the critical realist can acknowledge the facts of human knowing and pronounce the world mediated by meaning to be the real world; and he can do so only inasmuch as he shows that the process of experiencing, understanding, and judging is a process of self-transcendence.

Now we are not discussing a merely technical point in philosophy. Empiricism, idealism, and realism name three totally different horizons with no common identical objects. An idealist never means what an empiricist means, and a realist never means what either of them means. An empiricist may argue that quantum theory cannot be about physical reality; it cannot because it deals only with relations between phenomena. An idealist would concur and add that, of course, the same is true of all science and, indeed, of the whole of human knowing. The critical realist will disagree with both: a verified hypothesis is probably true; and what probably is true refers to what in reality probably is so. To change the illustration, What are historical facts? For the empiricist they are what was out there and was capable of being looked at. For the idealist they are mental constructions carefully based on data recorded in documents. For the critical realist they are events in the world mediated by true acts of meaning. To take a third illustration, What is a myth? There are psychological, anthropological, historical, and philosophic answers to the question. But there also are reductionist answers: myth is a narrative about entities not to be found within an empiricist, an idealist, a historicist, an existentialist horizon.

Enough of illustrations. They can be multiplied indefinitely, for philosophic issues are universal in scope, and some form of naive realism seems to appear utterly unquestionable to very many. As soon as they begin to speak of knowing, of objectivity, of reality, there crops up the assumption that all knowing must be something like looking. To be liberated from that blunder, to discover the self-transcendence proper to the human process of coming to know, is to break often long-ingrained habits of thought and speech. It is to acquire the mastery in one's own house that is to be had only when one knows precisely what one is doing when one is knowing. It is a conversion, a new beginning, a fresh start. It opens the way to ever further clarifications and developments.

Moral conversion changes the criterion of one's decisions and choices from satisfactions to values. As children or minors we are persuaded, cajoled, ordered, compelled to do what is right. As our knowledge of human reality increases, as our responses to human values are strengthened and refined, our mentors more and more leave us to ourselves so that our freedom may exercise its ever advancing thrust toward authenticity. So we move to the existential moment when we discover for ourselves that our choosing affects ourselves no less than the chosen or rejected objects, and that it is up to each of us to decide for himself what he is to make of himself. Then is the time for the exercise of vertical freedom and then moral conversion consists in opting for the truly good, even for value against satisfaction when value and satisfaction conflict. Such conversion, of course, falls far short of moral perfection. Deciding is one thing, doing is another. One has yet to uncover and root out one's individual, group, and general bias.[1] One has to keep developing one's knowledge of human reality and potentiality as they are in the existing situation. One has to keep distinct its elements of progress and its elements of decline. One has to keep scrutinizing one's intentional responses to values and their implicit scales of preference. One has to listen to criticism and to protest. One has to remain ready to learn from others. For moral knowledge is the proper possession only of morally good men and, until one has merited that title, one has still to advance and to learn.

Religious conversion is being grasped by ultimate concern. It is other-worldly falling in love. It is total and permanent self-surrender without conditions, qualifications, reservations. But it is such a surrender, not as an act, but as a dynamic state that is prior to and principle of subsequent acts. It is revealed in retrospect as an under-tow of existential consciousness, as a fated acceptance of a vocation to holiness, as perhaps an increasing

[1] See *Insight*, pp. 218–242.

simplicity and passivity in prayer. It is interpreted differently in the context of different religious traditions. For Christians it is God's love flooding our hearts through the Holy Spirit given to us. It is the gift of grace, and since the days of Augustine, a distinction has been drawn between operative and cooperative grace. Operative grace is the replacement of the heart of stone by a heart of flesh, a replacement beyond the horizon of the heart of stone. Cooperative grace is the heart of flesh becoming effective in good works through human freedom. Operative grace is religious conversion. Cooperative grace is the effectiveness of conversion, the gradual movement towards a full and complete transformation of the whole of one's living and feeling, one's thoughts, words, deeds, and omissions.[2]

As intellectual and moral conversion, so also religious conversion is a modality of self-transcendence. Intellectual conversion is to truth attained by cognitional self-transcendence. Moral conversion is to values apprehended, affirmed, and realized by a real self-trancendence. Religious conversion is to a total being-in-love as the efficacious ground of all self-transcendence, whether in the pursuit of truth, or in the realization of human values, or in the orientation man adopts to the universe, its ground, and its goal.

Because intellectual, moral, and religious conversions all have to do with self-transcendence, it is possible, when all three occur within a single consciousness, to conceive their relations in terms of sublation. I would use this notion in Karl Rahner's sense[3] rather than Hegel's to mean that what sublates goes beyond what is sublated, introduces something new and distinct, puts everything on a new basis, yet so far from interfering with the sublated or destroying it, on the contrary needs it, includes it, preserves all its proper features and properties, and carries them forward to a fuller realization within a richer context.

So moral conversion goes beyond the value, truth, to values

---

[2] On grace as operative and cooperative in St. Thomas, see *Theological Studies* 2(1941), 289–324; 3(1942), 69–88; 375–402; 533–578. In book form, B. Lonergan, *Grace and Freedom in Aquinas*, London: Darton, Longman & Todd, and New York: Herder & Herder, 1971.

[3] K. Rahner, *Hörer des Wortes*, München: Kösel, 1963, p. 40.

generally. It promotes the subject from cognitional to moral self-transcendence. It sets him on a new, existential level of consciousness and establishes him as an originating value. But this in no way interferes with or weakens his devotion to truth. He still needs truth, for he must apprehend reality and real potentiality before he can deliberately respond to value. The truth he needs is still the truth attained in accord with the exigences of rational consciousness. But now his pursuit of it is all the more secure because he has been armed against bias, and it is all the more meaningful and significant because it occurs within, and plays an essential role in, the far richer context of the pursuit of all values.

Similarly, religious conversion goes beyond moral. Questions for intelligence, for reflection, for deliberation reveal the eros of the human spirit, its capacity and its desire for self-transcendence. But that capacity meets fulfilment, that desire turns to joy, when religious conversion transforms the existential subject into a subject in love, a subject held, grasped, possessed, owned through a total and so an other-worldly love. Then there is a new basis for all valuing and all doing good. In no way are fruits of intellectual or moral conversion negated or diminished. On the contrary, all human pursuit of the true and the good is included within and furthered by a cosmic context and purpose and, as well, there now accrues to man the power of love to enable him to accept the suffering involved in undoing the effects of decline.

It is not to be thought, however, that religious conversion means no more than a new and more efficacious ground for the pursuit of intellectual and moral ends. Religious loving is without conditions, qualifications, reservations; it is with all one's heart and all one's soul and all one's mind and all one's strength. This lack of limitation, though it corresponds to the unrestricted character of human questioning, does not pertain to this world. Holiness abounds in truth and moral goodness, but it has a distinct dimension of its own. It is other-worldly fulfilment, joy, peace, bliss. In Christian experience these are the fruits of being in love with a mysterious, uncomprehended God. Sinfulness similarly is distinct from moral evil; it is the privation of total loving;

it is a radical dimension of lovelessness. That dimension can be hidden by sustained superficiality, by evading ultimate questions, by absorption in all that the world offers to challenge our resourcefulness, to relax our bodies, to distract our minds. But escape may not be permanent and then the absence of fulfilment reveals itself in unrest, the absence of joy in the pursuit of fun, the absence of peace in disgust—a depressive disgust with oneself or a manic, hostile, even violent disgust with mankind.

Though religious conversion sublates moral, and moral conversion sublates intellectual, one is not to infer that intellectual comes first and then moral and finally religious. On the contrary, from a causal viewpoint, one would say that first there is God's gift of his love. Next, the eye of this love reveals values in their splendor, while the strength of this love brings about their realization, and that is moral conversion. Finally, among the values discerned by the eye of love is the value of believing the truths taught by the religious tradition, and in such traditon and belief are the seeds of intellectual conversion. For the word, spoken and heard, proceeds from and penetrates to all four levels of intentional consciousness. Its content is not just a content of experience but a content of experience and understanding and judging and deciding. The analogy of sight yields the cognitional myth. But fidelity to the word engages the whole man.

Besides conversions there are breakdowns. What has been built up so slowly and so laboriously by the individual, the society, the culture, can collapse. Cognitional self-transcendence is neither an easy notion to grasp nor a readily accessible datum of consciousness to be verified. Values have a certain esoteric imperiousness, but can they keep outweighing carnal pleasure, wealth, power? Religion undoubtedly had its day, but is not that day over? Is it not illusory comfort for weaker souls, an opium distributed by the rich to quiet the poor, a mythical projection of man's own excellence into the sky?

Initially not all but some religion is pronounced illusory, not all but some moral precept is rejected as ineffective and useless, not all truth but some type of metaphysics is dismissed as mere talk. The negations may be true, and then they represent an effort to offset decline. But also they may be false, and then they are the beginning of decline. In the latter case some part of cultural achievement is being destroyed. It will cease being a familiar component in cultural experience. It will recede into a forgotten past for historians, perhaps, to rediscover and reconstruct. Moreover, this elimination of a genuine part of the culture means that a previous whole has been mutilated, that some balance has been upset, that the remainder will become distorted in an effort to compensate. Further, such elimination, mutilation, distortion will, of course, be admired as the forward march of progress, while the evident ills they bring forth are to be remedied, not by a return to a misguided past, but by more elimination, mutilation, distortion. Once a process of dissolution has begun, it is screened by self-deception and it is perpetuated by consistency. But that does not mean that it is confined to some single uniform course. Different nations, different classes of society, different age-groups can select different parts of past achievement for elimination, different mutilations to be effected, different distortions to be provoked. Increasing dissolution will then be matched by increasing division, incomprehension, suspicion, distrust, hostility, hatred, violence. The body social is torn apart in many ways, and its cultural soul has been rendered incapable of reasonable convictions and responsible commitments.

For convictions and commitments rest on judgments of fact and judgments of value. Such judgments, in turn, rest largely on beliefs. Few, indeed, are the people that, pressed on almost any point, must not shortly have recourse to what they have believed. Now such recourse can be efficacious only when believers present a solid front, only when intellectual, moral, and religious skeptics are a small and, as yet, uninfluential minority. But their numbers can increase, their influence can mount, their voices can take over the book market, the educational system, the mass media. Then believing begins to work not for but against intellectual, moral, and religious self-transcendence. What had been an uphill but universally respected course collapses into the peculiarity of an outdated minority.

3. DIALECTIC: THE ISSUE

The issue to be confronted in dialectic is twofold, for our functional specialties, history, interpretation, and special research are deficient in two manners.

Friedrich Meinecke has said that every historical work is concerned both with causal connections and with values but that most historians tend to be occupied principally either with causal connections or with values. Moreover, he claimed that history, as concerned with values, "... gives us the content, wisdom, and signposts of our lives."[4] Carl Becker went even further. He wrote: "The value of history is ... not scientific but moral: by liberating the mind, by deepening the sympathies, by fortifying the will, it enables us to control, not society, but ourselves—a much more important thing; it prepares us to live more humanely in the present and to meet rather than to foretell the future."[5] But the functional specialty, history, as we conceived it, was concerned with movements, with what in fact was going forward. It specialized on the end of the third level of intentional consciousness, on what happened. It had nothing to say about history as primarily concerned with values, and rightly so, inasmuch as history as primarily concerned with values pertains to a specialization not on the third but on the fourth level of intentional consciousness.

Similarly, our account of interpretation was a matter of understanding the thing, the words, the author, and oneself, of passing judgment on the accuracy of one's understanding, of determining the manner of expressing what one has understood. But besides so intellectual a hermeneutics, there also is an evaluative hermeneutics. Besides potential, formal, and full acts of meaning, there are also constitutive and effective acts of meaning. Now the apprehension of values and disvalues is the task not of understanding but of intentional response. Such response is all the fuller, all the more discriminating, the better a man one is, the more refined one's sensibility, the more delicate one's feelings.

[4] F. Stern, *The Varieties of History*, New York: Meridian, 1956, p. 272.

[5] Charlotte Smith, *Carl Becker: On History and the Climate of Opinion*, Ithaca, N.Y.: Cornell, 1956. p. 117.

9

So evaluative interpretation pertains to a specialty, not on the end of the second level of intentional consciousness, but on the end of the fourth level.

Such, then, is a first task of dialectic. It has to add to the interpretation that understands a further interpretation that appreciates. It has to add to the history that grasps what was going forward a history that evaluates achievements, that discerns good and evil. It has to direct the special research needed for such interpretation and for such history.

There is, as well, a second task. For our account of critical history promised univocal results only if historians proceeded from the same standpoint. But standpoints are many, and the many are of different kinds. There is the coloring that arises from the individuality of the historian and results in perspectivism. There is the inadequacy that is revealed when further data are uncovered and a better understanding achieved. There are, finally, the gross differences due to the fact that historians with opposed horizons are endeavoring to make intelligible to themselves the same sequence of events.

With such gross differences dialectic is concerned. They are not merely perspectival, for perspectivism results from the individuality of the historian, but these gross differences occur between opposed and even hostile classes of historians. They are not ordinarily to be removed by uncovering further data, for the further data, in all probability, will be as susceptible of opposed interpretations as the data at present available. The cause of the gross differences is a gross difference of horizon, and the proportionate remedy is nothing less than a conversion.

As history, so also interpretation does not promise univocal results. The interpreter may understand the thing, the words, the author, and himself. But if he undergoes conversion, he will have a different self to understand, and the new understanding of himself can modify his understanding of the thing, the words, and the author.

Special research, finally, is conducted with a view to particular exegetical or historical tasks. The horizons that guide the performance of the tasks also guide the performance of the research.

One easily finds what fits into one's horizon. One has very little ability to notice what one has never understood or conceived. No less than interpretation and history, the preliminary special research can reveal differences of horizon.

In brief, the first phase of theology is incomplete, if it is restricted to research, interpretation, and history. For as we have conceived these functional specialties, they approach but do not achieve an encounter with the past. They make the data available, they clarify what was meant, they narrate what occurred. Encounter is more. It is meeting persons, appreciating the values they represent, criticizing their defects, and allowing one's living to be challenged at its very roots by their words and by their deeds. Moreover, such an encounter is not just an optional addition to interpretation and to history. Interpretation depends on one's self-understanding; the history one writes depends on one's horizon; and encounter is the one way in which self-understanding and horizon can be put to the test.

4. DIALECTIC: THE PROBLEM

The presence or absence of intellectual, of moral, of religious conversion gives rise to dialectically opposed horizons. While complementary or genetic differences can be bridged, dialectical differences involve mutual repudiation. Each considers repudiation of its opposites the one and only intelligent, reasonable, and responsible stand and, when sufficient sophistication is attained, each seeks a philosophy or a method that will buttress what are considered appropriate views on the intelligent, the reasonable, the responsible.

There results a babel. All three types of conversion may be lacking; any one may be present, or any two, or all three. Even prescinding from differences in the thoroughness of the conversion, there are eight radically differing types. Moreover, every investigation is conducted from within some horizon. This remains true even if one does not know one operates from within a horizon, or even if one assumes that one makes no assumptions. Whether they are explicitly acknowledged or not, dialectically opposed horizons lead to opposed value judgments, opposed accounts of historical movements, opposed interpretations of authors, and different selections of relevant data in special research.

To a great extent natural science escapes this trap. It limits itself to questions that can be settled through an appeal to observation and experiment. It draws its theoretical models from mathematics. It aims at an empirical knowledge in which value judgments have no constitutive role. Still these advantages do not give complete immunity. An account of scientific method stands to cognitional theory as the less to the more general, so that no firm barrier separates science, scientific method, and general cognitional theory. So mechanist determinism used to be part of science; now it is a discarded philosophic opinion. But in its place there is Niels Bohr's doctrine of complementarity, which includes philosophic views on human knowledge and on reality, and any departure from Bohr's position involves still more philosophy.[6] Again, while physics, chemistry, biology do not make value judgments, still the transition from liberal to totalitarian regimes has made scientists reflect on the value of science and their rights as scientists, while military and other uses of scientific discoveries have made them advert to their duties.

In the human sciences the problems are far more acute. Reductionists extend the methods of natural science to the study of man. Their results, accordingly, are valid only in so far as a man resembles a robot or a rat and, while such resemblance does exist, exclusive attention to it gives a grossly mutilated and distorted view.[7] General system theory rejects reductionism in all its forms, but it still is aware of its unsolved problems; for systems engineering involves a progressive mechanization that tends to reduce man's role in the system to that of a robot, while systems generally can be employed for destructive as well as constructive ends.[8] Gibson Winter in his *Elements for a Social*

---

[6] P. A. Heelan, *Quantum Mechanics and Objectivity*, The Hague: Nijhoff, 1965, Chapter Three.

[7] F. W. Matson, *The Broken Image*, Garden City, N.Y.: Doubleday, 1966, Chapter Two.

[8] L. v. Bertalanffy, *General System Theory*, New York: Braziller, 1968, pp. 10, 52.

Ethic[9] has contrasted the diverging styles in sociology associated with the names of Talcott Parsons and C. Wright Mills. After noting that the difference in approach led to different judgments on existing society, he asked whether the opposition was scientific or merely ideological—a question, of course, that transported the discussion from the history of contemporary sociological thought into philosophy and ethics. Prof. Winter worked out a general account of social reality, distinguished physicalist, functionalist, voluntarist, and intentionalist styles in sociology, and assigned to each its sphere of relevance and effectiveness. Where Max Weber distinguished between social science and social policy, Prof. Winter distinguishes between philosophically grounded and graded styles in social science and, on the other hand, social policy grounded not only in social science but also in the value judgments of an ethics.

Both in the natural and in the human sciences, then, there obtrude issues that are not to be solved by empirical methods. These issues can be skirted or evaded with greater success in the natural sciences and less in the human sciences. But a theology can be methodical only if these issues are met head on. To meet them head on is the problem of our fourth functional specialty, dialectic.

5. DIALECTIC: THE STRUCTURE

The structure of dialectic has two levels. On an upper level are the operators. On a lower level are assembled the materials to be operated on.

The operators are two precepts: develop positions; reverse counter-positions. Positions are statements compatible with intellectual, moral, and religious conversion; they are developed by being integrated with fresh data and further discovery. Counter-positions are statements incompatible with intellectual, or moral, or religious conversion; they are reversed when the incompatible elements are removed.

Before being operated on, the materials have to be assembled, completed, compared, reduced, classified, selected. *Assembly*

[9] New York: Macmillan, 1966, pb. 1968.

includes the researches performed, the interpretations proposed, the histories written, and the events, statements, movements to which they refer. *Completion* adds evaluative interpretation and evaluative history; it picks out the one hundred and one "good things" and their opposites; it is history in the style of Burckhardt rather than Ranke.[10] *Comparison* examines the completed assembly to seek out affinities and oppositions. *Reduction* finds the same affinity and the same opposition manifested in a number of different manners; from the many manifestations it moves to the underlying root. *Classification* determines which of these sources of affinity or opposition result from dialectically opposed horizons and which have other grounds. *Selection*, finally, picks out the affinities and oppositions grounded in dialectically opposed horizons and dismisses other affinities and oppositions.

Now this work of assembly, completion, comparison, reduction, classification, and selection will be performed by different investigators and they will be operating from within different horizons. The results, accordingly, will not be uniform. But the source of this lack of uniformity will be brought out into the open when each investigator proceeds to distinguish between positions, which are compatible with intellectual, moral, and religious conversion and, on the other hand, counter-positions, which are incompatible either with intellectual, or with moral, or with religious conversion. A further objectification of horizon is obtained when each investigator operates on the materials by indicating the view that would result from developing what he has regarded as positions and by reversing what he has regarded as counter-positions. There is a final objectification of horizon when the results of the foregoing process are themselves regarded as materials, when they are assembled, completed, compared, reduced, classified, selected, when positions and counter-positions are distinguished, when positions are developed and counter-positions are reversed.

[10] On Burckhardt, E. Cassirer, *The Problem of Knowledge*, Philosophy, Science, and History since Hegel, New Haven: Yale, 1950, Chapter Sixteen; G. P. Gooch, *History and Historians in the Nineteenth Century*, London: Longmans, [2]1952, pp. 529–533.

6. DIALECTIC AS METHOD

There has been outlined the structure of a dialectic, and now there must be asked whether it satisfies the definition of method. Clearly enough, it presents a pattern of related and recurrent operations. But it is yet to be seen whether the results will be progressive and cumulative. Accordingly, let us see what happens, first, when the dialectic is implemented by a person that has undergone intellectual, moral, and religious conversion and, secondly, when it is implemented by a person that has not yet undergone intellectual or moral or religious conversion.

In the first case, the investigator will know from personal experience just what intellectual, moral, and religious conversion is. He will have no great difficulty in distinguishing positions from counter-positions. When he develops positions and reverses counter-positions, he will be presenting an idealized version of the past, something better than was the reality. Moreover, all such investigators will tend to agree and, as well, they will be supported in part by other investigators that have been converted in one or two of the areas but not in all three.

In the second case, the investigator may have only what Newman would call a notional apprehension of conversion, and so he might complain that dialectic is a very foggy procedure. But at least he would recognize radically opposed statements. In the area or areas, however, in which he lacked conversion, he would be mistaking counter-positions for positions and positions for counter-positions. When he proceeded to develop what he thought were positions and to reverse what he thought were counter-positions, in reality he would be developing counter-positions and reversing positions. While the implementation of dialectic in the first case led to an idealized version of the past, its implementation in the second case does just the opposite; it presents the past as worse than it really was. Finally, there are seven different ways in which this may be achieved, for the second case includes (1) those without any experience of conversion, (2) those with the experience of only intellectual or only moral or only religious conversion, and (3) those that lack only intellectual or only moral or only religious conversion.

Now let us make this contrast slightly more concrete. Our fourth functional specialty moves beyond the realm of ordinary empirical science. It meets persons. It acknowledges the values they represent. It deprecates their short-comings. It scrutinizes their intellectual, moral, and religious assumptions. It picks out significant figures, compares their basic views, discerns processes of development and aberration. As the investigation expands, there are brought to light origins and turning-points, the flowering and the decadence of religious philosophy, ethics, spirituality. Finally, while all viewpoints may not be represented, there is the theoretical possibility of the fourth functional specialty being carried out in eight quite different manners.

Such divergence, however, is not confined to future investigators. Positions and counter-positions are not just contradictory abstractions. They are to be understood concretely as opposed moments in ongoing process. They are to be apprehended in their proper dialectical character. Human authenticity is not some pure quality, some serene freedom from all oversights, all misunderstanding, all mistakes, all sins. Rather it consists in a withdrawal from unauthenticity, and the withdrawal is never a permanent achievement. It is ever precarious, ever to be achieved afresh, ever in great part a matter of uncovering still more oversights, acknowledging still further failures to understand, correcting still more mistakes, repenting more and more deeply hidden sins. Human development, in brief, is largely through the resolution of conflicts and, within the realm of intentional consciousness, the basic conflicts are defined by the opposition of positions and counter-positions.

Now it is only through the movement towards cognitional and moral self-transcendence, in which the theologian overcomes his own conflicts, that he can hope to discern the ambivalence at work in others and the measure in which they resolved their problems. Only through such discernment can he hope to appreciate all that has been intelligent, true, and good in the past even in the lives and the thought of opponents. Only through such discernment can he come to acknowledge all that was misinformed, misunderstood, mistaken, evil even in those with whom

252

he is allied. Further, however, this action is reciprocal. Just as it is one's own self-transcendence that enables one to know others accurately and to judge them fairly, so inversely it is through knowledge and appreciation of others that we come to know ourselves and to fill out and refine our apprehension of values.

Inasmuch, then, as investigators assemble, complete, compare, reduce, classify, select, they bring to light the dialectical opposi-tions that existed in the past. Inasmuch as they pronounce one view a position and its opposite a counter-position and then go on to develop the positions and reverse the counter-positions, they are providing one another with the evidence for a judgment on their personal achievement of self-transcendence. They reveal the selves that did the research, offered the interpretations, studied the history, passed the judgments of value.

Such an objectification of subjectivity is in the style of the crucial experiment. While it will not be automatically efficacious, it will provide the open-minded, the serious, the sincere with the occasion to ask themselves some basic questions, first, about others but eventually, even about themselves. It will make conversion a topic and thereby promote it. Results will not be sudden or startling, for conversion commonly is a slow process of maturation. It is finding out for oneself and in oneself what it is to be intelligent, to be reasonable, to be responsible, to love. Dialectic contributes to that end by pointing out ultimate differences, by offering the example of others that differ radically from oneself, by providing the occasion for a reflection, a self-scrutiny, that can lead to a new understanding of oneself and one's destiny.

7. THE DIALECTIC OF METHODS: PART ONE

Already we have remarked that the presence and absence of intellectual, moral, or religious conversion not only give rise to opposed horizons but also, with the advent of sophistication, generate opposed philosophies, theologies, methods, to justify and defend the various horizons.

Now the task of dealing with these conflicts pertains, not to the methodologists, but to theologians occupied in the fourth functional specialty. Moreover, the theologian's strategy will be, not to prove his own position, not to refute counter-positions, but to exhibit diversity and to point to the evidence for its roots. In this manner he will be attractive to those that appreciate full human authenticity and he will convince those that attain it. Indeed, the basic idea of the method we are trying to develop takes its stand on discovering what human authenticity is and showing how to appeal to it. It is not an infallible method, for men easily are unauthentic, but it is a powerful method, for man's deepest need and most prized achievement is authenticity.

It remains that the methodologist cannot totally ignore the conflict of philosophies or methods. Especially is this so when there are widely held views that imply that his own procedures are mistaken and even wrong-headed. Accordingly, I shall comment briefly, first, on certain contentions of linguistic analysis and, secondly, on certain conclusions that follow from idealist premises.

In a valuable paper presented at the twenty-third annual convention of the Catholic Theological Society of America Prof. Edward MacKinnon explained:

> Since the publication of Wittgenstein's *Philosophical Investigations* there has been a growing consensus that the meaningfulness of language is essentially public and only derivatively private. Unless this were so language could not serve as a vehicle for intersubjective communication. The meaning of a term, accordingly, is explained chiefly by clarifying its use, or the family of usages associated with it. This requires an analysis both of the way terms function within language, or a study of syntax, and also of the extralinguistic contexts in which its use is appropriate, or questions of semantics and pragmatics.
>
> A consequence of this position . . . is that the meaning of a word is not explicable by reference or reduction to private mental acts. The usual scholastic doctrine is that words have meaning *because* they express concepts. Meanings are primarily in concepts, private mental acts or states, and then derivatively in language which expresses such a concept. Within this view of language, transcendence does not present too formidable a linguistic problem. A word, such as "God" can mean a transcendent being, if this is what one

intends in using the word. Comforting as such a simple solution might be, it, unfortunately, will not work.[11]

This I find a clear and helpful basis of discussion. I wish to clarify my own position by adding a few remarks.

First, I do not believe that mental acts occur without a sustaining flow of expression. The expression may not be linguistic. It may not be adequate. It may not be presented to the attention of others. But it occurs. Indeed, Ernst Cassirer has reported that students of aphasia, agnosia, and apraxia universally have found these disorders of speech, knowledge, and action to be inter-related.[12]

Secondly, I have no doubt that the ordinary meaningfulness of ordinary language is essentially public and only derivatively private. For language is ordinary if it is in common use. It is in common use, not because some isolated individual happens to have decided what it is to mean, but because all the individuals of the relevant group understand what it means. Similarly, it is by performing expressed mental acts that children and foreigners come to learn a language. But they learn the language by learning how it ordinarily is used, so that their private knowledge of ordinary usage is derived from the common usage that essentially is public.

Thirdly, what is true of the ordinary meaningfulness of ordinary language is not true of the original meaningfulness of any language, ordinary, literary, or technical. For all language develops and, at any time, any language consists in the sedimentation of the developments that have occurred and have not become obsolete. Now developments consist in discovering new uses for existing words, in inventing new words, and in diffusing the discoveries and inventions. All three are a matter of expressed mental acts. The discovery of a new usage is a mental act expressed by the new usage. The invention of a new word is a mental act expressed by the new word. The communication of

[11] Edward MacKinnon, "Linguistic Analysis and the Transcendence of God," *Proceedings, Catholic Theological Society of America*, 23(1968), 30.

[12] E. Cassirer, *The Philosophy of Symbolic Forms*, New Haven: Yale, 1957, vol. III, p. 220.

the discoveries and inventions can be done technically by introducing definitions or spontaneously as when *A* utters his new verbal constellation, *B* responds, *A* grasps in *B*'s response how successful he was in communicating his meaning and, in the measure he failed, he seeks and tries out further discoveries and inventions. Through a process of trial and error a new usage takes shape, and, if there occurs a sufficiently broad diffusion of the new usage, then a new ordinary usage is established. Unlike ordinary meaningfulness, then, unqualified meaningfulness originates in expressed mental acts, is communicated and perfected through expressed mental acts, and attains ordinariness when the perfected communication is extended to a large enough number of individuals.

Fourthly, behind this confusion of ordinary meaningfulness and original meaningfulness there seems to lurk another. For two quite different meanings may be given to the statement that all philosophic problems are linguistic problems. If one conceives language as the expression of mental acts, one will conclude that philosophic problems have their source not only in linguistic expression but also in mental acts, and it could happen that one would devote much more attention to the mental acts than to the linguistic expression. But one may feel that mental acts are just occult entities or, if they really exist, that philosophers are going to keep on floundering indefinitely if they pay any attention to them or, at least, if they make them basic to their method. On a reductionist view, then, or on a stronger or weaker methodological option, one may decide to limit philosophic discourse or, at least, basic philosophic discourse to the usage of ordinary language illumined, perhaps, by the metalanguages of syntax, semantics, and pragmatics.

However, if one adopts this approach, one cannot account for the meaningfulness of language by appealing to its originating mental acts. That would be a simple solution. It would be a true solution. But it is not an admissible solution, for it puts mental acts at the basis of the meaningfulness of language and, thereby, it does precisely what the philosophic or the methodological decision prohibited. Moreover, within this horizon, it is not difficult to overlook the distinction between the meaningfulness of language that has become ordinary and the originating meaningfulness it possesses when it is becoming ordinary. On the basis of that oversight one can maintain that the meaningfulness of language is essentially public and only derivatively private.

8. THE DIALECTIC OF METHODS: PART TWO

We have been talking about mental acts and now we must note that such talk can occur in genetically distinct horizons. In any of these the talk may be correct or incorrect but, the more differentiated the horizon, the fuller, the more accurate, and the more explanatory will be the talk.

Of the genetically distinct horizons the principal ones have been indicated already in the sections on *Realms of Meaning* and *Stages of Meaning* in our third chapter on *Meaning*. In fully differentiated consciousness there are four realms of meaning. There is the realm of common sense with its meanings expressed in everyday or ordinary language. There is the realm of theory where language is technical, simply objective in reference, and so refers to the subject and his operations only as objects. There is the realm of interiority where language speaks indeed of the subject and his operations as objects but, none the less, rests upon a self-appropriation that has verified in personal experience the operator, the operations, and the processes referred to in the basic terms and relations of the language employed. Finally, there is the realm of transcendence in which the subject is related to divinity in the language of prayer and of prayerful silence.

Fully differentiated consciousness is the fruit of an extremely prolonged development. In primitive undifferentiated consciousness the second and third realms do not exist, while the first and fourth interpenetrate. Language refers primarily to the spatial, the specific, the external, the human, and only by special techniques is it extended to the temporal, the generic, the internal, the divine. The advent of civilization means an increasing differentiation of roles to be fulfilled and of tasks to be performed, an ever more elaborate organization and regulation to ensure fulfilment and performance, an ever denser population, and greater and greater abundance. With each of these changes the communicative, cognitive, effective, and constitutive functions of language expand while, as an added grace, literature develops and differentiates to celebrate human achievement and to deplore human evil, to exhort to high endeavor and to entertain man at leisure.

All this can go forward though thought and speech and action remain within the world of common sense, of persons and things as related to us, of ordinary language. But if man's practical bent is to be liberated from magic and turned towards the development of science, if his critical bent is to be liberated from myth and turned towards the development of philosophy, if his religious concern is to renounce aberrations and accept purification, then all three will be served by a differentiation of consciousness, a recognition of a world of theory. In such a world things are conceived and known, not in their relations to our sensory apparatus or to our needs and desires, but in the relations constituted by their uniform interactions with one another. To speak of things so conceived requires the development of a special technical language, a language quite distinct from that of common sense. No doubt, one has to begin from within the world of commonsense apprehension and speech. No doubt one frequently has to have recourse to this world. But also there is no doubt that these withdrawals and returns only ensure the gradual construction of a quite different mode of apprehension and of expression.

This differentiation of consciousness is illustrated by the Platonic contrast of the phenomenal and the noumenal worlds, of Aristotle's distinction and correlation of what is first for us and what is first absolutely, of Aquinas' hymns and his systematic theology, of Galileo's secondary and primary qualities, of Eddington's two tables.

In this differentiation, which knows only two realms, technical science, technical philosophy, technical theology are all three located in the realms of theory. All three operate principally with concepts and judgments, with terms and relations, with some approximation to the logical ideal of clarity, coherence, and rigor. All three, finally, deal primarily with objects and, while they may advert to the subject and his operations, still any systematic treatment, as in Aristotle and in Aquinas, is of the subject and the operations as objectified and, indeed, conceived metaphysically in terms of matter and form, of potency, habit, and act, of efficient and final causes.[13]

However, as science develops, philosophy is impelled to migrate from the world of theory and to find its basis in the world of interiority. On the one hand, science gives up any claim to necessity and truth. It settles for verifiable possibilities that offer an ever better approximation to truth. But, on the other hand, its success lends color to totalitarian ambitions, and science conceives its goal as the full explanation of all phenomena.

In this situation philosophy is left with the problems of truth and relativism, of what is meant by reality, of the grounds of theory and of common sense and of the relations between the two, of the grounds of specifically human sciences. It finds itself confronted with the fact that all human knowledge has a basis in the data of experience and, since science seems to have acquired at least squatters' rights to the data of sense, it will have to take its stand on the data of consciousness.

Now just as the world of theory is quite distinct from the world of common sense yet is constructed only through a manifold use of commonsense knowledge and ordinary language, so also the world of interiority is quite distinct from the worlds of theory and of common sense yet it is constructed only through a manifold use of mathematical, scientific, and commonsense knowledge and of both ordinary and technical language. As the world of common sense and its language provide the scaffolding for entering into the world of theory, so both the worlds of common sense and of theory and their languages provide the scaffolding for entering into the world of interiority. But while the transition from common sense to theory introduces us to entities that we do not directly experience, the transition from common sense and theory to interiority promotes us from consciousness of self to knowledge of self. Common sense and theory have mediated to us what is immediately given in

[13] See above, p. 95.

consciousness. Through them we have advanced from merely given operations and processes and unities to a basic system of terms and relations that distinguish and relate and name the operations and processes and unities and enable us to speak clearly, accurately, and explanatorily about them.

Such speech, however, is found clear and accurate and explanatory only by those that have done their apprenticeship. It is not enough to have acquired common sense and to speak ordinary language. One has also to be familiar with theory and with technical language. One has to examine mathematics, and discover what is happening when one is learning it and, again, what was happening as it was being developed. From reflecting on mathematics one has to go on to reflecting on natural science, discern its procedures, the relations between successive steps, the diversity and relatedness of classical and statistical methods, the sort of world such methods would reveal—all the while attending not merely to scientific objects but also attending, as well as one can, to the conscious operations by which one intends the objects. From the precision of mathematical understanding and thought and from the ongoing, cumulative advance of natural science, one has to turn to the procedures of common sense, grasp how it differs from mathematics and natural science, discern its proper procedures, the range of its relevance, the permanent risk it runs of merging with common nonsense. To say it all with the greatest brevity: one has not only to read *Insight* but also to discover oneself in oneself.

Let us now revert to the relations between language and mental acts. First, then, a language that refers to mental acts has to be developed. As we have noted, the Homeric hero is depicted, not as thinking, but as conversing with a god or goddess, with his horse or a river, with his heart or his temper. Bruno Snell's *The Discovery of Mind* recounts how the Greeks gradually developed their apprehension of man and eventually confronted the problems of cognitional theory. In Aristotle there exists a systematic account of the soul, its potencies, habits, operations, and their objects. In some respects it is startlingly accurate, but it is incomplete, and throughout it presupposes a metaphysics. It is in the world not of common sense and not of interiority but of theory. It is to be complemented by the fuller theory of Aquinas.

However, once consciousness has been differentiated and systematic thought and speech about mental acts have been developed, the capacities of ordinary language are vastly enlarged. Augustine's penetrating reflections on knowledge and consciousness, Descartes' *Regulae ad directionem ingenii,* Pascal's *Pensées,* Newman's *Grammar of Assent* all remain within the world of commonsense apprehension and speech yet contribute enormously to our understanding of ourselves. Moreover, they reveal the possibility of coming to know the conscious subject and his conscious operations without presupposing a prior metaphysical structure. It is this possibility that is realized when a study of mathematical, scientific, and commonsense operations bears fruit in experiencing, understanding, and affirming the normative pattern of related and recurrent operations by which we advance in knowledge. Once such an account of knowledge is attained, one can move from the gnoseological question (What are we doing when we are knowing?) to the epistemological question (Why is doing that knowing?) and from both to the metaphysical question (What do we know when we do it?).

From within the world of interiority, then, mental acts as experienced and as systematically conceived are a logical first. From them one can proceed to epistemology and metaphysics. From all three one can proceed, as we attempted in Chapter Three, to give a systematic account of meaning in its carriers, its elements, its functions, its realms, and its stages.

Still this priority is only relative. Besides the priority that is reached when a new realm of meaning is set up, there also is the priority of what is needed if that process of setting up is to be undertaken. The Greeks needed an artistic, a rhetorical, an argumentative development of language before a Greek could set up a metaphysical account of mind. The Greek achievement was needed to expand the capacities of commonsense knowledge and language before Augustine, Descartes, Pascal, Newman could make their commonsense contributions to our self-knowledge. The history of mathematics, natural science, and philosophy and, as well, one's own personal reflective engagement in all three are needed if both common sense and theory are to construct the scaffolding for an entry into the world of interiority.

The conditions, then, for using mental acts as a logical first are numerous. If one insists on remaining in the world of common sense and ordinary language or if one insists on not going beyond the worlds of common sense and of theory, one's decisions preclude the possibility of entering into the world of interiority. But such decisions on the part of any individual or group are hardly binding on the rest of mankind.

9. THE DIALECTIC OF METHODS: PART THREE

An *a priori* rejection of the present approach can stem from idealist tendencies no less than from linguistic analysis. Perhaps its clearest expression is to be found in the writings of Karl Jaspers who would contend that our self-appropriation is indeed an *Existenzerhellung*, a clarification of the subject's own reality, but it is not objective knowledge.

Now it is true, of course, that self-appropriation occurs through a heightening of consciousness and such a heightening reveals not the subject as object but the subject as subject. I should contend, however, that this heightening of consciousness proceeds to an objectification of the subject, to an intelligent and reasonable affirmation of the subject, and so to a transition from the subject as subject to the subject as object. Such a transition yields objective knowledge of the subject just as much as does any valid transition from the data of sense through inquiry and understanding, reflection and judgment. But while that is my view, it is not the view of the idealist tradition which Jaspers inherited.

To understand this tradition in its endless complexity is quite beyond our present concern. But some basic clarification must be attempted at least in terms of points already made. There are, then, two quite disparate meanings of the term, object. There is the object in the world mediated by meaning: it is what is intended by the question, and it is what becomes understood, affirmed, decided by the answer. To this type of object we are related immediately by our questions and only mediately by the operations relevant to answers, for the answers refer to objects only because they are answers to questions.

But there is another quite different meaning of the term, object. For besides the world mediated by meaning there also is a world of immediacy. It is a world quite apart from questions and answers, a world in which we lived before we spoke and while we were learning to speak, a world into which we try to withdraw when we would forget the world mediated by meaning, when we relax, play, rest. In that world the object is neither named nor described. But in the world mediated by meaning one can recollect and reconstitute the object of the world of immediacy. It is already, out, there, now, real. It is *already*: it is given prior to any questions about it. It is *out*: for it is the object of extraverted consciousness. It is *there*: as sense organs, so too sensed objects are spatial. It is *now*: for the time of sensing runs along with the time of what is sensed. It is *real*: for it is bound up with one's living and acting and so must be just as real as they are.

As there are two meanings of the word, object, so too there are two meanings of the word, objectivity. In the world of immediacy the necessary and sufficient condition of objectivity is to be a successfully functioning animal. But in the world mediated by meaning objectivity has three components. There is the experiential objectivity constituted by the givenness of the data of sense and the data of consciousness. There is the normative objectivity constituted by the exigences of intelligence and reasonableness. There is the absolute objectivity that results from combining the results of experiential and normative objectivity so that through experiential objectivity conditions are fulfilled while through normative objectivity conditions are linked to what they condition. The combination, then, yields a conditioned with its conditions fulfilled and that, in knowledge, is a fact and, in reality, it is a contingent being or event.

We have distinguished two worlds, two meanings of the word, object, two quite different criteria of objectivity. But when these distinctions are not drawn, there result a number of typical confusions. The naive realist knows the world mediated by meaning, but he fancies that he knows it by taking a good look at what is going on out there now. The naive idealist, Berkeley, concludes that *esse est percipi*. But *esse* is reality affirmed in the world mediated by meaning, while *percipi* is the givenness of an object in the world of immediacy. The rigorous empiricist, Hume, eliminates from the world mediated by meaning everything that is not given in the world of immediacy. The critical idealist, Kant, sees that a Copernican revolution is overdue. But, so far from drawing the needed distinctions, he only finds another more complicated manner of confusing things. He combines the operations of understanding and reason, not with the data of sense, but with sensitive intuitions of phenomena, where the phenomena are the appearing, if not of nothing, then of the things themselves which, while unknowable, manage to get talked about through the device of the limiting concept. The absolute idealist, Hegel, brilliantly explores whole realms of meaning; he gives poor marks to naive realists; but he fails to advance to a critical realism, so that Kierkegaard can complain that what is logical also is static, that movement cannot be inserted into a logic, that Hegel's system has room not for existence (self-determining freedom) but only for the idea of existence.

Kierkegaard marks a trend. Where he was concerned with faith, Nietzsche was with power, Dilthey with concrete human living, Husserl with the constitution of our intending, Bergson with his *élan vital*, Blondel with action, American pragmatists with results, European existentialists with authentic subjectivity. While the mathematicians were discovering that their axioms were not self-evident truths, while the physicists were discovering that their laws were not inevitable necessities but verifiable possibilities, the philosophers ceased to think of themselves as the voice of pure reason and began to be the representatives of something far more concrete and human. Or if they still stressed objective evidence and necessity, as did Husserl, they also were performing reductions that bracketed reality out of the question and concentrated on essence to ignore contingence.

There has resulted not so much a clarification as a shift in the meanings of the terms, objective and subjective. There are areas in which investigators commonly agree, such as mathematics and science; in such fields objective knowledge is obtainable. There are other areas, such as philosophy, ethics, religion, in which agreement commonly is lacking; such disagreement is explained by the subjectivity of philosophers, moralists, religious people. But whether subjectivity is always mistaken, wrong, evil, is a further question. Positivists, behaviorists, naturalists would tend to say that it is. Others, however, would insist on distinguishing between an authentic and an unauthentic subjectivity. What results from the former is neither mistaken nor wrong nor evil. It just is something quite different from the objective knowledge attainable in mathematics and in science.

In some such context as the foregoing one would have to agree with Jaspers' view that a clarification of subjectivity, however authentic, is not objective knowledge. Still that context survives only as long as there survive the ambiguities underlying naive realism, naive idealism, empiricism, critical idealism, absolute idealism. Once those ambiguities are removed, once an adequate self-appropriation is effected, once one distinguishes between object and objectivity in the world of immediacy and, on the other hand, object and objectivity in the world mediated by meaning and motivated by value, then a totally different context arises. For it is now apparent that in the world mediated by meaning and motivated by value, objectivity is simply the consequence of authentic subjectivity, of genuine attention, genuine intelligence, genuine reasonableness, genuine responsibility. Mathematics, science, philosophy, ethics, theology differ in many manners; but they have the common feature that their objectivity is the fruit of attentiveness, intelligence, reasonableness, and responsibility.

10. A SUPPLEMENTARY NOTE

We have distinguished four realms of meaning: common sense, theory, interiority, and transcendence. We have had occasion to distinguish such differentiations of consciousness as the resolution of common sense into common sense and theory and the further resolution of common sense and theory into common sense, theory, and interiority. But our remarks on transcendence as a differentiated realm have been fragmentary.

What I have referred to as the gift of God's love, spontaneously reveals itself in love, joy, peace, patience, kindness, goodness, fidelity, gentleness, and self-control. In undifferentiated consciousness it will express its reference to the transcendent both through sacred objects, places, times, and actions, and through the sacred offices of the shaman, the prophet, the lawgiver, the apostle, the priest, the preacher, the monk, the teacher. As consciousness differentiates into the two realms of common sense and theory, it will give rise to special theoretical questions concerning divinity, the order of the universe, the destiny of mankind, and the lot of each individual. When these three realms of common sense, theory, and interiority are differentiated, the self-appropriation of the subject leads not only to the objectification of experiencing, understanding, judging, and deciding, but also of religious experience.

Quite distinct from these objectifications of the gift of God's love in the realms of common sense and of theory and from the realm of interiority, is the emergence of the gift as itself a differentiated realm. It is this emergence that is cultivated by a life of prayer and self-denial and, when it occurs, it has the twofold effect, first, of withdrawing the subject from the realm of common sense, theory, and other interiority into a "cloud of unknowing" and then of intensifying, purifying, clarifying, the objectifications referring to the transcendent whether in the realm of common sense, or of theory, or of other interiority.

It is to be observed that, while for secular man of the twentieth century the most familiar differentiation of consciousness distinguishes and relates theory and common sense, still in the history of mankind both in the East and the Christian West the predominant differentiation of consciousness has set in opposition and in mutual enrichment the realms of common sense and of transcendence.

FOUNDATIONS

In Chapter Five on functional specialties, theology was conceived as reflection on religion and it was said to go forward in two phases. In a first, mediating phase, theological reflection ascertained what had been the ideals, the beliefs, the performance of the representatives of the religion under investigation. But in a second, mediated phase, theological reflection took a much more personal stance. It was no longer to be content to narrate what others proposed, believed, did. It has to pronounce which doctrines were true, how they could be reconciled with one another and with the conclusions of science, philosophy, history, and how they could be communicated appropriately to the members of each class in every culture.

It is with the basis of this much more personal stance that the fifth functional specialty, foundations, is concerned. Accordingly, we are seeking the foundations, not of the whole of theology, but of the three last specialties, doctrines, systematics, and communications. We are seeking not the whole foundation of these specialties—for they obviously will depend on research, interpretation, history, and dialectic—but just the added foundation needed to move from the indirect discourse that sets forth the convictions and opinions of others to the direct discourse that states what is so.

I. FOUNDATIONAL REALITY

Foundational reality, as distinct from its expression, is conversion: religious, moral, and intellectual. Normally it is intellectual conversion as the fruit of both religious and moral conversion; it is moral conversion as the fruit of religious conversion; and it is religious conversion as the fruit of God's gift of his grace.

Such conversion is operative, not only in the functional specialty, foundations, but also in the phase of mediating theology, in research, interpretation, history, and dialectic. However, in this earlier phase conversion is not a prerequisite; anyone can do research, interpret, write history, line up opposed positions. Again, when conversion is present and operative, its operation is implicit: it can have its occasion in interpretation, in doing history, in the confrontation of dialectic; but it does not constitute an explicit, established, universally recognized criterion of proper procedure in these specialties. Finally, while dialectic does reveal the polymorphism of human consciousness—the deep and unreconcilable oppositions on religious, moral, and intellectual issues—still it does no more: it does not take sides. It is the person that takes sides, and the side that he takes will depend on the fact that he has or has not been converted.

At its real root, then, foundations occurs on the fourth level of human consciousness, on the level of deliberation, evaluation, decision. It is a decision about whom and what you are for and, again, whom and what you are against. It is a decision illuminated by the manifold possibilities exhibited in dialectic. It is a fully conscious decision about one's horizon, one's outlook, one's world-view. It deliberately selects the frame-work, in which doctrines have their meaning, in which systematics reconciles, in which communications are effective.

Such a deliberate decision is anything but arbitrary. Arbitrariness is just unauthenticity, while conversion is from unauthenticity to authenticity. It is total surrender to the demands of the human spirit: be attentive, be intelligent, be reasonable, be responsible, be in love.

Again, it is not to be conceived as an act of will. To speak of an act of will is to suppose the metaphysical context of a faculty psychology. But to speak of the fourth level of human consciousness, the level on which consciousness becomes conscience, is to suppose the context of intentionality analysis. Decision is responsible and it is free, but it is the work not of a metaphysical will but of conscience and, indeed, when a conversion, the work of a good conscience.

Further, deliberate decision about one's horizon is high achievement. For the most part people merely drift into some contemporary horizon. They do not advert to the multiplicity of horizons. They do not exercise their vertical liberty by migrating from the one they have inherited to another they have discovered to be better.

Finally, although conversion is intensely personal, it is not purely private. While individuals contribute elements to horizons, it is only within the social group that the elements accumulate and it is only with century-old traditions that notable developments occur. To know that conversion is religious, moral, and intellectual, to discern between authentic and unauthentic conversion, to recognize the difference in their fruits—by their fruits you shall know them—all call for a high seriousness and a mature wisdom that a social group does not easily attain or maintain.

It follows that conversion involves more than a change of horizon. It can mean that one begins to belong to a different social group or, if one's group remains the same, that one begins to belong to it in a new way. Again, the group will bear witness to its founder or founders whence originated and are preserved its high seriousness and mature wisdom. Finally, the witness it bears will be efficacious in the measure that the group is dedicated not to its own interests but to the welfare of mankind. But how the group is constituted, who was the founder to whom it bears witness, what are the services it renders to mankind, these are questions not for the fifth functional specialty, foundations, but for the sixth, doctrines.

2. THE SUFFICIENCY OF THE FOUNDATIONAL REALITY

Foundations may be conceived in two quite different manners. The simple manner is to conceive foundations as a set of premises, of logically first propositions. The complex manner is to conceive foundations as what is first in any ordered set. If the ordered set consists in propositions, then the first will be the logically first propositions. If the ordered set consists in an ongoing, developing reality, then the first is the immanent and operative set of norms that guides each forward step in the process.

Now if one desires foundations to be conceived in the simple manner, then the only sufficient foundations will be some variation or other of the following style: One must believe and accept whatever the bible or the true church or both believe and accept. But X is the bible or the true church or both. Therefore, one must believe and accept whatever X believes and accepts. Moreover, X believes and accepts a, b, c, d,. . . . . Therefore, one must believe and accept a, b, c, d,. . . .

On the contrary, if one desires foundations for an ongoing, developing process, one has to move out of the static, deductivist style—which admits no conclusions that are not implicit in premisses—and into the methodical style—which aims at decreasing darkness and increasing light and keeps adding discovery to discovery. Then, what is paramount is control of the process. It must be ensured that positions are accepted and counterpositions are rejected. But that can be ensured only if investigators have attained intellectual conversion to renounce the myriad of false philosophies, moral conversion to keep themselves free of individual, group, and general bias,[1] and religious conversion so that in fact each loves the Lord his God with his whole heart and his whole soul and all his mind and all his strength.

Now there is no need here, I trust, to argue against the revival of a Denzinger theology or a conclusions theology. They offer necessary elements in theology but by themselves they are notoriously insufficient. On the other hand, it does seem necessary to insist that the threefold conversion is not foundational in the sense that it offers the premises from which all desirable conclusions are to be drawn. The threefold conversion is, not a set of propositions that a theologian utters, but a fundamental and momentous change in the human reality that a theologian is. It operates, not by the simple process of drawing inferences from premisses, but by changing the reality (his own) that the interpreter

[1] On bias, *Insight*, pp. 218–242.

has to understand if he is going to understand others, by changing the horizon within which the historian attempts to make the past intelligible, by changing the basic judgments of fact and of value that are found to be not positions but counter-positions.

Neither the converted nor the unconverted are to be excluded from research, interpretation, history, or dialectic. Neither the converted nor the unconverted are to follow different methods in these functional specialties. But one's interpretation of others is affected by one's understanding of oneself, and the converted have a self to understand that is quite different from the self that the unconverted have to understand. Again, the history one writes depends on the horizon within which one is attempting to understand the past; the converted and the unconverted have radically different horizons; and so they will write different histories. Such different histories, different interpretations, and their underlying different styles in research become the center of attention in dialectic. There they will be reduced to their roots. But the reduction itself will only reveal the converted with one set of roots and the unconverted with a number of different sets. Conversion is a matter of moving from one set of roots to another. It is a process that does not occur in the marketplace. It is a process that may be occasioned by scientific inquiry. But it occurs only inasmuch as a man discovers what is unauthentic in himself and turns away from it, inasmuch as he discovers what the fulness of human authenticity can be and embraces it with his whole being. It is something very cognate to the Christian gospel, which cries out: Repent! The kingdom of God is at hand.

3. PLURALISM IN EXPRESSION

While conversion manifests itself in deeds and in words, still the manifestation will vary with the presence or absence of differentiated consciousness. There results a pluralism in the expression of the same fundamental stance and, once theology develops, a multiplicity of the theologies that express the same faith. Such a pluralism or multiplicity is of fundamental impro-tance, both for the understanding of the development of religious traditions, and for an understanding of the impasses that may result from such development.

We recall, then, the four basic realms of meaning: the realm of common sense, the realm of theory, the realm of interiority, and the realm of transcendence. To these for present purposes may be added the realm of scholarship and the realm of art. Any realm becomes differentiated from the others when it develops its own language, its own distinct mode of apprehension, and its own cultural, social, or professional group speaking in that fashion and apprehending in that manner.

If we presume that every normal adult operates in the realm of common sense, then undifferentiated consciousness will operate only in the realm of common sense, while all cases of differentiated consciousness will operate both in the realm of common sense and in one or more other realms. Considering only the mathematically possible combinations, one can list some thirty-one different types of differentiated consciousness. There are five cases of singly differentiated consciousness; these operate in the realm of common sense and as well in the realm either of the transcendent or of art or of theory or of scholarship or of interiority. There are ten cases of doubly differentiated consciousness; then to the realm of common sense there are added the realms either of religion and art, or religion and theory, or religion and scholarship, or religion and interiority, or art and theory, or art and scholarship, or art and interiority, or theory and scholarship, or theory and interiority, or scholarship and interiority. There are ten more cases of triply differentiated consciousness, five cases of a fourfold differentiation of consciousness, and one case of a fivefold differentiation.

Undifferentiated consciousness develops in the manner of common sense. It achieves an accumulation of insights enabling one to speak and act in a manner appropriate to any of the situations that commonly arise in one's milieu and, on the other hand, to pause and figure things out when an unfamiliar situation comes along.

As a style of developing intelligence, common sense is common to mankind. But as a content, as a determinate understanding of man and his world, common sense is common not to mankind but to the members of each village, so that strangers appear strange and, the more distant their native land, the more strangely they appear to speak and act.

In their endless varieties common sense and ordinary language are not unaware of the realms of religion, art, theory, scholarship, interiority. But their apprehension of these realms is rudimentary and their expression vague. Such defects are remedied as consciousness attains an ever fuller differentiation, but this implies that each new differentiation will involve some remodeling of one's previous commonsense views on matters on which common sense is not competent. Not only does the more differentiated consciousness master more realms but also it understands the people that are at home in these realms. Inversely, less differentiated consciousness finds more differentiated consciousness beyond its horizon and, in self-defence, may tend to regard the more differentiated with that pervasive, belittling hostility that Max Scheler named *ressentiment*.

Religiously differentiated consciousness is approached by the ascetic and reached by the mystic. In the latter there are two quite different modes of apprehension, of being related, of consciously existing, namely, the commonsense mode operating in the world mediated by meaning and the mystical mode withdrawing from the world mediated by meaning into a silent and all-absorbing self-surrender in response to God's gift of his love. While this, I think, is the main component, still mystical attainment is manifold. There are many mansions within Teresa of Avila's *Interior Castle* and, besides Christian mystics, there are the mystics of Jewry, Islam, India, and the Far East. Indeed, Mircea Eliade has a book on shamanism with the subtitle, 'archaic techniques of ecstasy'.

Artistically differentiated consciousness is a specialist in the realm of beauty. It promptly recognizes and fully responds to beautiful objects. Its higher attainment is creating: it invents commanding forms; works out their implications; conceives and produces their embodiment.

Theoretically differentiated consciousness occurs in two

phases. In both of these phases objects are apprehended, not in their commonsense relations to us, but in their verifiable relations to one another. Hence, basic terms are defined implicitly by their relations to one another, and these relations in turn are established by an appeal to experience. However, in the first phase, the basic terms and relations pertain to a philosophy, and the sciences are conceived as further and fuller determinations of the objects of philosophy, as in Aristotelianism. In the second phase, the sciences are emancipated from philosophy; they discover their own basic terms and relations; and as that discovery matures, there occurs in a new setting the distinction Aristotle drew between the *priora quoad nos* and the *priora quoad se*. Eddington adverted to this distinction by speaking of his two tables: one of them was visible, palpable, brown, solid, and heavy; the other was mostly empty space with here and there an unimaginable wavicle.

The scholarly differentiation of consciousness is that of the linguist, the man of letters, the exegete, the historian. It combines the brand of common sense of its own place and time with a commonsense style of understanding that grasps the meanings and intentions in the words and deeds that proceeded from the common sense of another people, another place, or another time. Because scholarship operates in the commonsense style of developing intelligence, it is not trying to reach the universal principles and laws that are the goal of the natural sciences and the generalizing human sciences. Its aim is simply to understand the meaning intended in particular statements and the intentions embodied in particular deeds. Accordingly, the scholarly and the theoretical differentiations of consciousness are quite distinct.

Interiorly differentiated consciousness operates in the realms of common sense and of interiority. While theoretically differentiated consciousness seeks to determine its basic terms and relations by beginning from sense experience, interiorly differentiated consciousness, though it must begin from sense, eventually deserts this beginning to determine its basic terms and relations by adverting to our conscious operations and to the dynamic structure that relates them to one another. It is on such a basis that the present method is erected. It has been toward such a basis that modern philosophy has been groping in its efforts to overcome fourteenth-century skepticism, to discover its relationship to the natural and the human sciences, to work out a critique of common sense which so readily blends with common nonsense, and to place abstractly apprehended cognitional activity within the concrete and sublating context of human feeling and of moral deliberation, evaluation, and decision.

Each of the foregoing differentiations of consciousness can be incipient or mature or receding. In a devout life one can discern the forerunner of mystical experience, in the art lover the beginnings of creativity, in a wisdom literature the foreshadow of philosophic theory, in the antiquarian the makings of a scholar, in psychological introspection the materials of interiorly differentiated consciousness. But what has been achieved need not be perpetuated. The heroic spirituality of a religious leader may be followed by the routine piety of his later followers. Artistic genius can yield place to artistic humbug. The differentiated consciousness of a Plato or Aristotle can enrich a later humanism though the cutting edge of genuine theory does not live on. High scholarship can settle down to amassing unrelated details. Modern philosophy can migrate from theoretically to interiorly differentiated consciousness but it can also revert to the undifferentiated consciousness of the Presocratics and of the analysts of ordinary language.

I have been content to offer brief descriptions of each of the differentiations of consciousness. But besides such single differentiations, there are double, triple, fourfold, and fivefold differentiations. As there are ten types of double differentiation, ten more of triple differentiation, and five of fourfold differentiation, there are many different routes through which one might advance to the fivefold differentiation. Again, as each differentiation occurs, it takes over a realm of the universe and spontaneously requires of previous attainments a readjustment of their previous practice, which hitherto somehow or other had tried to make do in that realm. In particular, theoretically differentiated consciousness enriches religion with a systematic theology but it also liberates natural science from philosophic bondage by enabling it to work out its own basic terms and relations. Scholarship builds an impenetrable wall between systematic theology and its historical religious sources, but this development invites philosophy and theology to migrate from a basis in theory to a basis in interiority. In virtue of that migration, theology can work out a method that both grounds and criticizes critical history, interpretation, and research.

4. PLURALISM IN RELIGIOUS LANGUAGE

Besides the radical pluralism that results from the presence or absence of intellectual, moral, or religious conversion, there exists a more benign yet still puzzling variety that has its root in the differentiation of human consciousness.

The most common type by far is undifferentiated consciousness. To this type will always belong the vast majority of the faithful. Because it is undifferentiated, it is only puzzled or amused by the oracles of religiously differentiated consciousness, by the exertions of artists, by the subtleties of theorists, by the plodding labors of historians, and by the complex use of familiar words that results from an interiorly differentiated consciousness. Hence, to preach to this majority and to teach it one must use its own language, its own procedures, its own resources. Unfortunately these are not uniform. There are as many brands of common sense as there are languages, social or cultural differences, almost differences of place and time. So it is that to preach the gospel to all men calls for at least as many preachers as there are differing places and times, and it requires each of them to get to know the people to whom he or she is sent, their ways of thought, their manners, their style of speech. There follows a manifold pluralism. Primarily it is a pluralism of communications rather than of doctrines. But within the limits of undifferentiated consciousness, there is no communication of doctrine except through the rituals, narrative forms, titles, parables, metaphors that are effective in the given milieu.

An exception to this last statement must be noted. The educated classes in a society, such as was the Hellenistic, normally are instances of undifferentiated consciousness. But their education had among its sources the works of genuine philosophers, so that they could be familiar with logical principles and could take propositions as the objects on which they reflected and operated.

In this fashion Athanasius was able to include, among his many clarifications of the term, *homoousion*, a rule concerning propositions about the Father and the Son: *eadem de Filio, quae de Patre dicuntur, excepto Patris nomine.*[2]

Again, there can be introduced new technical terms, when the context makes their meaning clear. Thus in the decree of the council of Chalcedon there are introduced in the second paragraph the terms, person and nature. But the first paragraph leaves no room for doubt about what was meant. Repeatedly it insists that it is one and the same Son our Lord Jesus Christ that is perfect in divinity and the same perfect in humanity, truly God and the same truly man, consubstantial with the Father in his divinity and the same consubstantial with us in his humanity, born of the Father before the ages in his divinity and these last days the same . . . born of the Virgin Mary in his humanity.[3]

Now the meaning of this declaration is luminous, but to a logically trained mind it raises a question. Is the humanity the same as the divinity? If not, how can one and the same same be both human and divine? It is after these questions have been raised, that it becomes relevant to explain that a distinction can be drawn between person and nature, that divinity and humanity denote two different natures, that it is one and the same person that is both God and man. Such logical clarification is within the meaning of the decree. But if one goes on to raise metaphysical questions, such as the reality of a distinction between person and nature, not only is one moving beyond questions explicitly envisaged by the decree, but also one is being enticed out of undifferentiated consciousness and into the theoretically differentiated consciousness of a Scholasticism.

First, however, let us consider religiously differentiated consciousness. It <u>can</u> be content with the negations of an apophatic

<hr/>

[2] Athanasius, *Orat.* III *c. Arianos, MG* 26, 329 A.
[3] *DS* 301.

theology. For it is in love. On its love there are not any reservations or conditions or qualifications. By such love it is oriented
positively to what is transcendent in lovableness. Such a positive
orientation and the consequent self-surrender, as long as they are
operative, enable one to dispense with any intellectually apprehended object. And when they cease to be operative, the memory
of them enables one to be content with enumerations of what
God is not.[4]

It may be objected that *nihil amatum nisi praecognitum.* But
while that is true of other human love, it need not be true of the
love with which God floods our hearts through the Holy Spirit
he has given us (Rom. 5, 5). That grace could be the finding that
grounds our seeking God through natural reason and through
positive religion. It could be the touchstone by which we judge
whether it is really God that natural reason reaches[5] or positive
religion preaches. It could be the grace that God offers all men,
that underpins what is good in the religions of mankind, that
explains how those that never heard the gospel can be saved. It
could be what enables the simple faithful to pray to their
heavenly Father in secret even though their religious apprehensions are faulty. Finally, it is in such grace that can be found the
theological justification of Catholic dialogue with all Christians,
with non-Christians, and even with atheists who may love God
in their hearts while not knowing him with their heads.

Next, artistically differentiated consciousness, especially if
joined to religious sensibility, heightens religious expression. It
makes rituals solemn, liturgies stately, music celestial, hymns
moving, oratory effective, teaching ennobling.

Thirdly, there is theoretically differentiated consciousness. As
already explained, there was a slight tincture of this in the Greek
councils at Nicea, Ephesus, Chalcedon, Constantinople III. But

[4] See Karl Rahner, *The Dynamic Element in the Church*, Montreal: Palm, and
Freiburg: Herder, 1964, pp. 129 ff. More fully: William Johnston, *The Mysticism
of the Cloud of Unknowing*, New York, Rome, Tournai, Paris: Desclée, 1967.

[5] On the transition from the context of Vatican I to the contemporary context
on natural knowledge of God, see my paper, "Natural Knowledge of God,"
Proceedings of the Catholic Theological Society of America, 23(1968), 54–69.

in the medieval period there was developed in the universities a vast, systematic, and collaborative task of reconciling all that had been handed down in the church from the past. The bold speculative efforts of an Anselm had aimed at comprehension before a sufficiently broad basis of information had been obtained. A more precise approach was illustrated by Abaelard's *Sic et Non*, in which one hundred and fifty-eight propositions were both proved and disproved by arguments drawn from scripture, the Fathers, the councils, and reason.[6] From this dialectical display there was developed the technique of the *quaestio*: Abaelard's *Non* became *Videtur quod non*; his *Sic* became *Sed contra est*; to these were added a general response that outlined principles of solution and specific responses that applied the principles to each of the alleged pieces of evidence. Parallel to this development was the erudite activity of composing books of sentences that collected and classified relevant passages from scripture and tradition. When the technique of the *quaestio* was applied to the materials set forth in books of sentences, there resulted the commentaries and with them a new problem. There would be no point in reconciling the diverging materials in the books of sentences if the solutions to the multitudinous questions were themselves incoherent. There was needed, then, some conceptual system that would enable theologians to give coherent answers to all the questions they raised; and this need was met partly by adopting and partly by adapting the Aristotelian corpus.

Scholastic theology was a monumental achievement. Its influence in the Catholic church has been profound and enduring. Up to Vatican II, which preferred a more biblical turn of speech, it has provided much of the background of pontifical documents and conciliar decrees. Yet today by and large it is abandoned, partly because of the inadequacy of medieval aims, and partly because of the short-comings of the Aristotelian corpus.

The Scholastic aim of reconciling all the elements in its Christian inheritance had one grave defect. It was content with a logically and metaphysically satisfying reconciliation. It did not realize how much of the multiplicity in the inheritance constituted

---

[6] *ML* 178, 1339 ff.

not a logical or metaphysical problem but basically a historical problem.

On the other hand, so far was the Aristotelian corpus from providing either guidance for historical research or an understanding of the historicity of human reality, that it set forth its scientific ideal in terms of necessity. Moreover, this mistaken ideal infected not only Scholasticism but also much of modern thought. It was the discovery and acceptance of non-Euclidean geometry that brought mathematicians to acknowledge that their postulates or axioms were not necessary truths. It was quantum theory that led physicists to drop their talk about the necessary laws of nature. It was the depression of the nineteen thirties that obliged economists to retreat from their insistence on the iron laws of economics.

It is to be noted, however, that Aquinas was as little influenced by the ideal of necessity as had been Aristotle himself. His various commentaries, *quaestiones disputatae, summae*, fall under the description of research followed by a search for understanding. It was, perhaps, only in the wake of the Augustinian-Aristotelian controversy towards the end of the thirteenth century that Aristotle's *Posterior Analytics* was taken seriously with a consequent burst of skepticism to be followed by decadence.

Whatever the cause, Aquinas held an outstanding position in subsequent theology. Commentaries continued to be written on the sentences of Peter Lombard up to the end of the sixteenth century. But a diverging tradition was begun by Capreolus (*ob.* 1444) who wrote his commentary on Aquinas' commentary on Peter Lombard's sentences. A more radical departure was initiated by Cajetan (*ob.* 1534) who wrote his commentary on Aquinas' *Summa theologiae* to be followed in this practice by Bañez (*ob.* 1604), John of St. Thomas (*ob.* 1644), the Salmanticenses (1637 to 1700), Gonet (*ob.* 1681), and Billuart (*ob.* 1757). But for all the excellence of Aquinas and for all the erudition of these theologians, their procedure was unsound. Commentaries on a systematic work, such as was the *Summa theologiae*, are related only indirectly to Christian sources. The Reformation demanded a return to the gospel, but the proper meaning of that demand could be grasped only through the emergence of the scholarly differentiation of consciousness.

It is true, of course, that Melchior Cano (*ob. c.* 1560) in his *De locis theologicis* outlined a method of theology that involved direct study of all sources. But as the resulting manualist tradition reveals, direct study is not enough. There has to be discovered the historicity of human reality. There have to be worked out the techniques for reconstructing the diverging contexts presupposed by different persons, peoples, places, times. And when such techniques are mastered, it becomes apparent that the old-style treatises could be taught, not by any single professor, but only by a team.

The complexities of the scholarly differentiation of consciousness have been set forth in our chapters on *Interpretation, History, History and Historians,* and *Dialectics*. But such a presentation in turn presupposes interiorly differentiated consciousness, aware of its several kinds of operation and of the dynamic relations that organize their multiplicity into a functioning whole. For it is only through such awareness that there can be had either an accurate description of what scholars do or an adequate elimination of the confusions arising from mistaken theories of knowledge.

While elements of modern scholarship may be found here and there down the ages, its massive development was the work of the German Historical School of the nineteenth century. First its attention was directed to ancient Greece and Rome and to modern Europe. Gradually it penetrated biblical, patristic, medieval, and later religious studies. Long resisted in Catholic circles, today it is offered no serious opposition. The era dominated by Scholasticism has ended. Catholic theology is being reconstructed.

5. CATEGORIES

It has been pointed out that medieval theology turned to Aristotle for guidance and help in clarifying its thought and making it coherent. On the method we are proposing the source of basic clarification will be interiorly and religiously differentiated consciousness.

The transcendental notions are our capacity for seeking and, when found, for recognizing instances of the intelligible, the true, the real, the good. It follows that they are relevant to every object that we come to know by asking and answering questions.

While the transcendental notions make questions and answers possible, categories make them determinate. Theological categories are either general or special. General categories regard objects that come within the purview of other disciplines as well as theology. Special categories regard the objects proper to theology. The task of working out general and special categories pertains, not to the methodologist, but to the theologian engaged in this fifth functional specialty. The methodologist's task is the preliminary one of indicating what qualities are desirable in theological categories, what measure of validity is to be demanded of them, and how are categories with the desired qualities and validity to be obtained.

First, then, Christianity is a religion that has been developing for over two millenia. Moreover, it has its antecendents in the Old Testament, and it has the mission of preaching to all nations. Plainly, a theology that is to reflect on such a religion and that is to direct its efforts at universal communication must have a transcultural base.

Next, the transcendental method outlined in our first chapter is, in a sense, transcultural. Clearly it is not transcultural inasmuch as it is explicitly formulated. But it is transcultural in the realities to which the formulation refers, for these realities are not the product of any culture but, on the contrary, the principles that produce cultures, preserve them, develop them. Moreover, since it is to these realities we refer when we speak of *homo sapiens*, it follows that these realities are transcultural with respect to all truly human cultures.

Similarly, God's gift of his love (Rom. 5, 5) has a transcultural aspect. For if this gift is offered to all men, if it is manifested more or less authentically in the many and diverse religions of mankind, if it is apprehended in as many different manners as there are different cultures, still the gift itself as distinct from its manifestations is transcultural. For of other love it is true enough that it presupposes knowledge—*nihil amatum nisi praecognitum*. But God's gift of his love is free. It is not conditioned by human knowledge; rather it is the cause that leads man to seek knowledge of God. It is not restricted to any stage or section of human culture but rather is the principle that introduces a dimension of other-worldliness into any culture. All the same, it remains true, of course, that God's gift of his love has its proper counterpart in the revelation events in which God discloses to a particular people or to all mankind the completeness of his love for them. For being-in-love is properly itself, not in the isolated individual, but only in a plurality of persons that disclose their love to one another.

There exist, then, bases from which might be derived both general and special categories that in some measure are transcultural. But before attempting to indicate the manner in which such derivation might be achieved, let us first say something about the validity to be expected in the derivation.

First, with regard to the base for general theological categories in transcendental method, we have only to repeat what already has been said. The explicit formulation of that method is historically conditioned and can be expected to be corrected, modified, complemented as the sciences continue to advance and reflection on them to improve. What is transcultural is the reality to which such formulation refers, and that reality is transcultural because it is not the product of any culture but rather the principle that begets and develops cultures that flourish, as it also is the principle that is violated when cultures crumble and decay.

Secondly, with regard to the base of special theological categories, a distinction has to be drawn between being in love in an unrestricted manner (1) as it is defined and (2) as it is achieved. As it is defined, it is the habitual actuation of man's capacity for self-transcendence; it is the religious conversion that grounds both moral and intellectual conversion; it provides the real criterion by which all else is to be judged; and consequently one has only to experience it in oneself or witness it in others, to find in it its own justification. On the other hand, as it actually is achieved in any human being, the achievement is dialectical. It is authenticity as a withdrawal from unauthenticity, and the withdrawal is never complete and always precarious. The greatest of saints have not only their oddities but also their defects, and it is not some but all of us that pray, not out of humility but in truth,[7] to be forgiven our trespasses as we forgive those that trespass against us.

Accordingly, while there is no need to justify critically the charity described by St. Paul in the thirteenth chapter of his first epistle to the Corinthians, there is always a great need to eye very critically any religious individual or group and to discern beyond the real charity they may well have been granted the various types of bias that may distort or block their exercise of it.[8]

Thirdly, both with regard to transcendental method and with regard to God's gift of his love we have distinguished between an inner core, which is transcultural, and an outer manifestation, that is subject to variation. Needless to say, theological categories will be transcultural only in so far as they refer to that inner core. In their actual formulation they will be historically conditioned and so subject to correction, modification, complementation. Moreover, the more elaborate they become and the further they are removed from that inner core, the greater will be their precariousness. On what grounds, then, are they to be accepted and employed?

Before answering this question, there must be introduced the notion of the model or ideal-type. Models, then stand to the human sciences, to philosophies, to theologies, much as mathematics stands to the natural sciences. For models purport to be, not descriptions of reality, not hypotheses about reality, but simply interlocking sets of terms and relations. Such sets, in

---

[7] DS 230.

[8] On bias, see *Insight*, pp. 191–206, 218–242. More generally, see the manifold warnings against various forms of illusion in devotional and ascetical writings. While this tradition should be integrated with the findings of depth psychology, it is of great importance to be aware of current corrections of earlier views. See

fact, turn out to be useful in guiding investigations, in framing hypotheses, and in writing descriptions. Thus, a model will direct the attention of an investigator in a determinate direction with either of two results; it may provide him with a basic sketch of what he finds to be the case; or it may prove largely irrelevant, yet the discovery of this irrelevance may be the occasion of uncovering clues that otherwise might be overlooked. Again, when one possesses models, the task of framing an hypothesis is reduced to the simpler matter of tailoring a model to suit a given object or area. Finally, the utility of the model may arise when it comes to describing a known reality. For known realities can be exceedingly complicated, and an adequate language to describe them hard to come by. So the formulation of models and their general acceptance as models can facilitate enormously both description and communication.

Now what has been said about models, is relevant to the question concerning the validity of the general and special theological categories. First, such categories will form a set of interlocking terms and relations and, accordingly, they will possess the utility of models. Further, these models will be built up from basic terms and relations that refer to transcultural components in human living and operation and, accordingly, at their roots they will possess quite exceptional validity. Finally, whether they are to be considered more than models with exceptional foundational validity, is not a methodological but a theological question. In other words, it is up to the theologian to decide whether any model is to become an hypothesis or to be taken as a description.

6. GENERAL THEOLOGICAL CATEGORIES

If categories are to be derived, there is needed a base from which they are derived. The base of general theological categories is the attending, inquiring, reflecting, deliberating subject along

L. v. Bertalanffy, *General System Theory*, New York: Braziller, 1968, pp. 106 ff., 188 ff. A. Maslow, *Toward a Psychology of Being*, Princeton: Van Nostrand, 1962, esp. pp. 19–41. Ernest Becker, *The Structure of Evil*, New York: Braziller, 1968, pp. 154–166. Arthur Janov, *The Primal Scream*, New York: Putman, 1970.

with the operations that result from attending, inquiring, reflecting, deliberating and with the structure within which the operations occur. The subject in question is not any general or abstract or theoretical subject; it is in each case the particular theologian that happens to be doing theology. Similarly, the relevant attending, inquiring, reflecting, deliberating are the attending, inquiring, reflecting, deliberating that he has found to go on in himself; the consequent operations are the operations he has uncovered and identified in his own operating; and the structure within which the operations occur is the pattern of dynamic relations which, as he knows from his own experience, lead from one operation to the next. Finally, the subject is self-transcending. His operations reveal objects: single operations reveal partial objects; a structured compound of operations reveals compounded objects; and as the subject by his operations is conscious of himself operating, he too is revealed though not as object but as subject.

Such is the basic nest of terms and relations. Now there has been for millenia a vast multitude of individuals in whom such basic nests of terms and relations can be verified: for they too attend, understand, judge, decide. Moreover, they do so not in isolation but in social groups, and as such groups develop and progress and also decline, there is not only society but also history.

Further, the basic nest of terms and relations can be differentiated in a number of manners. So one can distinguish and describe: (1) each of the different kinds of conscious operation that occur; (2) the biological, aesthetic, intellectual, dramatic, practical, or worshipful patterns of experience within which the operations occur; (3) the different quality of the consciousness inherent in sensing, in operating intelligently, in operating reasonably, in operating responsibly and freely; (4) the different manners in which operations proceed towards goals: the manner of common sense, of the sciences, of interiority and philosophy, of the life of prayer and theology; (5) the different realms of meaning and the different worlds meant as a result of the various manners of proceeding: the world of immediacy, given in

FOUNDATIONS

immediate experience and confirmed by successful response; the world of common sense; the world of the sciences; the world of interiority and philosophy; the world of religion and theology; (6) the diverse heuristic structures within which operations accumulate towards the attainment of goals: the classical, statistical, genetic, and dialectical heuristic structures[9] and, embracing them all, the integral heuristic structure which is what I mean by a metaphysics;[10] (7) the contrast between differentiated consciousness that shifts with ease from one manner of operation in one world to another manner of operation in a different world and, on the other hand, undifferentiated consciousness which is at home in its local variety of common sense but finds any message from the worlds of theory, of interiority, of transcendence both alien and incomprehensible; (8) the difference between those that have or have not been converted religiously, or morally, or intellectually; (9) the consequent dialectically opposed positions and counter-positions, models, categories.

Such differentiation vastly enriches the initial nest of terms and relations. From such a broadened basis one can go on to a developed account of the human good, values, beliefs, to the carriers, elements, functions, realms, and stages of meaning, to the question of God, of religious experience, its expressions, its dialectical development.

Finally, since the basic nest of terms and relations is a dynamic structure, there are various ways in which models of change can be worked out. Fire, for instance, has been conceived as one of the four elements, as due to phlogiston, and as a process of oxydization. But while the answers have little in common, they are answers to the same question, What will you know when you understand the data on fire? More generally, the nature of any x is what one will know when the data on x are understood. So by turning to the heuristic notions behind common names, one finds the unifying principle of the successive meanings attributed to the name.[11]

Other illustrations mostly from *Insight* follow. Developments

[9] *Insight*, pp. 33–69, 217–244, 451–487, 530–594.
[10] Ibid., pp. 390–396.　　[11] Ibid., pp. 36 ff.

can be analysed as processes from initial global operations of low efficiency, through differentiation and specialization, to the integration of the perfected specialties. Revolutionary developments in some departments of thought can be schematized as successive higher viewpoints.[12] A universe in which both classical and statistical laws are verified will be characterized by a process of emergent probability.[13] Authenticity can be shown to generate progress, unauthenticity to bring about decline,[14] while the problem of overcoming decline provides an introduction to religion.[15] The problems of interpretation bring to light the notion of a potential universal viewpoint that moves over different levels and sequences of expression.[16]

7. SPECIAL THEOLOGICAL CATEGORIES

Let us now turn from deriving general theological categories to deriving special theological categories. In this task we have a model in the theoretical theology developed in the middle ages. But it is a model that can be imitated only by shifting to a new key. For the categories we want will pertain, not to a theoretical theology, but to a methodical theology.

To illustrate the difference, consider the medieval doctrine of grace. It presupposed a metaphysical psychology in terms of the essence of the soul, its potencies, habits, and acts. This presupposition represented the order of nature. But grace goes beyond nature and perfects it. Grace, accordingly, calls for special theological categories, and these must refer to supernatural entities, for grace is tied up with God's loving gift of himself to us, and that gift is due not to our natures but to God's free initiative. At the same time, these entities have to be prolongations perfecting our nature. Accordingly, they are habits and acts. Supernatural acts ordinarily proceed from supernatural operative habits (virtues) and supernatural operative habits proceed from the

[12] Ibid., pp. 13-19.   [13] Ibid., pp. 115-128, 259-262.
[14] Ibid., pp. 207-244.   [15] Ibid., pp. 688-703, 713-730.
[16] Ibid., pp. 562-594.

supernatural entitative habit (sanctifying grace) which, unlike the operative habits, is radicated not in the potencies but in the essence of the soul.

Now to effect the transition from theoretical to methodical theology one must start, not from a metaphysical psychology, but from intentionality analysis and, indeed, from transcendental method. So in our chapter on religion we noted that the human subject was self-trancendent intellectually by the achievement of knowledge, that he was self-transcendent morally inasmuch as he sought what was worth while, what was truly good, and thereby became a principle of benevolence and beneficence, that he was self-transcendent affectively when he fell in love, when the isolation of the individual was broken and he spontaneously functioned not just for himself but for others as well. Further we distinguished different kinds of love: the love of intimacy, of husband and wife, of parents and children; the love of mankind devoted to the pursuit of human welfare locally or nationally or globally; and the love that was other-wordly because it admitted no conditions or qualifications or restrictions or reservations. It is this other-worldly love, not as this or that act, not as a series of acts, but as a dynamic state whence proceed the acts, that constitutes in a methodical theology what in a theoretical theology is named sanctifying grace. Again, it is this dynamic state, manifested in inner and outer acts, that provides the base out of which special theological categories are set up.

Traditionally that dynamic state is manifested in three ways: the purgative way in which one withdraws from sinning and overcomes temptation; the illuminative way in which one's discernment of values is refined and one's commitment to them is strengthened; the unitive way in which the serenity of joy and peace reveal the love that hitherto had been struggling against sin and advancing in virtue.

The data, then, on the dynamic state of other-worldly love are the data on a process of conversion and development. The inner determinants are God's gift of his love and man's consent, but there also are outer determinants in the store of experience and in the accumulated wisdom of the religious tradition. If civil law recognizes adult responsibility at the age of twenty-one years, the professor of religious psychology at Louvain had it that man reaches genuine religious faith and a properly personal assumption of his inherited religion about the age of thirty.[17] But just as one can be a highly successful scientist and yet have very vague notions regarding his own intentional and conscious operations, so too a person can be religiously mature yet have to recall to mind his past life and study it in its religious moments and features before he can discern in it a direction, a pattern, a thrust, a call, to unworldliness. Even then his difficulties may not be at an end: he may be unable to associate any precise meaning with the words I have used; he may be too familiar with the reality of which I speak to connect it with what I say; he may be looking for something with a label on it, when he should simply be heightening his consciousness of the power working within him and adverting to its long-term effects.

But I do not think the matter is in doubt. In the realm of religious experience Olivier Rabut has asked whether there exists any unassailable fact. He found such a fact in the existence of love. It is as though a room were filled with music though one can have no sure knowledge of its source. There is in the world, as it were, a charged field of love and meaning; here and there it reaches a notable intensity; but it is ever unobtrusive, hidden, inviting each of us to join. And join we must if we are to perceive it, for our perceiving is through our own loving.[18]

The functional specialty, foundations, will derive its first set of categories from religious experience. That experience is something exceedingly simple and, in time, also exceedingly simplifying, but it also is something exceedingly rich and enriching. There are needed studies of religious interiority: historical, phenomenological, psychological, sociological. There is needed in the theologian the spiritual development that will enable him both to enter into the experience of others and to frame the terms and relations that will express that experience.

[17] A. Vergote, *Psychologie religieuse*, Brussels: Dessart, ³1969, p. 319.
[18] O. Rabut, *L'expérience religieuse fondamentale*, Tournai: Castermann, 1969, p. 168.

Secondly, from the subject one moves to subjects, their togetherness in community, service, and witness, the history of the salvation that is rooted in a being-in-love, and the function of this history in promoting the kingdom of God amongst men.

The third set of special categories moves from our loving to the loving source of our love. The Christian tradition makes explicit our implicit intending of God in all our intending by speaking of the Spirit that is given to us, of the Son who redeemed us, of the Father who sent the Son and with the Son sends the Spirit, and of our future destiny when we shall know, not as in a glass darkly, but face to face.

A fourth set of categories results from differentiation. Just as one's humanity, so too one's Christianity may be authentic or unauthentic or some blend of the two. What is worse, to the unauthentic man or Christian, what appears authentic, is the unauthentic. Here, then, is the root of division, opposition, controversy, denunciation, bitterness, hatred, violence. Here, too, is the transcendental base for the fourth functional specialty, dialectic.

A fifth set of categories regards progress, decline, and redemption. As human authenticity promotes progress, and human unauthenticity generates decline, so Christian authenticity—which is a love of others that does not shrink from self-sacrifice and suffering—is the sovereign means for overcoming evil. Christians bring about the kingdom of God in the world not only by doing good but also by overcoming evil with good (Rom. 12, 21). Not only is there the progress of mankind but also there is development and progress within Christianity itself; and as there is development, so too there is decline; and as there is decline, there also is the problem of undoing it, of overcoming evil with good not only in the world but also in the church.

So much for a sketch of general and special theological categories. As already noted, the task of a methodologist is to sketch the derivation of such categories, but it is up to the theologian working in the fifth functional specialty to determine in detail what the general and special categories are to be.

8. USE OF THE CATEGORIES

I have been indicating how general and special categories can be derived from a transcultural base. For general categories the base is the authentic or unauthentic man; attentive or inattentive, intelligent or slow-witted, reasonable or silly, responsible or irresponsible, with the consequent positions and counter-positions. For special categories the base is the authentic or unauthentic Christian, genuinely in love with God, or failing in that love, with a consequent Christian or unchristian outlook and style of living.

The derivation of the categories is a matter of the human and the Christian subject effecting self-appropriation and employing this heightened consciousness both as a basis for methodical control in doing theology and, as well, as an *a priori* whence he can understand other men, their social relations, their history, their religion, their rituals, their destiny.

The purification of the categories—the elimination of the unauthentic—is prepared by the functional specialty, dialectic, and it is effected in the measure that theologians attain authenticity through religious, moral, and intellectual conversion. Nor may one expect the discovery of some "objective" criterion or test or control. For that meaning of the "objective" is mere delusion. Genuine objectivity is the fruit of authentic subjectivity. It is to be attained only by attaining authentic subjectivity. To seek and employ some alternative prop or crutch invariably leads to some measure of reductionism. As Hans-Georg Gadamer has contended at length in his *Wahrheit und Methode*, there are no satisfactory methodical criteria that prescind from the criteria of truth.

The use of the general theological categories occurs in any of the eight functional specialties. The genesis of the special theological categories occurs seminally in dialectic and with explicit commitment in foundations. The commitment, however, is to the categories only as models, as interlocking sets of terms and relations. The use and the acceptance of the categories as hypothesis about reality or description of reality occur in doctrines, systematics, communications.

It is to be stressed that this use of the special categories occurs in interaction with data. They receive further specifications from the data. At the same time, the data set up an exigence for further clarification of the categories and for their correction and development.

In this fashion there is set up a scissors movement with an upper blade in the categories and a lower blade in the data. Just as the principles and laws of physics are neither mathematics nor data but the fruit of an interaction between mathematics and data, so too a theology can be neither purely *a priori* nor purely *a posteriori* but only the fruit of an ongoing process that has one foot in a transcultural base and the other on increasingly organized data.

So, as theology is an ongoing process, as religion and religious doctrine themselves develop, the functional specialty, foundations, will be concerned largely with the origins, the genesis, the present state, the possible developments and adaptations of the categories in which Christians understand themselves, communicate with one another, and preach the gospel to all nations.

12

DOCTRINES

Our sixth functional specialty is concerned with doctrines. We shall speak of the varieties of doctrines, of their functions, their variations, of the differentiation of human consciousness and the ongoing discovery of mind with consequently ongoing contexts, of the development, permanence, and historicity of dogma, of cultural pluralism and the unity of faith, and of the autonomy of the functional specialty named doctrines.

1. VARIETIES

A first step is to distinguish primary sources, church doctrines, theological doctrines, methodological doctrine, and the application of a methodological doctrine that results in a functional specialty named doctrines. Common to all is that they are taught. They differ and are distinguished because the teachers differ in the authority with which they teach.

In the primary sources a distinction is to be drawn between the doctrine of the original message and, on the other hand, doctrines about this doctrine. References to the original message may be found, for example, in I Cor. 15, 3 ff. and in Gal. 1, 6 ff. On the other hand, stages in the proclamation and application of this message yield doctrines about doctrine. Thus, there is the divine revelation in which God has spoken to us of old through his prophets and most recently in his Son (Heb. 1, 1.2). There is the church decree in which the decision of assembled Christians coincides with the decision of the Holy Spirit (Act 15, 28). There are apostolic traditions: Irenaeus, Tertullian, and Origen all appeal to the teaching given by the apostles to the churches they founded, and handed down from generation to generation.[1] There is the inspiration of the canonical scriptures that provided a far more accessible criterion once the canon had been formed and hermeneutical principles explained.[2]

Next, there are church doctrines. They have their antecedents both in New Testament confessions of faith[3] and in the decision of assembled Christians in Act 15, 28. In general they are not simple reaffirmations of scripture or tradition. However secure it may have seemed to urge with Pope Stephen "... *nihil innovetur nisi quod traditum est ...*" (*DS* 110), it remained that new questions did arise and that satisfactory answers were not forthcoming as long as one was content just to stand pat. Why this should be so is a large question to which some answer will be given in the sections on variations of doctrines and on the differentiations of consciousness. But one has only to peruse such a collection of conciliar and pontifical pronouncements as Denzinger's *Enchiridion Symbolorum* to observe that each is a product of its place and time and that each meets the questions of the day for the people of the day.

Thirdly, there are theological doctrines. Etymologically theology means a discourse about God. Within a Christian context it denotes a person's reflections on the revelation given in and by Christ Jesus. In the patristic period writers concerned themselves mainly with specific questions that currently were being ventilated, but towards its end there appeared such comprehensive works as John Damascene's *De fide orthodoxa*. In the medieval schools theology became methodical, collaborative, ongoing. Research and classification were undertaken in books of sentences. Interpretation in commentaries on the books of the Old and New Testaments and on the works of eminent writers.

---

[1] Irenaeus, *Adv. haer.*, I, 10, 2; III, 1–3; Harvey I, 92; II, 2 ff. Tertullian, *De praescr. haeret.*, 21. Origen, *De princ.*, *praef.* 1 & 2; Koetschau 7 f.

[2] Contrast the crisp principles of Clement of Alexandria (*Strom.* VIII, 2 ff.; Stählin III, 81 ff.) with the struggles of Irenaeus (*Adv. haer.* I, 3, 1.2.6; Harvey I, 24–26.31).

[3] See V. H. Neufeld, *The Earliest Christian Confessions*, Leiden: Brill, 1963, Volume V of *New Testament Tools and Studies* edited by B. M. Metzger.

Systematic theology sought to put order and coherence into the mass of materials assembled from scripture and tradition. It began, perhaps, with Abaelard's *Sic et non*, in which one hundred and fifty-eight propositions were both proved and disproved by arguments from scripture, from tradition, and from reason. In any case, Abaelard's *non* later became the *Videtur quod non* of the *quaestio*; his *sic* became the *Sed contra est*; there followed a statement of principles of solution or reconciliation; and finally the principles were applied to each of the conflicting sources. Now when the technique of the *quaestio* was applied to the materials in a book of sentences, there emerged a further need. The solutions to the endless questions had to be coherent with one another. There was needed some overall systematic view. It was to provide a substructure for such a view that theologians turned to Aristotle.

Fourthly, the methodological problems surfaced towards the end of the thirteenth century in a raucous knock-down controversy between Augustinians and Aristotelians. That controversy, so far from being settled, simply shifted into a permanent opposition between the Thomist and the Scotist schools, as did later the controversies between Catholics and Protestants, between Jesuits and Dominicans, and between the followers of different Protestant leaders. The needed solution to such ongoing differences is a theological method radical enough to meet head on the basic issues in philosophy. What is one doing when one is knowing? Why is doing that knowing? What does one know when one does it?

Though necessary, that is not enough. One must also ask what one is doing when one is doing theology, and one's answer must envisage not only the Christian encounter with God but also the historicity of Christian witness, the diversity of human cultures, the differentiations of human consciousness.

There is then a methodological doctrine. Just as theology reflects on revelation and church doctrines, so methodology reflects on theology and theologies. Because it reflects on theology and theologies, it has to mention both the revelation and the church doctrines on which the theologies reflect. But though it mentions them, it does not attempt to determine their content. That task it leaves to the church authorities and to the theologians. It is concerned to determine how theologians might or should operate. It is not concerned to predetermine the specific results all future generations must obtain.

There is a fifth variety of doctrines, the ones meant in the title of the present chapter. There are theological doctrines reached by the application of a method that distinguishes functional specialties and uses the functional specialty, foundations, to select doctrines from among the multiple choices presented by the functional specialty, dialectic.

2. FUNCTIONS

In the third chapter on meaning we distinguished the communicative, the effective, the constitutive, and the cognitive functions of meaning. Next, in the fourth chapter on religion we spoke both of an inner grace and of the outer word that comes to us from Christ Jesus. Because of its authoritative source, that word is doctrine. Because that source is one, the doctrine will be a common doctrine. Finally, such common doctrine will fulfil the communicative, effective, constitutive, and cognitive functions proper to meaning.

It is effective inasmuch as it counsels and dissuades, commands and prohibits. It is cognitive inasmuch as it tells whence we come, whither we go, how we get there. It is constitutive of the individual inasmuch as the doctrine is a set of meanings and values that inform his living, his knowing, his doing. It is constitutive of the community, for community exists inasmuch as there is a commonly accepted set of meanings and values shared by people in contact with one another. Finally, it is communicative for it has passed from Christ to the apostles and from the apostles to their successors and from these in each age to the flocks of which they were the pastors.

Further, there is the normative function of doctrines. Men may or may not be converted intellectually, morally, religiously. If they are not, and the lack of conversion is conscious and thorough-going, it heads for a loss of faith. But the unconverted may have no real apprehension of what it is to be converted. Sociologically they are Catholics or Protestants, but in a number of ways they deviate from the norm. Moreover, they may lack an appropriate language for expressing what they really are, and so they will use the language of the group with which they identify socially. There follows an inflation, or devaluation, of this language and so of the doctrine it conveys. Terms that denote what the unconverted is not, will be stretched to denote what he is. Doctrines that are embarrassing will not be mentioned in polite company. Conclusions that are unacceptable will not be drawn. Such unauthenticity can spread. It can become a tradition. Then persons, brought up in an unauthentic tradition, can become authentic human beings and authentic Christians only by purifying their tradition.

But against such deviations there is the normative function of doctrines. For the functional specialty, dialectic, deploys both the truth reached and the errors disseminated in the past. The functional specialty, foundations, discriminates between truth and error by appealing to the foundational reality of intellectual, moral, and religious conversion. The result of such discrimination is the functional specialty, doctrines, and so doctrines, based on conversion, are opposed to the aberrations that result from the lack of conversion. Accordingly, while the unconverted may have no real apprehension of what it is to be converted, at least they have in doctrines the evidence both that there is something lacking in themselves and that they need to pray for illumination and to seek instruction.

It is to be noted that the normative character of doctrines just indicated pertains to the functional specialty derived from the two previous specialties, dialectic and foundations. It is a normativeness that results from a determinate method. It is a normativeness distinct from that attributed to the opinions of theologians because of their personal eminence or because of the high esteem in which they are held in the church or among its officials. Finally, of course, the normativeness of any theological conclusion is distinct from and dependent on the normativeness attributed to divine revelation, inspired scripture, or church doctrine.

3. VARIATIONS

Anthropological and historical research has made us aware of the enormous variety of human social arrangements, cultures, mentalities. It follows that we, far more than many of our predecessors, are in a position to understand the variations that have taken place in the expression of Christian doctrines. For if the gospel is to be preached to all nations (Mt. 28, 19), still it is not to be preached in the same manner to all.[4] If one is to communicate with persons of another culture, one must use the resources of their culture. To use simply the resources of one's own culture is not to communicate with the other but to remain locked up in one's own. At the same time, it is not enough simply to employ the resources of the other culture. One must do so creatively. One has to discover the manner in which the Christian message can be expressed effectively and accurately in the other culture.

There is a further point. Once Christian doctrine has been introduced successfully within another culture, its subsequent development will further exploit the resources of that culture. The point is abundantly illustrated by Cardinal Daniélou's account of an orthodox Judaic Christianity that, in its apprehension of the Christian mysteries, employed the thought-forms and the stylistic genera of *Spätjudentum*. To conceive the Son and the Spirit as distinct persons, Judaic Christianity identified them with angels. And such and other strange concepts found expression in the form of exegesis, apocalypse, vision.[5] So too down the ages there have developed the idiosyncracies of local and national churches. Nor do such ongoing differences, once they are understood and explained, threaten the unity of faith. Rather they testify to its vitality. Doctrines that really are assimilated bear the stamp of those that assimilate them, and the absence of

---

[4] See the opening address of John XXIII at the second Vatican council. *AAS* 54(1962), 792, lines 8 ff.

[5] J. Daniélou, *Théologie du judéo-christianisme*, Tournai & Paris: Desclée, 1959; E.T. London: Darton, Longman & Todd, 1964. *Les symboles chrétiens primitifs*, Paris: du Seuil, 1961; E.T. London: Burns & Oates, and Baltimore: Helicon, 1964. *Études d'exégèse judéo-chrétienne*, Paris: Beauchesne, 1966.

such an imprint would point to a merely perfunctory assimilation.

While it is the missionary that above all must grasp and accept the fact of cultural differences, still the matter has another application. It arises when one's own culture has been undergoing change. Thus the contemporary notion of culture is empirical. A culture is a set of meanings and values informing a common way of life, and there are as many cultures as there are distinct sets of such meanings and values.

However, this manner of conceiving culture is relatively recent. It is a product of empirical human studies. Within less than one hundred years it has replaced an older, classicist view that had flourished for over two millenia. On the older view culture was conceived not empirically but normatively. It was the opposite of barbarism. It was a matter of acquiring and assimilating the tastes and skills, the ideals, virtues, and ideas, that were pressed upon one in a good home and through a curriculum in the liberal arts. It stressed not facts but values. It could not but claim to be universalist. Its classics were immortal works of art, its philosophy was the perennial philosophy, its laws and structures were the deposit of the wisdom and the prudence of mankind. Classicist education was a matter of models to be imitated, of ideal characters to be emulated, of eternal verities and universally valid laws. It sought to produce not the mere specialist but the *homo universale* that could turn his hand to anything and do it brilliantly.

The classicist is no pluralist. He knows that circumstances alter cases but he is far more deeply convinced that circumstances are somehow accidental and that, beyond them, there is some substance or kernel or root that fits in with classicist assumptions of stability, fixity, immutability. Things have their specific natures; these natures, at least in principle, are to be known adequately through the properties they possess and the laws they obey. Over and above the specific nature there is only individuation by matter, so that knowledge of one instance of a species is knowledge of any instance. What is true of species in general, also is true of the human species, of the one faith coming to us through Jesus Christ, through the one charity given through the gift of the Holy Spirit. So it was concluded that the diversity of peoples, cultures, social arrangements can involve only a difference in the dress in which doctrines are expressed, but cannot involve any diversity in church doctrine itself.

Now later we shall find that doctrines named dogmas are permanent, but our conclusion will not rest on classicist assumptions. Again, we are not relativists, and so we acknowledge something substantial and common to human nature and human activity; but that we place not in eternally valid propositions but in the quite open structure of the human spirit—in the ever immanent and operative though unexpressed transcendental precepts: Be attentive, Be intelligent, Be reasonable, Be responsible. Finally, human individuals differ from one another not only through individuation by matter but also in their mentalities their characters, their ways of life. For human concepts and human courses of action are products and expressions of acts of understanding, human understanding develops over time, such development is cumulative, and each cumulative development responds to the human and environmental conditions of its place and time. Classicism itself was on every notable and indeed noble instance of such cumulative development, but its claim to be the one culture of mankind can no longer be entertained.

4. DIFFERENTIATIONS OF CONSCIOUSNESS

To determine the starting-point, the process, the end-result of any particular development of doctrine calls for an exact historical investigation. To determine the legitimacy of any development calls for evaluational history; one has to ask whether or not the process was under the guidance of intellectual, moral, and religious conversion. But the deeper issue is the more general question that asks how is it that developments are possible. How is it that mortal man can develop what he would not know unless God had revealed it?

The basis for an answer to this question lies in what I have already referred to as the differentiation of consciousness. Already in the present work I have said not a little on this topic. But here

I have to return to it in somewhat fuller fashion, and I must apologize if I become repetitious.

A first differentiation arises in the process of growing up. The infant lives in a world of immediacy. The child moves exultingly into a world mediated by meaning. The commonsense adult never doubts that the real world is the world mediated by meaning. But he may not be too aware that it is mediated by meaning and, when he turns his hand to philosophy, he finds it very difficult to objectify the criteria by which he knows his statements to be true, and he easily commits the blunder of saying that he knows by taking a good look.

Next, there is not just one world mediated by meaning for, as human intelligence develops, it can discover new techniques in knowing. There is, however, a fundamental procedure that is practised spontaneously. I refer to it as common sense. There is the spontaneous process of teaching and learning that constantly goes forward in the individuals of a group. One notices, admires, tries to imitate, fails perhaps, watches or listens again, tries again and again till practice makes perfect. The result is an accumulation of insights that enable one both to deal successfully with recurrent situations and, as well, to notice what is novel is a new situation and to proceed to deal tentatively with that.

However, the situations that are recurrent vary with place and time. So there are as many brands of common sense as there are differing places and times. What is common to common sense is, not its content, but its procedure. In each of the very many brands there is a characteristic, self-correcting process of learning. Experience gives rise to inquiry and insight. Insight gives rise to speech and action. Speech and action sooner or later reveal their defects to give rise to further inquiry and fuller insight.

Thirdly, common sense is concerned with this world, with the immediate, the concrete, the particular. But God's gift of his love gives human living an orientation to what is transcendent in lovableness. This orientation manifests itself in uncounted manners and it can be distorted or rejected in as many more.

Fourthly, human knowing and feeling are incomplete without expression. The development, then, of symbols, of the arts, of a

literature is intrinsic to human advance. Already we have drawn
the reader's attention to a rich but concise illustration of this by
Bruno Snell in his *The Discovery of Mind*.[6]

Fifthly, there is the emergence of systematic meaning. Common sense knows the meanings of the words it employs, not
because it possesses definitions that obtain *omni et soli* but, as an
analyst would explain, because it understands how the words
might be employed appropriately. It was no paradox, then, that
neither Socrates nor his interlocutors were able to define words
that they constantly employed. Rather Socrates was opening the
way to systematic meaning which develops technical terms, assigns
them their interrelations, constructs models, and adjusts them
until there is reached some well-ordered and explanatory view
of this or that realm of experience. There result two languages,
two social groups, two worlds mediated by meaning. There is
the world mediated by commonsense meaning and there is the
world mediated by systematic meaning. There are the groups
that can employ both ordinary and technical language, and the
group that can employ only ordinary or commonsense language.

Sixthly, there is post-systematic literature. Within the culture
and influencing its education there have been developed systematic
views in logic, mathematics, science, philosophy. The systematic
views have grounded a critique of earlier common sense, literature, religion. The educated classes accept such a critique. Their
thinking is influenced by their cultural patrimony. But they
themselves are not systematic thinkers. They may on occasion
employ this or that technical term or logical technique. But their
whole mode of thought is just the commonsense mode.

Seventhly, there is the emergence of method. It consists in the
transposition of systematic meaning from a static to an ongoing,
dynamic context. Originally systems were constructed to endure.
They aimed at true and certain knowledge of what was necessarily so. But in modern times systems express, not what necessarily is so, but what intrinsically is hypothetical and in need of
verification. Again, they express, not what is expected to be
permanent, but what is expected to be revised and improved as

[6] Harvard University Press, 1953. Harper Torchbook, 1960.

further data are uncovered and better understanding is attaiend. Any given system, ancient or modern, is subject to logic. But the process from any given system to its successor is the concern of method.

Eighthly, there is the development of scholarship, of the skills of the linguist, the exegete, the historian. Unlike the natural scientist, the scholar does not aim at constructing a system, a set of universal principles and laws. He aims at coming to understand the common sense of another place and time. The understanding he reaches is itself of the same style and manner as his own original common sense. But its content is not the content of his own common sense but rather the content of the common sense of some distant land or some former time.

Ninthly, there is the development of post-scientific and post-scholarly literature. They stand to modern science and modern scholarship much as post-systematic literature stood to ancient system.

Tenthly, there is the exploration of interiority. It identifies in personal experience one's conscious and intentional acts and the dynamic relations that link them to one another. It offers an invariant basis for ongoing systems and a standpoint from which all the differentiations of human consciousness can be explored.

5. THE ONGOING DISCOVERY OF MIND: PART ONE

We have set forth a bare list of the differentiations of human consciousness. But these differentiations also characterize successive stages in cultural development and, as each earlier stage fails to foresee subsequent stages, the series as a whole may be named the ongoing discovery of mind. Finally, this series contributes not a little to an understanding of the development of doctrines, for doctrines have meaning within contexts, the ongoing discovery of mind changes the contexts, and so, if the doctrines are to retain their meaning within the new contexts, they have to be recast.

Accordingly, from a list of differentiations we have now to turn to a series of developments. We shall consider (1) the reinterpretation of symbolic apprehension, (2) philosophic purification of biblical anthropomorphism, (3) the occasional use of systematic meaning, (4) systematic theological doctrine, (5) church doctrine dependent on systematic theological doctrine, and in *Part Two* (6) the complexities of contemporary development.

By symbolic apprehension I here shall mean the apprehension of man and his world that is expressed in myth, saga, legend, magic, cosmogony, apocalypse, typology. The source of such apprehension, as already explained,[7] is the fact that prephilosophic and prescientific thought, while it can draw distinctions, cannot evolve and express an adequate account of verbal, notional, and real distinctions; further, it cannot distinguish between the legitimate and illegitimate uses of the constitutive and effective functions of meaning; the result is that it constructs its world symbolically.

Such construction, like metaphor, was not untrue. Indeed, later notions of truth had not yet been developed. The Hebrew thought of truth in terms of fidelity, and when he spoke of doing the truth he meant doing what was right. For the Greek truth was alētheia, what was not unnoticed, what was unconcealed, what was conspicuous. For a long time and for many the Homeric tales were conspicuous indeed.

Yet even in an age confined to symbolic apprehension, there was the possibility of rejecting the false and approximating to what is true. This consisted in reinterpreting the symbolic construct. Approximately the same materials would be employed and the same question answered. But there would be additions, eliminations, rearrangements that gave a new answer to the old question.

Such a reinterpretation, it is claimed, was effected by the Old Testament writers. They could use the traditions of neighboring peoples to provide themselves with the possibility of expression. But what they expressed was something quite different. The God of Israel played his role in a very real human history. Questions about creation and the last day were concerns with the beginning and the end of the story. There was no mention of a primeval battle of the gods, of a divine begetting either of kings or of an elected people, no cult of the stars or of

---

[7] See above, p. 93.

human sexuality, no sacralizing of the fruitfulness of nature.

Similarly in the New Testament, it is claimed, there did occur the use of symbolic representations also found in late Jewry and in Hellenistic Gnosticism. But these representations were used in a manner that kept them subordinate to Christian purposes and, when such subordination was lacking, they were submitted to the sharpest criticism and rejection.[8]

As reinterpretation occurs within the context of symbolic apprehension, so too it occurs within the context of philosophic concern. Xenophanes had noticed that men made their gods in their own image, and remarked that lions, horses, oxen would do likewise were they able to carve or to paint. It was the beginning of the long effort to conceive God, not on the analogy of matter, but on the analogy of spirit. So it was that Clement of Alexandria bid Christians to abstain from anthropomorphic conceptions of God even though they were to be found in scripture.[9]

Next, the Greek councils mark the beginning of a movement to employ systematic meaning in church doctrine. Thus, the church in the fourth century was being divided by an issue that had not been formulated in New Testament times. It met the issue by speaking of the consubstantiality of the Son with the Father. This, of course, is not some speculative flight concerned with an apprehension of the divine being or essence. It quite simply means that what is true of the Father also is true of the Son, except that the Son is not the Father. As Athanasius put it: *eadem de Filio quae de Patre dicuntur excepto Patris nomine.*[10] Or as the Preface for the Mass on Trinity Sunday put it: *Quod enim de tua gloria, revelante te, credimus, hoc de Filio tuo, hoc de Spiritu sancto sine differentia discretionis sentimus.*

Again, the council of Chalcedon, in the second paragraph of its decree, introduced the terms, person and nature. But subsequent theology has made very mysterious what, in the decree

---

[8] See Kurt Frör, *Biblische Hermeneutik*, München: Kaiser, 1961, ²1964, pp. 71 f.

[9] Clement, *Stromata*, V 11, 68, 3; *MG* 9, 103 B; Stählin II, 371,1 8 ff.; also V, 11, 71, 4; *MG* 110 A; Stählin II, 374, 15.

[10] Athanasius, *Orat. III c. Arianos*, 4; *MG* 26, 329 A.

itself, is quite simple and clear. For the first paragraph asserts that is one and the same Son our Lord Jesus Christ that is perfect in divinity and the same perfect in humanity, truly God and the same truly man, consubstantial with the Father in his divinity and the same consubstantial with us in his humanity, born of the Father before the ages in his divinity and these last days the same ... born of the Virgin Mary in his humanity.[11]

When in the next paragraph the decree speaks of person and natures, there is no doubt that the one person is the one and the same Son our Lord, and that the two natures are his divinity and his humanity. Still this statement can occur in a logical context, in an incipiently metaphysical context, and in a fully metaphysical context. When these contexts are not distinguished, when some of them are not even understood, Chalcedon's talk about person and nature can be made very mystifying.

There is a logical context. It simply operates on propositions. It may be illustrated by the account, given above, of the meaning of consubstantiality. It may be illustrated again by the later Christological doctrine of the *communicatio idiomatum*. On this showing, Chalcedon mentions person and nature because it is aware that people may ask whether divinity and humanity are one and the same and, if not, how is it that the Son our Lord Jesus Christ is one and the same. To forestall this doubt the council speaks of person and nature: the Son our Lord is one person; divinity and humanity are two natures.

There is an incipiently metaphysical context. About seventy-five years after Chalcedon, Byzantine theologians discovered that if Christ is one person with two natures then one of the natures must be personless. There followed not a little discussion of *enhypostasia* and *anhypostasia*, that is, of being a nature with and without being a person.[12]

There is a fully metaphysical context. It distinguishes verbal, notional, and real distinctions; it further distinguishes major and minor real distinctions; it divides minor real distinctions into the

[11] DS 301.

[12] Recent and original: D. B. Evans, *Leontius of Byzantium, An Origenist Christology*, Dumbarton Oaks, 1970. Distributed by J. J. Augustin, Publisher, Locust Valley, New York.

ordinary case and the analogical instance found in the mystery of the Incarnation; and, finally, it seeks the imperfect but very fruitful understanding of the mystery commended by the first Vatican council (*DS* 3016).

The fully metaphysical context emerges only in a late and fully self-conscious Scholasticism. But in its fundamental intention and style Scholasticism was a thorough-going effort to attain a coherent and orderly assimilation of the Christian tradition. The enormous differences between the two great figures, Anselm of Canterbury and Thomas Aquinas, were the result of a century and a half of unremitting labors to assemble and classify the data, to work towards an understanding of them in commentaries, to digest them by establishing the existence of questions and by seeking solutions for them, and to ensure the coherence of multitudinous solutions by using the Aristotelian corpus as a substructure.

Now the greater part of this work resembles the medieval anticipations of modern science. What has often been described as a transition from the implicit to the explicit, really was a transition of Christian consciousness from a lesser to a fuller differentiation. That consciousness had been differentiated by a common sense, by religion, by an artistic and literary culture, and by the slight dose of systematic meaning found in the Greek councils. In the medieval period it began to acquire a strong dose of systematic meaning. Terms were defined. Problems were solved. What had been lived and spoken of in one way, now became the object of reflex thought that reorganized, correlated, explained. About the middle of the twelfth century, Peter Lombard worked out a precise, explanatory meaning for the old and ambiguous name, sacrament, and in the light of this meaning discovered that there were seven sacraments in Christian practice. On each of these seven, traditional doctrines were collected, ordered, clarified, presented.

Again, the middle ages inherited from Augustine his affirmation of both divine grace and human liberty. For a long time it was difficult to say that there existed any finite thing that was not God's free gift. Though it was obvious that grace named not everything but something special, still lists of graces properly so called not only differed from one another but also betrayed not a little arbitrariness. At the same time it was very difficult for a theologian to say what he meant by liberty. Philosophers could define it as immunity from necessity. But theologians could not conceive liberty as free from the necessity of grace, or good without grace, or even evil with it. But what tortured the twelfth century found its solution in the thirteenth. About the year 1230 Philip the Chancellor completed a discovery that in the next forty years released a whole series of developments. The discovery was a distinction between two entitatively disproportionate orders: grace was above nature; faith was above reason; charity was above human good will; merit before God was above the good opinion of one's neighbors. This distinction and organization made it possible (1) to discuss the nature of grace without discussing liberty, (2) to discuss the nature of liberty without discussing grace, and (3) to work out the relations between grace and liberty.[13]

I have been sketching what may be considered the bright side of medieval theological development. I now must express some reservations. There can be little doubt that it was necessary for medieval thinkers to turn to some outside source to obtain a systematic substructure. There is little doubt that they could not do better than to turn to Aristotle. But today it is very evident that Aristotle has been superseded. Magnificently he represented an early stage of human development—the emergence of systematic meaning. But he did not anticipate the later emergence of a method that envisaged an ongoing succession of systems. He did not envisage the later emergence of a *Philologie* that made its aim the historical reconstruction of the constructions of mankind. He did not formulate the later ideal of a philosophy that was at once critical and historically-minded, that would cut to the roots

---

[13] On this process see my *Grace and Freedom: Operative Grace in the Thought of St. Thomas Aquinas*, London: Darton, Longman & Todd, and New York: Herder and Herder, 1971. The significance of Philip's distinction was that the two orders constituted the definition of grace and thereby eliminated the earlier extrinsic view that conceived grace as the liberation of liberty.

of philosophic disputes, and that would ground a view that embraced the differentiations of human consciousness and the epochs of human history.

Not only has Aristotle been superseded, but also certain defects have become manifest. His ideal of science in terms of necessity has been set aside not only by modern empirical science but also by modern mathematics. Again, there is to his thinking a certain blurring of the difference between the common names developed by common sense and the technical terms elaborated by explanatory science. Both of these defects, magnified several times, reappear in the fourteenth and fifteenth century Scholasticism. The excessively rigorous ideal of science offers some explanation for the emergence first of scepticism and then of decadence. The blurred distinction between common names and technical terms has some responsibility for the verbalism for which Scholasticism has been so bitterly reproached.

Church doctrines and theological doctrines pertain to different contexts. Church doctrines are the content of the church's witness to Christ; they express the set of meanings and values that inform individual and collective Christian living. Theological doctrines are part of an academic discipline, concerned to know and understand the Christian tradition and to further its development. As the two contexts are directed to quite distinct ends, so too they are unequal in extent. Theologians raise many questions that are not mentioned in church doctrines. Again, theologians may differ from one another though they belong to the same church. In Catholic circles, finally, the relations of theological schools to one another and to church doctrines is a carefully mapped terrain. What are called theological notes and ecclesiastical censures not only distinguish matters of faith and theological opinions but also indicate a whole spectrum of intermediate positions.[14]

Now from the middle ages right up to Vatican II the doctrines of the Catholic Church have been deriving from theology a precision, a conciseness, and an organization that in earlier times

[14] See E. J. Fortman, "Notes, theological", NCE 10, 523; and the systematic index to DS at H 1d and H 1bb, pp. 848 and 847.

they did not possess. In general, the meaning of these doctrines is not systematic but, commonly, it is post-systematic. One cannot infer what a church document must mean from one's knowledge of theology. At the same time any exact interpretation will presuppose a knowledge of theology. But it will also presuppose a knowledge of the *stylus curiae*. Finally, these presuppositions are necessary but not sufficient conditions. To know what church documents actually do mean calls for research and exegesis in each case.

No doubt, what readers would wish to find here is an account of the legitimacy of this influence of theology on church doctrine. But that, of course, is not a methodological but a theological question. What the methodologist may do, however, is point to the different contexts in which such questions have been raised. First, prior to the emergence of historically-mindedness, one had the alternatives of anachronism and archaism. The anachronist attributed to scripture and to the Fathers an implicit grasp of what the Scholastics discovered. The archaist, on the other hand, regarded as a corruption any doctrine that was not to be found in the plain meaning either of scripture or of scripture and patristic tradition. Secondly, as historical knowledge increased, various theories of development were worked out and applied with greater or less success. There is, however, a third option: it would contend that there can be many kinds of developments and that, to know them, one has to study and analyze concrete historical processes while, to know their legitimacy, one has to turn to evaluational history and assign them their place in the dialectic of the presence and absence of intellectual, moral, and religious conversion.

But at this point it is necessary to interrupt our sketch of the ongoing discovery of mind and to introduce the notion of ongoing contexts.

6. ONGOING CONTEXTS

Already a distinction has been drawn between material and formal context. Thus the canon of the New Testament is the material context of each of the books in the New Testament: it tells which are the other highly privileged areas of data on early Christianity. On the other hand, a formal context is reached through investigation: data give rise to questions; questions to opposed answers; opposed answers to further questions and further opposed answers. The puzzle keeps increasing, until a discovery is made. Gradually, things begin to fit together. There may occur a period of rapidly increasing insight. Eventually further questions begin to yield decreasing returns. A viewpoint is attained, and, while further questions can be asked, answers to them would not significantly modify what has already been ascertained. There has been built up a formal context: a set of interwoven questions and answers that reveal the meaning of a text.

Ongoing context arises when a succession of texts express the mind of a single historical community. Such an ongoing context necessitates a distinction between prior and subsequent context. Thus a statement may intend to deal with one issue and to prescind from other, further issues. But settling one does not burke the others. Usually it contributes to a clearer grasp of the others and to a more urgent pressure for their solution. According to Athanasius the council of Nicea used a non-scriptural term, not to set a precedent, but to meet an emergency. But the emergency lasted for some thirty-five years and, some twenty years after it had subsided, the first council of Constantinople felt it necessary to answer in a non-technical manner whether only the Son or also the Holy Spirit was consubstantial with the Father. Fifty years later at Ephesus, it was necessary to clarify Nicea by affirming that it was one and the same that was born of the Father and also born of the Virgin Mary. Twenty-one years later it was necessary to add that one and the same could be both eternal and temporal, both immortal and mortal, because he had two natures. Over two centuries later there was added the further clarification that the divine person with two natures also had two operations and two wills.

Such is the ongoing context of church doctrines that did not exist prior to Nicea but, bit by bit, came into existence subsequently to Nicea. It does not state what was intended at Nicea.

It does state what resulted from Nicea and what became in fact the context within which Nicea was to be understood.

As one may distinguish prior and subsequent stages in an ongoing context, so one ongoing context may be related to another. Of these relations the commonest are derivation and inter-action. Thus, the ongoing context that runs from Nicea to the third council of Constantinople derives from the doctrines of the first three centuries of Christianity but differs from them inasmuch as it employs a post-systematic mode of thought and expression. Again, the ongoing context of conciliar doctrines gave rise to a distinct but dependent context of theological doctrines. This presupposed the councils, distinguished Christ as God and Christ as man, and raised such questions as follow. Could Christ as man sin? Did he feel concupiscence? Was he in any way ignorant? Did he have sanctifying grace? To what extent? Did he have immediate knowledge of God? Did he know everything per-taining to his mission? Did he have freedom of choice?

Again, the theological context derived from the Greek councils expanded in the medieval schools to envisage the whole of scripture and tradition. It was not only ongoing, collaborative, and methodical but also dialectical. It was a context that em-braced mutually opposed schools of thought, that came to distinguish between opposition in theological doctrine and opposition in church doctrine, that agreed to differ on the former and declined to differ on the latter.

Finally, interacting contexts are represented by the context of theological doctrines and the context of church doctrines from the medieval period up to Vatican II. The theologians were under the influence of the church doctrines on which they reflected. Inversely, without the theologians, the church doctrines would not have had their post-systematic precision, conciseness, and organization.

7. THE ONGOING DISCOVERY OF MIND: PART TWO

The medieval decision to use the Aristotelian corpus as a substructure involved an integration of theology with a philo-sophy and with a detailed account of the material universe.

Such an integration offered the advantage of a unified world-view, but neither classicist culture nor Aristotelian thought inculcated the principle that unified world-views are subject to notable changes.

For centuries the Christian's image of himself and of his world was drawn from the first chapters of Genesis, from Jewish apocalyptic and Ptolemaic astronomy, and from the theological doctrines of the creation and immortality of each human soul. That image has been assaulted by novel scientific traditions stemming from Copernicus, Newton, Darwin, Freud, Heisenberg. It has been the great merit of Teilhard de Chardin to have recognized the Christian's need of a coherent image of himself in his world and to have contributed not a little towards meeting that need.

Once it was held that science was certain knowledge of things through their causes. Too often churchmen have presupposed that that definition was applicable to modern science. But modern science is not certain but probable. It attends to data rather than things. It speaks of causes but it means correlations and not end, agent, matter, form.

Once it was held that science was concerned with the universal and the necessary. Today in mathematics necessity is a marginal notion: conclusions indeed follow necessarily from their premisses; but basic premisses are freely chosen postulates and not necessary truths. In the early decades of this century scientists still spoke of the necessary laws of nature and even of the iron laws of economics. Quantum theory and Keynsian economics have put an end to that.

Scholarship once made its aim the attainment of humanistic eloquence. But early nineteenth-century *Philologie* set itself the goal of reconstructing the constructions of mankind. Its initial successes were in the fields of classical studies and of European history. But it has long since moved into the fields of biblical, patristic, and medieval studies. Its works are specialized, collaborative, ongoing, massive. What formerly was supposed to lie within the competence of a single dogmatic theologian, now can be undertaken only by a very large team.

There was a time when necessary principles were the acknowledged basis of philosophy, and these principles were identified with the self-evident propositions that were the basic premisses for philosophic deductions. Now it is true that there exist analytic propositions: if one defines A by the possession of a relation, R, to B, then there cannot be an A without a relation, R, to B. But it is equally true that there need exist no A with a relation, R, to B. For finite existence is known, not by defining terms, not by constructing analytic propositions, but by a process named verification.

Aristotle and his followers acknowledged special sciences that deal with beings of determinate kinds and a general science that dealt with being as being. Now the natural and human sciences aim at accounting for all the data of sense. Accordingly, if there is to be any general science, its data will have to be the data of consciousness. So there is effected the turn to interiority. The general science is, first, cognitional theory (what are you doing when you are knowing?), secondly, epistemology (why is doing that knowing?), and thirdly metaphysics (what do you know when you do it?). Such general science will be the general case of the methods of the special sciences and not, as in Aristotelianism, the general case of the content of the special sciences.

The foregoing shift to interiority was essayed in various manners from Descartes through Kant to the nineteenth-century German idealists. But there followed a still more emphatic shift from knowledge to faith, will, conscience, decision, action in Kierkegaard, Schopenhauer, Newman, Nietzsche, Blondel, the personalists, and the existentialists. The direction of this shift is correct in the sense that the fourth level of intentional consciousness—the level of deliberation, evaluation, decision, action——sublates the prior levels of experiencing, understanding, judging. It goes beyond them, sets up a new principle and type of operations, directs them to a new goal but, so far from dwarfing them, preserves them and brings them to a far fuller fruition.

Not only does the fourth level sublate the previous three, but also the previous three differ notably from the speculative intellect that was supposed to grasp self-evident and necessary truths. Such a speculative intellect could and did claim complete autonomy: bad will could hardly interfere with the apprehension of self-evident and necessary truth or with the necessary conclusions following from such truth. In fact, however, what human intelligence grasps in data and expresses in concepts is, not a necessarily relevant intelligibility, but only a possibly relevant intelligibility. Such intelligibility is intrinsically hypothetical and so always in need of a further process of checking and verifying before it can be asserted as *de facto* relevant to the data in hand. So it has come about that modern science is under the guidance of method, and the method that is selected and followed results not only from experiencing, understanding, and judging, but also from a decision.

I have been indicating in summary fashion a series of fundamental changes that have come about in the last four centuries and a half. They modify man's image of himself in his world, his science and his conception of science, his history and his conception of history, his philosophy and his conception of philosophy. They involve three basic differentiations of consciousness, and all three are quite beyond the horizon of ancient Greece and medieval Europe.

These changes have, in general, been resisted by churchmen for two reasons. The first reason commonly has been that churchmen had no real apprehension of the nature of these changes. The second reason has been that these changes commonly have been accompanied by a lack of intellectual conversion and so were hostile to Christianity.

Modern science is one thing and the extra-scientific opinions of scientists are another. Among the extra-scientific opinions of scientists up to the acceptance of quantum theory was a mechanist determinism that misrepresented nature and excluded human freedom and responsibility.[15]

Modern history is one thing and the philosophic assumptions of historians are another. H. G. Gadamer has examined the

---

[15] For an account of the scientists' philosophic successor to mechanist determinism, see P. A. Heelan, *Quantum Mechanics and Objectivity*, The Hague: Nijhoff, 1965.

assumptions of Schleiermacher, Ranke, Droysen, and Dilthey.[16] In more summary fashion Kurt Frör has stated that the work of historians in the earlier part of the nineteenth century was marked by a mixture of philosophic speculation and empirical research, and that what eliminated the speculation in the later part of the century was an ever more influential positivism.[17] The resultant historicism penetrated into biblical studies and there the resounding reactions were the work of Barth and Bultmann. Both acknowledged the significance of moral and religious conversion. In Barth this appeared in his contention that, while the bible was to be read historically, it also was to be read religiously; and religious reading was not merely a matter of pious feelings in the reader; it had also to attend to the realities of which the bible spoke.[18] In Bultmann, on the other hand, religious and moral conversion is the *existenziell* response to the appeal or challenge of the *kerygma*. But such a response is a subjective event, and its objectification results in myth.[19] While Bultmann is no ordinary positivist, for he knows about *verstehen*, still for him biblical study falls into two parts: there is the scientific part that is independent of religious belief; and there is the religious part that penetrates beneath the mythical objectifications of the bible to the subjective religious events to which it testifies.

In both Barth and Bultmann, though in different manners, there is revealed the need for intellectual as well as moral and religious conversion. Only intellectual conversion can remedy Barth's fideism. Only intellectual conversion can remove the secularist notion of scientific exegesis represented by Bultmann. Still intellectual conversion alone is not enough. It has to be made explicit in a philosophic and theological method, and such an explicit method has to include a critique both of the method of science and of the method of scholarship.

[16] H. G. Gadamer, *Wahrheit und Methode*, Tübingen: Mohr, 1960, pp. 162 ff.

[17] K. Frör, *Biblische Hermeneutik*, München: Kaiser, 1964, p. 28.

[18] Ibid., pp. 31 f.

[19] Ibid., pp. 34 ff. On the dualism in Bultmann's exegesis see Paul Minear, "The Transcendence of God and Biblical Hermeneutics," *Proceedings, Cath. Theol. Soc. Amer.*, 23(1968), 5 f.

8. THE DEVELOPMENT OF DOCTRINES

Already I have suggested that there is not some one manner or even some limited set of manners in which doctrines develop. In other words the intelligibility proper to developing doctrines is the intelligibility immanent in historical process. One knows it, not by *a priori* theorizing, but by *a posteriori* research, interpretation, history, dialectic, and the decision of foundations.

One cluster of manners, in which doctrines develop, I have named the ongoing discovery of mind. When consciousness constructs its world symbolically, it advances by reinterpreting traditional materials. When it leans towards philosophy, a Xenophanes or a Clement of Alexandria will rule anthropomorphism out of man's apprehension of the divine. The resulting purely spiritual apprehension of God will create a tension between biblical and later Christology, and the technical means available in a post-systematic culture may be employed to clarify the faith. The use of such technical means opens the door to a theology in which systematic meaning becomes predominant, and such theology in its turn can give to church doctrines a precision, a conciseness, and an organization that otherwise they would not possess. Finally, such a general involvement in the systematic can be undercut by the methodical, the scholarly, and the modern philosophic differentiations of consciousness to present the church with the dilemma of reverting to an antenicene Christology or of advancing to a thoroughly modern position.

However, the foregoing cluster, while it envisages not a little of doctrinal development, is not to be considered the whole story. Often enough development is dialectical. The truth is discovered because a contrary error has been asserted.

Again, doctrines are not just doctrines. They are constitutive both of the individual Christian and of the Christian community. They can strengthen or burden the individual's allegiance. They can unite or disrupt. They can confer authority and power. They can be associated with what is congenial or what is alien to a given polity or culture. It is not in some vacuum of pure spirit but under concrete historical conditions and circumstances that developments occur, and a knowledge of such conditions and circumstances is not irrelevant in the evaluational history that decides on the legitimacy of developments.

In closing this brief section, I note Prof. Geiselmann's view that the dogmas of the Immaculate Conception and of the Assumption of our Lady differ from those defined in ecumenical councils. The latter settle controverted issues. The former repeat what was already taught and celebrated in the whole Catholic church. Accordingly they are named by him "cultic".[20] Their sole effect was that the solemn teaching office now proclaims what formerly was proclaimed by the ordinary teaching office. Perhaps I might suggest that human psychology and specifically the refinement of human feelings is the area to be explored in coming to understand the development of Marian doctrines.

9. THE PERMANENCE OF DOGMAS

The permanence of the meaning of dogmas was taught in the constitution, Dei Filius, promulgated in the first Vatican council. This occurs in the last paragraph of the last chapter of the decree (DS 3020) and in the appended canon (DS 3043). Just what was meant, supposed, implied in this affirmation of permanent meaning, comes to light from a study of the constitution itself.

To the fourth and final chapter there were appended three canons. They reveal that the thrust of this chapter was directed against a rationalism that considered mysteries non-existent, that proposed to demonstrate the dogmas, that defended scientific conclusions opposed to church doctrines, that claimed the church had no right to pass judgment on scientific views, and that granted science the competence to reinterpret the church's dogmas (DS 3041–3043).

To deal with such rationalism the council had distinguished (1) the natural light of reason, (2) faith, (3) reason illumined by faith, and (4) reason operating beyond its competence. Something must be said on each of these.

[20] J. R. Geiselmann, "Dogma", Handbuch theologischer Grundbegriffe, edited by H. Fries, München: Kösel, 1962, I, 231.

Reason, then, or the natural light of reason has a range of objects within its reach (*DS* 3015). It can know with certitude of the existence of God (*DS* 3004), and it can know some but not all of the truths revealed by God (*DS* 3005, 3015). It should accept divine revelation (*DS* 3008), and such acceptance is in harmony with its nature (*DS* 3009). In no way does the church prohibit human disciplines from using their proper principles and methods within their own fields (*DS* 3019).

Faith is a supernatural virtue by which we believe to be true what God has revealed, not because we apprehend the intrinsic truth of what has been revealed, but because of the authority of God who reveals and can neither deceive nor be deceived (*DS* 3008). By faith that is both divine and catholic there are to be believed all that has been revealed by God in scripture or tradition and, as well, has been proposed to be believed as revealed either in a solemn pronouncement by the church or in the exercise of its ordinary and universal teaching office (*DS* 3011). Among the principal objects of faith are the mysteries hidden in God, which, were they not revealed, could not be known by us (*DS* 3015, cf. 3005).

Reason illumined by faith, when it inquires diligently, piously, soberly, reaches with God's help some extremely fruitful understanding of the mysteries. Such understanding rests on the analogy of things known naturally and on the interconnection of the mysteries with one another and with man's last end. But it never becomes capable of grasping them after the fashion it can understand the truths that lie within its proper range. For the divine mysteries by their very nature so exceed created intellect that, even given in relevation and accepted by faith, they remain as it were wrapped in the veil of faith (*DS* 3016).

It would seem to be the understanding attained by reason when illumined by faith that is praised in the quotation from Vincent of Lerins. For such understanding is of the mystery, and not of some human substitute, and so from the nature of the case it must be "... in suo dumtaxat genere, in eodem scilicet dogmate, eodem sensu eademque sententia" (*DS* 3020).

In contrast there is reason that steps beyond its proper bounds to invade and disturb the realm of faith (DS 3019). For the doctrine of faith, which God has revealed, has not been proposed as some sort of philosophic discovery to be perfected by human talent. It is a divine deposit, given to the spouse of Christ, to be guarded faithfully and declared infallibly. Hence there is ever to be retained that meaning of the sacred dogmas that once was declared by the church. From that meaning there is to be no departure under the pretext of some profounder understanding (DS 3020).

In the corresponding canon there is condemned anyone that says it is possible that eventually with the progress of science there may have to be given to the dogmas propounded by the church a meaning other than that which the church understands and understood (DS 3043).

First, then, there is affirmed a permanence of meaning: ". . . is sensus perpetuo est retinendus . . . nec umquam ab eo recedendum . . . in eodem scilicet dogmate, eodem sensu eademque sententia". (DS 3020). ". . . ne sensus tribuendus sit alius . . ." (DS 3043).

Secondly, the permanent meaning is the meaning declared by the church (DS 3020), the meaning which the church understood and understands (DS 3043).

Thirdly, this permanent meaning is the meaning of dogmas (DS 3020, 3043). But are dogmas revealed truths or revealed mysteries? The difference is that revealed mysteries lie beyond the competence of reason, but some revealed truths do not (DS 3005, 3015).

It would seem that the dogmas of DS 3020 and 3043 refer to the church's declarations of revealed mysteries. For the recurring contrast of the fourth chapter is between reason and faith. Only in the first paragraph (DS 3015) is there any mention of truths that are both of reason and of faith. Human disciplines would not be stepping beyond their proper bounds if they treated such truths (DS 3019). Nor can they be denied the status of a philosophic discovery to be perfected by human talent (DS 3020). Again, truths within reason's competence would seem capable of being known more accurately with the progress of science (DS 3043). Finally, it is only the mysteries that transcend the intelligence of the human mind (DS 3005), that stand beyond created intellect (DS 3016), that are accepted simply on God's authority (DS 3008), that could not be known unless they were revealed (DS 3015), that can admit no more than an analogous and imperfect understanding by human reason and then only when illumined by faith (DS 3016), that accordingly can claim to stand beyond the status of the products of human history.

Fourthly, the meaning of the dogma is not apart from a verbal formulation, for it is a meaning declared by the church. However, the permanence attaches to the meaning and not to the formula. To retain the same formula and give it a new meaning is precisely what the third canon excludes (DS 3043). Fifthly, it seems better to speak of the permanence of the meaning of dogmas rather than of its immutability. For permanence is the meaning of "... perpetuo retinendus ... numquam recedendum ... (ne) sensus tribuendus sit alius. ...." Again, it is permanence rather than immutability that is meant when there is desired an ever better understanding of the same dogma, the same meaning, the same pronouncement.

To conclude, there are two grounds for affirming the permanence of the meaning of revealed mysteries. There is the *causa cognoscendi*: what God has revealed and the church has infallibly declared, is true. What is true, is permanent: the meaning it possessed in its own context can never be denied truthfully.

There is also the *causa essendi*. The meaning of a dogma is not a datum but a truth. It is not a human truth but the revelation of a mystery hidden in God. One is denying divine transcendence if one fancies man has at his disposal the evidence that would enable him to substitute some other meaning for the meaning that has been revealed.

Such I believe is the doctrine of Vatican I on the permanence of the meaning of dogmas. It presupposes (1) that there exist mysteries hidden in God that man could not know unless they were revealed, (2) that they have been revealed, and (3) that the church has infallibly declared the meaning of what has been revealed. These presuppositions also are church doctrines. Their exposition and defence are tasks, not of a methodologist, but of a theologian.

IO. THE HISTORICITY OF DOGMAS

The constitution, *Dei Filius*, of Vatican I was occasioned by two currents in nineteenth-century Catholic thought. There were traditionalists that had little trust in human reason, and there were semi-rationalists who, while not denying the truths of faith, tended to place them within the competence of reason. Among the latter were Anton Günther, whose speculations attracted a wide following but were rejected by the Holy See (*DS* 2828 ff.), and Jakob Frohschammer, whose views on human perfectibility were no more acceptable (*DS* 2850 ff.; cf. 2908 f.). Such views were further pursued by Cardinal Franzelin both in the *votum* he presented to the preconciliar committee[21] and in the schema he presented for discussion in the early days of Vatican I.[22]

But as earlier we remarked about Nicea, so now we must repeat about Vatican I that its statements lie not only within the prior context of the thought of 1870 but also within the consequent context that attends to issues from which Vatican I saw fit to prescind. For Günther and Frohschammer in their different ways were concerned with historicity and specifically with the historicity of church doctrines. Vatican I was content to select an aspect of their views that was unacceptable. But it did not attempt to deal with the underlying issue of the historicity of dogma that since has come into prominence. We must ask, then, whether the doctrine of Vatican I on the permanence of the meaning of dogmas can be reconciled with the historicity that characterizes human thought and action.

---

[21] The *votum* has been published by Hermann J. Pottmeyer in his work, *Der Glaube vor dem Anspruch der Wissenschaft*, Freiburg: Herder, 1968. See the appendix especially pp. 50*, 51*, 54*, 55*. There is a valuable discussion of *DS* 3020 and 3043 on pp. 431–456.

[22] See Chapters Five, Six, Eleven, Twelve, and Fourteen of Franzelin's schema in Mansi 50, 62–69, and the abundant annotations, Mansi 50, 83 ff.

Briefly, the theoretical premisses from which there follows the historicity of human thought and action are (1) that human concepts, theories, affirmations, courses of actions are expressions of human understanding, (2) that human understanding develops over time and, as it develops, human concepts, theories, affirmations, courses of action change, (3) that such change is cumulative, and (4) that the cumulative changes in one place or time are not to be expected to coincide with those in another.

However, there is a notable difference between the fuller understanding of data and the fuller understanding of a truth. When data are more fully understood, there result the emergence of a new theory and the rejection of previous theories. Such is the ongoing process in the empirical sciences. But when a truth is more fully understood, it is still the same truth that is being understood. It is true that the sum of two and two is four. That same truth has been known in quite different contexts, say, by the ancient Babylonians, by the Greeks, and by modern mathematicians. But it is better understood by the modern mathematicians than it was by the Greeks, and in all likelihood it was better understood by the Greek thinkers than by the Babylonians.

Now the dogmas are permanent in their meaning because they are not just data but expressions of truths and, indeed, of truths that, were they not revealed by God, could not be known by man. Once they are revealed and believed, they can be better and better understood. But that ever better understanding is of the revealed truth and not of something else.

Nor is this opposed to the historicity of the dogmas. For dogmas are statements. Statements have meaning only within their contexts. Contexts are ongoing, and ongoing contexts are related principally by derivation and by interaction. Truths can be revealed in one culture and preached in another. They may be revealed in the styles and fashion of one differentiation of consciousness, defined by the church in the style and fashion of another differentiation, and understood by theologians in a third. What permanently is true, is the meaning of the dogma in the context in which it was defined. To ascertain that meaning there have to be deployed the resources of research, interpretation, history, dialectic. To state that meaning today one proceeds through foundations, doctrines, and systematics to communications. Communications finally are to each class in each culture and to each of the various differentiations of consciousness.

The permanence of the dogmas, then, results from the fact that they express revealed mysteries. Their historicity, on the other hand, results from the facts that (1) statements have meanings only in their contexts and (2) contexts are ongoing and ongoing contexts are multiple.

What is opposed to the historicity of the dogmas is, not their permanence, but classicist assumptions and achievements. Classicism assumed that culture was to be conceived not empirically but normatively, and it did all it could to bring about one, universal, permanent culture. What ended classicist assumptions was critical history. What builds the bridges between the many expressions of the faith is a methodical theology.

II. PLURALISM AND THE UNITY OF FAITH

There are three sources of pluralism. First, linguistic, social, and cultural differences give rise to different brands of common sense. Secondly, consciousness may be undifferentiated or it may be differentiated to deal expertly with some combination of such different realms as common sense, transcendence, beauty, system, method, scholarship, and philosophic interiority. Thirdly, in any individual at any given time there may exist the abstract possibility, or the beginnings, or greater or less progress, or high development of intellectual or moral or religious conversion.

There are two ways in which the unity of the faith may be conceived. On classicist assumptions there is just one culture. That one culture is not attained by the simple faithful, the people, the natives, the barbarians. None the less, career is always open to talent. One enters upon such a career by diligent study of the ancient Latin and Greek authors. One pursues such a career by learning Scholastic philosophy and theology. One aims at high office by becoming proficient in canon law. One succeeds by winning the approbation and favor of the right personages. Within this set-up the unity of faith is a matter of everyone subscribing to the correct formulae.

Such classicism, however, was never more than the shabby shell of Catholicism. The real root and ground of unity is being in love with God—the fact that God's love has flooded our inmost hearts through the Holy Spirit he has given us (Rom. 5, 5). The acceptance of this gift both constitutes religious conversion and leads to moral and even intellectual conversion.

Further, religious conversion, if it is Christian, is not just a state of mind and heart. Essential to it is an intersubjective, interpersonal component. Besides the gift of the Spirit within, there is the outward encounter with Christian witness. That witness testifies that of old in many ways God has spoken to us through the prophets but in this latest age through his Son (Heb. 1, 1.2).

Thirdly, the function of church doctrines lies within the function of Christian witness. For the witness is to the mysteries revealed by God and, for Catholics, infallibly declared by the church. The meaning of such declarations lies beyond the vicissitudes of human historical process. But the contexts, within which such meaning is grasped, and so the manner, in which such meaning is expressed, vary both with cultural differences and with the measure in which human consciousness is differentiated.

Such variation is familiar to us from the past. According to Vatican II revelation occurred not through words alone but through words and deeds.[23] The apostolic preaching was addressed not only to Jews in the thought-forms of *Spätjudentum* but also to Greeks in their language and idiom. While the New Testament writings spoke more to the heart than to the head, the Christological councils aimed solely at formulating the truths that were to guide one's mind and one's lips. When Scholastic theology recast Christian belief into a mould derived from Aristotle, it was deserting neither divine revelation nor scripture nor the councils. And if modern theologians were to transpose medieval theory into the categories derived from contemporary

[23] Second Vatican Council, *Dogmatic Constitution on Divine Revelation*, I, 2.

interiority and its real correlatives, they would be doing for our age what the greater Scholastics did for theirs.

In the past, then, there has existed a notable pluralism of expression. Currently in the church there is quietly disappearing the old classicist insistence on worldwide uniformity, and there is emerging a pluralism of manners in which Christian meaning and Christian values are communicated. To preach the gospel to all nations is to preach it to every class in every culture in the manner that accords with the assimilative powers of that class and culture.

For the most part such preaching will be to a consciousness that is little differentiated. So it will have to be as multiform as are the diverse brands of common sense generated by the many languages, social forms, and cultural meanings and values of mankind. In each case the preacher will have to know the brand of common sense to which he speaks, and he will have ever to keep in mind that, when consciousness is only slightly differentiated, coming to know does not occur apart from acting.

But if the faith is to be nourished in those with little education, it does not follow that the educated are to be neglected. Now just as the only way to understand another's brand of common sense is to come to understand the way in which he or she would understand, speak, act in any of the series of situations that commonly arise in his or her experience, so too the only way to understand another's differentiation of consciousness is to bring about that differentiation in oneself.

Further an exact grasp of another's mentality is possible only if one attains the same differentiation and lack of differentiation. For each differentiation of consciousness involves a certain re-modeling of common sense. Initially common sense assumes its own omnicompetence because it just cannot know better. But as successive differentiations of consciousness occur, more and more realms are controlled in the appropriate fashion and so are removed from the competence of common sense. Clarity and adequacy increase by bounds. One's initial common sense is purged of its simplifications, its metaphors, its myths, and its mystifications. With the attainment of full differentiation common sense is confined entirely to its proper realm of the immediate, the particular, the concrete.

However, there are many routes to full attainment and many varieties of partial attainment. Preaching the gospel to all means preaching it in the manner appropriate to each of the varieties of partial attainment and, no less, to full attainment. It was to meet the exigences proper to the beginnings of systematic meaning that Clement of Alexandria denied that the anthropomorphisms of scripture were to be taken literally. It was to meet the exigences of fully systematic meaning that medieval Scholasticism sought a coherent account of all the truths of faith and reason. It was to meet the exigences of contemporary scholarship that the second Vatican council decreed that the interpreter of scripture had to determine the meaning intended by the biblical writer and accordingly had to do so by understanding the literary conventions and cultural conditions of that writer's place and time.

The church, then, following the example of St. Paul, becomes all things to all men. It communicates what God has revealed both in the manner appropriate to the various differentiations of consciousness and, above all, in the manner appropriate to each of the almost endless brands of common sense. Still, these many modes of speech involve no more than a pluralism of communications for, though they are many, still all can be *in eodem dogmate, eodem sensu eademque sententia.*

Still, becoming all to all, even though it involves no more than a pluralism of communications, none the less is not without its difficulties. On the one hand, it demands a many-sided development in those that govern or teach. On the other hand, every achievement is apt to be challenged by those that fail to achieve. People with little notion of modern scholarship can urge that attending to the literary genre of biblical writings is just a fraudulent device for rejecting the plain meaning of scripture. Those with no taste for systematic meaning will keep repeating that it is better to feel compunction than to define it, even if those that attempt definition insist that one can hardly define what one does not experience. Those, finally, whose consciousness is unmitigated by any tincture of systematic meaning, will be unable to grasp the meaning of such dogmas as Nicea and they may gaily leap to the conclusion that what has no meaning for them is just meaningless.

Such difficulties suggest certain rules. First, because the gospel is to be preached to all, there must be sought the modes of representation and of expression appropriate to communicating revealed truth both to every brand of common sense and to every differentiation of consciousness. Secondly, no one, simply because of his faith, is obliged to attain a more fully differentiated consciousness. Thirdly, no one, simply because of his faith, is obliged to refrain from attaining an ever more differentiated consciousness. Fourthly, anyone may strive to express his faith in the manner appropriate to his differentiation of consciousness. Fifthly, no one should pass judgment on matters he does not understand, and no one with a less or a differently differentiated consciousness is capable of understanding accurately what is said by a person with a more fully differentiated consciousness.

Such pluralism will have little appeal to persons with a propensity to over-simplification. But the real menace to unity of faith does not lie either in the many brands of common sense or the many differentiations of human consciousness. It lies in the absence of intellectual or moral or religious conversion. The pluralism that results from lack of conversion is particularly perilous in three manners. First, when the absence of conversion occurs in those that govern the church or teach in its name. Secondly, when, as at present, there is going forward in the church a movement out of classicist and into modern culture. Thirdly, when persons with partially differentiated consciousness not only do not understand one another but also so extol system or method or scholarship or interiority or slightly advanced prayer as to set aside achievement and block development in the other four.

12. THE AUTONOMY OF THEOLOGY

What Karl Rahner refers to as *Denzingertheologie*, the late Pierre Charles of Louvain named Christian positivism. It conceived the function of the theologian to be that of a propagandist for church doctrines. He did his duty when he repeated, explained, defended just what had been said in church documents. He had no contribution of his own to make and so there could be no question of his possessing any autonomy in making it.

Now it is true, of course, that theology is neither a source of divine revelation nor an addition to inspired scripture nor an authority that promulgates church doctrines. It is also true that a Christian theologian should be an authentic human being and an authentic Christian and so will be second to none in his acceptance of revelation, scripture, and his church doctrine. But these premises do not lead to the conclusion that a theologian is just a parrot with nothing to do but repeat what has already been said.

From the history of theology it is clear that theologians treat many matters which church doctrines do not treat and that they have been the first to propound theological doctrines that, particularly in the Catholic church, provided the background and some part of the content of subsequent church doctrines. So it is that in our chapter on *Functional Specialties* we drew a distinction between religion and reflection on religion, identified such reflection with theology, and found theology so highly specialized that over and above field specialization and subject specialization we distinguished eight functional specialties.

The theologian, then, has a contribution of his own to make. Consequently, he possesses some autonomy, for otherwise he could make no contribution that was his own. Moreover, on the present account of theological method, there has been worked out the criterion that is to guide the theologian in the exercise of his autonomy. For the functional specialty, dialectic, assembles, classifies, analyzes the conflicting views of evaluators, historians, interpreters, researchers. The functional specialty, foundations, determines which views are the positions that proceed from the presence of intellectual, moral, and religious conversion, and which are the counter-positions that reveal its absence. In other words, each theologian will judge the authenticity of the authors of views, and he will do so by the touchstone of his own authenticity. This, of course, is far from a foolproof method. But it will tend to bring the authentic together; it will also tend to bring the unauthentic together and, indeed, to highlight their unauthenticity. The contrast between the two will not be lost on men of good will.

As autonomy calls for a criterion, so too it demands responsibility. Theologians are to be responsible for keeping their own house in order, for the influence they may exert on the faithful, and for the influence theological doctrine may have on church doctrine. They will fulfil this responsibility the more effectively, I believe, if they turn their thoughts to the topic of method and if, instead of waiting for the perfect method to be provided them, they adopt the best available and, in using it, come to discern its shortcomings and remedy its defects.

Now it may be thought that one endangers the authority of church officials if one acknowledges that theologians have a contribution of their own to make, that they possess a certain autonomy, that they have at their disposal a strictly theological criterion, and that they have grave responsibilities that will all the more effectively be fulfilled by adopting some method and working gradually towards improving it.

But I think the authority of church officials has nothing to lose and much to gain from the proposal. There is no loss in acknowledging the plain historical fact that theology has a contribution to make. There is much to be gained by recognizing autonomy and pointing out that it implies responsibility. For responsibility leads to method, and method if effective makes police work superfluous. Church officials have the duty to protect the religion on which theologians reflect, but it is up to the theologians themselves to carry the burden of making theological doctrine as much a matter of consensus as any other long-standing academic discipline.

There is a further aspect to the matter. Though a Roman Catholic with quite conservative views on religious and church doctrines, I have written a chapter on doctrines without subscribing to any but the doctrine about doctrine set forth in the first Vatican council. I have done so deliberately, and my purpose has been ecumenical. I desire it to be as simple as possible for theologians of different allegiance to adapt my method to their uses. Even though theologians start from different church confessions, even though their methods are analogous rather than similar, still that analogy will help all to discover how much they have in common and it will tend to bring to light how greater agreement might be achieved.

Finally, a distinction between dogmatic theology and doctrinal theology may serve to bring to focus points that repeatedly we have attempted to make. Dogmatic theology is classicist. It tends to take it for granted that on each issue there is one and only one true proposition. It is out to determine which are the unique propositions that are true. In contrast, doctrinal theology is historically-minded. It knows that the meaning of a proposition becomes determinate only within a context. It knows that contexts vary with the varying brands of common sense, with the evolution of cultures, with the differentiations of human consciousness, and with the presence or absence of intellectual, moral, and religious conversion. In consequence, it distinguished between the religious apprehension of a doctrine and the theological apprehension of the same doctrine. The religious apprehension is through the context of one's own brand of common sense, of one's own evolving culture, of one's undifferentiation or differentiation of consciousness, of one's own unceasing efforts to attain intellectual, moral, and religious conversion. In contrast, the theological apprehension of doctrines is historical and dialectical. It is historical inasmuch as it grasps the many different contexts in which the same doctrine was expressed in different manners. It is dialectical inasmuch as it discerns the difference between positions and counter-positions and seeks to develop the positions and to reverse the counter-positions.

13

SYSTEMATICS

THE seventh functional specialty, systematics, is concerned with promoting an understanding of the realities affirmed in the previous specialty, doctrines. Our remarks will fall under five headings. First, there is to be clarified the function of systematics. Secondly, there are to be listed the options that previous discussion has already closed. Thirdly, there is to be asked the relevance of any effort on the part of the human mind to understand transcendent mystery. Fourthly, there are the complexities that arise from the fact that systematic theology seeks an understanding not of data but of truths. Finally, there will be a brief indication of the manner in which a later systematics will continue, develop, revise earlier work.

I. THE FUNCTION OF SYSTEMATICS

For Kant understanding (*Verstand*) was the faculty of judgment. It is a view with antecedents in Plato and Scotus and, to a less extent, in Aristotle and Aquinas. For in the latter pair there is emphasized a distinction between two operations of intellect. In the first there are answered questions of the type, *Quid sit? Cur ita sit?* In the second there are answered questions of the type, *An sit? Utrum ita sit?* On this showing one is led to conceive understanding as the source not only of definitions but also of hypotheses, while it is by judgment that is known the existence of what has been defined, the verification of what a hypothesis proposes.

Now this distinction between understanding and judgment seems essential to an understanding of the Augustinian and

Anselmian precept, *Crede ut intelligas*. It does not mean, Believe that you may judge, for belief already is a judgment. It does not mean, Believe that you may demonstrate, for the truths of faith do not admit human demonstration. But very luminously it does mean, Believe that you may understand, for the truths of faith make sense to a believer and they seem to be nonsense to an unbeliever.

Out of the Augustinian, Anselmian, Thomist tradition, despite an intervening heavy overlay of conceptualism,[1] the first Vatican council retrieved the notion of understanding. It taught that reason illumined by faith, when it inquires diligently, piously, soberly, can with God's help attain a highly fruitful understanding of the mysteries of faith both from the analogy of what it naturally knows and from the interconnection of the mysteries with one another and with man's last end (*DS* 3016).

The promotion of such an understanding of the mysteries we conceive to be the principal function of systematics. This specialty presupposes doctrines. Its aim is not to add a further proof of doctrines *ex ratione theologica*. On the contrary, doctrines are to be regarded as established by the addition of foundations to dialectic. The aim of systematics is not to increase certitude but to promote understanding. It does not seek to establish the facts. It strives for some inkling of how it could possibly be that the facts are what they are. Its task is to take over the facts, established in doctrines, and to attempt to work them into an assimilable whole.

The classic example of this distinction between doctrines and systematics is provided by the fourth book of Aquinas' *Summa contra Gentiles*. There Chapters Two to Nine are concerned with the existence of God the Son, Chapters Fifteen to Eighteen with the existence of the Holy Spirit, Chapters Twenty-seven to Thirty-nine with the existence of the Incarnation. But Chapters Ten to Fourteen center in the question of the manner in which a

---

[1] On conceptualists, see my *Verbum: Word and Idea in Aquinas*, London: Darton, Longman & Todd, and Notre Dame: University of Notre Dame Press, 1967, Index, *s.v.*, p. 228. The key issue is whether concepts result from understanding or understanding results from concepts.

divine generation is to be conceived. Similarly, Chapters Nineteen to Twenty-five have to do with the manner of conceiving the Holy Spirit, and Chapters Forty to Forty-nine have to do with the systematics of the Incarnation.

Elsewhere Aquinas pointed out that a disputation could be directed to either of two ends. If directed to removing a doubt about what was so, then in theology one appealed principally to the authorities that the listener recognized. But if directed to the instruction of the student so that he be brought to an understanding of the truth in question, then one must take one's stand on the reasons that bring to light the ground of the truth and enable one to know how what is said is true. Otherwise, if the master settles the question only by an appeal to authorities, he will make his pupil certain of what is so; but so far from giving him any understanding or science, he will send him away empty.[2]

In contrast with medieval procedure, Catholics in recent centuries have not merely distinguished but even separated philosophy and theology. The result was two theologies: there was a natural theology in the philosophy course; there was a further systematic or speculative theology concerned with an orderly presentation of the mysteries of faith. I think the separation unfortunate. In the first place it was misleading. Time and again students took it for granted that systematic theology was just more philosophy and so of no religious significance. At the opposite pole there were those that argued that a natural philosophy does not attain the Christian God and, further, that what is not the Christian God is an intruder and an idol. In the second place, the separation weakened both natural theology and systematic theology. It weakened natural theology for abstruse philosophic concepts lose nothing of their validity and can gain enormously in acceptability when they are associated with their religious equivalents. It weakened systematic theology for the separation prevents the presentation of systematics as the Christian prolongation of what man can begin to know by his native powers. In the third place, the separation seems founded on a

[2] *Quodl.*, IV, q. 9, a. 3 (18).

mistake. As long as it is assumed that philosophy goes forward with such sublime objectivity that it is totally independent of the human mind that thinks it then, no doubt, there is something to be said for issuing a claim to such objectivity for preliminary matters of concern to the faith. But the fact of the matter is that proof becomes rigorous only within a systematically formulated horizon, that the formulation of horizons varies with the presence and absence of intellectual, moral, religious conversion, and that conversion is never the logical consequence of one's previous position but, on the contrary, a radical revision of that position.

Basically the issue is a transition from the abstract logic of classicism to the concreteness of method. On the former view what is basic is proof. On the latter view what is basic is conversion. Proof appeals to an abstraction named right reason. Conversion transforms the concrete individual to make him capable of grasping not merely conclusions but principles as well.

Again, the issue is one's notion of objectivity. If one considers logical proof to be basic, one wants an objectivity that is independent of the concrete existing subject. But while objectivity reaches what is independent of the concrete existing subject, objectivity itself is not reached by what is independent of the concrete existing subject. On the contrary, objectivity is reached through the self-transcendence of the concrete existing subject, and the fundamental forms of self-transcendence are intellectual, moral, and religious conversion. To attempt to ensure objectivity apart from self-transcendence only generates illusions.[3]

It may be objected, however, that this transition from the abstract to the concrete, from proof to conversion, does not square with the claim of the first Vatican council that through creatures God can be known with certainty by the natural light of human reason (DS 3004, 3026).

[3] The basic statement in this connection is by J. H. Newman, *An Essay in Aid of a Grammar of Assent*, London 1870, Paperback, Garden City, N.Y.: Doubleday, Image Books, 1958, Chapters Eight and Nine. See also his *Discussions and Arguments on Various Subjects*, London: Longmans, 1924: "Logic makes but a sorry rhetoric with the multitude; first shoot round corners and you may not despair of converting by a syllogism." This passage is quoted in the *Grammar*, p. 90.

In the first place, I would draw attention to the fact that the foregoing definition tacitly prescinds from the actual order in which we live. The third schema of *Dei Filius*, drawn up by Fr. Joseph Kleutgen, read in the canon: "... *per ea quae facta sunt, naturali ratione ab homine lapso certo cognosci et demonstrari posse* ..."[4] The final version, however, makes no mention of fallen man and, in view of the abstract classicism then prevalent, is perhaps most simply understood to refer to the state of pure nature.[5]

In the second place, with regard to the actual order in which we live, I should say that normally religious conversion precedes the effort to work out rigorous proofs for the existence of God. But I do not think it impossible that such proofs might be a factor facilitating religious conversion so that, by way of exception, certain knowledge of God's existence should precede the acceptance of God's gift of his love.

I have been advocating an integration of natural with systematic theology. But this is not to mean any blurring of distinctions. Separation is one thing, distinction is another. A man's body and soul can be distinct even though the man is still alive. Similarly, what is natural in a theologian's operations and what is supernatural, are distinct, even though one part is not assigned to a philosophy department and the other to a theology department. Again, there is the intelligibility of what cannot be otherwise, and there is the intelligibility of what can be otherwise; the two are distinct, even though a single explanation consists partly of one and partly of the other. Finally, there is the intelligibility within the reach of the human mind, and there is the intelligibility beyond it, and there is the intermediate, imperfect, analogous intelligibility that we can find in the mysteries of faith; the three are distinct but there is no occasion to separate them.

I would note that I am not proposing any novelty. I am proposing a return to the type of systematic theology illustrated

[4] See J. D. Mansi, *Sacrorum Conciliorum Nova et Amplissima Collectio* 53, 168.

[5] See my article, "*Natural Knowledge of God*", *Proceedings, Catholic Theological Society of America*, 23(1968), 54–69. Hermann Pottmeyer, *Der Glaube vor dem Anspruch der Wissenschaft*, Freiburg: Herder, 1968, pp. 168–204. David Coffey, "Natural Knowledge of God: Reflections on Romans I, 18–32", *Theological Studies* 31(1970), 674–691.

by Aquinas' *Summa contra Gentiles* and *Summa theologiae*. Both are systematic expressions of a wide-ranging understanding of the truths concerning God and man. Both are fully aware of the distinctions mentioned above. Neither countenances the separation that later was introduced.

If the aim of systematics is, as I hold, understanding, then it must present a single unified whole and not two separate parts that tend to overlook the primacy of conversion and tend to overemphasize the significance of proof.

2. CLOSED OPTIONS

From the very first chapter we have moved out of a faculty psychology with its options between intellectualism and voluntarism, and into an intentionality analysis that distinguishes four levels of conscious and intentional operations, where each successive level sublates previous levels by going beyond them, by setting up a higher principle, by introducing new operations, and by preserving the integrity of previous levels, while extending enormously their range and their significance.

Several consequences follow. The fourth and highest level is that of deliberation, evaluation, decision. It follows that the priority of intellect is just the priority of the first three levels of experiencing, understanding, and judging.

Secondly, it follows that the speculative intellect or pure reason is just an abstraction. Scientific or philosophic experiencing, understanding, and judging do not occur in a vacuum. They are the operations of an existential subject who has decided to devote himself to the pursuit of understanding and truth and, with greater or less success, is faithful to his commitment.

Thirdly, there arises the possibility of an exception to the old adage, *nihil amatum nisi praecognitum*. Specifically, it would seem that God's gift of his love (Rom. 5, 5) is not something that results from or is conditioned by man's knowledge of God. Far more plausibly it would seem that the gift may precede our knowledge of God and, indeed, may be the cause of our seeking knowledge of God.[6] In that case the gift by itself would be an orientation towards an unknown. Still, the orientation reveals its goal by its absoluteness: it is with all one's heart and all one's soul and with all one's mind and all one's strength. It is, then, an orientation to what is transcendent in lovableness and, when that is unknown, it is an orientation to transcendent mystery.

Now an orientation to transcendent mystery is basic to systematic theology. It provides the primary and fundamental meaning of the name, God. It can be the bond uniting all men despite cultural differences. It provides the origin for inquiry about God, for seeking assurance of his existence, for endeavoring to reach some understanding of the mysteries of faith. At the same time, it is quite in harmony with the conviction that no system we can construct will encompass or plumb or master the mystery by which we are held. As the fourth Lateran council declared: ". . . between creator and creature no similarity can be noted without a greater dissimilarity being noted" (DS 806). As the first Vatican council added: "The divine mysteries so exceed created intellect that, even when given in relevation and received by faith, they remain covered over by the very veil of faith itself . . ." (DS 3019).

Again, an orientation to transcendent mystery illuminates negative or apophatic theology which is content to say what God is not. For such a theology is concerned to speak about a transcendent unknown, a transcendent mystery. Its positive nourishment is God's gift of his love.

However, if there is to be an affirmative or kataphatic, as well as a negative or apophatic, theology, there must be confronted the question whether God is an object. Now certainly God is not an object in the naive realist sense of what is already out there now, or already up there now, or already in here now. Further he is not an object if one retreats from naive realism to an empiricism, a naturalism, a positivism, or an idealism. But if by an object one means anything that is intended in questions and known through correct answers, anything within the world mediated by meaning, then a distinction has to be drawn.

[6] Cf. Pascal's remark: "Take comfort, you would not be seeking me if you had not already found me". Pensées vii, 553.

On what I have called the primary and fundamental meaning of the name, God, God is not an object. For that meaning is the term of an orientation to transcendent mystery. Such an orientation, while it is the climax of the self-transcending process of raising questions, none the less is not properly a matter of raising and answering questions. So far from lying within the world mediated by meaning, it is the principle that can draw people out of that world and into the cloud of unknowing.[7]

However, withdrawal is for return. Not only can one's prayer consist in letting lapse all images and thoughts so as to permit God's gift of his love to absorb one, but also those that pray in that exhausting fashion can cease to pray and think back on their praying. Then they objectify in images and concepts and words both what they have been doing and the God that has been their concern.

But God comes within the world mediated by meaning in far more common ways. One's fundamental concern springs from God's gift of his love, but one's questions begin from the world and from man. Could the world be mediated by questions for intelligence if it did not have an intelligent ground? Could the world's facticity be reconciled with its intelligibility, if it did not have a necessary ground? Is it with man that morality emerges in the universe so that the universe is amoral and alien to man, or is the ground of the universe a moral being? Such questions invite answers and, as the questions intend, so too the answers can reveal an intelligent, necessary, moral ground of the universe.

Above all, in a religion that is shared by many, that enters into and transforms cultures, that extends down the ages, God will be named, questions about him will be asked, answers will be forthcoming. In still another manner God becomes an object in the very precise sense of what is intended in questions and known by correct answers. Nor is this meaning in any way invalidated

---

[7] I have found extremely helpful William Johnston's *The Mysticism of the Cloud of Unknowing*, New York, Rome, Tournai, Paris: Desclée, 1967. Readers wishing to fill out my remarks will find in his book a position very largely coherent with my own.

by the fact that naive realism, empiricism, positivism, idealism, or phenomenology cannot think of God and consequently cannot think of him as an object.

There is a still further consequence of the shift from a faculty psychology to intentionality analysis. It is that the basic terms and relations of systematic theology will be not metaphysical, as in medieval theology, but psychological. As has been worked out in our chapters on method, on religion, and on foundations, general basic terms name conscious and intentional operations. General basic relations name elements in the dynamic structure linking operations and generating states. Special basic terms name God's gift of his love and Christian witness. Derived terms and relations name the objects known in operations and correlative to states.

The point to making metaphysical terms and relations not basic but derived is that a critical metaphysics results. For every term and relation there will exist a corresponding element in intentional consciousness. Accordingly, empty or misleading terms and relations can be eliminated, while valid ones can be elucidated by the conscious intention from which they are derived. The importance of such a critical control will be evident to anyone familiar with the vast arid wastes of theological controversy.

The positive function of a critical metaphysics is twofold. On the one hand it provides a basic heuristic structure, a determinate horizon, within which questions arise. On the other hand, it provides a criterion for settling the difference between literal and metaphorical meaning and, again, between notional and real distinctions.[8]

Since knowledge of intentional consciousness can develop, it follows that the whole foregoing structure admits development and thereby escapes rigidity. At the same time, the structure ensures continuity, for the possibility of development is the possibility of revising earlier views, and the possibility of revising earlier views is the continuing existence of the structure already

[8] On the meaning of heuristic structure, of reality, and of real and notional distinctions, see *Insight*, Chapters Two, Fourteen, and Sixteen.

determined. Finally, the approach eliminates any authoritarian basis for method. One can find out for oneself and in oneself just what one's conscious and intentional operations are and how they are related to one another. One can discover for oneself and in oneself why it is that performing such and such operations in such and such manners constitutes human knowing. Once one has achieved that, one is no longer dependent on someone else in selecting one's method and in carrying it out. One is on one's own.

3. MYSTERY AND PROBLEM

Man's response to transcendent mystery is adoration. But adoration does not exclude words. Least of all, does it do so when men come together to worship. But the words, in turn, have their meaning within some cultural context. Contexts can be ongoing. One ongoing context can be derived from another. Two ongoing contexts can interact. Accordingly, while mystery is very different from the problems of common sense, of science, of scholarship, of much philosophy, still the worship of God and, more generally, the religions of mankind stand within a social, cultural, historical context and, by that involvement, generate the problems with which theologians attempt to deal.

Our reflections on the differentiation of human consciousness have brought to light some of the general types of context within which religious and theological discourse occur. The expression of man's apprehension of God can be largely symbolic; then inadequacies of expression are corrected by reinterpretation, by so modifying the symbol that undesired meanings are excluded and desired meanings are elucidated. Next, in the Presocratic world of a Xenophanes or the post-systematic world of Clement of Alexandria anthropomorphic speech about God will be discredited. The biblical God that stands or is seated, that has a right hand and a left, that waxes angry and repents, is not taken literally. God is conceived in terms of the transcendental notions of intelligibility, truth, reality, goodness. Such rethinking of God the Father entails a rethinking of his Son, and the rethinking of the Son generates a tension between the Son as rethought and the Son as depicted in the New Testament. There followed the crises provoked by Arius, by Nestorius, by Eutyches, and the post-systematic pronouncements of Nicea, Ephesus, and Chalcedon. The minimal use of technical expressions in the Greek councils and the late Byzantine and Syrian concern with theology as a whole prepared the way for the total rethinking of Christian doctrine in systematic terms by medieval theologians. There resulted a legacy that interacted with the ongoing context of church doctrines up to the second Vatican council. Meanwhile, modern science had eliminated much of the biblical apprehension of man and his world. Modern scholarship had kept revising the interpretation of biblical, patristic, medieval, and subsequent sources. Modern philosophy entailed a radical shift in systematic thinking.

Accordingly, while mystery is not to be confused with problem, the ongoing contexts within which mystery is adored and adoration is explained are anything but free from problems. Least of all at the present time is the existence of problems to be ignored. For now problems are so numerous that many do not know what to believe. They are not unwilling to believe. They know what church doctrines are. But they want to know what church doctrines could possibly mean. Their question is the question to be met by systematic theology.

The answer to that question is a gradual increase of understanding. A clue is spotted that throws some light on the matter in hand. But that partial light gives rise to further questions, the further questions to still further answers. The illuminated area keeps expanding for some time but eventually still further questions begin to yield diminishing returns. The vein of ore seems played out. But successive thinkers may tackle the whole matter over again. Each may make a notable contribution. Eventually perhaps there arrives on the scene a master capable of envisaging all the issues and of treating them in their proper order.

That order is not the order in which the solutions were discovered. For the course of discovery is roundabout. Subordinate issues are apt to be solved first. Key issues are likely to be overlooked until a great deal has been achieved. Quite distinct from the order of discovery is the order of teaching. For a teacher postpones solutions that presuppose other solutions. He begins with the issues whose solution does not presuppose the solution of other issues.

Such was the *ordo disciplinae* that Aquinas wanted in theology books for beginners.[9] To give a brief illustration we note that in the first book of the *Scriptum super Sententias* there is no separation of the treatment of God as one and of God as Trinity; at random questions regard either the first or the second. But in the *Summa contra Gentiles* a systematic separation is effected: the first book deals solely with God as one; Chapters Two to Twenty-six of the fourth book deal solely with God as Trinity. In the first part of the *Summa theologiae* questions 2 to 26 regard God as one, while questions 27 to 43 regard the Trinity. What in the *Contra Gentiles* was treated in very separate books, in the *Summa theologiae* is united in a continuous stream. For questions 27 to 29 are still concerned with God, while the elements of trinitarian theory are gradually constructed. Question 27 asks, not whether the Son proceeds from the Father, but whether there are processions in God. Question 28 asks whether these processions give rise to relations in God. Question 29 asks whether these relations are persons.[10]

Not only does the order of teaching or exposition differ from the order of discovery, but also the terms and relations of systematic thought express a development of understanding over and above the understanding had either from a simple inspection or from an erudite exegesis of the original doctrinal sources. So in Thomist trinitarian theory such terms as procession, relation, person have a highly technical meaning. They stand to these terms as they occur in scriptural or patristic writings much as in modern physics the terms, mass and temperature, stand to the adjectives, heavy and cold.

The existence of this divergence between religious sources and theological systems is a necessary consequence of the view

[9] See Aquinas, *Summa theologiae, Prologus.*
[10] I have treated the matter more fully in my *Verbum: Word and Idea in Aquinas,* pp. 206 ff.

expressed in the first Vatican council that, while it is the same dogma, meaning, position that is being understood, still that understanding grows and advances down the ages (*DS* 3020). In our chapter on *Doctrines*, we were concerned to affirm the permanence of dogma despite the historically shifting contexts within which dogmas were understood and expressed. In the present chapter on *Systematics* we have to advert to the reverse side of the coin, and, while maintaining the permanence of dogmas, attend principally to systematic developments.

Such developments occur in widely differing contexts. They were initiated in the ancient Greco-Roman and Byzantine worlds. They reached a high perfection in the statically conceived systems of medieval thought. They are being invited to emerge within the ongoing context of modern science, modern scholarship, and modern philosophy.

Unfortunately, though very humanly, all such developments are under the sign of contradiction. No less than understanding, misunderstanding can express itself systematically. Again, while genuine understanding tends to be unique, misunderstanding tends to be a manifold. Just as there are conflicting interpretations, conflicting histories, conflicting foundations, conflicting doctrines, so too one is to expect an array of conflicting systems.

To deal with such multiplicity, once more one must appeal to dialectic. One has to assemble the manifold, ascertain differences, reduce differences to their grounds. Such grounds may lie in some social, cultural, historical context, in the native endowment or the formation of given authors, in the presence or absence of intellectual, moral, or religious conversion, in the manner in which the method and task of systematic theology were conceived. On the basis of such analysis and in the light of one's own foundations and method one will judge which systems express positions and which express counter-positions.

4. UNDERSTANDING AND TRUTH

Already we have had occasion to distinguish data and facts. Data are given to sense or to consciousness. They are the given just as given. They are, of course, hardly noticed unless they fit in with one's understanding and have a name in one's language. At the same time, with an appropriate development of understanding and language, they will be noticed and, if important from some viewpoint, they will be insisted upon.

While data are just a single component in human knowledge, facts result from the conjunction of three distinct levels. Facts have the immediacy of what is given, the precision of what is somehow understood, conceived, named, the stubbornness of what is affirmed because a virtually unconditioned has been reached.

Now one can understand data and one can understand facts. The understanding of data is expressed in hypotheses, and the verification of hypotheses leads to probable assertions. The understanding of facts is a more complicated matter, for it supposes the existence of two types or orders of knowledge, where the facts of the first type supply the data for the second type. Thus, in critical history we distinguished two inquiries: a first inquiry aimed at finding out where one's witnesses got their information, how they checked it, how competently they used it; this was followed by a second inquiry that employed the evaluated information to construct an account of what was going forward in a given milieu at a given place and time. Similarly, in natural science one can start from the facts of commonsense knowledge and use them as the data for the construction of scientific theories; and inversely one can return from scientific theory through applied science, engineering, technology to bring about the transformation of the commonsense world.

Now the peculiarity of such understanding of facts is that two orders or types of knowledge call for two applications of the notion of truth. There is the truth of the facts in the first order or type. There is also the truth of the account or explanation reached in the second type or order. Moreover, while initially the second depends on the first, ultimately the two are interdependent, for the second can lead to a correction of the first. The critical historian's discovery of what was going forward can lead him to revise his evaluation of his witnesses. The scientific account of physical reality can involve a revision of commonsense views.

Far more complicated is the case of our eight, directly or indirectly, interdependent, functional specialties. Each of the eight is the work of all four levels of intentional consciousness. Consequently, each of the eight results from experience, insights, judgments of fact, and judgments of value. At the same time each is a specialty inasmuch as each is concerned to perform one of eight tasks. So research is concerned to make the data available. Interpretation to determine their meaning. History to proceed from meaning to what was going forward. Dialectic to go to the roots of conflicting histories, interpretations, researches. Foundations to distinguish positions from counter-positions. Doctrines to use foundations as a criterion for deciding between the alternatives offered by dialectic. Systematics to seek an understanding of the realities affirmed in doctrines.

Our present concern is with doctrines and systematics. Both aim at understanding the truth, but they do so in different manners. Doctrines aims at a clear and distinct affirmation of religious realities: its principal concern is the truth of such an affirmation; its concern to understand is limited to the clarity and distinctness of its affirmation. On the other hand, systematics aims at an understanding of the religious realities affirmed by doctrines. It wants its understanding to be true, for it is not a pursuit of misunderstanding. At the same time, it is fully aware that its understanding is bound to be imperfect, merely analogous, commonly no more than probable.

There are, then, in doctrines and systematics two instances of truth and two instances of understanding. Doctrines are concerned to state clearly and distinctly the religious community's confession of the mysteries so hidden in God that man could not know them if they had not been revealed by God.[11] Assent to such doctrines is the assent of faith, and that assent is regarded by religious people as firmer than any other. At the same time, the measure of understanding accompanying the assent of faith

[11] On confessions of faith in the New Testament, see V. H. Neufeld, *The Earliest Christian Confessions*, Leiden: Brill, 1963, vol. V of *New Testament Tools and Studies* edited by B. M. Metzger.

traditionally is recognized as highly variable. Irenaeus for instance acknowledged that one believer could be far more articulate than another, but he denied that the former was more a believer or the latter less a believer.[12]

In contrast, the views set forth in a systematic theology are commonly considered no more than probable, but the understanding to be reached is to be on the level of one's times. In the medieval period it was static system. In the contemporary world it has to be at home in modern science, modern scholarship, and modern philosophy.

Here perhaps may be inserted brief answers to the accusations often made against systematic theology, that it is speculative, irreligious, fruitless, élitist, irrelevant. Now a systematic theology can be speculative, as is clear from German idealism; but the systematic theology we advocate is really quite a homely affair. It aims at an understanding of the truths of faith, a *Glaubensverständnis*. The truths of faith envisaged are church confessions. Again, a systematic theology can become irreligious. This is particularly true when its main emphasis is, not conversion, but proof, or when positions are taken and maintained out of individual or corporate pride. But when conversion is the basis of the whole theology, when religious conversion is the event that gives the name, God, its primary and fundamental meaning, when systematic theology does not believe it can exhaust or even do justice to that meaning, not a little has been done to keep systematic theology in harmony with its religious origins and aims. Thirdly, systematic theology has its fruitless aspects, for just as understanding can be systematized, so too can misunderstanding. As the former type of system will be attractive to those that understand, so too the latter type will be attractive to the usually larger number of those that do not understand. Dialectic cannot be simply exorcized. But at least one no longer is totally at its mercy, when one methodically acknowledges the existence of such dialectic, sets up criteria for distinguishing between positions and counter-positions, and invites everyone to magnify the

[12] See *Adv. haer.* I, 10, 3; Harvey I, 84–96.

accuracy or inaccuracy of his judgments by developing what he thinks are positions and by reversing what he thinks are counter-positions. Fourthly, systematic theology is élitist: it is difficult, as also are mathematics, science, scholarship, philosophy. But the difficulty is worth meeting. If one does not attain, on the level of one's age, an understanding of the religious realities in which one believes, one will be simply at the mercy of the psychologists, the sociologists, the philosophers, that will not hesitate to tell believers what it really is in which they believe. Finally, systematic theology is irrelevant, if it does not provide the basis for the eighth functional specialty, communications. But to communicate one must understand what one has to communicate. No repetition of formulas can take the place of understanding. For it is understanding alone that can say what it grasps in any of the manners demanded by the almost endless series of different audiences.

5. CONTINUITY, DEVELOPMENT, REVISION

Four factors make for continuity. Of these one first may consider the normative structure of our conscious and intentional acts. In saying that the structure is normative I mean, of course, that it can be violated. For such acts may be directed, not to what truly is good, but to maximizing individual or group advantage. Again, they may be directed, not to the truth that is affirmed because a virtually unconditioned has been grasped, but to any of the misconceptions of truth that have been systematized in sundry philosophies: naive realism, empiricism, rationalism, idealism, positivism, pragmatism, phenomenology, existentialism. Finally, they may be directed, not to increasing human understanding, but to satisfying the "objective" or the "scientific" or the "meaningful" norms set up by some logic or method that finds it convenient to leave human understanding out of the picture.

The structure, then, of our conscious and intentional operations can be violated in various manners. There results the dialectic of positions and counter-positions. But the fact of this dialectic only objectifies and manifests the need for man to be authentic. At once, it invites him to intellectual and to moral conversion, while it points to the social and the cultural failure of those peoples that have insisted they could get along very well with neither intellectual nor moral conversion.

A second factor in continuity is God's gift of his love. It is a gift, not something due to our natures, but something that God freely bestows. It is given in various measures. But it is ever the same love, and so it ever tends in the same direction, to provide a further factor for continuity.

A third factor is the permanence of dogma. The mysteries that God alone knows, that he has revealed, that the church has defined, may in the course of time become better understood. But what is to be understood, is not some item within the ambit of human knowledge. It is just what God has revealed, and so dogma in this sense is permanent. Human understanding of it has ever to be in eodem dogmate, eodem sensu eademque sententia (DS 3020).

A fourth factor making for continuity is the occurrence in the past of genuine achievement. I have done two studies of the writings of St. Thomas Aquinas. One on *Grace and Freedom*, the other on *Verbum*. Were I to write on these topics today, the method I am proposing would lead to several significant differences from the presentation by Aquinas. But there also would exist profound affinities. For Aquinas' thought on grace and freedom and his thought on cognitional theory and on the trinity were genuine achievements of the human spirit. Such achievement has a permanence of its own. It can be improved upon. It can be inserted in larger and richer contexts. But unless its substance is incorporated in subsequent work, the subsequent work will be a substantially poorer affair.

Besides continuity there is development. There is the less conspicuous type of development that arises when the gospel is preached effectively to a different culture or to a different class in the same culture. There is the more conspicuous type of development that arises from the various differentiations of human consciousness. Finally, there are the fruits as well as the evils of dialectic. Truth can come to light, not because truth has been sought, but because a contrary error has been affirmed and repulsed.

Besides continuity and development, there also is revision. All development involves some revision. Further, because a theology is the product not simply of a religion but of a religion within a given cultural context, theological revisions may have their origin, not primarily in theological, but rather in cultural developments. So at the present time theological development is fundamentally a long delayed response to the development of modern science, modern scholarship, modern philosophy.

There exists, however, a distinct question. Even though fundamentally current theological revision is just an adaptation to cultural change, there remains the possibility that these adaptations will in turn imply still further revisions. Thus, the shift from a predominately logical to a basically methodical viewpoint may involve a revision of the view that doctrinal developments were "implicitly" revealed.[13] Again, just as the Alexandrian school refused to take literally the anthropomorphisms of the bible to bring about a philosophically based demythologization, so it may be asked whether modern scholarship may not bring about further demythologizations on exegetical or historical grounds. Such questions, of course, are very large indeed. Unmistakably they are theological. They accordingly lie outside the scope of the present work on method.

[13] See J. R. Geiselmann, "Dogma", *Handbuch theologischer Grundbegriffe*, hrsg. v. H. Fries, München: Kösel, 1962; I, 235.

14

COMMUNICATIONS

THEOLOGY has been conceived as reflection on religion and, indeed, in the present age as a highly differentiated and specialized reflection. After *research*, which assembles the data thought relevant, and *interpretation*, which ascertains their meaning, and *history*, which finds meanings incarnate in deeds and movements, and *dialectic*, which investigates the conflicting conclusions of historians, interpreters, researchers, and *foundations*, which objectifies the horizon effected by intellectual, moral, and religious conversion, and *doctrines*, which uses foundations as a guide in selecting from the alternatives presented by dialectic, and *systematics*, which seeks an ultimate clarification of the meaning of doctrine, there finally comes our present concern with the eighth functional specialty, *communications*.

It is a major concern, for it is in this final stage that theological reflection bears fruit. Without the first seven stages, of course, there is no fruit to be borne. But without the last the first seven are in vain, for they fail to mature.

Having insisted on the great importance of this final specialty, I must at once recall the distinction between the methodologist and the theologian. It is up to the theologians to carry out both the first seven specialties and no less the eighth. The methodologist has the far lighter task of indicating what the various tasks of theologians are and how each presupposes or complements the others.

Concretely, if the reader wishes to contemplate theologians at work in our eighth functional specialty, I would refer him to the five-volume *Handbuch der Pastoraltheologie* edited by F. X. Arnold,

F. Klostermann, K. Rahner, V. Schurr, and L. Weber.[1] In contrast, the concern of the methodologist is simply to present an account of the underlying ideas and directives that seem relevant to such monumental efforts.

1. MEANING AND ONTOLOGY

In our third chapter we distinguished four functions of meaning: it is cognitive, constitutive, communicative, effective.

Such functions have their ontological aspect. In so far as meaning is cognitive, what is meant is real. In so far as it is constitutive, it constitutes part of the reality of the one that means: his horizon, his assimilative powers, his knowledge, his values, his character. In so far as it is communicative, it induces in the hearer some share in the cognitive, constitutive, or effective meaning of the speaker. In so far as it is effective, it persuades or commands others or it directs man's control over nature.

Such ontological aspects pertain to meaning, no matter what its content or its carrier. They are found then in all the diverse stages of meaning, in all the diverse cultural traditions, in any of the differentiations of consciousness, and in the presence and absence of intellectual, moral, and religious conversion. Again, they pertain to meaning, whether its carrier is intersubjectivity or art or symbol or exemplary or abominable conduct or everyday or literary or technical language.

2. COMMON MEANING AND ONTOLOGY

Community is not just an aggregate of individuals within a frontier, for that overlooks its formal constituent, which is common meaning. Such common meaning calls for a common field of experience and, when that is lacking, people get out of touch. It calls for common or complementary ways of understanding and, when they are lacking, people begin to misunderstand, to distrust, to suspect, to fear, to resort to violence. It calls for common judgments and, when they are lacking, people

---

[1] Freiburg-Basel-Wien: Herder I, 1964; II-1 and II-2, 1966; III, 1968; IV, 1969. Some 2652 pages in all.

reside in different worlds. It calls for common values, goals, policies and, when they are lacking, people operate at cross-purposes.

Such common meaning is doubly constitutive. In each individual it is constitutive of the individual as a member of the community. In the group of individuals it is constitutive of the community.

The genesis of common meaning is an ongoing process of communication, of people coming to share the same cognitive, constitutive, and effective meanings. On the elementary level this process has been described as arising between the self and the other when, on the basis of already existing intersubjectivity, the self makes a gesture, the other makes an interpretative response, and the self discovers in the response the effective meaning of his gesture.[2] So from intersubjectivity through gesture and interpretation there arises common understanding. On that spontaneous basis there can be built a common language, the transmission of acquired knowledge and of social patterns through education, the diffusion of information, and the common will to community that seeks to replace misunderstanding with mutual comprehension and to change occasions of disagreement into occasions of non-agreement and eventually of agreement.[3]

As common meaning constitutes community, so divergent meaning divides it. Such division may amount to no more than a diversity of culture and the stratification of individuals into classes of higher and lower competence. The serious division is the one that arises from the presence and absence of intellectual, moral, or religious conversion. For a man is his true self inasmuch as he is self-transcending. Conversion is the way to self-transcendence. Inversely, man is alienated from his true self inasmuch as he refuses self-transcendence, and the basic form of ideology is the self-justification of alienated man.

[2] See Gibson Winter, *Elements for a Social Ethic*, New York: Macmillan, 1966, pb. 1968, pp. 99 ff.

[3] See R. G. Collingwood, *The New Leviathan*, Oxford: Clarendon, 1942, ⁵1966, p. 181 and *passim* on Platonic dialectic.

Needless to say, the unconverted and especially those that deliberately refused conversion will want to find some other root for alienation and ideology. Indeed, they will want to suggest, directly or indirectly, that self-transcendence is a case or the case of alienation and that ideology is at root the attempt to justify self-transcendence. Once more, then, we are confronted with the radical dialectical opposition that was our concern in our chapter on the fourth functional specialty.

Now, however, our interest is not in dialectic as affecting theological opinions but in dialectic as affecting community, action, situation. It affects community for, just as common meaning is constitutive of community, so dialectic divides community into radically opposed groups. It affects action for, just as conversion leads to intelligent, reasonable, responsible action, so dialectic adds division, conflict, oppression. It affects the situation, for situations are the cumulative product of previous actions and, when previous actions have been guided by the light and darkness of dialectic, the resulting situation is not some intelligible whole but rather a set of misshapen, poorly proportioned, and incoherent fragments.[4]

Finally, the divided community, their conflicting actions, and the messy situation are headed for disaster. For the messy situation is diagnosed differently by the divided community; action is ever more at cross-purposes; and the situation becomes still messier to provoke still sharper differences in diagnosis and policy, more radical criticism of one another's actions, and an ever deeper crisis in the situation.

3. SOCIETY, STATE, CHURCH

Society is studied by sociologists and social historians, the church is studied by ecclesiologists and church historians, the state is studied by political theorists and political historians.

What is studied by historians is particular, concrete, ongoing. It is partly constituted by meaning, and consequently it is changed by any change in its constitutive meaning. Further, it is subject

---

[4] On this topic see *Insight*, pp. 191–206, 218–232, 619–633, 687–730.

to the distortion and corruption of alienation and ideology, and it may be weakened and destroyed by ridicule and rejection.

On an ancient and traditional view, society is conceived as the organized collaboration of individuals for the pursuit of a common aim or aims. On the basis of this very general definition various kinds of society are distinguished and, among them, the church and the state which are named "perfect" societies on that ground that each in its own sphere possesses ultimate authority. It is to be observed that on this view church and state are not parts within a larger whole but simply instances within a larger class.

For the sociologist or social historian, however, anything that pertains to the togetherness of human beings is regarded as social. It follows that society must always be conceived concretely and, indeed, the fewer the groups of men living in total isolation from other men, the more there tends to exist a single human society that is worldwide.

It may be objected that this is a merely material view of society, but the objection may be easily countered by adding as formal component the structure of the human good described in Chapter Two. As the reader may recall, the structure stands on three levels. On a first level one considers the needs and capacities of individuals, their operations which within society become cooperations, and the resultant recurrent instances of the particular good. On a second level one considers their plasticity and perfectibility, their training for assuming roles and performing tasks within already understood and accepted modes and styles of cooperating, and their actual performance which results in the functioning or malfunctioning of the good of order. On a third level one considers individuals as free and responsible, adverts to their basic options for self-transcendence or for alienation, examines their personal relations with other individuals or groups within the society, and notes the terminal values they bring about in themselves and encourage in others.

Since all human beings have needs, and since needs are far better met through cooperation, the social structure of the good is a universal phenomenon. But it is realized in an enormous variety of stages of technological, economic, political, cultural, and religious development. Advance occurs first in pockets. Next it is diffused across frontiers. Finally, as it is generalized, interdependence grows. The intensification of interdependence leads one to think of society as international, while smaller units such as the empire, the nation, the region, megalopolis, the city begin to be thought of as parts of society.

The ideal basis of society is community, and the community may take its stand on a moral, a religious, or a Christian principle. The moral principle is that men individually are responsible for what they make of themselves, but collectively they are responsible for the world in which they live. Such is the basis of universal dialogue. The religious principle is God's gift of his love, and it forms the basis of dialogue between all representatives of religion. The Christian principle conjoins the inner gift of God's love with its outer manifestation in Christ Jesus and in those that follow him. Such is the basis of Christian ecumenism.

While the ideal basis of society is community, while society does not survive without a large measure of community, it remains that community is imperfect. For the larger and more complex society becomes, the longer and more exacting becomes the training needed for a fully responsible freedom to be possible. To ignorance and incompetence there are added alienation and ideology. Egoists find loop-holes in social arrangements, and they exploit them to enlarge their own share and diminish the share of others in current instances of the particular good. Groups exaggerate the magnitude and importance of their contribution to society. They provide a market for the ideological façade that would justify their ways before the bar of public opinion. If they succeed in their deception, the social process is distorted. What is good for this or that group, is mistakenly thought to be good for the country or for mankind, while what is good for the country or for mankind is postponed or mutilated. There emerge the richer classes and the poorer classes, and the richer become ever richer, while the poorer sink into misery and squalor. Finally, practical people are guided by common sense. They are immersed in the particular and concrete. They have little grasp of large movements or of long-term trends. They are anything but ready to sacrifice immediate advantage for the enormously greater good of society in two or three decades.

To cope with the problem of imperfect community society develops first procedures and then agencies which have histories of their own. In the modern pluralist democracies there are numerous bodies that largely are self-governing and that pursue any of the specialized ends that have resulted either from the spontaneities of human nature or from the differentiations brought about by human development. Such bodies train personnel, offer roles and set tasks within already understood and accepted styles and modes of cooperation, make their contribution to the good of order by which recurrent needs are met and in which terminal values arise, and in the light of ongoing results revise their procedures.

All such bodies, however, are subject to sovereign states. Such states are territorial divisions within human society. They are ruled by governments that perform legislative, executive, judicial, and administrative functions. When well run, they promote the good of order within society, and they penalize those that violate it.

But, as already remarked, the ideal basis of society is community. Without a large measure of community, human society and sovereign states cannot function. Without a constant renewal of community, the measure of community already enjoyed easily is squandered. There are needed, then, individuals and groups and, in the modern world, organizations that labor to persuade people to intellectual, moral, and religious conversion and that work systematically to undo the mischief brought about by alienation and ideology. Among such bodies should be the Christian church and to it in its contemporary situation we now turn.

4. THE CHRISTIAN CHURCH AND ITS CONTEMPORARY SITUATION

The Christian church is the community that results from the outer communication of Christ's message and from the inner gift of God's love. Since God can be counted on to bestow his

see JHN's
PPS - V.2.
p. 216
(top)

grace, practical theology is concerned with the effective communication of Christ's message.

The message announces what Christians are to believe, what they are to become, what they are to do. Its meaning, then, is at once cognitive, constitutive, effective. It is cognitive inasmuch as the message tells what is to be believed. It is constitutive inasmuch as it crystallizes the hidden inner gift of love into overt Christian fellowship. It is effective inasmuch as it directs Christian service to human society to bring about the kingdom of God.

To communicate the Christian message is to lead another to share in one's cognitive, constitutive, effective meaning. Those, then, that would communicate the cognitive meaning of the message, first of all, must know it. At their service, then, are the seven previous functional specialties. Next, those that would communicate the constitutive meaning of the Christian message, first of all, must live it. For without living the Christian message one does not possess its constitutive meaning; and one cannot lead another to share what one oneself does not possess. Finally, those that communicate the effective meaning of the Christian message, must practise it. For actions speak louder than words, while preaching what one does not practise recalls sounding brass and tinkling cymbal.

The Christian message is to be communicated to all nations. Such communication presupposes that preachers and teachers enlarge their horizons to include an accurate and intimate understanding of the culture and the language of the people they address. They must grasp the virtual resources of that culture and that language, and they must use those virtual resources creatively so that the Christian message becomes, not disruptive of the culture, not an alien patch superimposed upon it, but a line of development within the culture.

Here the basic distinction is between preaching the gospel and, on the other hand, preaching the gospel as it has been developed within one's own culture. In so far as one preaches the gospel as it has been developed within one's own culture, one is preaching not only the gospel but also one's own culture. In so far as one is preaching one's own culture, one is asking others not only to accept the gospel but also renounce their own culture and accept one's own.

Now a classicist would feel it was perfectly legitimate for him to impose his culture on others. For he conceives culture normatively, and he conceives his own to be the norm. Accordingly, for him to preach both the gospel and his own culture, is for him to confer the double benefit of both the true religion and the true culture. In contrast, the pluralist acknowledges a multiplicity of cultural traditions. In any tradition he envisages the possibility of diverse differentiations of consciousness. But he does not consider it his task either to promote the differentiation of consciousness or to ask people to renounce their own culture. Rather he would proceed from within their culture and he would seek ways and means for making it into a vehicle for communicating the Christian message.

Through communication there is constituted community and, conversely, community constitutes and perfects itself through communication. Accordingly, the Christian church is a process of self-constitution, a *Selbstvollzug*. While there still is in use the medieval meaning of the term, society, so that the church may be named a society, still the modern meaning, generated by empirical social studies, leads one to speak of the church as a process of self-constitution occurring within worldwide human society. The substance of that process is the Christian message conjoined with the inner gift of God's love and resulting in Christian witness, Christian fellowship, and Christian service to mankind.

Further, the church is a structured process. As does human society, it trains personnel. It distinguishes roles and assigns to them tasks. It has developed already understood and accepted modes of cooperation. It promotes a good of order in which Christian needs are met regularly, sufficiently, efficiently. It facilitates the spiritual and cultural development of its members. It invites them to transform by Christian charity their personal and group relations. It rejoices in the terminal values that flow from their lives.

The church is an out-going process. It exists not just for itself but for mankind. Its aim is the realization of the kingdom of God not only within its own organization but in the whole of human society and not only in the after life but also in this life.

The church is a redemptive process. The Christian message, incarnate in Christ scourged and crucified, dead and risen, tells not only of God's love but also of man's sin. Sin is alienation from man's authentic being, which is self-transcendence, and sin justifies itself by ideology. As alienation and ideology are destructive of community, so the self-sacrificing love that is Christian charity reconciles alienated man to his true being, and undoes the mischief initiated by alienation and consolidated by ideology.

This redemptive process has to be exercised in the church and in human society generally. It will regard the church as a whole and, again, each of its parts. Similarly, it will regard human society as a whole and, again, its many parts. In each case ends have to be selected and priorities determined. Resources have to be surveyed and, when they are inadequate, plans for their increase have to be made. Conditions need to be investigated under which the resources will be deployed for the attainment of the ends. Plans have to be drawn up for the optimal deployment of resources under the existing conditions for the attainment of ends. Finally, the several plans in the several areas and in the church as a whole have to be coordinated.

In the foregoing fashion the Christian church will become not only a process of self-constitution but also a fully conscious process of self-constitution. But to do so it will have to recognize that theology is not the full science of man, that theology illuminates only certain aspects of human reality, that the church can become a fully conscious process of self-constitution only when theology unites itself with all other relevant branches of human studies.

The possibility of each integration is a method that runs parallel to the method in theology. Indeed, the functional specialties of research, interpretation, and history can be applied to the data of any sphere of scholarly human studies. The same three specialties when conceived, not as specialties, but simply as experience, understanding, and judgment, can be applied to the data of any sphere of human living to obtain the classical principles and laws or the statistical trends of scientific human studies.

Now as in theology, so too in historical and empirical human studies scholars and scientists do not always agree. Here too, then, there is a place for dialectic that assembles differences, classifies them, goes to their roots, and pushes them to extremes by developing alleged positions while reversing alleged counter-positions. Theological foundations, which objectify the horizon implicit in religious, moral, and intellectual conversion, may now be invoked to decide which really are the positions and which really are the counter-positions. In this fashion any ideological intrusion into scholarly or scientific human studies is filtered out.

The notion of dialectic, however, may play a further role. It can be an instrument for the analysis of social process and the social situation. The social historian will ferret out instances in which ideology has been at work. The social scientist will trace its effects in the social situation. The policy maker will devise procedures both for the liquidation of the evil effects and for remedying the alienation that is their source.

The advantage of the second use of dialectic is that the work of the historian and the scientist leads directly to policy. Alienation and ideology are destructive of community; community is the proper basis of society; hence to seek the elimination of alienation and ideology is to promote the good of society.

However, both uses of dialectic would seem to be necessary. The first use gives social scientists and historians a first-hand acquaintance with alienation and ideology; the dialectic is applied to their own work. Just as the psychiatrist in his didactic learns about neurosis in himself, so too the social historian and scientist will have sharper eyes for alienation and ideology in the processes they study, if similar phenomena have been criticized in their own work.

Corresponding to doctrines, systematics, and communications in theological method, integrated studies would distinguish policy making, planning, and the execution of the plans. Policy is concerned with attitudes and ends. Planning works out the optimal use of existing resources for attaining the ends under given conditions. Execution generates feedback. This supplies scholars and scientists with the data for studies on the wisdom of policies and the efficacy of the planning. The result of such attention to feedback will be that policy making and planning become ongoing processes that are continuously revised in the light of their consequences.

We have been indicating a method, parallel to the method of theology, for integrating theology with scholarly and scientific human studies. The aim of such integration is to generate well-informed and continuously revised policies and plans for promoting good and undoing evil both in the church and in human society generally. Needless to say, such integrated studies will have to occur on many levels, local, regional, national, international. The principles of subsidiarity will require that at the local levels problems will be defined and, in so far as possible, solutions worked out. Higher levels will provide exchange centers, where information on successful and unsuccessful solutions is accumulated to be made available to inquiries and so prevent the useless duplication of investigations. They will also work on the larger and more intricate problems that have no solution at the lower levels, and they will organize the lower levels to collaborate in the application of the solutions to which they conclude. Finally, there is a general task of coordination, of working out in detail what kinds of problem are prevalent, at what level they are best studied, how all concerned on any given type of issue are to be organized for a collaborative effort.

I have been speaking mainly of the redemptive action of the church in the modern world. But no less important is its constructive action. In fact, the two are inseparable, for one cannot undo evil without also bringing about the good. Still one will be taking a very superficial and rather sterile view of the constructive side of Christian action, if one thinks only of forming policies, planning operations, and carrying them out. There is the far more arduous task (1) of effecting an advance in scientific knowledge, (2) of persuading eminent and influential people to consider the advance both thoroughly and fairly, and (3) of having them convince practical policy makers and planners both that the advance exists and that it implies such and such revisions of current policies and planning with such and such effects.

In conclusion let me say that such integrated studies correspond to a profound exigence in the contemporary situation. For ours is a time of ever increasing change due to an ever increasing expansion of knowledge. To operate on the level of our day is to apply the best available knowledge and the most efficient techniques to coordinated group action. But to meet this contemporary exigence will also set the church on a course of continual renewal. It will remove from its action the widespread impression of complacent irrelevance and futility. It will bring theologians into close contact with experts in very many different fields. It will bring scientists and scholars into close contact with policy makers and planners and, through them with clerical and lay workers engaged in applying solutions to the problems and finding ways to meet the needs both of Christians and of all mankind.

5. THE CHURCH AND THE CHURCHES

I have been speaking vaguely of the Christian church. In fact, the church is divided. There exist different confessions of faith. There are defended different notions of the church. Different groups cooperate in different ways.

Despite such differences there exist both a real and an ideal unity. The real unity is the response to the one Lord in the one Spirit. The ideal unity is the fruit of Christ's prayer: ". . . may they all be one . . ." (John 17, 21). At the present time that fruit is ecumenism.

In so far as ecumenism is a dialogue between theologians, our chapters on *Dialectic* and on *Doctrines* indicate the methodical notions that have occurred to us. But ecumenism also is a dialogue between churches and then largely it operates within the framework of the World Council of Churches and under the directives of particular churches. Illustrative of such directives is the decree on ecumenism issued by the second Vatican council.

While the existence of division and the slowness in recovering unity are deeply to be lamented, it is not to be forgotten that division resides mainly in the cognitive meaning of the Christian message. The constitutive meaning and the effective meaning are matters on which most Christians very largely agree. Such agreement, however, needs expression and, while we await common cognitive agreement, the possible expression is collaboration in fulfilling the redemptive and constructive roles of the Christian church in human society.

INDEX

Abaelard, 279, 297

Aberrations and affective development, 65; and transvaluation of symbols, 66; of feelings, 33

Absolute and judgment, 16, 35; and objectivity, 263; truth, reality, holiness, 116

Abstract and conception, 11; an experiential pattern may be, 61; logic in classicism, 338-39. Transcendental notions not a., 23-24, 36

Absurd, objective situation as, 55; universe, and despair, 105

Academic, theology as, 3. A. theology necessary, 139

Acculturation, historian unexempted from, 223; and common meaning, 79

Act(s), agent is agent because in, 96; manifest state of love, 106; of meaning, 74, 78, 86, 92, 245. Movement is incomplete a., 96. A. of sensing and understanding have potential meaning, 74. A. of understanding and judgment, 77, 336

Acts of the Apostles, cp. 15, v. 28, 295, 296; cp. 28, v. 26, 162

Action and active meaning, 74. Group action, 177-78, 367

Acton, Lord, 164

Adaptation assimilation and adjustment, 27

Adler, 67

Adoration, 344

Affective development and aberration, 65-66; fulfilment, 39, 52; self-transcendence, 289

Affirmation of experience, understanding etc., 15. Rational a. and reflective understanding, 74-76

Agnostic investigation of God, 103

Aigrisse, G., 68

Alétheia, 306

Alienation and disregard of transcendental precepts, 55; and ideology, 55, 357-59, 361, 364; remedies for, 34

Alphabet makes words visible, 92; as visual sign, 28

Already-out there-now-real, 263

Ambivalent fusion of theory and common-sense world, 98

Amnesia and history, 181

Anachronism and doctrines, 312

Analogy, advance from mimesis to, 87; of methods in theology, 333; of science, 3-4; use by historians of, 225-27

Analysts, *see* Linguistic a.

Ancient modes of meaning, 172-73

Angel, E., 69

Anhypostasia, 308

Anselm of Canterbury, 279, 309, 336

Anthropomorphic gods, 91

Anthropomorphisms of Bible, 353; *see* Biblical

Aphasia and motor disturbances, 86; agnosia and apraxia, disorders related to, 255

252; and faith, 117; and judgments of value, 37–38; major and minor, 80; never a secure possession, 110, 252, 284; as particular, 111; and progress, 288; and subjectivity, 265, 291; and terminal and originating values, 51. Thematic of a. as basic to method, 254. A. or unauthentic tradition, 80, 162, 299

Authority of church officials, 332

Autobiography and history, 182–84

Awareness of self, 8–10; of artist, 63

Awe evoked by mystery, 106. Mystery of love and a., 112, 113, 119

Bañez, 280

Barbarians, xi, 326

Barth, K., 318

Baudouin, C., 67, 68

Baur, C., 143

Beauty, and artistically differentiated consciousness, 273; pursued in art, 13

Becker, C., 194–96, 203–5, 208, 215–16, 221–23, 232, 245

Becker, E., 285

Behaviourists and cognitional myth, 214; and existence of operations, 16

Being, conditions for the affirmation of, 75. Contingent and necessary b., 101. Cosmological myth and divine b., 90. B. in love, 105, 109, 113, 291, *see* Gift of God's love. Parmenides and b., 91. Spheres of b., 75. Transcendental notion of b., and mystery, 110

Belief(s), 41–47; and appropriation of one's heritage, 41. Breakdown of b., 244. Faith and b., 123. False b., 44; B. and generation of knowledge, 43; and the historian, 216, 233; and maps, 42; mistaken, 47;

and progress and decline, 44; and science, 42. Religious b., 118–19. B. and understanding, 335–36. Universal b., 223. B. in world mediated by meaning, 238

Benz, E., 88, 108, 110

Berger, P., 223

Bergson, 264

Berkeley, 264

Bernard, C., 207

Bernheim, E., 199–201. B.'s rule, 221

Berry, G. G., 200

Bertalanffy, L. von, 248, 285

Betti, E., 153

Bias, as block to charity, 284; as block to development, 231; and common fund of knowledge, 43–44; definition of, 231; and love of evil, 40; and the historian, 217, 230–31. Individual, group, general b., 53, 217, 240, 270. B. and moral conversion, 242, 270. Subjective b. in history, 214

Biblical anthropomorphism, philosophic purification of, 305, 307, 319, 329. B. theology, 171–72

Billuart, 280

Biography and history, 183–84

Biologist, 82

Binswanger, L., 69

Blondel, 96, 264, 316

Boeckh, A., 209, 210

Bohr, N., 248

Borsch, F. H., 90

Breakdowns and conversions, 243–44

Brentano, 96

Brown, D. M., 106

Buckle, 201

Buddhism, 109

Bultmann, R., 158, 169, 186, 196, 318

Burckhardt, 250

Butterfield, H., 194

Byzantine theologians: and christ-ology, 308; and systematic thought, 345

Cajetan, 280
Calculus of pleasures and pains, 50
Callimachus, 98
Cano, M., 281
Capacity for self-transcendence: its fulfilment, 105-6; is transcendental notions, 104; is unrestricted questioning, 106. Individual c., 48
Capreolus, 280
Carrier(s) of meaning: different, 64; combined in incarnate meaning, 73. C. of the word, 112
Castelli, E., 113
Categorial differs from transcendental mode of intending, 11. Metaphysics not c. speculation, 25. C. precepts, 20. Scholastic predicamentals as c., 13. Transcendental and c. sources of meaning, 73
Categories, bases of, 282-83; defined and illustrated, 11. C. in foundations, 282-93. Derivation of theological c., 292. General theological c.: basic terms and relations, 286; differentiated, 286-87; models with, 287-88. C. and religious experience, 290. Special theological c.: base of, 283-84, 289; and data, 293; and Father, Son, Spirit, 291; five sets of, 289-91; genesis of, 292; model in medieval, 288, and progress and decline, 291. Theoretical c., 107. Transcultural aspect of c., 282, 284-5. Use of c., 285, 292-293
Cassirer, E., 86-87, 92, 96, 173, 250, 255
Catholicism and classicism, 327
Catholics and Protestants: and

method, 297; in merely sociological sense, 299
Causa cognoscendi et essendi and revealed mysteries, 323
Causal connections in history, 245
Causes and non-intentional states, 30. Aristotelian c., 11. Efficient and final c., 37-38, 259. C. and the historian, 230; and modern science, 315. C. not perceived, 16
Chardin, T. de, 315
Charles, P., 330
Charity blocked by bias, 284; not needing critical justification, 284. Religious c. and human pride, 117
Child and emergence of fourth level of consciousness, 121
Certitude, not aim of systematics, 336
Chalcedon, 138, 277-78, 307-8, 345
Change, models of, 287
Christian message, 362; studies, 150
Christians, agreement of in constitutive and effective meaning, 368; disagreement of in cognitive meaning, 368; self-image of, challenged by modern science, 315
Christianity and authenticity, 291. Conflicts in movements of C., 129. Early C. and identification of theology and religion, 140. C., horizons and conversion, 131-32. C. mirrored in theology, 139. Need for transcultural base of mission of C., 282. C. and entrance of God into history, 119
Christology, development in, as ongoing context, 313-14; tensions up to present in, 319-20
Church, Christian: as community resulting from outer communication of Christ's message, 361; constructive action of, 366-68; doctrines of, *see* Doctrines; divided,

367; identity and unity of, 367–68; as institutional framework, 48; outgoing, 363; as perfect society, 359; self-constitution of, 363; teaching of, 150, *see also* Doctrines; twentieth-century problems of, 140

Circle, hermeneutical, *see* Hermeneutical

City State as ideal type, 227

Civilization and world of common sense, 257–58. Ancient high c., 89–90. C. in decline, 54. Speculative accounts of c., 68

Classicism, abstract logic in, 338–39; mistakenly views culture, 124, 302, 326, 363; opposed to historicity of dogma, 326

Classicist, and control of meaning, 29; never departs from accepted terminology, 123; notion of culture as normative, etc., xi, 124, 301; and opposition of theory and common sense, 84

Classics in religion, letters, etc, founding traditions, demanding conversion, 161–62

Classification in dialectic, 250; medieval, 296; by subject specialization, 140

Clement of Alexandria, 296, 307, 319, 329, 344

Cloud of unknowing, 266, 342

Coffee, D., 339

Cognitional being, dynamic structure of, xii, 12–13, 15–16; myth, 213–14, 238–39. C. operations, *see* Operations. C. process; objectification of, 14–19, 77; and transcendental method, 4, 77; self-transcendence, 45, 104, 122, 233, 239, 252, 289. C. theory: answers question What am I doing when I am knowing?, 25, 83, 261, 287, 316; basic terms and relations, 21,

120, 343; differences in, 21, 76; and interpretation, 127, 154; and reality, knowledge, objectivity, 20, 213–14; revision of, 18–19, 22; source of root differences in theories of history, 180, 197–98. *See also* Mind, Questions, Self-transcendence, etc.

Cognitive function of meaning, 76: and communication of feelings, 90; and constitutive function, 89. C. and moral self-transcendence, 104

Collaboration in method, xi; and self-transcendence, 35, 104

Collingwood, R. G., 164–66, 175, 188, 204–6, 208, 218–19, 226, 357

Common meaning, *see* Meaning. C. sense: analysis of c.s. procedures and transcendental method, 83; blind to long-term consequences, 53. Brands of c.s., 276. Clash of c.s. with theory, 84. C.s. and full differentiation of consciousness, 328–29. Generalities of c.s., 230. Group c.s., 72. Humanism of c.s. from philosophy, 99. Interiority, foundation distinct from c.s., 85. C.s. and interpretation, 160–61. Modes of cognitional operations in c.s., 154, 303–5. C.s. and proverbs, 230. Realm of c.s., 81–85, 114–15, 120, 257, 265–66, 272. C.s. and research, 149; and scholarship, 233–34, 305; and scientific explanation, 349; as style of developing intelligence, 271, 303–5; as spontaneous procedure, 303. World of c.s., 95–96, 107, 257–59, 303–4. World's work done by c.s., 97

Commitment and categories, 292; and the good, 50; rests on judgment of value, 244

Communicatio Idiomatum, 308

Communications(s) and art, 132; of the Christian message, 362;

differentiated according to media, 136; of feelings, 90; as functional specialty, 132–33, 168–69; and the gospel, 300, 330; and history, 194; Internal c., 66–67, 74. Material meaning of c. in theology, 132. Pluralism in c., 276. C. and preaching, 328, 362; and pre-critical history, 185. C. presupposes understanding, 351. Problems of c. for Church, 140. C. of specialists, Transcultural base of c., 282. Use of models in c., 285

Communicative function of meaning, 78–79, 89–90

Community and common meaning, 79. Conversion and c., 130. C. and the development of language, 67. Dialectic as affecting c., 358. Formal constituent of c., 356. C. and ideal basis of society, 360–61. Religious c. and expression, 118. C. and social value, 32. Substance of c., 50. Subjects in c., 291. Traditions of c., 81

Complementarity (Bohr), 248

Complementary differences in horizon, 236

Compréhension (Aron), 206

Comte, A., 201

Concepts pertain to answer, 103; transcendental, 11–12; and understanding, 336

Conception and insight, 10–11

Conceptualism and Vatican I, 336

Concern, ultimate, 106, 241

Concrete dealt with in dialectics, 129, C. experiential pattern, 61. Transcendental notions as c., 23–24

Conflicts and dialectic, 129, 141–42, 347; ground of, 141

Connotation of transcendentals, 11

Conscience, bad, 121. Consciousness as c., 268–69. Decision, work of

good c., 269. Happy or unhappy c., 35. Peaceful or uneasy c., 40

Conscious intentionality, drive of, 30; dynamism of, 12, 34, 73; focused by words, 70–71, 82. Fulfilment of c.i., 105–6, 109, 111. C.i. making objects present, 8, 212. C.i. and mode of common sense, 85. C.i. moulded by language, 71. Question of God and c.i., 103. C.i. and self-transcendence, 38. Sensible expression and c.i., 86. C.i. and transcendental notions, 12, 34, 73. *See also* Levels of c.i.

Consciousness as cognitional event, 8; as conscience, 268–69. Classical c., 84. C. and data of philosophy, 95. Differentiated c.: and academic theology, 139; artistically, 273; artistically and with religious sensibility, 278; competence with, 273; and critical exigence, 84; interiorly, 274; long development of, 257–62; many types of, 272, 275; and obligations in faith, 330. Realms of worlds of meaning of d.c., 257–62. Religiously d.c., 278. D.c. and research, 150. Scholarly d.c., 274, 281, 305. Theoretically d.c., 273–74, 304. Unity of d.c., 84. *See also* Differentiation of c., Empirical c.: and higher animals, 9; just experience, 106. C.a fourfold experience, 14–15. Heightening of c.: difficulty of, 15; and religiosity, 290; and transcendental method, 25, 83. C. as key to constructing stages of meaning, 85. Levels of c., *see* Levels of conscious intentionality. C. of love of God, 121. C. of mystery, 106. C. and mystical mode of apprehension, 273. Mythic c., 92. Native spontaneities of c., 18. Operations of c. as

is dialectical, 284; as criterion by which all else defined, 283–84; efficacious ground of self-transcendence, 241; and guidance, 123; as operative grace, 107, 241; and proof of existence of God, 338; sublating moral c., 242–43; and ultimate concern, 241. *See also* C., intellectual, moral, religious; Gift of God's love. Self-transcendence and c., *see* Self-transcendence. Social dimension of c., 142. C., a transformation of subject, 130

Conviction and breakdowns, 244
Cooperation and institutions, roles, tasks, 48
Cooperative grace, 107, 241
Copernican revolution: in history 205–6; and Kant, 264. C. theory, 176
Copernicus, 176, 315
Copleston, F., 92, 95
Core of religious expression, 114. Transcultural core, 283–84
Corinthians I, cp. 13, v. 12, 135; cp. 15, v. 3, 295
Cosmogenesis, 103
Cosmogonies, 98
Coulanges, de, 227
Councils of Church, Christological, 327; *See also under place names and* Greek
Counter-positions and presentation of past, 251; and statements incompatible with conversion, 249; and systematics, 347; *see also* Positions
Creation, purpose of, 116; questions about, 306
Creativity in art, 273, 275; in imagination 10. Method as collaborative c., xi; c. in thinkers rare, 98
Crede ut intelligas, 336
Criteria, critical subject gives himself over to, 10. Transcendent

exigence and c. for deliberation, 84. C. and transcendental notions, 35

Critical exigence, 83; function of method, 20. C. ground of common sense and theory, 85. C. History: Credible testimonies and c.h., 195. Critical understanding of c.h., 193. Double process from data to facts in c.h., 202, 348. C.h. ending classicist assumptions, 326. C.h. as heuristic, ecstatic, selective, critical, constructive, 188–89, 193, 195; as objective knowledge of past, 195; of second degree, 193–94. Techniques of c.h., 195. C.h. as understanding: of sources, 189; of what was going on, 189. C. rationality, 10. Two meanings of c., 188. C. use of sources, 189
Criticism, art, 63. C. of author and tradition, 162. External and internal c., 200. C. as function of dialectic, 130. C. and the good, 36. Historical c., 199. Inner and outer c., 199–200. C. and philosophy, 129. Textual c., 126, 133
Crowe, F. E., 7, 71
Culture(s), classical and modern, 2, 29, 301–2; classicist view of, xi, 124, 301–2, 315, 326, 363; empirical notion of, xi, 124, 300–2; function of, 32. God and constructs of c., 29. Meaning of smile invariant in c., 60. Meanings as intrinsic component of c., 78. Pluralist view of c., 363
Cultural achievement destroyed in breakdown, 244. Condition of possibility of c. advance, 12. Cultural development: stages of, 305–19; and Piaget, 29–30. C. movements, 128. Variants and invariants of c. change, 11–12

INDEX

Damascene, J., 296
Daniélou, J., 300
Darwin, 315
Data, of consciousness, 72, 201–2. D, distinct from facts, 201–3, 347–48. D. as evidence, 186–87. Process from d. to results in theology, 126. D. relevant to theology, 149–50. D. of sense: explanation by sciences, 94; fulfilling conditions for affirmation, 75; inquired about, 86, 201–2; potentially intelligible, 74; provoke inquiry, 10
Decision and active meaning, 74; and authenticity, 121; about experiencing, understanding, etc., 14; and distinction between knowing and deciding, 90. D. and foundations, 268–69. D. and responsibility, 121
Decline and conversion, 243–44; cumulative, 55, 81. Education and d., 55. Feelings and d., 40. D. of good order, 54. Mass media and d., 55, 244. Progress and d., 52–55. D. and unauthenticity, 288
de Finance, J., 40, 237
Definition, names and Socratic concern, 70, 82
de la Potterie, 186
Deliberation and liberty, 50; operation on fourth level, 6, 9, 340. D. about value and question of God, 101. D. and transcendent exigence, 84
Demagogue and incarnate meaning, 73
Democracies, modern, 361
Demonic, 111
Demythologization and transcendental method, 21; and modern scholarship, 353
Denotation of categories and transcendentals, 11

Denzinger, 169, 296. D. theology, 270, 330
Department specialization, 126
Depth psychology and bias, 231, 284
Descamps, A., 171, 172
Descartes, 96, 223, 261, 316
Description of intentional operations incomplete, 19. Model not a d., xii, 227, 292
Detachment in art, 63; incarnate in the subject, 10
Determinism and decline, 117
Development, academic, 139; affective, 65. D. and bias, 231. Change of stage of meaning and d., 94. Cumulative d., 81. Definition of d., 138. Degrees of d., 29. Doctrinal d., 305–319, 353. Dialectic d. of religion, 110. End of d., 140. Fact of d., 352. Goal of d., 183. Legitimacy of d., see History, evaluational. Possibility of d., 343. Shift to theoretic d., 72. Systematic d., 347. D. of theology, 138–44, 353
Developments, revolutionary, 288
Dialectic, aim of, 129. D. and community, 358. D. compares and criticizes, 138. D. and conflicting doctrines, 252, 347. D. and conflicts, 129, 141, 235. D. and conversion, 224, 237–44, 251–53, 287, D. and differences in horizon, 224. 236–37, 247. D. and dynamic unities, 114. D. as ecumenical, 130, 136; as a functional speciality, 112, 128–30; and heuristic structures, 141. D. and history, 227, 346. D. and human sciences, 248–49. Implementation of d., 251–52. D. and interpretation, 246. The issue of d., 245–47. D. and irreducible differences, 129. D. of Jew and Greek, of master and slave, 51.

13   377

unrestricted capacity, 105–6, 109, 111

Given, world of given as given, 76

Glory of God, 116–17

Glaubens-verständnis, 350

Gnosticism, pronouncements on, restrained by discovery, 192. Symbolic representations in, 307

God(s) and analogy, 307. G. and apophatic theology, 277–78, 341. G. in Aquinas, 346. G. and atheist, 103. G. and conversion, 107, 240–41, 327, 350. G. and culture, 29. Demonic cult of G., 111. Entrance of G. into history, 119. Existence of God, 102–3, 116, 339. Fundamental meaning of name G., 341, 350. Glory of G., 116–17. G. as ground of universe, 101, 342. Hierophanies reveal g., 108. G. and kataphatic theology, 341. Love of G., 39, 84, 116; *see also* Gift. G. as mystery, 341. G. as object, 341–43. G. of persons, 108. Proof of existence of G., 102–3, 116, 339. Question of G., 39, 101–3, 116, 287, 342. G. as reached by subjectivity, 29. Remote G., 110. G. and religious expression, 118. Self-disclosure of G., 119. G. as self-transcending, 116. G. and transcendental notions, 344. G. and values, 106, 116. G. within world mediated by questions, 342

Goetz, J., 110, 111

Goethe, 209

Gonet, 280

Gooch, G. P., 186, 197, 250

Good, concrete, 27, 36, 93. G. and criticism, 36, 84. G. discerned by responsibility, 11. Human g.: agreeable and disagreeable, 31; individual and social, 47, 52, 55, 359; and moral conversion, 104,

240; structure of 47–52, 359; *see also* Beliefs, Feelings, Values. G. of order: deterioration of, 54; and history, 184; in institutions, 49; present function of, 181; and social values, 31; as terminal value, 50; not utopia, 49. Particular g., 48. Theoretical g., 94. Transcendental concept of g., 12. Transcendental notion of g., 36

Goodness beyond criticism, 36. G. pursued in morals, 13. G. as quality of supreme being, 109. Transcendental notion of g., 344

Gospel(s) and Bultmann, 158. G. and interpretation, 153–54. G. and modes of communication, 300, 330

Grace, Aquinas' theology of, 165–66, 352. G. and conversion, 123. G. and freedom, 352. G. and God's gift of love, 107, 241, 288; *see* Gift. G. and human development, 39. G. as liberation, 310. G. and medieval problematic of liberty, 309–10. G. and metaphysical categories, 288. Operative and cooperative g., 107, 241, 288–89. Sanctifying g., 289

Grammar and Aristotle's categories and logic, 71. G. and the study of words, 92. G. and the young, 122

Greek(s) achievement, 261. G. and cognitional theory, 260. G. Councils, 307–9, 313–14. G. discovery of mind, 90–98, 305–12, 314–18

Ground(s) for eightfold division of theology, 133–36. G. of universe, 103, 342

Group(s), activity of, 211. Analysis of technical proficiency of g., 30. Behaviour of g., 231. G. and conversion, 239. G. egoism, 54. First stage of meaning and g., 89. God of g., 108. G. and incarnate meaning, 73. Mathematical notion of

and history, 220–24. H. and holiness, 103. H. and interpretation, 161, 163. H. and liberty, 40. H. and limits of knowledge and interest, 235–37. H. and love, 106. H. of metaphysics, 343. Multiplicity of h., 269. Objectification of h., 250. Opposed h., 247. H. and question of God, 103. H. and realms of meaning, 257–62. H. as structured resultant of past, towards future, 237. H. and talk about mental acts, 257–62. H. and values, 247

Horney, K., 34, 68
Hostie, R., 34
Huber, W., 67
Human: becoming h., 97. H. culture, 124. H. development: in holiness, 116; through resolution of conflicts, 252. H. expectations, beyond grave, 116. Expressions of religious experience h., 108. H. inquiry and functional specialities, 134. Human knowledge: a compound, 12, 181, 348; historical character of, 43; and historical facts, 202; social character of, 41. H. living, *see Leben,* Living. H. mind, *see* Mind. H. sciences: and dialectic, 248–49; and history, 180, 211–212; and meaning, 154; and method, 3, 23, 249. H. spirit: open structure of, 302; philosophy as reconstructing constructions of, 210. H. studies: data of, 210; distinction from natural sciences, 212; distinguished from religious studies, 149–150; empirical, 301
Humanism, 97–99, 275
Humanist and question of God, 103
Hume, D., 16, 21, 222
Hünermann, P., 198, 210
Hypnosis, 59

Hypotheses and belief, 42. H. and ideal types (models), xii, 227, 284–85, 292. H. in natural science, 4–5. H. and sphere of being, 75
Husserl, E., 80, 96, 212, 264

'I' and 'thou' transformed into 'we', 33. 'I' and 'thou' and prior 'we', 57
Idea, what is sought by inquiry, 10
Ideal constructs, and stages of meaning, 85; and ideal-types, 228; and transcendental method, 227. I. of logic, 138, 258. I-types: and categories, 284–85, 287–88, 292; description of, 284–85; grand scale i.-t., 229; and hypotheses, xii, 227, 284–85, 292; and mathematics, 284; and the historian, 224, 227–28; and Toynbee, 228; *see* Models
Idealism, as a complication (remediable, 206) in Collingwood, 174. I. as counter to appropriation of third cognitional level, 213. I. and dialectic, 202. I. and empiricism, 214. German i., 316, 350. I. and interiority, 316. Moral i., 38. I. as naming a horizon, 239. I. and terms of meaning, 76
Idealization and art, 63
Identification, emotional, 58. I. and hypnosis, primitive mentality, sexual intercourse, 59
Ideological warfare, 178
Ideology and alienation, 55, 357–59, 361, 364. Basic form of i., 357–58. I. and conversion, 52. I. and decline, 117. I. and evil, 40. I. and faith, 117. I. and sociology, 249
Identity, consciousness and, 177. I. crisis of community, 168. I. of group, 182. The subject and i., 181
Idol and overemphasis of immanence, 111

functional specialties, 133; and philosophy, 95; and question of God, 103, 106–7. I. response: and feelings, 30–31, 38, 58; and goals, 30; and values, 38, 245–46. I. self-transcendence, 38

Intentionality analysis: and faculty psychology, 96, 340–43; and Husserl, 212; and transition to methodical theology, 289. Conscious i., *see* Conscious

Interdependence of functional specialties, 141

Interdisciplinary problems, 22–23, 132, 366

Interest and horizon, 236–37. I. and language, 70

Interiority, appropriation of, 83. I. and critical exigence, 84. I. as foundation of common sense, theory and philosophy, 85. I. as ground of distinction between worlds, 107. I. as invariant basis of ongoing systems, 305. Realm of i., 114–15, 257, 265–66, 272. Religious interiority: need for study of, 290; removing controversy, 115. Shift to i., 316, 327–28. I. and theologian, *see* Theologian and method. World of i.: entry into, 261–62; and God's love, 107, *see* Gift; language of, 257–62; and mental acts, 261; presuppositions of, 261–62; verification in, 257

Internal communication, 66–67

Interpretation and cognitional theory, 127, 154; and common sense, 160–61; and contexts, 183; and controversy, 158; and conversion, 246; and expression, 74, 154, 212; and human sciences, 154; and hermeneutics, 127, 153, 155, 159–60. Historical **i.,** 199, 214. Mediation of i., 157–58. I. and meaning,

126–27. Problems of i., 153–55. I. and potential universal viewpoint, 288. I. and reconstruction, 203. Systems of i. in psychology, 67–68. I and understanding words, author, self, 158–62, 189

Intersubjectivity, carrier of the word, 112. I. and communications, 59, 254, 357. I. and conversion, 327. I. and embodiment of meaning, 61, 70, 73–74

Introspection and heightening of awareness, 15. Myth of i., 8. I. as objectifying consciousness, 9

Intuitionism in interpretation, 157

Irenaeus, 295, 296, 350

Islam, 109

Isocrates, 97

Isomorphism, 21

Janov, A., 68, 285

Jaspers, K., 262, 265

Jesuit controversies with Dominicans, 297

Jesus Christ, 297, 298, 301; person and nature in, 307–8

Jewish apocalyptic, 315

Jonah, 66

John XXIII, 300

John of St Thomas, 280

Johnston, W., 29, 278, 342

Judaic Christianity, 300

Judaism, 109

Judgment(s) and absence of further relevant questions, 166. J. and belief, 42, 244. Doctrines as j., 132. J. of fact, 9–10, 45. J. as full act of meaning, 74–76. Historical j., 191–93. J. and Husserl, 212. J. and interpretation, 162–67. J. and the unconditioned, 75–76, 84, 102, 202, 213. J. of value: and active meaning, 74; and authenticity in moral self-transcendence, 36–41; and commitment, 244; and community, 50; and doctrines, 132; and feelings, 37–38, 166; from Faith, 119; and natural science, 248; a reality in moral order, 73; and social policy, 249; true and false, 37, 40, 233. J. and world mediated by meaning, 77

Jung, K., 67

Justice and decline, 54

Kant, 14, 96, 158, 210, 264, 316, 335

Kantian tradition identifying *verstehen* and judgment, 158

Keller, H., 70

Kenoboskion manuscripts, 192

Kerygma, 318

Keynsian economics, 315

Kierkegaard, 80, 96, 264, 316

Kingdom of God, 291

Kitagawa, J., 69, 88, 108

Kleutgen, J., 339

Klostermann, F., 356

Knowing, elementary and compound, 12, 181, 348. K. and idealism, 238–39. K. and objectivity, 20. K. and self-transcendence, 239. K. transformed by love of God, 106; *see* Gift. K. and the unconditioned, 75–76; *see* Unconditioned

Knowledge, evidence for account of, 83. K. in exegesis, 156. K. and Faith, 115. Historical k., *see* Historical. Historical character of k., 43. Immanently generated k., 43, 46–47. K. and interest, 235–37. K. and love, 122–23. Possibility of k., 210. Social character of k., 43. Sociology of k., 41. K. and value, 38. *See also* Gift, Human, Judgment. etc

Known unknown, 77

Koetschau, 296

Labour, division of, 72

Lake, F., 68

Langer, S., 61, 64

Langlois, C., 200, 201

Language analysts, *see* Linguistic. L. and common sense, 230, 257–62. L. and data, 348. Development of l., 86–87, 92. Early l., 86–90, 92. L. as expression, 10, 114, 256, 260–61. L. of historical explanation, 230. Literary l., 72, 255, 258, 304. L. and meaning, 70, 78, 112, 254–62. L. and meditation, 28. Ordinary l., 72, 81–82, 85, 230, 255–62. L. and realms of meaning, 257–62. Scriptural l., 138. Specialization of l., 72, L. and tradition, 80. Technical l., 72, 82, 255, 258, 260, 304. L. and the unconverted, 299. Use of l., 76–77

Laplace, 226

Laws, classical, 226, 288; civil, 289–90; and existential decision, 121; and good of order, 48–49; and the historian, 230; statistical, 6, 288

Learning process: and conversion, 155, 161; and hermeneutics, 209; in research, 149; self-correcting, 159–60, 208–9, 303; in understanding words, 158–59. L. theory, for exegesis, 156–58

Leben, Dilthey on, 210; as objectification, 211

Lebensphilosophie 212

Leontius of Byzantium, 308

Levels of conscious intentionality, four, 9, 14–15, 19, 73, 120–21, 232, 340; emergence of fourth, 121, 245–47, 316; and functional specialties, 133–36; as related, 120; and revision (of objectification) of, 19; and sources of meaning, 73; and transcendental notions, 11–12, 34–35

Levi-Strauss, C., 11

Mansi, 339
Maps, 42
Mark, St., ch. 12, v. 30, 105
Marrou, H.-I., 201, 206-8, 215-18, 220, 227-29
Mary, Virgin, 277, 308, 313
Maslow, A., 29, 39, 52, 69, 285
Mass-excitement, 58. M.-media, 55, 99
Materialism and cognitional myth, 214
Mathematics, non-necessity in, 280, 315. M. and heuristic structures, 141. M. and unacknowledged insights, 216
Mathematical sphere of being, 75-76
Matthew, St., ch. 7, v. 20, 119; ch. 28, v. 19, 300
Matson, F. W., 248
Matter, and form, 96, 259. M. is pure potency, 96
Maturity, religious, 290
Maxwell, 82
May, R., 69, 111
Mazlish, B., 201, 229
Meaning, acts, of, 74, 78. Active, m., 74. Ancient modes of m., 172. Carriers of m., 57 ff, 178, 356. Changes of m., 78. M. as cognitive, 76, 356, 362. Common m., 78, 111-12, 178, 211, 356-58. M. as communicative, 78, 356, 362. M. and community, 74, 178. M. and the concrete, 178, 211. M. as constitutive, 78, 178, 180, 306, 356, 362. M. and culture, see Culture. M. of doctrines, 298, 312, 314. M. of dogma, 322-26. M. as effective, 74-75, 89, 245, 306, 356, 362. M. as efficient, 77-78, 89. Elemental m., 63, 67. Elements of m., 73-76, 172, 178. M. and feelings, 31, 90. Functions of m., 76-78, 178, 306, 356. M. and historical investiga-

tion, 178. M. and human living, 139, 210-11. M. and human sciences, 135. Incarnate m., 73, 166. Intersubjective m., 59-61. Inward m., 211. M. and language, 254-57. Linguistic m., 60, 67, 70-73. Literal m., 343. Meanings of m. 178. M. and meant, 74. Metaphorical m., 343. Modes of m., 172. M. and myth, 89. M. and ontology, 356. Outward m., 211. Performative m., 75, 106. Permanence of m., 302, 320-24. M. and philosophy, 95. Potential m., 74. Realms of m., 81-85, 120, 257-62, 265, 272, 286. Religious m., 78, 112. M. of smile, 59-60. Sources of m., 73. Stages of m., 85-99, 108, 112, 173, 178. Stating of m., 167 ff. Systematic m., 305-10, 329-30. M. of a text, 167, 169. M. and the universal, 178. World mediated by m., 28, 30-31, 35, 76-77, 89, 92-93, 95-96, 112, 221, 238-39, 262-64, 303. Worlds of m., 257-62
Media and communications, 133, 136. Mass m., 55, 99
Mechanist determinism, 248, 317
Mediation of immediacy, 77. Notion of mediation, 28. M. and world, 76
Medieval schools and theological context, 314
Meinecke, 232-3, 245
Memory of group, 177, 181. M. and history, 181. M. of individual, 177
Menander, 98
Mental acts, 254-61: as logical first, 262; and new linguistic usage, 255-56, 260; occur in genetically distinct horizons, 257-59; as private, 254-57
Mendelbaum, M., 196
Message, Christian, 362, 368

Palmer, R. E., 210, 211
Pantheist, 59
Papal encyclicals, xii
Parmenides, 91
Participation in art, 64
Parsons, T., 249
Pascal, 115, 261, 341
Past, idealized versions of, 251. Objective knowledge of p., 195. Reconstruction of p., 183. Similarity of p. with present, 225. P. and perspectivism, 220
Pathology, supposed instances of, 222–23. P. of symbolic consciousness, 86
Pattern(s), alien, 62. P. in art, 61, 64. P. of experience, 29, 286. P. of movements, 59. P. of operations, 4, 6, 13, 17
Paul, St., 105, 162, 284, 329
Pavlov, 68
Peace, 39, 105, 242, 166 see Gift
Perception and early language, 87. P. and experiential pattern, 61. P. has an orientation of its own, 59
Performative meaning, 75, 106
Person(s), authentic, 51. Chaledonian doctrine of p., 277. P. and conversion, 130. P. emergent on fourth level of intentionality, 10. P. and incarnate meaning, 73. P. meet in dialectic, 252. P. and moral self-transcendence, 104. P. and nature in Christ, 307–8. P. in trinitarian theology, 346
Personal relations, 48, 50–51
Personalists, 316
Perspective in historical investigation, 187, 192
Perspectivism, accounts for different histories, 224. Definition of p., 216–18. P. and individuality of historian, 246. P. and relativism, 217

Phenomenalism and cognitional myth, 214
Phenomenology of a smile, 59–61
Philanthropia, 97
Philip the chancellor, 310
Philologie, 210, 310, 315
Philologists, 96
Philosophic problems not entirely linguistic, 256. P. purification of biblical anthropomorphisms, 305, 307. P. theory and humanism, 99
Philosophies, opposed, grounded in presence or absence of conversion, 253
Philosophy, Aristotelian, 310–11, 316. Data of p., 95, 259. P. and decline, 55; and historical inquiry, 225; and humanism, 98–99; and human sciences, 259; and interiority, 85, 95, 276, 316; and linguistic feedback, 97; and meaning, 29, 78; and method, xi, 25; and sciences, 94, 96, 275, 316. P. reflects on worlds, 92. Role of p., 24, 95. P. and self-evident principles, 316. P. and theology, 24, 337–40; see also Theologian and method. P. in world of theory, 258
Physics and categories, 11; and functional specialization, 126; and reshaping of senses, 67
Piaget, J., 27–29
Piron, H., 67
Pius IX, 150
Plato, 82, 92, 95, 98, 258, 275, 335
Plautus, 98
Pluralism and classical culture, 301–2; and communications, 276, 329; and conversions, 276, 326, 328, 330; and cultural traditions, 363. Developmental p., 150. P. and expression 271–76, 328. P. and faith, 326–30. Radical p., 276. P. in religious language, 276–81.

Scholarship, aim of, 274. S. and common sense, 233–34, 305. Definition of s., 233–34. Development of s., 305. S. and human studies, 364

Scholasticism, defects of later, 311. S. and emergence of metaphysical context, 309. Spirit of s., 172. S. and systematic meaning, 329. Theology of s.: abandoned, 279; as developing, 138; inauthenticity in, 80. S. and theoretic, 277

Schopenhauer, 96, 316

Schurr, V., 356

Science(s), Aristotle's views on, see Aristotle. S. and belief, 42. S. as autonomous, 94–95. S. and causes, 315. Classical and empirical notions of s., 315–16. S. and communications, 132. Data of s., 94, 135, 316. S. and dialectic, 252. S. as explanation, 94, 129. S. fiction, 99. General and special s., 316. S. and history, see History. Human s., 3, 23, 154, 180, 210–12, 248–49. S. and human mind, 4. S. and inauthenticity, 80. Method of s. and cognitional theory, 133, 248. Modern s.: autonomy of, 96; and correlations, 315; and extra-scientific opinion, 317; and humanism, 99; medieval anticipation of, 309; and method, xi, 259; probable, not necessary, 315. Natural s., 3–4, 23, 94, 141, 179–80, 259. S. as ongoing process, 94, 325. S. and ordinary language, 85. S. and philosophy, 85, 94–96, 274. S. and scholarship, 233–34. Value of s., 83. S. and value, 248. Unification of s., 24, 94. S. and world mediated by meaning, 77–78. S. and world of theory, 258–59.

Scissors movements, with categories in theology, 293

Scotist school, 297

Scotus, 335

Scripture, anachronism and archaism, 313; as data of theology, 150; and history of religion, 154; inspired, 296, 299; language of, 138; rarely quoted, xii

Seignobos, C., 200, 201

Selbstvollzug, Church as, 363

Self-appropriation, arduous, 167; and the book Insight, 7, 17, 260; as primary function of philosophy, 95; process of, 6–7, 13–16, 262, 265; and therapy, 34; and transcendental method, 83–85; and religious experience, 266

Self-awareness, 9

Self-correcting process of learning, 159–60, 208–9, 303

Self-destruction, 111

Self-determination, 50

Self-disclosure of God, 119

Self-knowledge, achievement of, 7, 260; and differentiated consciousness, 84; and feelings, 33; and interpretation, 161, 167; and method in theology, see Theologian and method; and revision, 18–19; rudimentary, 84

Self-revelation of historian, 220. S. of subject, 286

Self-sacrificing love, 55, 113, 117, 242, 291, 342, 364

Self-surrender, 105, 240

Self-transcendence, as achievement, 35, 41, 51, 104, 111. Affective s., 289. S. and alienation, 359. S. as base of categories, 286. Cognitional s., 45, 114, 122, 233, 239, 243, 252, 289. S. and conversion, 239, 241, 243, 283, 338, 357. S. and decline, 55. S. and faith, 117. S. of God,

116. Ground of s., 241. Judgment on s., 253. S. as interpersonal, 253. S. as moral, 38, 45, 104, 121–22, 233, 252, 289, 338, 357. S. and objectivity, 37, 338. S. and originating value, 51, 116, 242. S. revealing subject, 286. S. and religious conversion, 241, 338, 357. S. and theological conflict, 252. S. and value, 31–32, 37, 51
Self-understanding, tested in encounter, 247
Seminar, value of, 170
Semi-rationalists and Vatican I, 324
Sensations, produced at will, 15
Senses, as apparatus, 61; as attending, 11; and experiencing subject, 62; and Parmenides, 92; and science, 62; *see* Data
Sensism and cognitional myth, 214
Set of operations, 125; of terms and relations, *see* Terms
Sexual and emotional identification, 59; and immediacy, 77; and love of God, 111
Shakespeare, 209
Shamanism, 273
Shintoism, 108
Sic et non, 279, 297
Sign, conventional, 70
Signification, indicative, 86
Silence and love, 113. S. and prayer, 257, 265–66, 342
Simeon Stylites, 222
Simmel, G., 139, 206
Simon, B., 87, 88
Sin and alienation, 364. Human s., 117
Sinfulness, 242–43
Sitz im leben, 183
Skills, 27–30, 48
Smile, phenomenology of, 59–61
Smith, C., 196, 215–16, 221, 232, 245
Snell, B., 90, 97, 98, 173, 260, 304

Snyder, P. L., 194, 203
Social character of human knowledge, 43. S. institutions, 48–49, 78. S. progress and decline, 52–55. S. realism, 62. S. science, 231, 248–49. S. structure, 365–67
Socialization, as growth through common meaning, 79; historians not exempted from, 223
Society, basis of, 360; and cosmological myth, 90; and good of order, 48, 359, 361; studied by sociologists, 249, 358–59
Sociology and ethics, 248–49. S. of knowledge, 41. S. and natural sciences, 180. Styles of s., 248–49
Sophists, 92
Soul, Aristotelian account of, 95–96, 259–60; medieval analysis of, 288, 315
Sources, critical use of, 189; imperfect in history, 201. History starts from, returns to, s., 205. Religious s. and theological system, 346. S. of religious expression, 114
Space, absolute, 176. S. and art, 63. S. and early expression, 108. S. and experience, 104
Spätjudentum, 300, 327
Specialization, types of, 125
Specialties, *see* Functional specialties
Speculative intellect, *see* Intellect
Spheres of being, 75
Spinoza, 96
Spirit, *see* Holy, Human
Spiritual director and religious conversion, 123
Spontaneity and intersubjectivity, 57, 70. S. of operations, 18
Stages of cultural development, 30; of meaning, 85–99, 108
Stählin, 296, 307
State of being in love, *see* Gift, Love.

S. as institution, 48, 78. Non-intentional s., 30. S. and perfect society, 359

Stating meaning of text, basic exegetical operation: and doctrines and systematics, 169–70; by exegete *qua* exegete, 167, 169–71; in explanatory mode, 172–73; to exegetes, 170; to pupils, 170–71; to theological community, 171–73

Statistical frequencies, 226. S. heuristic structure, 287

Stephen, Pope, 296

Stekel, W., 34

Stern, F., 197, 201, 220, 245

Stinnette, C. R., 169

Structure(s), cognitional, *see* Cognitional. Heuristic s., *see* Heuristic. S. of human good, 47–52, 359. S. of human inquiry, 133. S. of human spirit, 302. Ontological s., 21. S. of subject's world, 71. S. of world mediated by meaning, 77

Stylus Curiae, 312

Subject and art, 62–63; and community, 29; and conversion, 130; and language, 71–72; 88; as operator, 7; present to self, 8; revealed, 14–16, 286. S. specialization, 126, 140, 145. Unity of a s., 138

Subjectivity and objective knowledge, 265, 292. Objectification of s., 253, 259, 262. S. of philosophers, 265. S. reaching for God, 29. S. and value, 233

Sublation, in conversions, 241–43; in levels of consciousness, 316, 340

Substratum, in Aristotle, 177

Supernatural-natural, medieval distinction, 309–10

Symbiosis of mother and child, 121

Symbolic apprehension, reinterpretation of, 305–7, 344. S. representations, 307

Symbols, ascensional and compound, 65; carriers of the word, 112; defined, 64; and inner communication, 66–67; interpretation of 67–69; laws of, 73; and logic, 66; meaning of, 74; and older theology, 120; pathology of, 86

Syrian theology, 345

Systematic exigence, 82–83, 96. S. function of transcendental method, 21. S. mode of cognitional operations, 153–54. S. meaning, 304–10, 314, 329. S. theologian, 137.

Systematics, aim of, 132, 345, 349–50. S. and communications, 142. S. and conflicts, 348. Closed options in s., 340–44. Continuity and development of s., 351–53. S. distinguished from doctrines, 336–37. Function of s., 335–40

Task(s) of apologist, 123; of cognitional theorist, 161; and community, 361; of dialectic, 245–46; of exegete, 156, 178; of historian, 178, 184, 198; and human good, 48, 50; of intentional response, 245; of methodologist, 282, 312, 355; of modern theology, 327–28; of textual critic, 133, 168, 199; of theology, 136–37, 169, 194, 282, 355; *see also* Theologian and method

Teachers in church, 329

Teaching and order of discovery, 346

Technical advance, 90. T. language, 71–73

Technology and science, 99

Terence, 98

Teresa of Avila, 273

Terminal values, 51, 116

Term(s), in interiority, 120. T. of meaning, 75–76. T. and relations; basic (general and special), 286, 343: of cognitional theory, 21, 120, 343;

11-273 For Mom + Dad